Bruce Schneier continues to amaze me with his passion, intelligence and versatility.

In *Liars and Outliers*, Bruce explores a subject far removed from the comfortable field of cryptography, deep at the heart of security—how we create trust. Experienced security professionals will readily recognize that human factors are often far more important than technology in creating trustworthy systems. This book is an overdue examination of the network of social controls that shape trust and security; providing a great framework for thinking about the role of social pressures in creating trust. For those of us working to secure systems, it provides a vital model for thinking about how we can understand, respond to, and shape the social forces that impact security.

Bruce argues the advance of technology in our hyperconnected world creates the potential to widen the security gap between defectors and defenders, but also provides us with tools for closing this gap. I think that expanding the scope of security from technology to social forces will also help narrow this gap.

Bruce has challenged everyone from Amazon to the TSA. I hope you enjoy this book and that it challenges you to think more broadly about the means you can employ to help create secure systems.

Sincerely,

Andy Ellis
Chief Security Officer, Akamai Technologies

"This fascinating book gives an insightful and convincing framework for understanding security and trust."　　　　　　　　　　　　　　　　　—Jeff Yan
Founding Research Director, Center for Cybercrime and Computer Security
Newcastle University

"By analyzing the moving parts and interrelationships among security, trust, and society, Schneier has identified critical patterns, pressures, levers, and security holes within society. Clearly written, thoroughly interdisciplinary, and always smart, *Liars and Outliers* provides great insight into resolving society's various dilemmas."　　　　　　　　　　　　　　　　　　　　　　　　—Jerry Kang
Professor of Law, UCLA

"By keeping the social dimension of trust and security in the center of his analysis, Schneier breaks new ground with an approach that's both theoretically grounded and practically applicable."　　　　　　　　　　　　　　—Jonathan Zittrain
Professor of Law and Computer Science, Harvard University
and author of *The Future of the Internet—And How to Stop It*

"Eye opening. Bruce Schneier provides a perspective you need to understand today's world."　　　　　　　　　　　　　　　　　　　—Steven A. LeBlanc
Director of Collections, Harvard University
and author of *Constant Battles: Why We Fight*

"An outstanding investigation of the importance of trust in holding society together and promoting progress. *Liars and Outliers* provides valuable new insights into security and economics."　　　　　　　　　　　　　　　　　—Andrew Odlyzko
Professor, School of Mathematics, University of Minnesota

"What Schneier has to say about trust—and betrayal—lays a groundwork for greater understanding of human institutions. This is an essential exploration as society grows in size and complexity."　　　　　　　　　　　　　　　—Jim Harper
Director of Information Policy Studies, CATO Institute
and author of *Identity Crisis: How Identification Is Overused and Misunderstood*

"Society runs on trust. *Liars and Outliers* explains the trust gaps we must fill to help society run even better."　　　　　　　　　　　　　　—M. Eric Johnson
Director, Glassmeyer/McNamee Center for Digital Strategies
Tuck School of Business at Dartmouth College

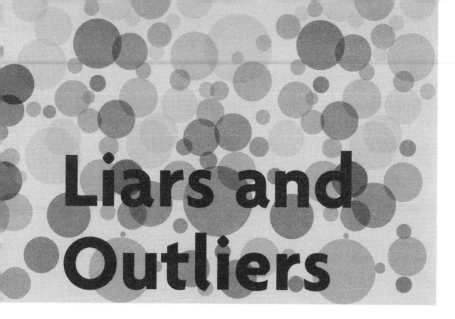

Liars and Outliers

Enabling the Trust That Society Needs to Thrive

Bruce Schneier

WILEY

John Wiley & Sons, Inc.

Liars and Outliers: Enabling the Trust That Society Needs to Thrive

Published by
John Wiley & Sons, Inc.
10475 Crosspoint Boulevard
Indianapolis, IN 46256
www.wiley.com

Published by John Wiley & Sons, Inc., Indianapolis, Indiana

Published simultaneously in Canada

ISBN: 978-1-118-64360-0
The material for this book was previously printed under the ISBN 978-1-118-14330-8.

Manufactured in the United States of America

10 9 8 7 6 5 4 3 2 1

For general information on our other products and services please contact our Customer Care Department within the United States at (877) 762-2974, outside the United States at (317) 572-3993 or fax (317) 572-4002.

Wiley also publishes its books in a variety of electronic formats and by print-on-demand. Not all content that is available in standard print versions of this book may appear or be packaged in all book formats. If you have purchased a version of this book that did not include media that is referenced by or accompanies a standard print version, you may request this media by visiting http://booksupport .wiley.com. For more information about Wiley products, visit us at www.wiley.com.

Library of Congress Control Number: 2011944879

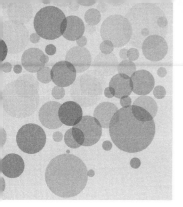

Credits

Executive Editor
Carol Long

Project Editor
Tom Dinse

Senior Production Editor
Debra Banninger

Copy Editor
Kim Cofer

Editorial Manager
Mary Beth Wakefield

Freelancer Editorial Manager
Rosemarie Graham

Marketing Manager
Ashley Zurcher

Business Manager
Amy Knies

Production Manager
Tim Tate

Vice President and Executive Group Publisher
Richard Swadley

Vice President and Executive Publisher
Neil Edde

Associate Publisher
Jim Minatel

Project Coordinator, Cover
Katie Crocker

Proofreader
Nancy Carrasco

Indexer
Johnna Dinse

Cover Designer
Ryan Sneed

Cover Concept
Luke Fretwell

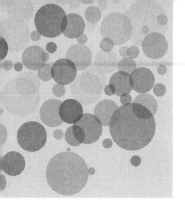

Contents

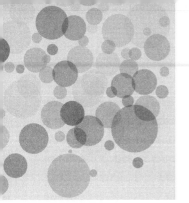

A Note
for Readers

This book contains both notes and references. The notes are explanatory bits that didn't make it into the main text. These are indicated by superscript numbers in both the paper and e-book formats. The references are not indicated at all in the main text; they are collected at the back of the book, organized by printed page number and a bit of quoted text.

Overview

Just today, a stranger came to my door claiming he was here to unclog a bathroom drain. I let him into my house without verifying his identity, and not only did he repair the drain, he also took off his shoes so he wouldn't track mud on my floors. When he was done, I gave him a piece of paper that asked my bank to give him some money. He accepted it without a second glance. At no point did he attempt to take my possessions, and at no point did I attempt the same of him. In fact, neither of us worried that the other would. My wife was also home, but it never occurred to me that he was a sexual rival and I should therefore kill him.

Also today, I passed several strangers on the street without any of them attacking me. I bought food from a grocery store, not at all concerned that it might be unfit for human consumption. I locked my front door, but didn't spare a moment's worry at how easy it would be for someone to smash my window in. Even people driving cars, large murderous instruments that could crush me like a bug, didn't scare me.

Most amazingly, this worked without much overt security. I don't carry a gun for self-defense, nor do I wear body armor. I don't use a home burglar alarm. I don't test my food for poison. I don't even engage in conspicuous displays of physical prowess to intimidate other people I encounter.

It's what we call "trust." Actually, it's what we call "civilization."

All complex ecosystems, whether they are biological ecosystems like the human body, natural ecosystems like a rain forest, social ecosystems like an open-air market, or socio-technical ecosystems like the global financial system or the Internet, are deeply interlinked. Individual units within those ecosystems are interdependent, each doing its part and relying on the other units to do their parts as well. This is neither rare nor difficult, and complex ecosystems abound.

At the same time, all complex ecosystems contain parasites. Within every interdependent system, there are individuals who try to subvert the system to their own ends. These could be tapeworms in our digestive tracts, thieves in a bazaar, robbers disguised as plumbers, spammers on the Internet, or companies that move their profits offshore to evade taxes.

Within complex systems, there is a fundamental tension between what I'm going to call cooperating, or acting in the group interest; and what I'll call defecting, or acting against the group interest and instead in one's own self-interest. Political philosophers have recognized this antinomy since Plato. We might individually want each other's stuff, but we're collectively better off if everyone respects property rights and no one steals. We might individually want to reap the benefits of government without having to pay for them, but we're collectively better off if everyone pays taxes. Every country might want to be able to do whatever it wants, but the world is better off with international agreements, treaties, and organizations. In general, we're collectively better off if society limits individual behavior, and we'd each be better off if those limits didn't apply to us individually. That doesn't work, of course, and most of us recognize this. Most of the time, we realize that it is in our self-interest to act in the group interest. But because parasites will always exist—because some of us steal, don't pay our taxes, ignore international agreements, or ignore limits on our behavior—we also need security.

Society runs on trust. We all need to trust that the random people we interact with will cooperate. Not trust completely, not trust blindly, but be reasonably sure (whatever that means) that our trust is well-founded and they will be trustworthy in return (whatever *that* means). This is vital. If the number of parasites gets too large, if too many people steal or too many people don't pay their taxes, society no longer works. It doesn't work both because there is so much theft that people can't be secure in their property, and because even the honest become suspicious of everyone else. More importantly, it doesn't work because the social contract breaks down: society is no longer seen as providing the required benefits. Trust is largely habit, and when there's not enough trust to be had, people stop trusting each other.

The devil is in the details. In all societies, for example, there are instances where property is legitimately taken from one person and given to another: taxes, fines, fees, confiscation of contraband, theft by a legitimate but despised ruler, etc. And a societal norm like "everyone pays his or her taxes" is distinct from any discussion about what sort of tax code is fair. But while we might disagree about the extent of the norms we subject ourselves to—that's what politics is all about—we're collectively better off if we all follow them.

Of course, it's actually more complicated than that. A person might decide to break the norms, not for selfish parasitical reasons, but because his moral compass tells him to. He might help escaped slaves flee into Canada because slavery is wrong. He might refuse to pay taxes because he disagrees with what his government is spending his money on. He might help laboratory animals escape because he believes animal testing is wrong. He might shoot a doctor who performs abortions because he believes abortion is wrong. And so on.

Sometimes we decide a norm breaker did the right thing. Sometimes we decide that he did the wrong thing. Sometimes there's consensus, and sometimes we disagree. And sometimes those who dare to defy the group norm become catalysts for social change. Norm breakers rioted against the police raids of the Stonewall Inn in New York in 1969, at the beginning of the gay rights movement. Norm breakers hid and saved the lives of Jews in World War II Europe, organized the Civil Rights bus protests in the American South, and assembled in unlawful protest at Tiananmen Square. When the group norm is later deemed immoral, history may call those who refused to follow it heroes.

In 2008, the U.S. real estate industry collapsed, almost taking the global economy with it. The causes of the disaster are complex, but were in a large part caused by financial institutions and their employees subverting financial systems to their own ends. They wrote mortgages to homeowners who couldn't afford them, and then repackaged and resold those mortgages in ways that intentionally hid real risk. Financial analysts, who made money rating these bonds, gave them high ratings to ensure repeat rating business.

This is an example of a failure of trust: a limited number of people were able to use the global financial system for their own personal gain. That sort of thing isn't supposed to happen. But it did happen. And it will happen again if society doesn't get better at both trust and security.

Failures in trust have become global problems:

- The Internet brings amazing benefits to those who have access to it, but it also brings with it new forms of fraud. Impersonation fraud—now called identity theft—is both easier and more profitable than it was pre-Internet. Spam continues to undermine the usability of e-mail. Social networking sites deliberately make it hard for people to effectively manage their own privacy. And antagonistic behavior threatens almost every Internet community.

- Globalization has improved the lives of people in many countries, but with it came an increased threat of global terrorism. The terrorist attacks of 9/11 were a failure of trust, and so were the government overreactions in the decade following.

- The financial network allows anyone to do business with anyone else around the world; but easily hacked financial accounts mean there is enormous profit in fraudulent transactions, and easily hacked computer databases mean there is also a global market in (terrifyingly cheap) stolen credit card numbers and personal dossiers to enable those fraudulent transactions.

- Goods and services are now supplied worldwide at much lower cost, but with this change comes tainted foods, unsafe children's toys, and the outsourcing of data processing to countries with different laws.

- Global production also means more production, but with it comes environmental pollution. If a company discharges lead into the atmosphere—or chlorofluorocarbons, or nitrogen oxides, or carbon dioxide—that company gets all the benefit of cheaper production costs, but the environmental cost falls on everybody else on the planet.

And it's not just global problems, of course. Narrower failures in trust are so numerous as to defy listing. Here are just a few examples:

- In 2009–2010, officials of Bell, California, effectively looted the city's treasury, awarding themselves unusually high salaries, often for part-time work.

- Some early online games, such as Star Wars Galaxy Quest, collapsed due to internal cheating.

- The senior executives at companies such as WorldCom, Enron, and Adelphia inflated their companies' stock prices through fraudulent accounting practices, awarding themselves huge bonuses but destroying the companies in the process.

What ties all these examples together is that the interest of society was in conflict with the interests of certain individuals within society. Society had some normative behaviors, but failed to ensure that enough people cooperated and followed those behaviors. Instead, the defectors within the group became too large or too powerful or too successful, and ruined it for everyone.

●   ●   ●

This book is about trust. Specifically, it's about trust within a group. It's important that defectors not take advantage of the group, but it's also important for everyone in the group to trust that defectors won't take advantage.

"Trust" is a complex concept, and has a lot of flavors of meaning. Sociologist Piotr Sztompka wrote that "trust is a bet about the future contingent actions of others." Political science professor Russell Hardin wrote: "Trust involves giving discretion to another to affect one's interests." These definitions focus on trust between individuals and, by extension, their trustworthiness.[1]

When we trust people, we can either trust their intentions or their actions. The first is more intimate. When we say we trust a friend, that trust isn't tied to any particular thing he's doing. It's a general reliance that, whatever the situation, he'll do the right thing: that he's trustworthy. We trust the friend's intentions, and know that his actions will be informed by those intentions.[2]

The second is less intimate, what sociologist Susan Shapiro calls *impersonal trust*. When we don't know someone, we don't know enough about her, or her underlying motivations, to trust her based on character alone. But we can trust her future actions.[3] We can trust that she won't run red lights, or steal from us, or cheat on tests. We don't know if she has a secret desire to run red lights or take our money, and we really don't care if she does. Rather, we know that she is likely to follow most social norms of acceptable behavior because the consequences of breaking these norms are high. You can think of this kind of trust—that people will behave in a trustworthy manner even if they are not inherently trustworthy—more as confidence, and the corresponding trustworthiness as compliance.[4]

In another sense, we're reducing trust to consistency or predictability. Of course, someone who is consistent isn't necessarily trustworthy. If someone is a habitual thief, I don't trust him. But I do believe (and, in another sense of the word, trust) that he will try to steal from me. I'm less interested in that aspect of trust, and more in the positive aspects. In *The Naked Corporation*, business strategist Don Tapscott described trust, at least in business, as the expectation that the other party will be honest, considerate, accountable, and transparent. When two people are consistent in this way, we call them cooperative.

In today's complex society, we often trust systems more than people. It's not so much that I trusted the plumber at my door as that I trusted the systems that produced him and protect me. I trusted the recommendation from my insurance company, the legal system that would protect me if he did rob my house, whatever the educational system is that produces and whatever insurance system bonds skilled plumbers, and—most of all—the general societal systems that inform how we all treat each other in society. Similarly, I trusted the banking system, the corporate system, the system of police, the system of traffic laws, and the system of social norms that govern most behaviors.[5]

This book is about trust more in terms of groups than individuals. I'm not really concerned about how specific people come to trust other specific people. I don't care if my plumber trusts me enough to take my check, or if I trust that driver over there enough to cross the street at the stop sign. I'm concerned with the general level of impersonal trust in society. Francis Fukuyama's definition nicely captures the term as I want to use it: "Trust is the expectation that arises within a community of regular, honest, and cooperative behavior, based on commonly shared norms, on the part of other members of that community."

Sociologist Barbara Misztal identified three critical functions performed by trust: 1) it makes social life more predictable, 2) it creates a sense of community, and 3) it makes it easier for people to work together. In some ways, trust in society works like oxygen in the atmosphere. The more customers trust merchants, the easier commerce is. The more drivers trust other drivers, the smoother traffic flows. Trust gives people the confidence to deal with strangers: because they know that the strangers are likely to behave honestly, cooperatively, fairly, and sometimes even altruistically. The more trust is in the air, the healthier society is and the more it can thrive. Conversely, the less trust is in the air, the sicker society is and the more it has to contract. And if the amount of trust gets too low, society withers and dies. A recent example of a systemic breakdown in trust occurred in the Soviet Union under Stalin.

I'm necessarily simplifying here. Trust is relative, fluid, and multidimensional. I trust Alice to return a $10 loan but not a $10,000 loan, Bob to return a $10,000 loan but not to babysit an infant, Carol to babysit but not with my house key, Dave with my house key but not my intimate secrets, and Ellen with my intimate secrets but not to return a $10 loan. I trust Frank if a friend vouches for him, a taxi driver as long as he's displaying his license, and Gail as long as she hasn't been drinking. I don't trust anyone at all with my computer password. I trust my brakes to stop the car, ATM machines to dispense money from my account, and Angie's List to recommend a qualified plumber—even though

I have no idea who designed, built, or maintained those systems. Or even who Angie is. In the language of this book, we all need to trust each other to follow the behavioral norms of our group.

Many other books talk about the value of trust to society. This book explains how society establishes and maintains that trust.[6] Specifically, it explains how society enforces, evokes, elicits, compels, encourages—I'll use the term *induces*—trustworthiness, or at least compliance, through systems of what I call *societal pressures*, similar to sociology's social controls: coercive mechanisms that induce people to cooperate, act in the group interest, and follow group norms. Like physical pressures, they don't work in all cases on all people. But again, whether the pressures work against a particular person is less important than whether they keep the scope of defection to a manageable level across society as a whole.

A manageable level, but not too low a level. Compliance isn't always good, and defection isn't always bad. Sometimes the group norm doesn't deserve to be followed, and certain kinds of progress and innovation require violating trust. In a police state, everybody is compliant but no one trusts anybody. A too-compliant society is a stagnant society, and defection contains the seeds of social change.

This book is also about security. Security is a type of a societal pressure in that it induces cooperation, but it's different from the others. It is the only pressure that can act as a physical constraint on behavior regardless of how trustworthy people are. And it is the only pressure that individuals can implement by themselves. In many ways, it obviates the need for intimate trust. In another way, it is how we ultimately induce compliance and, by extension, trust.

It is essential that we learn to think smartly about trust. Philosopher Sissela Bok wrote: "Whatever matters to human beings, trust is the atmosphere in which it thrives." People, communities, corporations, markets, politics: everything. If we can figure out the optimal societal pressures to induce cooperation, we can reduce murder, terrorism, bank fraud, industrial pollution, and all the rest.

If we get pressures wrong, the murder rate skyrockets, terrorists run amok, employees routinely embezzle from their employers, and corporations lie and cheat at every turn. In extreme cases, an untrusting society breaks down. If we get them wrong in the other direction, no one speaks out about institutional injustice, no one deviates from established corporate procedure, and no one popularizes new inventions that disrupt the status quo—an oppressed society stagnates. The very fact that the most extreme failures rarely happen in the modern industrial world is proof that we've largely gotten societal pressures right. The failures that we've had show we have a lot further to go.

Also, as we'll see, evolution has left us with intuitions about trust better suited to life as a savannah-dwelling primate than as a modern human in a global high-tech society. That flawed intuition is vulnerable to exploitation by companies, con men, politicians, and crooks. The *only* defense is a rational understanding of what trust in society is, how it works, and why it succeeds or fails.

*   *   *

This book is divided into four parts. In Part I, I'll explore the background sciences of the book. Several fields of research—some closely related—will help us understand these topics: experimental psychology, evolutionary psychology, sociology, economics, behavioral economics, evolutionary biology, neuroscience, game theory, systems dynamics, anthropology, archaeology, history, political science, law, philosophy, theology, cognitive science, and computer security.

All these fields have something to teach us about trust and security.[7] There's a lot here, and delving into any of these areas of research could easily fill several books. This book attempts to gather and synthesize decades, and sometimes centuries, of thinking, research, and experimentation from a broad swath of academic disciplines. It will, by necessity, be largely a cursory overview; often, the hardest part was figuring out what *not* to include. My goal is to show where the broad arcs of research are pointing, rather than explain the details—though they're fascinating—of any individual piece of research.[8]

In the last chapter of Part I, I will introduce societal dilemmas. I'll explain a thought experiment called the Prisoner's Dilemma, and its generalization to societal dilemmas. Societal dilemmas describe the situations that require intra-group trust, and therefore use societal pressures to ensure cooperation: they're the central paradigm of my model. Societal dilemmas illustrate how society keeps defectors from taking advantage, taking over, and completely ruining society for everyone. It illustrates how society ensures that its members forsake their own interests when they run counter to society's interest. Societal dilemmas have many names in the literature: collective action problem, Tragedy of the Commons, free-rider problem, arms race. We'll use them all.

Part II fully develops my model. Trust is essential for society to function, and societal pressures are how we achieve it. There are four basic categories of societal pressure that can induce cooperation in societal dilemmas:

*   *Moral pressure.* A lot of societal pressure comes from inside our own heads. Most of us don't steal, and it's not because there are armed guards

and alarms protecting piles of stuff. We don't steal because we believe it's wrong, or we'll feel guilty if we do, or we want to follow the rules.

- *Reputational pressure.* A wholly different, and much stronger, type of pressure comes from how others respond to our actions. Reputational pressure can be very powerful; both individuals and organizations feel a lot of pressure to follow the group norms because they don't want a bad reputation.

- *Institutional pressure.* Institutions have rules and laws. These are norms that are codified, and whose enactment and enforcement is generally delegated. Institutional pressure induces people to behave according to the group norm by imposing sanctions on those who don't, and occasionally by rewarding those who do.

- *Security systems.* Security systems are another form of societal pressure. This includes any security mechanism designed to induce cooperation, prevent defection, induce trust, and compel compliance. It includes things that work to prevent defectors, like door locks and tall fences; things that interdict defectors, like alarm systems and guards; things that only work after the fact, like forensic and audit systems; and mitigation systems that help the victim recover faster and care less that the defection occurred.

Part III applies the model to the more complex dilemmas that arise in the real world. First I'll look at the full complexity of competing interests. It's not just group interest versus self-interest; people have a variety of competing interests. Also, while it's easy to look at societal dilemmas as isolated decisions, it's common for people to have conflicts of interest: multiple group interests and multiple societal dilemmas are generally operating at any one time. And the effectiveness of societal pressures often depends on why someone is considering defecting.

Then, I'll look at groups as actors in societal dilemmas: organizations in general, corporations, and then institutions. Groups have different competing interests, and societal pressures work differently when applied to them. This is an important complication, especially in the modern world of complex corporations and government agencies. Institutions are also different. In today's world, it's rare that we implement societal pressures directly. More often, we delegate someone to do it for us. For example, we delegate our elected officials to pass laws, and they delegate some government agency to implement those laws.

In Part IV, I'll talk about the different ways societal pressures fail. I'll look at how changes in technology affect societal pressures, particularly security. Then I'll look at the particular characteristics of today's society—the Information Society—and explain why that changes societal pressures. I'll sketch what the future of societal pressures is likely to be, and close with the social consequences of too much societal pressure.

This book represents my attempt to develop a full-fledged theory of coercion and how it enables compliance and trust within groups. My goal is to suggest some new questions and provide a new framework for analysis. I offer new perspectives, and a broader spectrum of what's possible. Perspectives frame thinking, and sometimes asking new questions is the catalyst to greater understanding. It's my hope that this book can give people an illuminating new framework with which to help understand how the world works.

●   ●   ●

Before we start, I need to define my terms. We talk about trust and security all the time, and the words we use tend to be overloaded with meaning. We're going to have to be more precise...and temporarily suspend our emotional responses to what otherwise might seem like loaded, value-laden, even disparaging, words.

The word *society*, as used in this book, isn't limited to traditional societies, but is any group of people with a loose common interest. It applies to societies of circumstance, like a neighborhood, a country, everyone on a particular bus, or an ethnicity or social class. It applies to societies of choice, like a group of friends, any membership organization, or a professional society. It applies to societies that are some of each: a religion, a criminal gang, or all employees of a corporation. It applies to societies of all sizes, from a family to the entire planet. All of humanity is a society, and everyone is a member of multiple societies. Some are based on birth, and some are freely chosen. Some we can join, and to some we must be invited. Some may be good, some may be bad—terrorist organizations, criminal gangs, a political party you don't agree with—and most are somewhere in between. For our purposes, a society is just a group of interacting *actors* organized around a common attribute.

I said actors, not people. Most societies are made up of people, but sometimes they're made up of groups of people. All the countries on the planet are a society. All corporations in a particular industry are a society. We're going to be talking about both societies of individuals and societies of groups.

Societies have a collection of *group interests*. These are the goals, or directions, of the society. They're decided by the society in some way: perhaps formally—either democratically or autocratically—perhaps informally by the group. International trade can be in the group interest. So can sharing food, obeying traffic laws, and keeping slaves (assuming those slaves are not considered to be part of the group). Corporations, families, communities, and terrorist groups all have their own group interests. Each of these group interests corresponds to one or more norms, which is what each member of that society is supposed to do. For example, it is in the group interest that everyone respect everyone else's property rights. Therefore, the group norm is not to steal (at least, not from other members of the group[9]).

Every person in a society potentially has one or more *competing interests* that conflict with the group interest, and *competing norms* that conflict with the group norm. Someone in that we-don't-steal society might really want to steal. He might be starving, and need to steal food to survive. He just might want other people's stuff. These are examples of *self-interest*. He might have some competing *relational interest*. He might be a member of a criminal gang, and need to steal to prove his loyalty to the group; here, the competing interest might be the group interest of another group. Or he might want to steal for some higher moral reason: a competing *moral interest*—the Robin Hood archetype, for example.

A *societal dilemma* is the choice every actor has to make between group interest and his or her competing interests. It's the choice we make when we decide whether or not to follow the group norm. Those who do *cooperate*, and those who do not *defect*. Those are both loaded terms, but I mean them to refer only to the action as a result of the dilemma.

Defectors—the liars and outliers of the book's title—are the people within a group who don't go along with the norms of that group. The term isn't defined according to any absolute morals, but instead in opposition to whatever the group interest and the group norm is. Defectors steal in a society that has declared that stealing is wrong, but they also help slaves escape in a society where tolerating slavery is the norm. Defectors change as society changes; defection is in the eye of the beholder. Or, more specifically, it is in the eyes of everyone else. Someone who was a defector under the former East German government was no longer in that group after the fall of the Berlin Wall. But those who followed the societal norms of East Germany, like the Stasi, were—all of a sudden—viewed as defectors within the new united Germany.

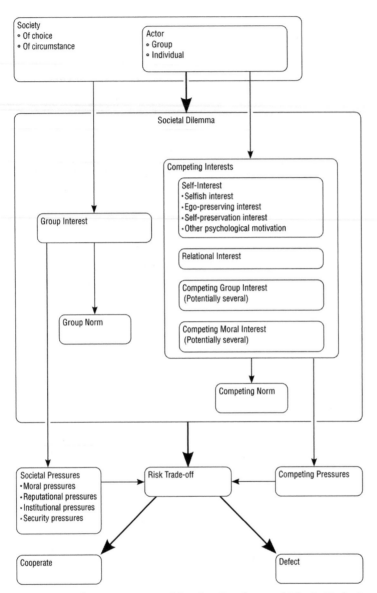

Figure 1: The Terms Used in the Book, and Their Relationships

Criminals are defectors, obviously, but that answer is too facile. Everyone defects at least some of the time. It's both dynamic and situational. People can cooperate about some things and defect about others. People can cooperate with one group they're in and defect from another. People can cooperate today and defect tomorrow, or cooperate when they're thinking clearly and defect when they're reacting in a panic. People can cooperate when their needs are cared for, and defect when they're starving.

When four black North Carolina college students staged a sit-in at a whites-only lunch counter inside a Woolworth's five-and-dime store in Greensboro, in 1960, they were criminals. So are women who drive cars in Saudi Arabia. Or homosexuals in Iran. Or the 2011 protesters in Egypt, who sought to end their country's political regime. Conversely, child brides in Pakistan are not criminalized and neither are their parents, even though in some cases they marry off five-year-old girls. The Nicaraguan rebels who fought the Sandinistas were criminals, terrorists, insurgents, or freedom fighters, depending on which side you supported and how you viewed the conflict. Pot smokers and dealers in the U.S. are officially criminals, but in the Netherlands those offenses are ignored by the police. Those who share copyrighted movies and music are breaking the law, even if they have moral justifications for their actions.

Defecting doesn't necessarily mean breaking government-imposed laws. An orthodox Jew who eats a ham and cheese sandwich is violating the rules of his religion. A Mafioso who snitches on his colleagues is violating *omertà*, the code of silence. A relief worker who indulges in a long, hot shower after a tiring journey, and thereby depletes an entire village's hot water supply, unwittingly puts his own self-interest ahead of the interest of the people he intends to help.

What we're concerned with is the overall *scope of defection*. I mean this term to be general, comprising the number of defectors, the rate of their defection, the frequency of their defection, and the intensity (the amount of damage) of their defection. Just as we're interested in the general level of trust within the group, we're interested in the general scope of defection within the group.

Societal pressures are how society ensures that people follow the group norms, as opposed to some competing norms. The term is meant to encompass everything society does to protect itself: both from fellow members of society, and non-societal members who live within and amongst the society. More generally, it's how society enforces intra-group trust.

The terms *attacker* and *defender* are pretty obvious. The predator is the attacker, the prey is the defender. It's all intertwined, and sometimes these terms can get a bit muddy. Watch a martial arts match, and you'll see each person defending against his opponent's attacks while at the same time hoping his own attacks get around his opponent's defenses. In war, both sides attack and defend at the tactical level, even though one side might be attacking and the other defending at the political level. These terms are value-neutral. Attackers can be criminals trying to break into a home, superheroes raiding a criminal mastermind's stronghold, or cancer cells metastasizing their way through a hapless human host. Defenders can be a family protecting its home from invasion, the criminal mastermind protecting his lair from the superheroes, or a posse of leukocytes engulfing opportunistic pathogens they encounter.

These definitions are important to remember as you read this book. It's easy for us to bring our own emotional baggage into discussions about security, but most of the time we're just trying to understand the underlying mechanisms at play, and those mechanisms are the same, regardless of the underlying moral context.

Sometimes we need the dispassionate lens of history to judge famous defectors like Oliver North, Oskar Schindler, and Vladimir Lenin.

PART I
The Science of Trust

A Natural History of Security

Our exploration of trust is going to start and end with security, because security is what you need when you don't have any trust and—as we'll see—security is ultimately how we induce trust in society. It's what brings risk down to tolerable levels, allowing trust to fill in the remaining gaps.

You can learn a lot about security from watching the natural world.

- Lions seeking to protect their turf will raise their voices in a "territorial chorus," their cooperation reducing the risk of encroachment by other predators for the local food supply.

- When hornworms start eating a particular species of sagebrush, the plant responds by emitting a molecule that warns any wild tobacco plants growing nearby that hornworms are around. In response, the tobacco plants deploy chemical defenses that repel the hornworms, to the benefit of both plants.

- Some types of plasmids secrete a toxin that kills the bacteria that carry them. Luckily for the bacteria, the plasmids also emit an antidote; and as long as a plasmid secretes both, the host bacterium survives. But if the plasmid dies, the antidote decays faster than the toxin, and the bacterium dies. This acts as an insurance policy for the plasmids, ensuring that bacteria don't evolve ways to kill them.

In the beginning of life on this planet, some 3.8 billion years ago, an organism's only job was to reproduce. That meant growing, and growing required energy. Heat and light were the obvious sources—photosynthesis appeared 3 billion years ago; chemosynthesis is at least a half a billion years older than that—but consuming the other living things floating around in the primordial ocean worked just as well. So life discovered predation.

We don't know what that first animal predator was, but it was likely a simple marine organism somewhere between 500 million and 550 million years ago. Initially, the only defense a species had against being eaten was to have so many individuals floating around the primordial seas that enough individuals were left to reproduce, so that the constant attrition didn't matter. But then life realized it might be able to avoid being eaten. So it evolved defenses. And predators evolved better ways to catch and eat.

Thus security was born, the planet's fourth oldest activity after eating, eliminating, and reproducing.

Okay, that's a pretty gross simplification, and it would get me booted out of any evolutionary biology class. When talking about evolution and natural selection, it's easy to say that organisms make explicit decisions about their genetic future. They don't. There's nothing purposeful or teleological about the evolutionary process, and I shouldn't anthropomorphize it. Species don't realize anything. They don't discover anything, either. They don't decide to evolve, or try genetic options. It's tempting to talk about evolution as if there's some outside intelligence directing it. We say "prehistoric lungfish first learned how to breathe air," or "monarch butterflies learned to store plant toxins in their bodies to make themselves taste bad to predators," but it doesn't work that way. Random mutation provides the material upon which natural selection acts. It is through this process that individuals of a species change subtly from their parents, effectively "trying out" new features. Those innovations that turn out to be beneficial—air breathing—give the individuals a competitive advantage and might potentially propagate through the species (there's still a lot of randomness in this process). Those that turn out to be detrimental—the overwhelming majority of them—kill or otherwise disadvantage the individual and die out.

By "beneficial," I mean something very specific: increasing an organism's ability to survive long enough to successfully pass its genes on to future generations. Or, to use Richard Dawkins's perspective from *The Selfish Gene*, genes that helped their host individuals—or other individuals with that gene—successfully reproduce tended to persist in higher numbers in populations.

If we were designing a life form, as we might do in a computer game, we would try to figure out what sort of security it needed and give it abilities accordingly. Real-world species don't have that luxury. Instead, they try new attributes randomly. So instead of an external designer optimizing a species' abilities based on its needs, evolution randomly walks through the solution space and stops at the first solution that works—even if just barely. Then it climbs upwards in the fitness landscape until it reaches a local optimum. You get a lot of weird security that way.

You get teeth, claws, group dispersing behavior, feigning injury and playing dead, hunting in packs, defending in groups (flocking and schooling and living in herds), setting sentinels, digging burrows, flying, mimicry by both predators and prey, alarm calls, shells, intelligence, noxious odors, tool using (both offensive and defensive),[1] planning (again, both offensive and defensive), and a whole lot more.[2] And this is just in largish animals; we haven't even listed the security solutions insects have come up with. Or plants. Or microbes.

It has been convincingly argued that one of the reasons sexual reproduction evolved about 1.2 billion years ago was to defend against biological parasites. The argument is subtle. Basically, parasites reproduce so quickly that they overwhelm any individual host defense. The value of DNA recombination, which is what you get in sexual reproduction, is that it continuously rearranges a species' defenses so parasites can't get the upper hand. For this reason, a member of a species that reproduces sexually is much more likely to survive than a species that clones itself asexually—even though such a species will pass twice as many of its genes to its offspring as a sexually reproducing species would.

Life evolved two other methods of defending itself against parasites. One is to grow and divide quickly, something that both bacteria and just-fertilized mammalian embryos do. The other is to have an immune system. Evolutionarily, this is a relatively new development; it first appeared in jawed fish about 300 million years ago.[3]

A surprising number of evolutionary adaptations are related to security. Take vision, for example. Most animals are more adept at spotting movement than picking out details of stationary objects; it's called the orienting response.[4] That's because things that move may be predators that attack, or prey that needs to be attacked. The human visual system is particularly good at spotting animals.[5] The human ability, unique on the planet, to throw things long distances is another security adaptation. Related is what's called the size-weight misperception: the illusion that easier-to-throw rocks are perceived to be lighter than they are. It's related to our ability to choose good projectiles. Similar stories could be told about many human attributes.[6]

The predator/prey relationship isn't the only pressure that drives evolution. As soon as there was competition for resources, organisms had to develop security to defend their own resources and attack the resources of others. Whether it's plants competing with each other for access to the sun, predators fighting over hunting territory, or animals competing for potential mates, organisms had to develop security against others of the same species. And again, evolution resulted in all sorts of weird security. And it works amazingly well.

Security on Earth went on more or less like this for 500 million years. It's a continual arms race. A rabbit that can run away at 30 miles per hour—in short bursts, of course—is at an evolutionary advantage when the weasels and stoats can only run 28 mph, but at an evolutionary disadvantage once predators can run 32 mph.

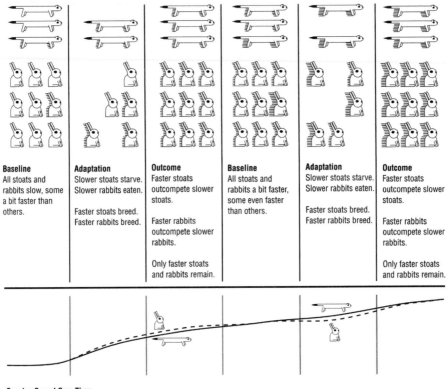

Baseline	Adaptation	Outcome	Baseline	Adaptation	Outcome
All stoats and rabbits slow, some a bit faster than others.	Slower stoats starve. Slower rabbits eaten. Faster stoats breed. Faster rabbits breed.	Faster stoats outcompete slower stoats. Faster rabbits outcompete slower rabbits. Only faster stoats and rabbits remain.	All stoats and rabbits a bit faster, some even faster than others.	Slower stoats starve. Slower rabbits eaten. Faster stoats breed. Faster rabbits breed.	Faster stoats outcompete slower stoats. Faster rabbits outcompete slower rabbits. Only faster stoats and rabbits remain.

Species Speed Over Time
Absolute speed increases. Relative speed remains relatively constant.

Figure 2: The Red Queen Effect in Action

It's different when the evolutionary advantage is against nature. A polar bear has thick fur because it's cold in the Arctic. And it's thick to a point, because the Arctic doesn't get colder in response to the polar bear's changes. But that same polar bear has fur that appears white so as to better sneak up on seals. But a better camouflaged polar bear means that only more wary seals survive and reproduce, which means that the polar bears need to be even better at camouflage to eat, which means that the seals need to be more wary, and on and on and on up to some physical upper limit on camouflage and wariness.

This only-relative evolutionary arms race is known as the Red Queen Effect, after Lewis Carroll's race in *Through the Looking-Glass*: "It takes all the running you can do, to keep in the same place." Predators develop all sorts of new tricks to catch prey, and prey develop all sorts of new tricks to evade predators. The prey get more poisonous, so their predators get more poison-resistant, so the prey get even more poisonous. A species has to continuously improve just to survive, and any species that can't keep up—or bumps up against physiological or environmental constraints—becomes extinct.

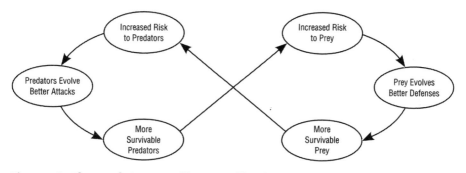

Figure 3: The Red Queen Effect Feedback Loop

Along with becoming faster, more poisonous, and bitier, some organisms became smarter. At first, a little smarts went a long way. Intelligence allows individuals to adapt their behaviors, moment by moment, to suit their environment and circumstances. It allows them to remember the past and learn from experience. It lets them be individually adaptive. No one has a date, but vertebrates first appeared about 525 million years ago—and continued to improve on various branches of the tree of life: mammals (215 million years ago), birds (75 million years ago), primates (60 million years ago), the genus *Homo* (2.5 million years ago), and then humans (somewhere between 200,000 and 450,000 years ago, depending on whose evidence you believe). When it comes to security, as with so many things, humans changed everything.

Let's pause for a second. This isn't a book about animal intelligence, and I don't want to start an argument about which animals can be considered intelligent, or what about human intelligence is unique, or even how to define the word "intelligence." It's definitely a fascinating subject, and we can learn a lot about our own intelligence by studying the intelligence of other animals. Even my neat intelligence progression from the previous paragraph might be wrong: flatworms can be trained, and some cephalopods are surprisingly smart. But those topics aren't really central to this book, so I'm going to elide them. For my purposes, it's enough to say that there is a uniquely human intelligence.[7]

And humans take their intelligence seriously. The brain only represents 3% of total body mass, but uses 20% of the body's total blood supply and 25% of its oxygen. And—unlike other primates, even—we'll supply our brains with blood and oxygen at the expense of other body parts.

One of the things intelligence makes possible is cultural evolution. Instead of needing to wait for genetic changes, humans are able to improve their survivability through the direct transmission of skills and ideas. These memes can be taught from generation to generation, with the more survivable ideas propagating and the bad ones dying out. Humans are not the only species that teaches its young, but humans have taken this to a new level.[8] This caused a flowering of security ideas: deception and concealment; weapons, armor, and shields; coordinated attack and defense tactics; locks and their continuous improvement over the centuries; gunpowder, explosives, guns, cruise missiles, and everything else that goes "bang" or "boom"; paid security guards and soldiers and policemen; professional criminals; forensic databases of fingerprints, tire tracks, shoe prints, and DNA samples; and so on.

It's not just intelligence that makes humans different. One of the things that's unique about humans is the extent of our socialization. Yes, there are other social species: other primates, most mammals and some birds.[9] But humans have taken sociality to a completely different level. And with that socialization came all sorts of new security considerations: concern for an ever-widening group of individuals, concern about potential deception and the need to detect it, concern about one's own and others' reputations, concern about rival groups of attackers and the corresponding need to develop groups of defenders, recognition of the need to take preemptive security measures against potential attacks, and after-the-fact responses to already-occurred attacks for the purpose of deterring others in the future.[10]

Some scientists believe that this increased socialization actually spurred the development of human intelligence.[11] Machiavellian Intelligence Theory—you might also see this called the Social Brain Hypothesis—holds that we evolved intelligence primarily in order to detect deception by other humans. Although the "Machiavellian" term came later, the idea first came from psychologist Nicholas Humphrey. Humphrey observed that wild gorillas led a pretty simple existence, with abundant and easily harvested food, few predators, and not much else to do but eat, sleep, and play. This was in contrast to gorillas in the laboratory, which demonstrated impressive powers of creative reasoning. So the obvious question is: what's the evolutionary advantage of being intelligent and clever if it's not required in order to survive in the wild? Humphrey proposed that the primary role of primate intelligence and creativity was to deal with the complexities of living with other primates. In other words, we evolved smarts not to outsmart the world, but to outsmart each other.

It's more than that. As we became more social, we needed to learn how to get along with each other: both cooperating with each other and ensuring everyone else cooperates, too. It involves understanding each other. Psychologist Daniel Gilbert describes it very well:

> We are social mammals whose brains are highly specialized for thinking about others. Understanding what others are up to—what they know and want, what they are doing and planning—has been so crucial to the survival of our species that our brains have developed an obsession with all things human. We think about people and their intentions; talk about them; look for and remember them.

This makes evolutionary sense. Intelligence is a valuable survival trait when you have to deal with the threats from the natural world. But intelligence is an even more valuable survival trait when you have to deal with the threats from other intelligent individuals. An intelligent adversary is a different animal, so to speak, than an unintelligent adversary. An intelligent attacker is adaptive. An intelligent attacker can learn about its prey. An intelligent attacker can make long-term plans. An intelligent adversary can predict your defenses and incorporate them into his plans. If you're being attacked by an intelligent human, your most useful defense is to also be an intelligent human. Our ancestors grew smarter because those around them grew smarter, and the only way to keep up was to become even smarter.[12] It's a Red Queen Effect in action.

In primates, the frequency of deception is directly proportional to the size of a species' neocortex: the "thinking" part of the mammalian brain. That is, the bigger the brain, the greater the capacity for deception. The human brain has a neocortex that's four times the size of its nearest evolutionary relative. Eighty percent of our brain is neocortex, compared to 50% in our nearest existing relative and 10% to 40% in non-primate mammals.[13]

And as our neocortex grew, the complexity of our social interactions grew as well. Primatologist Robin Dunbar has studied primate group sizes. Dunbar examined 38 different primate genera, and found that the volume of the neocortex correlates with the size of the troop. He established that the mean human group size is 150.[14] This is the Dunbar number: the number of people with whom we can have explicit and personal encounters, whose history we can remember, and with whom we can experience some level of intimacy.[15] Of course, it's an average. You personally might be able to keep track of more or fewer. This number appears regularly in human society: it's the estimated size of a Neolithic farming village; the size at which Hittite settlements split; and it's a basic unit in professional armies, from Roman times to the present day. It's the average size of people's Christmas card lists. It's a common department size in modern corporations.

So as our ancestors got smarter, their social groups got larger. Chimpanzees live in groups of approximately 60 individuals. *Australopithecus*—our ancestor from 4.5 million years ago—had an average group size of 70 individuals. When our first tool-using ancestors appeared 2 million years ago, the group size grew to 80. *Homo erectus* had a mean group size of 110, and Neanderthals 140. *Homo sapiens*: 150.

One hundred and fifty people is a lot to keep track of, especially if they're all clever, sneaky, duplicitous, and—as it turns out—murderous. There is a lot of evidence—both from the anthropological record and from ethnographic studies of contemporary primitive cultures—that humans are innately quite violent, and that intertribal warfare was endemic in primitive society. Several studies estimate that 15–25% of prehistoric males died in warfare.[16]

Economist Paul Seabright postulates that intelligence and murderousness are mutually reinforcing. The more murderous a species is, the greater the selective benefit of intelligence; smarter people are more likely to survive their human adversaries. And the smarter someone is, the more an adversary wants to kill him—and not just make him submit, as other species do.

Looking at the average weight of humans and extrapolating from other animals, humans should primarily hunt medium-sized rodents; indeed, early humans primarily hunted small game. And hunting small game is much more efficient for a bunch of reasons.[17] Even so, all primitive societies hunt large game: antelopes, walrus, and so on. The theory is that although large-game hunting is less efficient, the skill set is the same as what's required for intertribal warfare. The groups that excelled at large-game hunting were more likely to survive the endemic warfare that existed in our evolutionary past. Group hunting also reinforced social bonds, which are a useful group survival trait.

A male killing another male of the same species—especially an unrelated male—eliminates a sexual rival. If you have fewer sexual rivals, you have more of your own offspring. Natural selection favors murderousness. On the other hand, attempting to murder another individual of the same species is dangerous; you might get yourself killed in the process. This means fewer offspring, which implies a counterbalancing natural selection against murderousness.

It's another Red Queen Effect, this one involving murder. Evolutionary psychologist David Buss writes:

> As the motivations to murder evolved in our minds, a set of counter-inclinations also developed. Killing is a risky business. It can be dangerous and inflict horrible costs on the victim. Because it's so bad to be dead, evolution has fashioned ruthless defenses to prevent being killed, including killing the killer. Potential victims are therefore quite dangerous themselves. In the evolutionary arms race, homicide victims have played a critical and unappreciated role—they pave the way for the evolution of anti-homicide defenses.

There is considerable debate about how violent we really are, with the majority opinion coming down on the "quite violent" side, especially among males from ages 16 to 24. On the other hand, some argue that human violence has declined over the millennia, primarily due to the changing circumstances that come with civilization. We do know it's been traditionally very hard to convince soldiers to kill in war, and our experience with post-traumatic stress disorder shows that it has long-lasting ill effects. Our violence may be innate, but it depends a lot on context. We're comparable with other primates.[18]

But if we are so naturally murderous, how did our prehistoric ancestors come to trust each other? We know they did, because if they hadn't, society would never have developed. People would never have gathered into groups that extended past immediate family, let alone into villages and towns and cities. Division of labor would have never evolved, because people couldn't trust others to do their parts. We would never have established trade with the strangers we occasionally encountered, let alone with companies based halfway across the planet. Friendships wouldn't exist. Societies based on either geography or interest would be impossible. Any sort of governmental structure: forget it. It doesn't matter how big your neocortex is or how abstractly you can reason: unless you can trust others, your species will forever remain stuck in the Stone Age.

The answer to that question will make use of the concepts presented in this chapter—the Red Queen Effect, the Dunbar number, our natural intelligence and murderousness—and it will make use of security. It turns out that trust in society isn't easy, and that we're still getting it wrong.

The Evolution of Cooperation

Two of the most successful species on the planet are humans and leafcutter ants of Brazil. Evolutionary biologist Edward O. Wilson has spent much of his career studying the ants, and argues that their success is due to division of labor.[1] There are four different kinds of leafcutter workers: gardeners, defenders, foragers, and soldiers. Each type of ant is specialized to its task, and together the colony does much better than colonies of non-specialized ant species.

Humans specialize too, and—even better—we can adapt our specialization to the situation. A leafcutter ant is born to a particular role; we get to decide our specialization in both the long and short term, and change it if it's not working out for us.[2]

Division of labor is an exercise in trust. A gardener leafcutter ant has to trust that the forager leafcutter ants will bring leaf fragments back to the nest. I, specializing right now in book writing, have to trust that my publisher is going to print this book and bookstores are going to sell it. And that someone is going to grow food that I can buy with my royalty check. If I couldn't trust literally millions of nameless, faceless other people, I couldn't specialize.

Brazilian leafcutter ant colonies evolved trust and cooperation because they're all siblings. We had to evolve it the hard way.

• • •

We all employ both cooperating and defecting strategies. Most of the time our self-interest and group interest coincide, and we act in accordance with the group norm. Only sometimes do we act in some competing norm. It depends on circumstance, and it depends on who we are. Some of us are more cooperative, more honest, more altruistic, and fairer. And some of us are less so. There isn't one dominant survival strategy that evolution has handed down to us; we have the flexibility to switch between different strategies.

One way to think of the relationship between society as a whole and its defectors is as a parasitic relationship. Take the human body as an example. Only 10% of the total number of cells in our human bodies are us—human cells with our particular genome. The other 90% are symbionts, genetically unrelated organisms.[3] Our relationship with them ranges from mutualism (we both benefit) to commensalism (one benefits) to parasitism (one benefits and the other is harmed). The society of our bodies needs the cooperators to survive, and at the same time spends a lot of energy defending itself against the defectors.

Extending the analogy even further, our social systems are filled with parasites as well. Parasites steal stuff instead of buying it. They take more than their share in a communal situation. They overstay their welcome on their Aunt Faye's couch. They incur unsustainable debt, confident that bankruptcy laws—or some expensive lawyers—will enable them to bail out on their creditors when the going gets tough.

Parasites are all over the Internet. Crime is a huge business. Spammers are parasitic on e-mail. Griefers in online games are parasitic on more conventional players. File sharers copy music instead of paying for it; they're parasitic on the music industry, getting the benefit of commercial music without giving back any money in return.

Excepting the smallest and simplest cases, every society has parasites living inside it. And there is an evolutionary advantage to being a parasite as long as there aren't too many of them and they aren't too good at it.

Being a parasite is a balancing act. Biological parasites do best if they don't immediately kill their hosts, but instead let them survive long enough for the parasites to spread to additional hosts. Ebola is too successful, so it fails as a species. The common cold does a much better job of spreading itself; it infects, and in the end kills, far more people by being much less "effective." Predators do best if they don't kill enough prey to wipe out the entire species. Spammers do better if they don't clog e-mail to the point where no one uses it anymore, and rogue banks are more profitable if they don't crash the entire economy. All parasites do better if they don't destroy whatever system they've latched themselves onto. Parasites thrive only if they don't thrive *too well*.

There's a clever model from game theory that illustrates this: the Hawk-Dove game. It was invented by geneticists John Maynard Smith and George R. Price in 1971 to explain conflicts between animals of the same species. Like most game theory models, it's pretty simplistic. But what it illuminates about the real world is profound.

The game works like this. Assume a population of individuals with differing survival strategies. Some cooperate and some defect. In the language of the game, the defectors are hawks. They're aggressive; they attack other individuals, and fight back if attacked. The cooperators are doves. They're pacific; they share with other doves, and retreat when attacked. You can think about this in terms of animals competing for food. When two doves meet, they cooperate and share food. When a hawk meets a dove, the hawk takes food from the dove. When two hawks meet, they fight and one of them randomly gets the food and the other has some probability of dying from injury.[4]

Set some initial parameters in the simulation: the value of sharing, the chance and severity of harm if two hawks fight each other, and so on. Program this model into a computer, set proportions for the initial population—50% hawks and 50% doves, for example—and let individuals interact with each other over multiple iterations.

What's interesting about this simulation is that neither strategy is guaranteed to dominate. Both hawks and doves can be successful, depending on the initial parameters. If the value of the food stolen is greater than the risk of death, the whole population becomes hawks. That is, if everyone is starving, people take what they can from each other without worrying about the consequences. Add a single dove, and it immediately starves. But as food gets less valuable (e.g., more plentiful) or fighting gets more dangerous, the population stabilizes into a mixture of hawks and doves. The more dangerous fighting is, the fewer hawks there will be. If food is reasonably plentiful and fighting reasonably dangerous, the population stabilizes into a mixture of mostly doves and fewer hawks. But unless you plug some really unrealistic numbers into the simulation—like starting out with a population entirely of doves—there will always be at least a few hawks in the mix.

This makes sense. Imagine a society made up entirely of cooperative doves. They share food whenever they meet each other, never stealing from one another. Now add a single hawk to the society. He does great. He steals food from all the doves, and since no one ever fights back, he has no risk of dying. It's the best survival strategy ever.

Now add a second hawk. The strategy is still pretty effective; if the population is large enough, the two hawks will never even meet. But as the number of hawks grows, the chance of two of them encountering each other—and one of them dying in the resultant fight—increases. At some point, and the exact point depends on the parameters, there are enough other hawks around that being a hawk is as dangerous as being a dove has become. That's the stable percentage of hawks in the population.

Aside from making fighting more deadly or food less valuable, there are other ways to affect the percentages of hawks and doves. If doves can recognize hawks and refuse to engage, the population will have fewer hawks. If doves can survive hawk attacks without losing their food—by developing defenses, by learning to be sneaky—the population will have fewer hawks. If there is a way for doves to punish hawks, the population will have fewer hawks. If there is a way for doves to do even better if they work together, the population will have fewer hawks. If hawks can gang up on doves profitably, the population will have more hawks. In general, we get fewer hawks if we increase the benefits of being a dove and/or raise the costs of being a hawk, and we get more hawks if we do the reverse. All of this makes intuitive sense, and shouldn't come as a surprise.

And while a population consisting entirely of doves is stable, you can only get there if you start the game out that way. And if you assume that individuals in the game can think strategically and change their strategies as people can—doves can become hawks, and hawks can become doves—then an all-dove population is no longer stable. A physicist would describe an all-dove population as an unstable equilibrium. Given how easily a dove can become a hawk, it's very unstable. There will always be at least a minority of hawks.

The Hawk-Dove game is a model, and not intended to explain how cooperation evolved. However, several lessons can be learned by extrapolating the Hawk-Dove game into the real world. Any society will have a mix of people who cooperate and share, and people who defect and steal. But as the penalty, or cost, for attempting to steal, and failing, increases—it could be dying, it could be being jailed, it could be something else—there will be fewer defectors. Similarly, as the benefit of stealing increases—either in the value of what the thief gets, or in the probability he'll succeed in stealing—there will be more thieves.

In the real world, there are gradations of hawkishness. One person might murder someone to take his money; another might rob a person but let him live. A third might just shortchange him in some business transaction, or take an unfair share at the family dinner. Those are all hawkish behaviors, but they're not the same. Also, no one is 100% hawk or 100% dove; they're individual mixtures, depending on circumstance.[5]

If the benefit of being a hawk is greater than the risk of being a hawk, then hawks become the dominant strategy. Doves can't survive, and everyone becomes a hawk. That's anarchy: Hobbes's "war of all against all." In human terms, society falls apart. If we want to maintain a society based on cooperation, we need to ensure that the rate of defection stays small enough to allow society to remain cohesive.

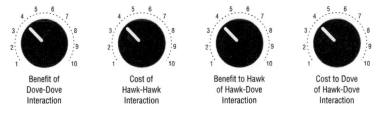

| Benefit of Dove-Dove Interaction | Cost of Hawk-Hawk Interaction | Benefit to Hawk of Hawk-Dove Interaction | Cost to Dove of Hawk-Dove Interaction |

Figure 4: Metaphorical Knobs to Control a Hawk-Dove Game

You can think of these parameters as knobs that control the rate of defection. We might not think of it in those terms, but it's what we do all the time in the real world. Want fewer burglars? Increase the prison term for burglary, put more policemen on the street, or subsidize burglar alarms. Willing to live with more burglars? Understaff police departments, make it easier for burglars to fence stolen merchandise, or convince people to keep more cash at home.[6] These are all societal pressures. So are increasing or decreasing social inequality, and teaching respect for other people's property in school.

In our world, the costs and benefits of being a defector vary over time. As we develop new security technologies, and as the defectors develop new ways around them, society stabilizes with a different scope of defection. Similarly, as we develop new systems—Internet banking, for example—and defectors develop new ways to attack them, society stabilizes with a still different scope of defection. If the police force gets better at arresting speeders, there will be fewer of them. If someone invents a radar detector or if cars handle better at higher speeds, there will be more speeders.[7]

We'll talk about this more in later chapters. The important point for right now is that no matter how hard we make life for the hawks among us—shunning them, removing them from society completely, making it less likely they will profit from their aggressive tactics—we will never be able to get the hawk percentage down to zero. Yes, we can make it very unprofitable to be a hawk, but if the percentage drops too low, being a hawk will become a more advantageous strategy. And because we humans are intelligent and adaptable, someone will figure that out and switch strategies.

Defectors are endemic to all complex systems. This is one of the dominant paradigms of life. We need to recognize that all of our complex human systems, whether they are millennia-old social systems or modern socio-technical systems, will always have parasites. There will always be a group of people who will try to take without giving back. The best we can hope for is to do what our bodies do, and what every natural ecosystem does: keep those parasites down to a tolerable level.

It's not even clear that natural selection favors the society with a minimum of hawk-like behavior. Hawks have value to society. In fact, if societies are in conflict with each other, it is evolutionarily advantageous to have some aggressive individuals. When war breaks out, the society with more hawks is likely to prevail. Again, think back to the primitive world in which we evolved. If you assume, as many anthropologists do, that tribal warfare was endemic among human societies, then having a substantial percentage of hawks around was valuable. Yes, they took advantage of the doves in peacetime, but they ensured the survival of those doves in wartime. Of course, we're now stuck with too many hawks because of the evolutionary pressures of 100,000 years ago.

●   ●   ●

I'm about to lump a lot of human traits together: cooperation, altruism, kindness, trustworthiness, and fairness. They're different, but all prosocial behaviors—behaviors intended to help others—and they're the glue that holds human society together. While psychologists put fine distinctions on them, considering them as facets of a whole is more useful for our purposes. They are all precursors of trust, and what allowed us to take the concept of specialization to a level unprecedented on our planet.

Figuring out how these traits evolved is an open question. Sure, they're great for our species as a whole, but that doesn't affect evolution. What matters for evolution is whether a particular characteristic helps the reproductive success of individuals with that characteristic. Kindness might be useful for society, but if it didn't result in kind people reproducing more successfully than unkind people, it would be bred out of the species pretty quickly.

There is an obvious evolutionary advantage in trusting kin: people with whom you share genetic material. If you have a gene, then your close relatives are likely to have that same gene. A gene that, on balance, makes it more likely for you to help your close relatives pass their genes on to future generations will also be more likely to be passed on to future generations—assuming, of course, that the help it provides outweighs the cost to provide it. For example, if a lioness is genetically predisposed to suckle her sister's offspring, there's a good chance that her nieces and nephews share the genes responsible for that behavior, and will pass them on to their own offspring.

The natural world is filled with examples of animals trusting, helping, and behaving altruistically with each other. Not just ants: many insects defend their nests or hives with their lives. Some animals who live in groups and fear predation—prairie dogs, ground squirrels, some monkeys, assorted herd animals, and many birds—alert the group with an alarm call if they spot a predator. Other animals hunt in groups. Most of these examples turn out to be kin helping kin.[8]

Extending this tendency towards non-kin is much more difficult.[9] Archaeologists have a four-stage model of the human process. Stage one happened 6 million years ago, when empathy and a motivation to help others developed in a common ancestor of humans and chimpanzees. Stage two began 1.8 million years ago; compassion can be seen in both short-term caring for sick individuals and special treatment for the dead. Stage three is much more recent; around 500,000 or 400,000 years ago, humans became dependent on group hunting, and started exhibiting long-term care for the injured and the infirm. Stage four occurred in modern humans starting 120,000 years ago, when compassion extended to strangers, animals, and sometimes even objects: religious objects, antiques, family heirlooms, etc. It probably didn't extend much past groups bigger than the Dunbar number of 150 until the invention of agriculture, about 10,000 years ago—I guess that's a fifth stage.

Still, that doesn't tell us how or why it eventually did.

There are two basic types of non-kin cooperation. The first is mutualism.[10] In some species, unrelated individuals cooperate because together they can perform tasks they couldn't do by themselves. A pack might hunt together because it can kill larger prey than the members could individually. Unrelated elephants help each other move objects they could not move alone.

Within a species, there's a tendency for individuals to cooperate by limiting their behavior. In many species, males fight each other for the prize of mating with a female. Primates fight to determine who is in charge of the tribe. In my house, the two cats fight to determine who gets to sit in the sunny chair. All these fights are serious, but tend to be non-injurious and are governed by ritual: roaring contests in red deer, claw-waving in male fiddler crabs, shell-rapping in hermit crabs. This is because these ritualized battles are often more about getting information about the other individual than actually fighting, and a non-lethal battle is often a more survivable strategy. The Hawk-Dove game can model these types of conflicts: if the risk of being a hawk is great enough, it makes evolutionary sense to be a dove even if your opponent is a hawk, because it's more survivable to retreat than to fight.[11]

So maybe we became smart enough to realize that cooperation usually beat defection as a survival skill, and modified our behavior accordingly. Those who could make that trade-off were more likely to pass their genes on to the next generation. This cooperation extended slowly outwards, from the immediate family group to more distant relatives to kith to familiar strangers—and over time, to unfamiliar strangers. And that cooperation slowly turned into trust.

Intelligence alone doesn't explain our trust of non-kin, though. Raw intelligence makes people calculating, but not necessarily honest or compassionate.[12] The missing ingredient is called *reciprocal altruism*. This is the second basic type of non-kin cooperation, and means that we tend to treat people as we have been treated.

Reciprocal altruism isn't limited to humans. Vampire bats must ingest blood every 60 hours or they'll die. If a bat can't find its own meal, a non-kin bat will often regurgitate some of its undigested blood and feed it to the hungry bat, knowing that another bat will regurgitate food for it at some later time. Then, the bats pay attention. They have large frontal lobes in their brains that they use to remember which other bats have shared blood with them in the past. A bat is more likely to share blood with a bat that has shared blood with it previously. Similarly, animals such as dogs, cats, horses, and some birds remember who was nice to them.

Think about our ancestors and their relationship with others living in their community. Cheating is valuable to the individual in the short term. But a person living in that community had an additional incentive not to cheat: if he did, he squandered his chance at future cooperation with his victim, and risked his reputation with the community. If the benefits of future cooperation are great enough, it makes evolutionary sense for non-kin to help each other if they can be reasonably sure they will be repaid at a later date.

A reasonable question, then, is whether altruism in the purest sense of the word really exists, or if it's all based on some anticipated reward or punishment. Perhaps Mother Teresa wasn't really altruistic; she expected her reward in Heaven. Perhaps our instinct to protect our children isn't really altruistic; it's because we expect them to care for us in our old age. We don't consider vampire bats altruistic; they expect repayment at some future date. Even the mother who sacrifices her life for her child might just be ensuring that her genes survive.

If we simplify, the psychological theory of transactional analysis holds that people expect some sort of return—either emotional or material—from their apparent altruism and kindness. So we rescue a stranger from a burning building because we expect to survive and be praised, and we give money to charity because it makes us feel virtuous. You can argue that whenever we act in the group interest, it's because we know we're better off when we do.

There's even an alternate theory that explains altruistic behavior without any need for pure, selfless altruism. Biologist Amotz Zahavi's handicap principle explains costly "signals" within species. If you're an individual of above-average fitness, it makes evolutionary sense to spend some of that surplus on costly and hard-to-fake signals to advertise that fact to a potential mate. This holds true for a peacock's tail and a stag's antlers, as well as for a human's apparently altruistic acts. So the man who rescues a stranger from a burning building is advertising his kindness and physical prowess, and the woman who gives money to charity is advertising her wealth. We do know that agreeableness is a trait desired by others in a mate; kind people are more likely to reproduce.

This seems an irrelevant exercise, rather like debating whether or not there is such a thing as free will.[13] George Price, one of the inventors of the Hawk-Dove game, was unable to accept altruism's selfish basis, and spent much of his later life trying to demonstrate how wrong his mathematical model was. He gave his money away to strangers, let the homeless live in his house, and eventually committed suicide from depression. I think a more optimistic viewpoint is in order. People behave in ways that are altruistic, empathic, kind, trustworthy, fair, and cooperative. We do these things even though we don't have to. Yes, we have evolved into a species that finds these traits desirable. Yes, this is primarily reciprocal. Yes, we are also intelligent and calculating, but this is precisely the point. We have the ability to decide whether to be prosocial or not, and most of us, most of the time, decide positively. And we call these behaviors "altruism," "kindness," and "cooperation." We trust because others are trustworthy.

Humans seem to have evolved along these lines, overcoming the murderousness that accompanied our increasing intelligence. There is an enormous amount of laboratory research on altruism, fairness, cooperation, and trust. Experimenters have subjects play a variety of bargaining games where they divide a pot of money amongst themselves, with different outcomes depending on whether or not they act in the group interest or in self-interest. These have names like the

Ultimatum game[14], the Dictator game[15], the Trust game[16], and the Public Goods game[17], all with many different variants designed to tease out a particular aspect of human prosocial behavior.[18] The general results seem to be that:

- People tend to be fair-minded.[19] They routinely reduce their own rewards in order to be fair to other players.
- People tend to want to punish unfairness, even at their own personal expense.[20] We have a sense of justice and responsibility, and we react negatively to those who act contrary to that sense. In many instances people also reduce their own reward in order to punish someone whom they perceive to be as acting unfairly.
- People tend to follow social or cultural norms with respect to these prosocial behaviors.[21] Definitions of fairness are cultural. People are more likely to be altruistic in a game that emphasizes altruism, and selfish in a game that emphasizes selfishness. Levels of trust and trustworthiness vary across cultures.
- People tend to be more trusting and altruistic with people they think they know and can identify with—even just a little bit—than with anonymous strangers.[22]
- External factors matter a lot. In experiments, people were kinder after they found a coin, traveled up an escalator (as opposed to traveling down), or watched a video of flying through clouds (as opposed to watching a video of driving on the ground).

Of course—and this is important to remember—these are typical results, and there is a wide variety of behavior among individual people.[23] This matches our experience in the world.

Neuroscience may also help explain altruism, most recently using mirror neurons. These are neurons in our brain that fire both when we perform an action[24] and when we observe someone else performing the same action. First discovered in 1992, mirror neurons are theorized to be critical in imitation and learning, language acquisition, developing a theory of mind, empathy, and a variety of other prosocial behaviors.

Additionally, a large body of neuroscience research supports the notion that we are altruistic innately, even if we receive no direct benefit, because at a deep level we want to be. Studies using functional magnetic resonance imaging (fMRI) show that the amygdala, the primitive part of the brain associated with fear and anger, is involved in decisions about fairness and justice. And it's probably not an unrelated side-effect that people who observe others acting either fairly or unfairly rate the fair people as significantly more agreeable, likeable, and attractive than the unfair people. We treat each other altruistically because it gives us pleasure to do so.

We not only innately trust, but we want to be trusted. A lot of this is intellectually calculated, but it goes deeper than that. Our need to be trusted is innate. There's even a biological feedback loop. Researchers have found that oxytocin— a hormone released during social bonding—naturally increases in a person who perceives that he is trusted by others. Similarly, artificially increasing someone's oxytocin level makes her more trusting.

The philosopher and economist Adam Smith expressed a similar sentiment 300 years ago:

> How selfish so ever man may be supposed, there are evidently some principles in his nature, which interest him in the fortune of others, and render their happiness necessary to him, though he derives nothing from it except the pleasure of seeing it.

Of course, human trust isn't all-or-nothing. It's contextual, calibrated by our ability to calculate costs and benefits. A lot of our willingness to trust non-kin is calibrated by the society we live in. If we live in a polite society where trust is generally returned, we're at ease trusting first. If we live in a violent society where strangers are hostile and untrustworthy, we don't trust so easily and require further evidence that our trust will be reciprocated.

Our trust rules can be sloppy. We're more likely to trust people who are similar to us: look like us, dress like us, and speak the same language. In general, we're more likely to trust in familiar situations. We also generalize: if we have a good experience with people of a particular nationality or a particular profession, we are likely to trust others of the same type. And if we have a bad experience, we're likely to carry that mistrust to others of the same type.[25] These rules of thumb might not make logical sense in today's diverse world, but they seem to have been good ideas in our evolutionary past.

This is all good, but we have a chicken-and-egg problem. Until people start trusting non-kin, there is no evolutionary advantage to trusting non-kin. And until there's an evolutionary advantage to trusting non-kin, people won't be predisposed to trust non-kin. Just as a single hawk in a Hawk-Dove game can take advantage of everybody, a single dove in a Hawk-Dove game gets taken advantage of by everybody. That is, the first trusting person who engages with a group of untrustworthy people isn't going to do very well.

It turns out that cooperative behavior can overcome these problems. Mathematical biologist Martin A. Nowak has explored the evolution of cooperation using mathematics, computer models, and experiments, and has found four different mechanisms by which altruistic behavior can spontaneously evolve in non-kin groups:

- *Direct reciprocity.* Being altruistic towards you now is a good strategy because you'll be altruistic towards me later.
- *Indirect reciprocity.* Being altruistic towards you now is a good strategy because my reputation as an altruistic individual will increase, and someone else will be altruistic towards me later.[26]
- *Network reciprocity.* Being altruistic towards you now is a good strategy because we are both in a group whose members are altruistic to each other, and being part of that group means that someone else will be altruistic towards me later.
- *Group selection.* Being altruistic towards you now is a good strategy because we're both part of a group whose members are altruistic to each other, and our group of altruists is more likely to survive than a group of non-altruists.[27]

What methods work depend on how much it costs for one individual to help another, how beneficial the help is, and how likely it is that helpful individuals meet and recognize each other in the future. And, depending on details, there are several plausible biological models of how this sort of thing might have jump-started itself. Exactly how this evolved in humans is debated.[28] Philosopher Patricia Churchland suggests four coexistent characteristics of our pre-human ancestors that make all of Nowak's mechanisms likely: "loose hierarchy and related easygoing temperament, cooperative parenting extending to cooperating with the group, sexual selection, and lethal intergroup competition." The last one is especially interesting; our murderousness helped make us cooperative.

What's likely is that all six mechanisms—Nowak's four, kin selection, and Zahavi's handicap principle—were working at the same time. Also that there was a strong positive-feedback loop, as we became smarter and more social. Each individual mechanism contributes a bit towards the evolution of cooperation, which makes resultant individuals better able to pass their genes on to the next generation, which selects for a little more contribution from each mechanism, which makes resultant individuals even better able to pass their genes on, and so on. And these processes, especially group selection, work on both the genetic and cultural levels.

We became trustworthy, well...most of the time. We trusted others, well... most of the time. And, as we'll see, we used security to fill in the gaps where otherwise trust would fail. In a way, humans domesticated themselves.[29]

A Social History of Trust

Trust is rare on this planet. Here's primatologist Robert Sapolsky:

> When baboons hunt together they'd love to get as much meat as possible, but they're not very good at it. The baboon is a much more successful hunter when he hunts by himself than when he hunts in a group because they screw up every time they're in a group. Say three of them are running as fast as possible after a gazelle, and they're gaining on it, and they're deadly. But something goes on in one of their minds—I'm anthropomorphizing here—and he says to himself, "What am I doing here? I have no idea whatsoever, but I'm running as fast as possible, and this guy is running as fast as possible right behind me, and we had one hell of a fight about three months ago. I don't quite know why we're running so fast right now, but I'd better just stop and slash him in the face before he gets me." The baboon suddenly stops and turns around, and they go rolling over each other like Keystone cops and the gazelle is long gone because the baboons just became disinhibited. They get crazed around each other at every juncture.

We're not like that. Not only do we cooperate with people we know, we cooperate with people we've never even met. We treat strangers fairly, altruistically sometimes. We put group interest ahead of our own selfishness. More importantly, we control other people's selfish behaviors.

We do this through a combination of our own prosocial impulses and the societal pressures that keep us all in line. This is what allowed for the hunter-gatherer societies of prehistory, the civilization of history, and today's globalization.

But while our cultures evolved, our brains did not. As different as our lives are from those of the primitive hunter-gatherers who lived in Africa 100,000 years ago, genetically we have barely changed at all.[1] There simply hasn't been enough time. As Matt Ridley writes in *The Red Queen*:

Inside my skull is a brain that was designed to exploit the conditions of an African savanna between 3 million and 100,000 years ago. When my ancestors moved into Europe (I am a white European by descent) about 100,000 years ago, they quickly evolved a set of physiological features to suit the sunless climate of northern latitudes: pale skin to prevent rickets, male beards, and a circulation relatively resistant to frostbite. But little else changed. Skull size, body proportions, and teeth are all much the same as they are in a San tribesman from southern Africa. And there is little reason to believe that the grey matter inside the skull changed much, either. For a start, 100,000 years is only three thousand generations, a mere eye blink in evolution, equivalent to a day and a half in the life of bacteria. Moreover, until very recently the life of a European was essentially the same as that of an African. Both hunted meat and gathered plants. Both lived in social groups. Both had children dependent on their parents until their late teens. Both passed wisdom down with complex languages. Such evolutionary novelties as agriculture, metal, and writing arrived less than three hundred generations ago, far too recently to have left much imprint on my mind.

It is this disconnect between the speed of cultural evolution and memes—intragenerationally fast—and the speed of genetic evolution—glacially slow, literally—that make trust and security hard. We've evolved for the trust problem endemic to living in small family groups in the East African highlands in 100,000 BC. It's 21st century New York City that gives us problems.[2]

Our brains are sufficiently neuroplastic that we can adapt to today's world, but vestiges of our evolutionary past remain. These cognitive biases affect how we respond to fear, how we perceive risks (there's a whole list of them in Chapter 15), and how we weigh short-term versus long-term costs and benefits. That last one is particularly relevant to decisions about cooperation and defection. Psychological studies show that we have what's called a hyperbolic discounting rate: we often prefer lower payoffs sooner to higher payoffs later. As we saw in the previous chapter, decisions to cooperate often involve putting our long-term interests ahead of our short-term interests. In some ways, this is unnatural for us.

●   ●   ●

As we saw in the previous chapter, any system of cooperators also includes some defectors. So as we as a species became more cooperative, we evolved strategies for dealing with defectors.

Making this happen isn't free. We have evolved a variety of different mechanisms to induce cooperation, the societal pressures I'll discuss in Chapters 6 through 10. Francis Fukuyama wrote: "Widespread distrust in society...imposes a kind of tax on all forms of economic activity, a tax that high-trust societies do not have to pay." It's a tax on the honest. It's a tax imposed on ourselves by ourselves, because, human nature being what it is, too many of us would otherwise become hawks and take advantage of the rest of us. And it's an expensive tax.[3]

James Madison famously wrote: "If men were angels, no government would be necessary." If men were angels, no security would be necessary. Door locks, razor wire, tall fences, and burglar alarms wouldn't be necessary. Angels never go where they're not supposed to go. Police forces wouldn't be necessary. Armies? Countries of angels would be able to resolve their differences peacefully, and military expenses would be unnecessary.

Currency, that paper stuff that's deliberately made hard to counterfeit, wouldn't be necessary, as people could just write down how much money they had.[4] Angels never cheat, so nothing more would be required. Every security measure that isn't designed to be effective against accident, animals, forgetfulness, or legitimate differences between scrupulously honest angels could be dispensed with.

We wouldn't need police, judges, courtrooms, jails, and probation officers. Disputes would still need resolving, but we could get rid of everything associated with investigating, prosecuting, and punishing crime. Fraud detection would be unnecessary: the parts of our welfare and healthcare system that make sure people fairly benefit from those services and don't abuse them; and all of the anti-shoplifting systems in retail stores.

Entire industries would be unnecessary, like private security guards, security cameras, locksmithing, burglar alarms, automobile anti-theft, computer security, corporate security, airport security, and so on. And those are just the obvious ones; financial auditing, document authentication, and many other things would also be unnecessary.

Not being angels is expensive.

We don't pay a lot of these costs directly. The vast majority of them are hidden in the price of the things we buy. Groceries cost more because some people shoplift. Plane tickets cost more because some people try to blow planes up. Banks pay out lower interest rates because of fraud. Everything we do or buy costs more because some sort of security is required to deliver it.

Even greater are the non-monetary costs: less autonomy, reduced freedom, ceding of authority, lost privacy, and so on. These trade-offs are subjective, of course, and some people value them more than others. But it's these costs that lead to social collapse if they get too high.

Security isn't just a tax on the honest, it's a very expensive tax on the honest. If all men were angels, just think of the savings!

●   ●   ●

It wasn't always like this. Security used to be cheap. Societal pressures used to be an incidental cost of society itself. Many of our societal pressures evolved far back in human prehistory, well before we had any societies larger than extended family groups. We touched on these mechanisms in the previous chapter: both the moral mechanisms in our brains that internally regulate our behavior, and the reputational mechanisms we all use to regulate each other's behavior.

Morals and reputation comprise our prehistoric toolbox of societal pressures. They are informal, and operate at both conscious and subconscious levels in our brains: I refer to the pair of them, unenhanced by technology, as *social pressures*. They evolved together, and as such are closely related and intertwined in our brains and societies. From a biological or behaviorist perspective, there's a reasonable argument that my distinction between moral and reputational systems is both arbitrary and illusory, and that differentiating the two doesn't make much sense. But from our perspective of inducing trust, they are very different.

Despite the prevalence of war, violence, and general deceptiveness throughout human history—and the enormous amount of damage wrought by defectors—these ancient moral and reputational systems have worked amazingly well. Most of us try not to treat others unfairly, both because it makes us feel bad and because we know they'll treat us badly in return. Most of us don't steal, both because we feel guilty when we do and because there are consequences if we get caught. Most of us are trustworthy towards strangers—within the realistic constraints of the society we live in—because we recognize it's in our long-term interest. And we trust strangers because we recognize it is in their interest to act trustworthily. We don't want a reputation as an untrustworthy, or an untrusting, person.

Here's an example from early human prehistory: two opposing tendencies that would cause society to fall apart if individuals couldn't trust each other. On one hand, we formed pair bonds for the purpose of child-rearing. On the other hand, we had a primarily gender-based division of labor that forced men and women to separate as they went about their different hunting and gathering tasks. This meant that primitive humans needed to trust that everyone honored the integrity of these pair bonds, since individuals often couldn't be around to police them directly. The difficulty in resolving those opposing tendencies is known as Deacon's Paradox.[5]

No, anthropologists don't have unrealistic views on the sanctity of marriage. They know that illicit affairs go on all the time.[6] But they also realize that such indiscretions occur with much less frequency than they would if mating weren't largely based on pair-bonding.[7] Most people are honest most of the time, and most pair bonds are respected most of the time. Deacon singled out one particular human capability—the ability to form symbolic contracts—as the particular mechanism that polices sexual fidelity. This isn't just about two people deciding to cohabitate, share food, and produce and raise offspring. It's about two people making a public declaration of commitment in marriage ceremonies, and enlisting other members of the community to simultaneously recognize and promote the stability of their pair bond. Because everyone has a stake in supporting sexual fidelity within the community, everyone keeps an eye on everyone else and punishes illicit matings.

This is an example of a social pressure. It's informal and ad hoc, but it protects society as a whole against the potentially destabilizing individual actions of its members. It protects society from defectors, not by making them disappear, but by keeping their successes down to a manageable rate. Without it, primitive humans wouldn't have trusted each other enough to establish gender-based division of labor and, consequently, could never have coalesced into communities of both kith and kin.

Other examples include being praised for good behavior, being gossiped about and snubbed socially for bad behavior, being shamed, shunned, killed, and—this is much the same as being killed—ostracized and cast out of the group.

I'm omitting a lot of detail, and there are all sorts of open research questions. How did these various social pressures evolve? When did they first appear, and how did their emergence separate us from the other primates—and other protohumans?[8] How did trust affect intelligence, and how did intelligence affect trust? For our purposes, it's enough to say that they evolved to overcome our increased deceptiveness and murderousness.

In a primitive society, these social pressures are good enough. When you're living in a small community, and objects are few and hard to make, it's pretty easy to deal with the problem of theft. If Alice loses a bowl at the same time Bob shows up with an identical bowl, everyone in the community knows that Bob stole it from Alice and can then punish Bob. The problem is that these mechanisms don't scale. As communities grow larger, as they get more complex, as social ties weaken and anonymity proliferates, this system of theft prevention—morals keeping most people honest, and informal detection, followed by punishment, leading to deterrence to keep the rest honest—starts to fail.

Remember the Dunbar number? Actually, Dunbar proposed several natural human group sizes that increase by a factor of approximately three: 5, 15, 50, 150, 500, and 1,500—although, really, the numbers aren't as precise as all that. The layers relate to both the intensity and intimacy of relationships, and the frequency of contact.

The smallest, three to five, is a *clique*: the number of people from whom you would seek help in times of severe emotional distress. The 12-to-20 person group is the *sympathy group*: people with whom you have a particularly close relationship. After that, 30 to 50 is the typical size of hunter-gatherer overnight camps, generally drawn from a single pool of 150 people. The 500-person group is the *megaband*, and the 1,500-person group is the *tribe*; both terms are common in ethnographic literature. Fifteen hundred is roughly the number of faces we can recognize, and the typical size of a hunter-gatherer society.[9]

Evolutionary psychologists are still debating Dunbar's findings, and whether there are as many distinct levels as Dunbar postulates. Regardless of how this all shakes out, for our purposes it's enough to notice that as we move from smaller group sizes to larger ones, our informal social pressures begin to fail, necessitating the development of more formal ones. A family doesn't need formal rules for sharing food, but a larger group in a communal dining hall will. Small communities don't need birth registration procedures, marriages certified by an authority, laws of inheritance, or rules governing real-estate transfer; larger communities do. Small companies don't need employee name badges, because everyone already knows everyone else; larger companies need them and many other rules besides.

To put it another way, our trust needs are a function of scale. As the number of people we dealt with increased, we no longer knew them well enough to be able to trust their intentions, so our prehistoric trust toolbox started failing. As we developed agriculture and needed to trust more people over increased distance—physical distance, temporal distance, emotional distance—we needed additional societal pressures to elicit trustworthiness at this new scale. As the number of those interactions increased, and as the potential damage the group could do to the individual increased, we needed even more. If humans were incapable of developing these more formal societal pressures, societies either would have stopped growing or would have disintegrated entirely.

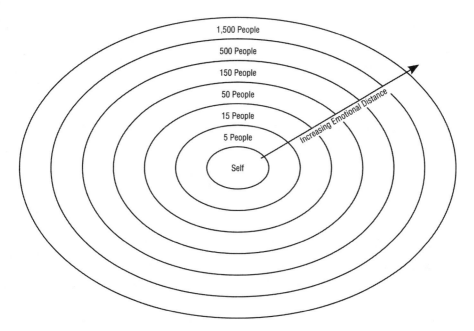

Figure 5: Dunbar Numbers

Agriculture required protecting resources, through violence if necessary. Luckily, two things happened. We invented institutions—government, basically—and we developed technology. Both of them allowed for human societies to grow larger without tearing themselves apart.

Institutions formalized reputational pressure. With government came laws, enforcement, and formal punishment. I'm not implying that the original purpose of government was facilitating trust, only that part of what these formal institutions did was codify the existing societal norms. This codification is a trust mechanism.

History has forgotten all of these early institutions. Some were undoubtedly civil. Some were religious.[10] No one knows the details of how our ancestors made the transition from an extended family to a tribe of several extended families, because they happened thousands of years before anyone got around to inventing writing. Certainly there's overlap between formal reputational and early institutional pressures. It's enough to say that we made the transition, and that we augmented moral and reputational pressures with institutional pressures.[11]

This was a critical development, one that gives us the ability to trust people's actions, even if we can't trust their intentions. We reinforced our informal recognition of pair bonds with formal marriage through religious and civil institutions. We added laws about theft, and prescribed specific punishments. A lot of this, at least initially, is formalizing reputational mechanisms so that they scale to larger groups. But something important happens in the transition: institutional pressures require institutions to implement them. Society has to designate a subset of individuals to enforce the laws. Think of elders, guards, police forces, and judicial systems; priests also take on this role.

Institutions also enabled the formation of groups of groups, and subgroups within groups. So small tribes could become part of larger political groupings. Individual churches could become part of a larger religious organization. Companies could have divisions. Government organizations could have departments. Empires could form, and remain stable over many generations. Institutions scale in a way that morals and reputation do not, and this has allowed societies to grow at a rate never before seen on the planet.

The second force that allowed society to scale was technology—both technology in general and security technology specifically. Security systems are the final way we induce trust. Early security mechanisms included building earthen berms, wearing animal skins as camouflage, and digging pit traps. In one sense, security isn't anything new; we learned in Chapter 2 that it's been around almost as long as life itself. That primitive sort of security is what you might call natural defenses, focused on the individual. But when societies got together and realized they could, as a group, implement security systems, security became a form of societal pressure. In a sense, security technologies allow natural defenses to scale to protect against intra-group defection.

Technology also allowed informal social pressures to scale and become what I call societal pressures. Morals could be written down and passed from generation to generation. Reputation could similarly be recorded, and transferred from one person to another. This sort of thing depends a lot on technology: from the Bible and letters of introduction, to online debates on morality, to entries on the Angie's List database.

A good way to think about it is that both institutional pressure and security systems allow us to overcome the limitations of the Dunbar numbers by enabling people to trust systems instead of people. Instead of having to trust individual merchants, people can trust the laws that regulate merchants. Instead of having to evaluate the trustworthiness of individual borrowers, banks and other lending institutions can trust the credit rating system. Instead of trusting that people won't try to rob my house, I can trust the locks on my doors and—if I want to turn it on—my burglar alarm.

Technology changes the efficacy of societal pressures in another way as well. As soon as the different systems of societal pressure themselves need to be secured, it becomes possible for a defector to attack those security systems directly. Once there's a technologically enhanced system of reputational pressure, that system needs to be protected with security technology. So we need signet rings and wax seals to secure letters of introduction, and computer security measures that keep the Angie's List database from being hacked. Similarly, once forensic measures exist to help enforce laws, those forensic measures can be directly targeted. So burglars wear gloves to keep from leaving fingerprints, and file down VINs to prevent stolen cars from being tracked.

There's a bigger change that results from society's increased scale. As society moved from informal social pressures to more formal societal pressures—whether institutional pressures and security systems, or technologically enhanced moral and reputational pressures—the nature of trust changed. Recall our two definitions of trust from Chapter 1: trust of intentions and trust of actions. In smaller societies, we are usually concerned with trust in the first definition. We're intimately familiar with the people we're interacting with, and have a good idea about their intentions. The social pressures induce cooperation in specific instances, but are also concerned with their overall intentions. As society grows and social ties weaken, we lose this intimacy and become more concerned with trust in the second definition. We don't know who we're interacting with, and have no idea about their intentions, so we concern ourselves with their actions. Societal pressures become more about inducing specific actions: compliance.

Compliance isn't as good as actual trustworthiness, but it's good enough. Both elicit trust.

Also through history, technology allowed specialization, which encouraged larger group sizes. For example, a single farmer could grow enough to sustain more people, permitting even greater specialization. In this and other ways, general technological innovations enabled society to grow even larger and more complex. Dunbar's numbers remain constant, but postal services, telegraph, radio, telephone, television, and now the Internet have allowed us to interact with more people than ever before. Travel has grown increasingly fast and increasingly long distance over the millennia, and has allowed us to meet more people face-to-face. Countries have gotten larger, and there are multinational quasi-governmental organizations. Governments have grown more sophisticated. Organizations have grown larger and more geographically dispersed. Businesses have gotten larger; now there are multinational corporations employing hundreds of thousands of people controlling assets across several continents. If your Facebook account has substantially more than 150 friends, you probably only have a superficial connection with many of them.[12]

Technology also increases societal complexity. Automation and mass distribution mean one person can affect more people and more of the planet. Long-distance communication, transport, and travel mean that people can affect each other even if they're far away. Governments have gotten larger, both in terms of geographical area and level of complexity. Computer and networking technology mean that things happen faster, and information that might once have been restricted to specialists can be made available to a worldwide audience. These further increases in scale have a major effect on societal pressures, as we'll see in Chapter 16.

None of this is to say that societal pressures result in a fair, equitable, or moral society. The Code of Hammurabi from 1700 BC, the first written code of laws in human history, contains some laws that would be considered barbaric today: if a son strikes his father, his hands shall be hewn off; if anyone commits a robbery and is caught, he shall be put to death; if anyone brings an accusation of any crime before the elders, and does not prove what he has charged, he shall, if a capital offense is charged, be put to death. And world history is filled with governments that have oppressed, persecuted, and even massacred their own people. There's nothing to guarantee that the majority actually approves of these laws; societal interest and societal norms might be dictated by an authoritarian ruler. The only thing societal pressures guarantee is that, in the short run at least, society doesn't fall apart.

Furthermore, societal pressures protect a society from change: bad, good, and indeterminate. Cooperators are, by definition, those who follow the group norm. They put the group interest ahead of any competing interests, and by doing so, make it harder for the group norm to change. If the group norm is unsustainable, this can fatally harm society in the long run.

Remember that society as a whole isn't the only group we're concerned about here. Societal pressures can be found in any group situation. They're how a group of friends protect themselves from greedy people at communal dinners. They enable criminal organizations to protect themselves from loose cannons and potential turncoats within their own ranks. And they're how a military protects itself from deserters and insubordinates, and how corporations protect themselves from embezzling employees.

Societal Dilemmas

Here are some questions related to trust:

- During a natural disaster, should I steal a big-screen TV? What about food to feed my family?
- As a kamikaze pilot, should I refuse to kill myself? What if I'm just a foot soldier being ordered to attack a heavily armed enemy bunker?
- As a company employee, should I work hard or slack off? What if the people around me are slacking off and getting away with it? What if my job is critical and, by slacking off, I harm everyone else's year-end bonuses?

There's a *risk trade-off* at the heart of every one of these questions. When deciding whether to cooperate and follow the group norm, or defect and follow some competing norm, an individual has to weigh the costs and benefits of each option. I'm going to use a construct I call a societal dilemma to capture the tension between group interest and a competing interest.

What makes something a societal dilemma, and not just an individual's free choice to do whatever he wants and risk the consequences, is that there are societal repercussions of the trade-off. Society as a whole cares about the dilemma, because if enough people defect, something extreme happens. It might be bad, like widespread famine, or it might be good, like civil rights. But since a societal dilemma is from the point of view of societal norms, by definition it's in society's collective best interest to ensure widespread cooperation.

Let's start with the smallest society possible: two people. Another model from game theory works here. It's called the Prisoner's Dilemma.[1]

Alice and Bob are partners in crime, and they've both been arrested for burglary.[2] The police don't have enough evidence to convict either of them, so they bring them into separate interrogation rooms and offer each one a deal. "If you betray your accomplice and agree to testify against her," the policeman says, "I'll let you go free and your partner will get ten years in jail. If you both betray each other, we don't need your testimony, and you'll each get six years in jail. But if you cooperate with your partner and both refuse to say anything, I can only convict you on a minor charge—one year in jail."[3]

Neither Alice nor Bob is fully in charge of his or her own destiny, since the outcome for each depends on the other's decision. Neither has any way of knowing, or influencing, the other's decision; and they don't trust each other.

Imagine Alice evaluating her two options: "If Bob stays silent," she thinks, "then it would be in my best interest to testify against him. It's a choice between no jail time versus one year in jail, and that's an easy choice. Similarly, if Bob rats on me, it's also in my interest to testify. That's a choice between six years in jail versus ten years in jail. Because I have no control over Bob's decision, testifying gives me the better outcome, regardless of what he chooses to do. It's obviously in my best interest to betray Bob: to confess and agree to testify against him." That's what she decides to do.

Bob, in a holding cell down the hall, is evaluating the same options. He goes through the same reasoning—he doesn't care about Alice any more than she cares about him—and arrives at the same conclusion.

So both Alice and Bob confess. The police no longer need either one to testify against the other, and each spends six years in jail. But here's the rub: if they had both remained silent, each would have spent only one year in jail.

Societal Dilemma: Prisoners confessing.	
Society: A group of two prisoners.	
Group interest: Minimize total jail time for all involved.	Competing interest: Minimize individual jail time.
Group norm: To cooperate with the other prisoner and remain silent.	Corresponding defection: Testify against the other.

The Prisoner's Dilemma encapsulates the conflict between group interest and self-interest. As a pair, Alice and Bob are best off if they both remain silent and spend only one year in jail. But by each following his or her own self-interest, they both end up with worse outcomes individually.

The only way they can end up with the best outcome—one year in jail, as opposed to six, or ten—is by acting in their group interest. Of course, that only makes sense if each can trust the other to do the same. But Alice and Bob can't.

Borrowing a term from economics, the other prisoner's jail time is an *externality*. That is, it's an effect of a decision not borne by the decision maker. To Alice, Bob's jail time is an externality. And to Bob, Alice's jail time is an externality.

I like the prisoner story because it's a reminder that cooperation doesn't imply anything moral; it just means going along with the group norm. Similarly, defection doesn't necessarily imply anything immoral; it just means putting some competing interest ahead of the group interest.

Basic commerce is another type of Prisoner's Dilemma, although you might not have thought about it that way before. Cognitive scientist Douglas Hofstadter liked this story better than prisoners, confessions, and jail time.

> Two people meet and exchange closed bags, with the understanding that one of them contains money, and the other contains a purchase. Either player can choose to honor the deal by putting into his or her bag what he or she agreed, or he or she can defect by handing over an empty bag.

It's easy to see one trust mechanism that keeps merchants from cheating: their reputations as merchants. It's also easy to see a measure that keeps customers from cheating: they're likely to be arrested or at least barred from the store. These are examples of societal pressures, and they'll return in the next chapters.

This example illustrates something else that's important: societal dilemmas are not always symmetrical. The merchant and a customer have different roles, and different options for cooperating and defecting. They also have different incentives to defect, and different competing norms.

Here's a societal dilemma involving two companies. They are selling identical products at identical prices, with identical customer service and everything else. Sunoco and Amoco gasoline, perhaps. They are the only companies selling those products, and there's a fixed number of customers for them to divvy up. The only way they can increase their market share is by advertising, and any increase in market share comes at the expense of the other company's. For simplicity's sake, assume that each can spend either a fixed amount on advertising or none at all; there isn't a variable amount of advertising spending that they can do. Also assume that if one advertises and the other does not, the company that advertises gains an increase in market share that more than makes up for the advertising investment. If both advertise, their investments cancel each other out and market share stays the same for each. Here's the question: advertise or not?

It's the same risk trade-off as before. From Alice's perspective, if she advertises and Bob does not, she increases her market share. But if she doesn't advertise and Bob does, she loses market share. She's better off advertising, regardless of what Bob does. Bob makes the same trade-off, so they both end up advertising and see no change in market share, when they would both have been better off saving their money.

Societal Dilemma: Advertising.	
Society: Two companies selling the same product.	
Group interest: Maximize profits. Group norm: To not engage in a costly and fruitless advertising arms race, and not advertise.	Competing interest: Maximize profits at the expense of the other company. Corresponding defection: Advertise.

This is your basic arms race, in which the various factions expend effort just to stay in the same place relative to each other. The USA and the USSR did this during the Cold War. Rival political parties do it, too.

If you assume the individuals can switch between strategies and you set the parameters right, the Hawk-Dove game is a Prisoner's Dilemma. When pairs of individuals interact, they each have the choice of cooperating (being a dove) or defecting (being a hawk). Both individuals know that cooperating is the best strategy for them as a pair, but that individually they're each better off being a hawk.

Not every interaction between two people involves a Prisoner's Dilemma. Imagine two drivers who are both stuck because a tree is blocking the road. The tree is too heavy for one person to move on his own, but it can be moved if they work together. Here, there's no conflict. It is in both their selfish interest and their group interest to move the tree together. But Prisoner's Dilemmas are common, and once you're primed to notice them, you'll start seeing them everywhere.[4]

● ● ●

The basic Prisoner's Dilemma formula involves two people who must decide between their own self-interest and the interest of their two-person group. This is interesting—and has been studied extensively[5]—but it's too simplistic for our purposes. We are more concerned with scenarios involving larger groups, with dozens, hundreds, thousands, even millions of people in a single dilemma.

Here's a classic societal dilemma: overfishing. As long as you don't catch too many fish in any area, the remaining fish can breed fast enough to keep up with demand. But if you start taking too many fish out of the water, the remaining fish can't breed fast enough and the whole population collapses.

If there were only one fisher, she could decide how much fish to catch based on both her immediate and long-term interests. She could catch all the fish she was able to in one year, and make a lot of money. Or she could catch fewer fish this year, making less money, but ensuring herself an income for years to come. It's a pretty easy decision to make—assuming she's not engaged in subsistence fishing—and you can imagine that in most instances, the fisher would not sacrifice her future livelihood for a short-term gain.

But as soon as there's more than one boat in the water, things become more complicated. Each fisher not only has to worry about overfishing the waters herself, but whether the other fishers are doing the same. There's a societal dilemma at the core of each one of their decisions.

Societal Dilemma: Overfishing.	
Society: A group of fishers all fishing out of the same waters.	
Group interest: The productivity of the fishing waters over the long term. Group norm: To limit individual catches.	Competing interest: Short-term profit. Corresponding defection: Take more than your share of fish.

Fisher Alice's trade-off includes the same elements as Prisoner Alice's trade-off. Alice can either act in her short-term self-interest and catch a lot of fish, or act in the group interest of all the local fishers and catch fewer fish. If everyone else acts in the group interest, then Alice is better off acting in her own selfish interest. She'll catch more fish, and fishing stocks will remain strong because she's the only one overfishing. But if Alice acts in the group interest while others act in their self-interest, she'll have sacrificed her own short-term gain for nothing: she'll catch fewer fish, and the fishing stocks will still collapse due to everyone else's overfishing.

Her analysis leads to the decision to overfish. That makes sense, but—of course—if everyone acts according to the same analysis, they'll end up collapsing the fishing stocks and ruining the industry for everyone. This is called a *Tragedy of the Commons*, and was first described by the ecologist Garrett Hardin in 1968.[6]

A Tragedy of the Commons occurs whenever a group shares a limited resource: not just fisheries, but grazing lands, water rights, time on a piece of shared exercise equipment at a gym, an unguarded plate of cookies in the kitchen. In a forest, you can cut everything down for maximum short-term profit, or selectively harvest for sustainability. Someone who owns the forest can make the trade-off for himself, but when an unorganized group together owns the forest there's no one to limit the harvest, and a Tragedy of the Commons can result.

A Tragedy of the Commons is more complicated than a two-person Prisoner's Dilemma, because the other fishers aren't making this decision collectively. Instead, each individual fisher decides for himself what to do. In the two-person dilemma, Alice had to try to predict what Bob would do. In this larger dilemma, many more outcomes are possible.

Assume there are 100 fishers in total. Any number from 0 through 100 could act in their selfish interest and overfish. Harm to the group would increase as the scope of overfishing increases, regardless of what Alice does. Alice would probably not be harmed at all by 1 fisher overfishing, and she would be significantly harmed if all 99 chose to do the same. Fifty overfishers would cause some amount of harm; 20, a lesser amount. There are degrees of overfishing. Twenty fishers who each overfish by a small amount might do less damage to the fish stocks than 5 who take everything they can out of the water. What matters here is the scope of defection: the number of overfishers, but also the frequency of overfishing, and the magnitude of each overfishing incident.

At some scope of defection, stocks will be so depleted that everyone's catch in future years will be jeopardized. There's more at stake than whether Alice gets her fair share. In game theory, this is called a non-zero-sum game because wins and losses don't add up to zero: there are outcomes where everyone loses, and loses big.[7] A fishery is non-zero-sum. Other societal dilemmas might seem like zero-sum games with a finite resource: if one person takes more, others get less. But even in these instances, there is a potential for catastrophe in widespread defection. If a community can't share a common water resource, everyone's crops will die because farmers can't plan on water use. If a few people constantly hog the exercise equipment, others won't come to the gym, which will lose membership and close. If someone consistently takes all the cookies, Mother will stop baking them. Remember: it's a bad parasite that kills its host.

The non-zero-sum property is an essential aspect of a societal dilemma. The group result barely depends on any single person's actions. Alice's cooperation or defection doesn't appreciably change the number of overfishers, nor is it likely to collapse the fishing stocks. It's the actions of the group that determine the overall result; at some point, the effects of the overfishers on the group will change from nothing to irreversible damage.

It's also possible that the group will not reach that point, even if all the members take as much fish as they want. There might not be enough fishers in the waters, or fishing technology might not be efficient enough. All the members of the group might be able to fish as much as they possibly can without affecting each other or future fishing stocks. But at some point, either the waters will get crowded enough or the fishers will get technologically advanced enough that the Tragedy of the Commons dilemma will occur.

The disconnect between Alice's individual actions and the effect of the group's actions as a whole makes societal dilemmas even harder to solve in larger groups. Under a rational economic analysis, it makes no sense for Alice to cooperate. The group will do whatever it does, regardless of her actions, and her individual cooperation or defection won't change that. All she's really deciding is whether to seize or forgo the short-term benefits of defecting.

Societal Dilemma: Tragedy of the Commons.	
Society: Some group of people, either a society of interest or a society of circumstance.	
Group interest: That the common resource not run out, and be available for all.	Competing interest: Get as much of that resource as possible in the short term.
Group norm: Cooperate and share that resource within its sustainability limits..	Corresponding defection: Take as much of that shared resource as you can.

In a Tragedy of the Commons, people acting in their self-interest harm the group interest. There's another type of societal dilemma, where people can receive the benefit of those who act in the group interest without having to act in the group interest themselves. It's called the *free-rider problem*.

Whooping cough (otherwise known as pertussis) is a good example. It's both almost entirely preventable and almost entirely untreatable. Early in the 20th century, before the establishment of widespread vaccination programs, it was one of the most feared illnesses, and it remains a significant cause of death in developing countries. Compared to other vaccines, the pertussis vaccine isn't actually very effective at conferring immunity to any one individual. The standard infant schedule calls for four shots. After the first shot, about 30% become immune; after two, 50%; and even after all four shots have been administered, only about 90% of individuals have enough antibodies to fight off the disease.

What's more, vaccination is not without risk. The original pertussis vaccine carried a small risk of neurological damage. It has since been replaced with a safer vaccine, but a minuscule risk of adverse reactions still persists, as it does with any vaccine. In the late 1960s and early 1970s, adverse vaccine reactions received a lot of attention in the media, most notably in Sweden, Japan, and the UK. Parents began to refuse vaccinations for their children, and doctors were often powerless to persuade them that the benefits outweighed the risks.

One of the primary benefits of vaccination is herd immunity. If almost everyone is vaccinated against a particular disease, there's no way for it to take hold in the community. Even if someone gets the disease, it's unlikely he will be able to infect others. Parents who refuse to have their children vaccinated do not only endanger their own children; they increase the risk of infection for everyone in the community. This increases, of course, as more parents opt out of vaccination programs. And while this is true for any vaccinated disease, the danger is particularly acute for whooping cough because the vaccine doesn't confer complete immunity and isn't recommended for the youngest infants or for those who are immune-compromised.

Between 1974 and 1979, the rate of pertussis vaccination among Swedish infants dropped precipitously, from 90% to 12%. Correspondingly, the incidence of whooping cough in Swedish children under four skyrocketed from 0.05% in 1975—effectively zero—to 3.4% by 1983. Sweden went from a country that had all but eradicated whooping cough to a country with a 1 in 30 infection rate.

When parents decide whether or not to immunize their child, they are faced with a societal dilemma. They can choose to cooperate and vaccinate their child, or they can choose to defect and refuse. As long as most children are vaccinated, a child is better off not being immunized: he avoids the chance of adverse effects, but reaps the benefit of herd immunity. But if there are too many defectors, everyone suffers the increased risk of epidemics. And it's a non-zero-sum game; there's a point where epidemics suddenly become much more likely.

Societal Dilemma: Vaccination.	
Society: Society as a whole.	
Group interest: No epidemics. Group norm: Vaccinate.	Competing interest: Avoid the small risk of adverse side effects (encephalopathy, allergic or autoimmune reactions, or—in extreme cases—contracting the disease from the vaccination).
	Corresponding defection: Avoid vaccination.

A free rider receives the benefit of everyone else's cooperation without having to cooperate himself. Think of a single person in the community who doesn't pay his taxes; he gets all the benefits of the public institutions those taxes pay for—police and fire departments, road construction and maintenance, regulations to keep his food and workplace safe, a military—without having to actually pay for them.

But as more and more people stop paying their taxes, the government can provide fewer and fewer of those services—services that would be much more expensive or impossible for individuals to provide on their own—and the benefit of free riding is reduced. In the extreme, the whole system collapses.

Imagine a condominium without smoke detectors. The first tenant to install one is a sucker, because even though he pays for his detector, the building can burn down from a fire started elsewhere. The last tenant to install one is a fool, because he already receives the benefits of everyone else's detectors without having to pay anything.

It's easy to dismiss those original two-person examples as the responsibility of the two people alone. Alice and Bob can decide whether to rat on each other in jail, or whether to cheat each other when they buy and sell sealed bags. No one else needs to get involved. There's certainly no reason for society to get involved. Let the buyer and seller beware.

Society becomes involved because a broader societal dilemma emerges from Alice's and Bob's decisions. Let's look at the sealed bag exchange, focusing on customer Alice. She can either cooperate by paying for her purchase, or defect by defrauding merchant Bob. Yes, that decision most directly affects Bob, but—thinking more broadly about theft and society—it affects everyone.

Societal Dilemma: Defrauding merchants.	
Society: Those who buy and sell goods.	
Group interest: For commerce to operate smoothly.	Competing interest: Get stuff without having to pay for it.
Group norm: Don't defraud merchants.	Corresponding defection: Defraud merchants.

It's not that society cares about any particular thief; rather, society wants property rights to be respected. Note that it doesn't matter what sort of property rights deserve respect. There could be communal property, there could be personal property, and there could be everything in-between. What's important for society is for everyone to respect what society decides are the property rules that make collective life work, and then for everybody to be able to trust that those rules will be followed.[8]

Similarly, if we focus on merchant Bob, we can see that he is in a corresponding societal dilemma with the society composed of all the other merchants: he can either treat his customers fairly or he can defraud them. Society doesn't want dishonest merchants; not only because we don't want to be defrauded, but also because we know that our entire system of commerce hinges on trust.

The alternative just wouldn't work. Merchants would stop doing transactions with all customers, not just with Alice. And customers would stop doing transactions with all merchants. Or they could both implement expensive and time-consuming bag-checking procedures that require them to each hire someone to help them perform transactions. And so on. Without trust, commerce collapses.

Even prisoners can have a broader community with a stake in whether or not prisoners confess. A criminal organization won't be concerned with Alice or Bob personally, but with members' loyalty to the organization. The organization as a whole benefits if it is viewed by individual members as an association in which they can trust others to keep their secrets, even at great personal cost.

Societal Dilemma: Criminals testifying against each other.	
Society: The criminal organization.	
Group interest: To minimize the amount of jail time for the society.	Competing interest: To minimize personal jail time.
Group norm: Don't testify against each other.	Corresponding defection: Testify against each other in exchange for reduced jail time.

The interesting thing about these dilemmas is that, looking at them in isolation, there's no logical solution. Thinking back to the prisoners, there is no analysis by which cooperation makes sense. Because they can't trust each other, they both end up confessing. This is the fundamental problem with cooperation: trust is unnatural, and it's not in the individual's short-term self-interest. This problem is why cooperation is so rare in the natural world, why it took so long to develop in humans, and why we have developed societal pressures as a way to enforce cooperation and hold society together.

PART II
A Model of Trust

Societal Pressures

I n game theory, Prisoner's Dilemmas have no solution. Because the two prisoners, or the merchant and customer, can't trust each other, they both end up defecting. The larger societal dilemmas—the arms race, the Tragedy of the Commons, and the free-rider problem—are similarly unsolvable. Defecting is the only course that makes logical sense, even though the end result will be disastrous for the entire group.

But that's not how people generally operate. We cooperate all the time. We engage in honest commerce, although Enron and AIG and Countrywide are some pretty spectacular exceptions. Most of us don't overfish, even though the few of us who do have depleted the ocean's stocks. We mostly vaccinate our children, despite the minor risk of an adverse reaction. Sometimes, even, we don't rat on each other in prison.[1]

Prisoner's Dilemmas involve a risk trade-off between group interest and self-interest, but it's generally only a dilemma if you look at it very narrowly. For most people, most of the time, there's no actual dilemma. We don't stand at the checkout line at a store thinking: "Either the merchant is selling me a big screen TV, or this box is secretly filled with rocks. If it's rocks, I'm better off giving him counterfeit money. And if it has a TV, I'm still better off giving him counterfeit money." Generally, we just pay for the TV, put it in our car, and drive home. And if we're professional check forgers, we don't think through the dilemma, either. We pay for the TV with a bad check, put it in our car—I suppose it's a getaway car this time—and drive back to our lair.

The problem isn't with people; the problem is with the dilemma.[2] Societal dilemmas are choices between group interest and some competing individual interest. It assumes the individuals are only trying to minimize their jail time, or maximize their fishing catch or short-term profits. But in the real world, people are more complicated than that. Our competing interests are more nuanced and varied, and they're subjective and situational. We try to maximize things other than our selfish self-interest. And our societal dilemmas are part of our ongoing relationships with other people.

Society solves societal dilemmas by making it in people's best interest to act in the group interest. We do this so naturally and so easily that we don't even notice the dilemma. Because of laws and police, it's not obviously better to steal a big screen TV than go without. Because of how everyone will react, it's not obviously smarter to betray a friend. Sure, no jail time is better than risking six years in jail, and catching more fish is better than catching fewer fish, but even those assessments fail to capture the richness of human emotion. Is no jail time but a reputation as a stool pigeon better than six years in jail? Is catching more fish but contributing to the degradation of the oceans better than catching fewer fish, even if everyone else is catching more than you? It depends. It depends on who you are. It depends on what you are. It depends on where you are.

Another famous dilemma illustrates this. The Stag Hunt was first formulated by Jean-Jacques Rousseau in 1754. In his scenario, a small group of hunters—it could be two and it could be more; it doesn't matter—are hunting a stag together. As would be obvious to readers of his day, everyone needs to work together in order to pull this off.

> If it was a matter of hunting deer, everyone well realized that he must remain at his post; but if a rabbit happened to pass within reach of one of them, we cannot doubt that he would have gone off in pursuit of it without scruple and, having caught his own prey, he would have cared very little about having caused his companions to lose theirs.

What makes this different than the Prisoner's Dilemma is that the benefit of cooperation is more than the benefit of defection: a stag is much more food, even divided a few ways, than a rabbit. It would seem there's no actual dilemma; for all players, cooperate–cooperate is better than any other option. In the real world, however, defections happen in this sort of cooperative game all the time. It seems to make no sense.

Rousseau, too, ignored the variety and subjectivity of the hunters' competing interests. It's not obvious—for all people all the time—that a share of a stag is better than a whole rabbit. Sure, it's more meat, but that's not the only consideration. First of all, the stag isn't a done deal. The choice is between a guaranteed rabbit—they're small and easy to catch—and the possibility, maybe even the probability, of a share of a stag. Is our intrepid hunter Alice an optimist or a pessimist? Does she want to stalk stag for hours, or does she want to snare her rabbit, go home, and do something she really enjoys with the rest of her day? Maybe she's tired. Maybe she's bored. Maybe she doesn't even like the taste of stag, and has a great rabbit stew recipe she's been dying to try. (Me, I like the one in Julia Child's *The Way to Cook*.) Maybe she is happy to forgo the rabbit for a stag, but doesn't trust that her fellow hunters will do the same. The point is that it's not for Rousseau to conclude which of these considerations matter to the hunters; the hunters get to decide for themselves. And they're all going to decide differently.

Another dilemma is called the Snowdrift Dilemma, sometimes called Chicken.[3] Two drivers are trapped by a snowdrift; each can either cooperate by shoveling or defect by remaining in his own car. If both remain in their cars, both remain stuck. If at least one of them shovels, both are freed; and two shovelers will get the job done much faster and more reliably than one. But unlike a Prisoner's Dilemma, it's in each driver's best interest to cooperate, even if the other defects.[4]

It turns out there are several different dilemmas[5]—generally called social dilemmas or coordination games—whose differences depend on the relative value of the various outcomes. Those nuances make a huge difference to game theorists, but are less important to everyday people. We make trade-offs based on what we want to do.[6]

When you look at the details of players' competing interests, motivations, and priorities, you often realize they might not be playing the same game. What might be a Prisoner's Dilemma for Alice could be a Snowdrift for Bob. What might be a Snowdrift for Alice might be a Stag Hunt for Bob. For Alice, cooperating might be the obviously smart thing to do. She might feel bad about herself if she defected. She might be afraid of what her friends would think if she defected. There might be a law against defecting, and she might not want to risk the jail time. She'll have her own particular trade-off: her own subjective values about cooperating and defecting. Bob might cooperate or defect for completely different reasons. And even if Bob and Alice are playing the same game today, they might each play a different game tomorrow. The complexities of these societal dilemmas are much more complicated than simple game theory models.

Think back to the baboon story at the start of Chapter 4. Notice the societal dilemma:

Societal Dilemma: Gazelle hunting.	
Society: Society of baboons.	
Group interest: Tasty gazelle meat for everyone.	Competing interest: Gaining an advantage over a fellow baboon.
Group norm: Hunt cooperatively.	Corresponding defection: Attack a fellow baboon during the hunt.

One of the great achievements of our species is our ability to solve societal dilemmas. In a way, we solve them by cheating. That is, we don't solve them within the parameters of the game. Instead, we modify the game to eliminate the dilemma. Recall the two drivers stuck behind a fallen tree that neither one can move by himself. They're not in a Prisoner's Dilemma. They're not even in a Snowdrift Dilemma. In their situation, their selfish interest coincides with the group interest—they're going to move the tree and get on with their lives. The trick to solving societal dilemmas is make them look like that. That's what societal pressures do: they're how society puts its thumb on the scales.

●   ●   ●

Solving societal dilemmas often means considering the people involved and their situations more broadly. The sealed-bag exchange is no longer a Prisoner's Dilemma if we assume the people involved have a sufficiently strong conscience.

Alice might be thinking: "If I assume Bob will cooperate, I have two choices. If I cooperate, I'll get my purchase and feel good about cooperating with Bob. If I defect, I'll get my purchase for free but I'll feel guilty about cheating Bob. That guilty feeling is worse than giving up the money, so it makes sense for me to cooperate. On the other hand, if I assume Bob will cheat me, my two choices look like this: If I cooperate, Bob will take my money and I'll feel stupid and angry for cooperating with a cheat. If I defect, I won't get my purchase and will feel guilty for trying to cheat Bob. That stupid feeling for being cheated is a little worse than the guilty feeling for trying to cheat Bob—who turned out to be a cheat himself. But Bob is making this same analysis, and he doesn't want to feel guilty about cheating me, either. So he's not going to defect."

And indeed, Bob makes the same analysis and also cooperates, although—most likely—they both don't consciously decide anything and both just behave honestly and trust each other to do the same. Maybe I have the emotions wrong—they could be motivated by a moral compass, by a sense of fairness, or by altruism towards the other person. In any case, dilemma solved.

Those guilty feelings come from inside our heads. Feelings of guilt are a societal pressure, one that works to varying degrees in each of us.

Moral pressure isn't the only thing we use to solve societal dilemmas. All of the considerations that make cooperation more attractive and defection less attractive are societal pressures. These include the rewards society directs towards cooperators and the penalties it directs towards defectors, the legal punishments society metes out to defectors, and the security measures that make defecting difficult to pull off and even more difficult to get away with.[7]

Societal Dilemma: Stealing.	
Society: Society as a whole.	
Group interest: Respect property rights. Group norm: Don't steal.	Competing interest: Get stuff without having to pay for it. Corresponding defection: Steal.
To encourage people to act in the group interest, society implements these societal pressures: Moral: People feel good about being honest and bad about stealing. People have been taught religious admonitions like "Thou shalt not steal." Reputational: Society shuns people who have a reputation for being thieves. Institutional: Stealing is illegal, and society punishes thieves. Security: Door locks, burglar alarms, and so on.	

Of course, there's a lot more going on, and I'll discuss that in later chapters. The real world isn't this simplistic; any analysis of human interaction must take circumstances into account. If Alice is a tourist in a foreign country, Bob might cheat her anyway. If the dollar value of cheating is high enough, either Alice or Bob might decide that cheating is worth more than the negative feelings that result from cheating. In Chapter 3, I said that trust is contextual; all of that analysis applies here.

For most of us, it is more worthwhile to cooperate than to defect. It can be a better strategy for us, given what we know about the people who share in our dilemma.[8] And, for different and equally valid reasons, some of us find defection to be more valuable than cooperation. Not universally, not all of the time, but at that moment for that person and that particular trade-off. There are no actual dilemmas; there are just individual subjective risk trade-offs.

Here are six different ways societal pressures can reduce the scope of defection—which I'll illustrate using the example of Alice potentially cheating a merchant.

- *Pressures that increase the actual or perceived difficulty of defecting.* Actual commerce usually doesn't happen inside sealed bags. Bob takes various additional security precautions to minimize the risk that Alice might cheat. Bob requires her to pay with hard-to-forge currency, or runs her credit card through a third-party authentication system. Window bars and burglar alarms make it harder for Alice to steal from Bob.
- *Pressures that raise the consequences of defecting.* These would be largely implemented after the fact; think prison terms, fines, cutting off a thief's hand,[9] and social ostracism. Even if they never catch anyone, the police can make it difficult and expensive to commit a crime; every heist movie demonstrates this entertainingly.
- *Pressures that reduce the actual or expected benefits of defecting.* Exploding ink cartridges can make stolen garments less useful to thieves, and daily ATM withdrawal limits restrict how much a thief can steal.
- *Pressures that limit the damage caused by the defections that happen.* Bob won't keep a lot of cash in his store. He might even store some of his expensive inventory elsewhere. He'll also have an insurance policy that will help him resume normal business quickly after a theft.
- *Pressures that increase the benefits of cooperating.* Reputation serves this function; Alice derives value from being known in society as honest and honorable in her business dealings, more so if she is part of the same society as the merchant she patronizes. Certainly Alice's credit rating is a part of her reputation. We also have a powerful need to conform to the group.
- *Pressures that lower the costs of cooperating.* Society makes it easy to cooperate. Stores make check-out stands easy to find. Unforgeable paper money and credit cards make it easy to conduct commerce, as opposed to a barter system, or needing to lug around a sackful of gold and silver. Or think of the iTunes store, which makes it easy to buy music legitimately online.

There's a lot of overlap here, and many of these techniques are tightly coupled. When you reduce the benefits of defecting, you almost certainly reduce the frequency of defecting.

Difficulty of Defecting   Consequence of Defecting   Benefit of Defecting   Damage from Defecting   Benefit of Cooperating

Figure 6: Societal Pressure Knobs

Think back to the Hawk-Dove game, and the knobs society can use to set the initial parameters. The categories in that figure are all individual knobs, and societal pressures provide a mechanism for the group to control those knobs. In theory, if the knobs are calibrated perfectly, society will get the exact scope of defection it's willing to tolerate.

There are many ways to sort societal pressures. The system I'm using sorts them by origin: moral pressures, reputational pressures, institutional pressures, and security systems.[10] These are categories you've certainly felt yourself. We feel moral pressure to do the right thing or—at least—to not do the wrong thing. Reputational pressure is more commonly known as peer pressure, but I mean any incentives to cooperate that stem from other people. Institutional pressure is broader and more general: the group using rules to induce cooperation. Security systems comprise a weird hybrid: it's both a separate category, and it enhances the other three categories.

The most important difference among these four categories is the scale at which they operate.

- *Moral pressure works best in small groups.* Yes, our morals can affect our interactions with strangers on the other side of the planet, but in general, they work best with people we know well.
- *Reputational pressure works well in small- and medium-sized groups.* If we're not at least somewhat familiar with other people, we're not going to be

able to know their reputations. And the better we know them, the more accurately we will know their reputations.

- *Institutional pressure works best in larger-sized groups.* It often makes no sense in small groups; you're unlikely to call the police if your kid sister steals your bicycle, for example. It can scale to very large groups—even globally—but with difficulty.
- *Security systems can act as societal pressures at a variety of scales.* They can be up close and personal, like a suit of armor. They can be global, like the systems to detect international money laundering. They can be anything in between.

I'm being deliberately vague about group sizes here, but there definitely is a scale consideration with societal pressures. And because the increasing scale of our society is one of the primary reasons our societal pressure systems are failing, it's important to keep these considerations in mind.

Another difference between the categories of societal pressure is that they operate at distinct times during a security event. Moral pressure can operate either before, during, or after an individual defects. Reputational, as well as most institutional, pressure operates after the defection, although some institutional pressure operates during. Security can operate before, during, or after.

Any measures that operate during or after the event affect the trade-off through a feedback loop. Someone who knows of the negative outcome—perhaps ostracism due to a bad reputation, or a jail sentence—either through direct knowledge or through seeing it happen to someone else, might refrain from defecting in order to avoid it. This is deterrence.

All of this, and more, is illustrated in the complicated block diagram below. Along the bottom axis is the timeline: before, during, and after defection. Along the left are the different categories of societal pressure: moral and reputational (considered together), institutional, and security systems. The traits/tendencies box represents the physical and emotional aspects of people that make them more or less likely to defect. Natural defenses are aspects of targets that make them more or less difficult to attack. Neither of these are societal pressure systems, but I include them for the sake of completeness.

An example might be useful here. Alice is deciding whether to burglarize a house. The group interest is for her not to burglarize the house, but she has some competing interest—it doesn't matter what it is—that makes her want to burglarize the house. Different pressures affect her risk trade-off in different ways.

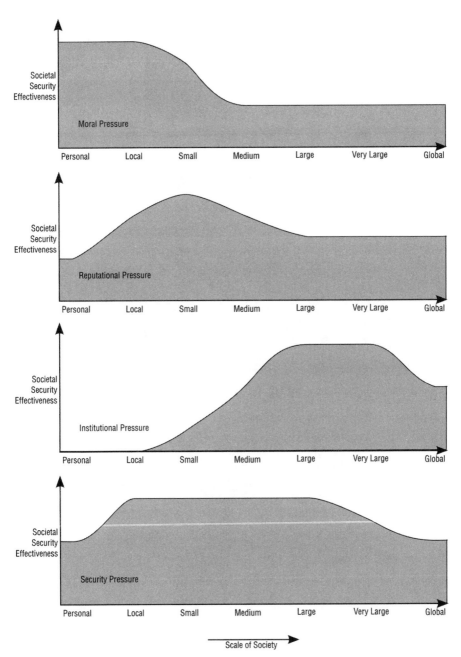

Figure 7: The Scale of Different Societal Pressures

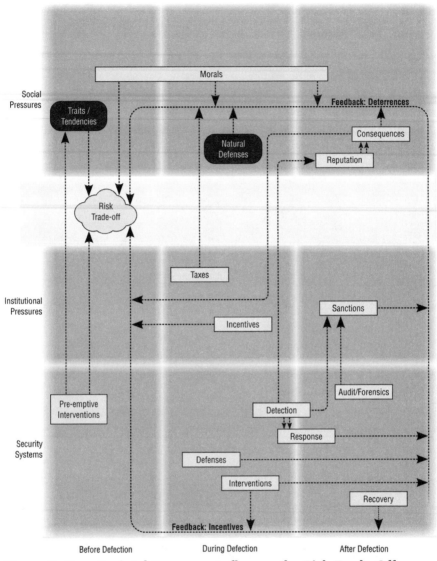

Figure 8: How Societal Pressures Influence the Risk Trade-Off

- Traits/tendencies. If Alice is afraid of heights, she won't try to break in through a second-story window. If she has a broken leg, she probably won't try to break in at all. These considerations operate before defection, at the point of the risk trade-off, when she's deciding whether or not to burglarize the house. (Note that this is not societal pressure.)

- Natural defenses operate during the burglary. Maybe the owner of the house is home and might tackle Alice. (Again, note that this is not societal pressure.)
- Most moral pressures operate at the point of the risk trade-off, or decision: Alice's sense of fairness, sense of right and wrong, and desire to obey the law. Some operate during the actual burglary: feelings of empathy, for example. Some operate after she's committed her crime: guilt, shame, and so on.
- Reputational pressures, assuming she's caught, operate after she's done burglarizing the house. They stem from the reactions and responses of others.
- Institutional pressures also operate after she's done burglarizing the house. Think of laws and mechanisms to punish the guilty in this case.
- Security systems can operate before, during, or after. Preemptive interventions, including incarcerating Alice before she commits the crime or forcing her to take some mood-altering medication that makes her not want to burglarize houses, operate before. Defenses operate during: door locks and window bars make it harder for her to burglarize the house. Detection systems can operate during or after: a burglar alarm calls a response that may or may not come in time. Interventions, like camouflage and authentication systems, operate during as well. Forensic systems operate afterwards, and may identify Alice as the burglar. There's one more type of security system: recovery systems that operate after a burglary can provide a perverse incentive to those aware that the consequences of their misbehavior can be mitigated at no cost to themselves. If Alice knows the house owner can easily recover from a burglary—maybe he has a lot of money, or good insurance—she's more likely to burglarize him.

Systems that work during or after the burglary usually have a deterrence effect. Alice is less likely to burglarize a house if she knows the police are diligent and jail sentences are severe. Or if she knows there's a homeowner who is skilled at karate, or has a burglar alarm.

These categories are not meant to be rigid. There are going to be societal pressures that don't fit neatly into any one category. That's okay; these categories are more meant to be a way of broadly understanding the topic as a whole than a formal taxonomy.

In the next four chapters, I'll outline each type of societal pressure in turn. I'll talk about how they work, and how they fail.

Societal pressure failures occur when the scope of defection is either too high or too low: either there are too many burglaries, or we're spending too much money on security to prevent burglary. This is not the same as individual burglaries; if someone's house was burglarized, it's not necessarily a societal security failure. Remember, we can never get the number of hawks down to zero; and sooner or later, further reducing their number becomes prohibitively expensive.

In some ways, societal pressures are like a group's immune system. Like antibodies, T cells, and B cells, they defend society as a whole against internal threats without being particularly concerned about harm to individual members of the group. The protection is not perfect, but having several different mechanisms that target different threats in different ways—much as an immune system does—makes it stronger.

Moral Pressures

Looking back at all the elections I've had the opportunity to vote in, there has never been one whose outcome I affected in any way. My voting has never even changed the vote percentages in any perceptible way. If I decided to never vote again, democracy wouldn't notice. It would certainly be in my best interest not to vote. Voting is a pain. I have to drive to the polling place, stand in line, then drive home.[1] I'm a busy guy.

Voting is a societal dilemma. For any single individual, there are no benefits to voting. Yes, your vote counts—it just doesn't matter. The rare examples of small elections decided by one vote don't change the central point: voting isn't worth the trouble. But if no one voted, democracy wouldn't work.

Still, people vote. It makes sense if 1) the voters see a difference between the two candidates, and 2) they care at least a little bit about the welfare of their fellow citizens. Studies with actual voters bear this out.[2]

Societal Dilemma: Voting.	
Society: Society as a whole.	
Group interest: A robust democracy. Group norm: Vote.	Competing interest: Do what you want to do on election day. Corresponding defection: Don't bother voting.
To encourage people to act in the group interest, society implements these societal pressures:	
Moral: People tend to feel good when they vote and bad when they don't vote, because they care about their welfare and that of their fellow citizens.	

Caring about the welfare of your fellow citizens is an example of a moral pressure.[3] To further increase voter turnout, society can directly appeal to morals. We impress upon citizens the importance of the issues at stake in the election; we even frame some of the issues in explicitly moral terms. We instill in them a sense of voting as a civic duty. We evoke their sense of group membership, and remind them that their peers are voting. We even scare them, warning that if they don't vote, the remaining voters—who probably don't agree with them politically—will decide the election.

Murder is another societal dilemma. There might be times when it is in our individual self-interest to kill someone else, but it's definitely in the group interest that murder not run rampant. To help prevent this from happening, society has evolved explicit moral prohibitions against murder, such as the Sixth (or Fifth, in the Roman Catholic and Lutheran traditional number) Commandment, "Thou shalt not kill."

Morality is a complex concept, and the subject of thousands of years' worth of philosophical and theological debate. Although the word "moral" often refers to an individual's values—with "moral" meaning "good," and "immoral" meaning "bad"—I am using the term "morals" here very generally, to mean any innate or cultural guidelines that inform people's decision-making processes as they evaluate potential trade-offs.[4] These encompass conscious and unconscious processes, explicit rules and gut feelings, deliberate thoughts, and automatic reactions. These also encompass internal reward mechanisms, for both cooperation and defection. Looking back at Figure 8 in Chapter 6, there is going to be considerable overlap between morals and what I called "traits/tendencies"—I hope to ignore that as well. As we saw in Chapter 3, all sorts of physiological processes make us prone to prosocial behaviors like cooperation and altruism. I'm lumping all of these under the rubric of morals.

And while morals can play a large part in someone's risk trade-off, in this chapter I am just focusing on how morals act as a societal pressure system to reduce the scope of defection. In Chapter 11, I'll discuss how morals affect the decision to cooperate or defect more broadly.

Beliefs that voting is the right thing to do, and that murdering someone is wrong, are examples of moral pressure: a mechanism designed to engage people's sense of right and wrong. Natural selection has modified our brains so that trust, altruism, and cooperation feel good, but—as we well know—that doesn't mean we're always trustworthy, altruistic, and cooperative. In both of the above examples, voting and murder, morals aren't very effective. With voting, a large defection rate isn't too much of a problem. U.S. presidential elections are decided by about half the pool of eligible voters.[5] Elections for lesser offices are decided by an even smaller percentage. But while this is certainly a social issue, the harm non-voters cause is minimal.

With murder, the number of defectors is both smaller and more harmful. In 2010, the murder rate in the U.S. was 5.0 per 100,000 people. Elsewhere in the world, it ranges from 0.39 per 100,000 in the relatively murder-free nation of Singapore, to an astonishing 58 per 100,000 in El Salvador.

●   ●   ●

Morals affect societal dilemmas in a variety of ways. They can affect us at the time of the risk trade-off, by making us feel good or bad about a particular cooperate/defect decision. They can affect us after we've made the decision and during the actual defection: empathy for our victims, for example. And they can affect us after the defection, through feelings of guilt, shame, pride, satisfaction, and so on. Anticipating moral feelings that may arise during and after defection provides either an incentive to cooperate or a deterrent from defection.

At the risk of opening a large philosophical can of worms, I'll venture to say that morals are unique in being the only societal pressure that makes people "want to" behave in the group interest. The other three mechanisms make them "have to."

There are two basic types of morals that affect risk trade-offs, one general and the other specific. First, the general. The human evolutionary tendencies toward trust and cooperation discussed in Chapter 3 are reflected in our moral, ethical, and religious codes. These codes vary wildly, but all emphasize prosocial behaviors like altruism, fairness, cooperation, and trust. The most general of these is the Golden Rule: "Do unto others what you would have them do unto you." Different groups have their own unique spin on the Golden Rule, but it's basically an admonition to cooperate with others. It really is the closest thing to a universal moral principle our species has.[6]

Moral reminders don't have to be anything formal. They can be as informal as the proverbs—which are anything but simplistic—that we use to teach our children; and cultures everywhere have proverbs about altruism, diligence, fidelity, and being a cooperating member of the community.[7] The models of the world we learn sometimes have moral components, too.

This can go several ways. You might learn not to defecate upstream of your village because you've been taught about cholera, or because you've been taught that doing so will make the river god angry. You might be convinced not to throw down your weapon and leave your fellow pikemen to face the charge alone either by a love for your comrades-at-arms like that for your brothers, or by knowledge that pikemen who run from charging horsemen get lanced in the back—not to mention what happens to deserters.

Traditionally, religion was the context where society codified and taught its moral rules. The Judeo-Christian tradition has the Ten Commandments, and Buddhism the Four Noble Truths. Muslims have the Five Pillars of Islam. All of these faiths call for the indoctrination of children in their teachings. Religion even exerts a subtle influence on the non-religious. In one experiment, theists and atheists alike gave more money away—to an anonymous stranger, not to charity—when they were first asked to unscramble a jumbled sentence containing words associated with religion than when the sentence contained only religion-neutral words. Another found less cheating when they were asked to recall the Ten Commandments. A third experiment measured cheating behavior as a function of belief in a deity. They found no difference in cheating behavior between believers and non-believers, but found that people who conceived of a loving, caring, and forgiving God were much more likely to cheat than those who conceived of a harsh, punitive, vengeful, and punishing God.[8]

Often, morals are not so much prescriptions of specific behaviors as they are meta rules. That is, they are more about intention than action, and rarely dictate actual behaviors. Is the Golden Rule something jurors should follow? Should it dictate how soldiers ought to treat enemy armies? Many ethicists have long argued that the Golden Rule is pretty much useless for figuring out what to do in any given situation.

Our moral decisions are contextual. Even something as basic as "Thou shalt not kill" isn't actually all that basic. What does it mean to kill someone? A more modern translation from the original Hebrew is "Thou shalt not murder," but that just begs the question. What is the definition of murder? When is killing not murder? Can we kill in self-defense, either during everyday life or in war-time? Can we kill as punishment? What about abortion? Is euthanasia moral? Is assisted suicide? Can we kill animals? The devil is in the details. This is the stuff that philosophers and moral theologians grapple with, and for the most part, we can leave it to them. For our purposes, it's enough to note that general moral reminders are a coarse societal pressure.

Contextualities are everywhere. Prosocial behaviors like altruism and fairness may be universal, but they're expressed differently at different times in each culture. This is important. While morals are internal, that doesn't mean we develop them naturally, like the ability to walk or grasp. Morals are taught.

They're memes and they do evolve, subject to the rules of natural selection, but they're not genetically determined.

Or maybe some are. There's a theory that we have a moral instinct that's analogous to our language instinct. Across cultures and throughout history, all moral codes have rules in common; the Golden Rule is an example. Others relevant to this book include a sense of fairness, a sense of justice, admiration of generosity, prohibition against murder and general violence, and punishment for wrongs against the community. Psychologist and animal behaviorist Marc Hauser even goes so far as to propose that humans have specific brain functions for morals, similar to our language centers.[9] And psychologist Jonathan Haidt proposes five fundamental systems that underlie human morality.

- *Harm/care systems.* As discussed in Chapter 3, we are naturally predisposed to care for others. From mirror neurons and empathy to oxytocin, our brains have evolved to exhibit altruism.
- *Fairness/reciprocity systems.* Also discussed in Chapter 3, we have natural notions of fairness and reciprocity.
- *In-group/loyalty systems.* Humans have a strong tendency to divide people into two categories, those in our group ("us") and those not in our group ("them"). This has serious security ramifications, which we'll talk about in the section on group norms later in the chapter, and in the next chapter about group membership.
- *Authority/respect systems.* Humans have a tendency to defer to authority and will follow orders simply because they're told to by an authority.
- *Purity/sanctity systems.* This is probably the aspect of morality that has the least to do with security, although patriarchal societies have used it to police all sorts of female behaviors. Mary Douglas's *Purity and Danger* talks about how notions of purity and sanctity operate as stand-ins for concepts of unhealthy and dangerous, and this certainly influences morals.

You can think of these systems as moral receptors, and compare them to taste and touch receptors. Haidt claims an evolutionary basis for his categories, although the evidence is scant. While there may be an innate morality associated with them, they're also strongly influenced by culture. In any case, they're a useful partitioning of our moral system, and they all affect risk trade-offs.

These five fundamental systems are also influenced by external events. Spontaneous cooperation is a common response among those affected by a natural disaster or other crisis. For example, there is a marked increase in solidarity during and immediately after a conflict with another group, and the U.S. exhibited that solidarity after the terrorist attacks of 9/11. This included a general increase in prosocial behaviors such as spending time with children, engaging in religious activities, and donating money. Crime in New York dropped. There was also an increase in in-group/out-group divisions, as evidenced by an increase in hate crimes against Muslims and other minorities throughout the country.

Some of our moral pressure is very strong. Kin aversion, the particular disgust we have for the idea of mating with people we grew up with, works without any prompting or ancillary security.[10] So does our tendency to feel protective impulses towards children, which can extend to small animals and even dolls. This makes sense. We avoided incest and looked after our offspring for millions of years before we became human. These strong moral inclinations can be deliberately tapped. Think of evocations of kin relationships to foster cooperation: blood brothers, brothers in Christ, and so on. Or how cartoon animals are so often drawn with the big-head-big-eyes look of babies in an attempt to make them more universally likeable.

A lot of our morals are cultural. For example, while fairness is a universal human trait, notions of fairness differ among groups, based on variables like community size and religious participation. Psychologist Joseph Henrich used a cooperation game to study notions of fairness, altruism, and trust among the Machiguenga tribesmen deep in the Peruvian Amazon. While Westerners tended to share a lucky find with someone else, the tribesmen were more likely to keep it to themselves. In both instances, the actions were perceived as fair by others of the same culture.[11]

Think back to the various societal dilemmas we've discussed so far. Many of them have a moral component that encourages people to cooperate. We're taught—or conditioned, depending on what social science theory you believe—that stealing and fraud are wrong, although different cultures have different definitions of property. We're taught that taking more than our fair share is wrong: whatever "fair" means in our culture. We're taught that sitting idly by while others do all the work is wrong, although no one accuses the incapacitated, the infirm, the elderly, or infants of being immoral. Even criminals have moral codes that prohibit ratting on each other.

Of course, the effectiveness of these rules depends largely on individual circumstances, and some of them—such as "honor among thieves," or the politeness rule against taking the last item on a communal plate of food—are notoriously weak. But there would be even less honor among thieves if the phrase didn't exist to remind them of their moral obligation to the group.

Moral pressure can do better, though. In addition to general admonitions to cooperative behavior, other measures specifically remind people of their moral obligations to the group, such as the obligation to vote. For example, think about the signs in restaurant bathrooms that read, "Employees must wash hands before returning to work."[12] Another example are the signs that remind people not to litter. My favorite is "Don't mess with Texas," one of the best advertising slogans ever.

Of course, signs warning "No shoplifting," or "Shoplifting is a crime," primarily remind shoplifters that they run the risk of getting caught and going to jail; more about that in a couple of chapters. These reminders nonetheless have an unmistakable moral component. And, more precisely, public service announcements that deliberately invoke people's feelings of guilt and shame have been shown to be effective in changing behavior.

One afternoon at a historic monument in Rome, I saw a sign advising visitors: "This is your history. Please don't graffiti it." That sign was an artifact of a societal dilemma: it's fun to carve one's name into the rock wall, but if everyone does that, historic monuments will soon look ugly. The difference between selfish interest and group interest is small in this case; for some people, a simple reminder is enough to tip the scales in favor of the group.

●   ●   ●

Group norms are themselves a form of moral societal pressure. Voting turnout rates range from as high as 92% in Austria to as low as 48% in the United States. Yes, some countries make voting mandatory and use other categories of social pressure to get people to vote, and we'll talk about those in the next chapter; but these are rates in countries where voting is entirely optional.

The "Don't mess with Texas" slogan is so good because it doesn't just remind people not to litter. It reinforces the group identity of Texans both as people who don't leave messes and who are not to be messed with.

We not only absorb our moral codes and definitions of right and wrong from the group; the group also transmits cues about cooperation and defection and what it means to act in a trustworthy manner. People are more likely to suppress their self-interest in favor of the group interest if they feel that others are doing so as well, and they're less likely to do so if they feel that others are taking advantage of them. The psychological mechanism for this is unclear, but certainly it is related to our innate sense of fairness. We generally don't mind sacrificing for the group, as long as we're all sacrificing fairly. But if we feel like we're being taken advantage of by others who are defecting, we're more likely to defect as well.

If you see your neighbor watering his lawn during a drought restriction and getting away with it, your sense of fairness is offended. To restore fairness, you have two options: you can turn him in, or you can take the same benefit for yourself. You have to live with your neighbor, so defecting is easier. (Recall the phrase "if you can't beat 'em, join 'em.")

Psychologist Andrew Colman called this the Bad Apple Effect.[13] Any large group is likely to contain a few bad apples who will defect at the expense of the group interest and inspire others to do likewise. If someone is speeding, or littering, or watering his lawn in spite of water-use restrictions, others around him are more likely to do the same.

This can occasionally create a positive-feedback loop, driven by individual differences in how people evaluate their risk trade-off. The first defectors provide a small additional incentive for everyone else to defect. Because there are always some people who are predisposed to cooperate, but just barely, that incentive may push them over to the defecting side. This, in turn, can result in an even greater incentive for everyone else to defect —a cascade that can sometimes lead to mass defection and even a mob mentality.

Both experiment and observation bear this out. Littering is a societal dilemma: it is in everyone's self-interest to drop his or her own trash on the ground—carrying it to a can is bothersome—but if everyone did that, the streets would be a mess. People are more likely to litter if there is a small amount of litter already on the ground, and two or three times more likely to litter if there is a lot. Just seeing a single person litter, or seeing someone pick up litter, modifies behavior. In a recent book, James B. Stewart points to the current epidemic of lying by public figures, and blames it for the general breakdown of ethics in America: when lying is believed to be normal, more people lie. In psychological experiments, a single unpunished free rider in a group can cause the entire group to spiral towards less and less cooperation. These patterns reflect the human tendency to adhere not only to social norms, but to moral norms. In Islam, announcing that you've sinned is itself a sin.[14]

This effect can motivate cooperation, too. For years, society has tried to encourage people to conserve energy. It's another societal dilemma: we're better off collectively if we conserve our natural resources, but each of us individually is better off if we use as much as we want. Even more selfishly, if I use as much as I want and everyone else conserves, I get all the benefits of conservation without actually having to do anything. Awareness campaigns have worked somewhat to mitigate this problem, but not enough.

Every month, included in my electric bill, is a chart comparing my electricity usage to my neighbors' average usage. It tells me if I'm using more, or less, electricity than average. On the face of it, why should I care? Electricity isn't free. The more I use, the more I pay. And aside from the savings from lower bills—which exist even without the chart—I get no personal benefit for conserving, and incur no penalty for not conserving.

But the chart works. People use less energy when they can compare their energy usage with that of their neighbors.[15] That's because there actually is a benefit and a penalty, albeit entirely inside the heads of those receiving the bill: their competitive nature, their desire to conform to group norms, and so on.

Similarly, people are more likely to pay their taxes if they think others are paying their taxes as well. People are more likely to vote, less likely to overfish, more likely to get immunized, and less likely to defraud their customers if they think these practices are the group norm. This isn't peer pressure; in these cases, the risk trade-off is made in secret. Of course, this sort of thing works even better when the group knows whether or not you've cooperated or defected, but that's the subject of the next chapter.

Morals can be influenced by a powerful ruler, or a ruling class, or a priestly class. Especially if you can manipulate people's in-group/out-group designations, some awful things can be done in the name of morality: slavery and genocide are two examples.[16] Interestingly, genocide is often precipitated by propaganda campaigns that paint the victims as vermin or otherwise less than human: undeserving of the moral predispositions people have towards other people.

Psychologist Simon Baron-Cohen maintains that in psychopaths, cruelty and evil stem from a failure or absence of empathy. Extending this notion into our model, a person is more inclined to cooperate if he feels empathy with the other people in the group, and is more inclined to defect if he doesn't feel that empathy. Both general moral rules and specific moral reminders serve to enhance empathy to the group, by reminding people of both their moral principles and the group interest.[17]

●   ●   ●

For more than ten years, economist Paul Feldman brought bagels into his workplace and sold them on the honor system. He posted prices that people were expected to pay, securing the system by nothing more than the bagel-eaters' morals.[18] Although it was easy to take a bagel without paying, Feldman succeeded in collecting about 90% of the posted price, resulting in much more profit than if he had to pay someone to sell the bagels and guard the money. He eventually turned this into a full-time business, selling food on the honor system to 140 companies in the Washington, DC, area.

Societal pressure based on morals largely succeeds because of who we are as human beings. When we meet someone for the first time, we tend to cooperate. We act trustworthy because we know it's right, and we similarly extend some amount of trust. We tip in restaurants. We pay for our bagels. We follow social norms simply because they *are* social norms. This is all contextual, of course, and we're not stupid about it. But it is our nature.

Philosopher Emmanuel Levinas said that morality is grounded in face-to-face interactions. In general, moral pressure works best at close range. It works best with family, friends, and other intimate groups: people whose intentions we can trust. It works well when the groups are close in both space and time. It works well when it's immediate: in crises and other times of stress. It works well with groups whose members are like each other, whether ethnically, in sharing an interest, or some other trait. Even having a common enemy works in this regard.

Think about the chart that shows my energy use compared to my neighbors'. It doesn't compare me to the rest of the world, or even to my country. It compares me to my neighbors, the people most like me.

Morals sometimes work at long range. After the 2011 earthquake and tsunami in Japan, people turned in thousands of wallets and safes found in the rubble, filled with $78 million in cash. People regularly protest working conditions at factories, or give to relief efforts, or fight social injustices, in other countries halfway across the planet. People have moral beliefs that encompass all of humanity, or all animals, or all living creatures. We are a species that is capable of profound morality.

We are also a species capable of profound immorality. And while moral pressure works, it also regularly fails. When it does, it fails for several specific reasons:

People vary in their individual behavior. Sure, most people will cooperate most of the time, but some people will defect some of the time, and almost everyone will defect once in a while.

Morals often conflict. We'll talk about this more in Chapter 11. Sometimes defectors are people whose morals lead to different imperatives than those reached by the cooperators. These people will be largely unaffected by societal moral pressure. Society will have an easier time convincing a potential thief that stealing is wrong than it will have convincing an abolitionist that slavery is good.

Morals often overreach. It's relatively easy to use morals to enforce basic prosocial behaviors, because those are aligned with what's already in our brains. Enforcing arbitrary moral codes is much harder. If the group norm goes against any of Haidt's five fundamental moral systems, more people will have conflicting morals, and more will defect.

Throughout history, totalitarian regimes have attempted to impose moral codes on their citizens, suppressing some heretofore acceptable behaviors and inventing new obligations. Perhaps the most well-known modern example of an authoritarian attempt to reorient popular moral sensibilities was the Soviet Union's unsuccessful prohibition on the practice of religion, which threatened to undermine materialist Communist ideology. This kind of thing isn't rare. When I visited Myanmar in 1991, I saw large billboards everywhere, courtesy of the government's "People's Desire Campaign," exhorting the populace to believe and act in all sorts of pro-government ways. These campaigns often just drive the behaviors underground.

Morals can be manipulated. Confidence tricksters, in particular, manipulate the very same traits that make us cooperate: kindness, altruism, fairness.

Morals scale badly. They fail as societies become larger and the moral ties that bind their members weaken.

Remember Baron-Cohen's theory of empathy. As the group gets larger and more anonymous, there's less empathy. Joseph Stalin said, "the death of one man is a tragedy, the death of millions is a statistic"; similarly, we have trouble thinking about large groups in the same moral way we think of the people closest to us.

All of these reasons make morals the weakest of the societal pressures. Morals are the societal pressure that works "when no one is watching." They determine whether we keep a wallet that no one saw us find and pick up, whether we litter on a deserted street, whether we conserve energy or crank up the air conditioning, and whether we help ourselves to a bagel on a tray in an empty break room.

When nothing other than moral pressure influences a societal dilemma, the number of defectors will be at its largest. However, opportunities for individuals to make moral choices when they are unobserved represent only a small portion of societal dilemmas. We humans are a social species, and more often than not someone *is* watching. And that makes an enormous difference.

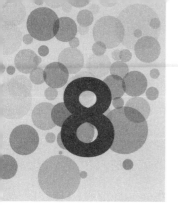

8 Reputational Pressures

From the perspective of trust, societal dilemmas involve a Red Queen Effect. On one hand, defectors should evolve to be better able to fool cooperators. And on the other, cooperators should evolve to better recognize defectors. It's a race between the ability to deceive and the ability to detect deception.

There's a lot of research on detecting deception, and humans seem not to be very good at it. There are exceptions, and people can learn to be better at it—but in general, we can't tell liars from truth-tellers. Like the Lake Wobegon children who are all above average, most of us think we're much better at detecting deception than we actually are. We're better, but still not great, at predicting cooperators and defectors.[1]

This is surprising. The Red Queen Effect means both sides improve in order to stay in place, yet in this case, defectors have the upper hand. A possible reason is that we have developed another method for figuring out who to trust and who not to. We're a social species, and in our evolutionary past we interacted with the same people over and over again. We don't have to be that good at predicting bad behavior, because we're really good at detecting it after the fact—and using reputation to punish it.[2]

In fact, our brains have specially evolved to deal with cheating after the fact. Perhaps the most vivid demonstration of this can be seen with the Wason Selection Task. The test compares people's ability to solve a generic logical reasoning problem with their ability to solve the same problem presented in a framework of detecting cheaters: for example, "if Alice went to Boston, she took the train" versus "if Alice is served alcohol, she is over 21." People are generally much better at solving the latter. Additionally, fMRI scans of the brains performing this task show that we have specific brain circuitry for cheater detection.

Think back to how contrived and artificial the sealed bag exchange from Chapter 5 seemed. That's because there's more going on than short-term decision making. Commerce isn't a one-time event. It happens again and again, day after day, often between the same people. We know the individuals and companies with whom we interact, maybe personally, maybe casually, maybe by their brand. Everyone has a reputation, and it's important. While morals are part of the reason we cooperate with each other, the preponderance of the evidence—both observational and experimental—supports the hypothesis that we cooperate primarily because we crave reward (engagement) and fear punishment (exclusion) from other members of our group.[3]

Bob depends on his reputation as an honest merchant. If he cheats Alice, she won't do business with him again. Even worse, she'll tell her friends.[4] Bob couldn't survive as a merchant if he had a reputation as a cheater. If we assume that the cost to Bob's reputation if he defects is greater than the value of the item being purchased, he has no dilemma. He is better off cooperating, regardless of what Alice does. Reputation is such a major factor for Bob that he almost certainly allows Alice to reverse the transaction after the fact, a process commonly known as returning the purchase.[5] This is the fundamental threat of damage to your reputation. A business works to make its customers happy, because it knows its reputation will be damaged if it doesn't deliver. Customers, knowing this is true, are more willing to trust the business.[6]

Societal Dilemma: Cheating customers.	
Society: Group of merchants/society as a whole.	
Group interest: Merchants are trusted. Group norm: Don't cheat customers.	Competing interest: Maximize short-term profits. Corresponding defection: Cheat customers when possible.
To encourage people to act in the group interest, society implements these societal pressures: Moral: Guilt, shame, sense of fairness, kindness, etc. Reputational: Merchants want to be seen as trustworthy. Customers share their experiences with merchants, making merchants less likely to cheat customers so as to retain their good reputation.	

Customer reputation used to be a bigger deal than it is today. When commerce was transacted entirely in local markets with local merchants, in situations where buyers and sellers knew each other and knew they would need to do business with each other many times in the future, reputation mattered just as much to the customer as it did to the merchant. In today's world of global commerce, where potential customers may be located a half a world away, customer reputation matters much less than merchant reputation. Means for ascertaining the integrity of potential customers are coming back, though. Online reputation systems, like eBay's feedback mechanism, gave both merchants and customers reputation information about each other. (In 2008, eBay changed this, and no longer allows merchants to give feedback on customers, citing abuse of the process by merchants.)

We take our reputations very seriously, and spend a lot of time and effort maintaining them, sometimes defending them to the point of death.[7] We go to these extremes because we recognize that if we want others to trust us and cooperate with us, we need a good reputation. So we keep our reputation clean, cover up blemishes, or fake our reputation completely.

Tellingly, psychological and brain research both show that we remember negative information about people more vividly, with more detail, and for a longer time than positive information. It seems that knowing who will defect is more important than knowing whom to trust.

We're also good at keeping up with the reputation of others. There's a theory that gossip originated as a mechanism for learning about the reputations of others and helping us know whom to trust. Of course, gossip requires language. Humans are unique on the planet for our ability to gossip,[8] and humans everywhere on the planet are enthusiastic about it. It tells us who is likely to be cooperative and who is not, so we know whom to interact with. It helps establish group interests and group norms. It works as a societal pressure system, too; both observational studies and experiments show that gossip helps keep people in line. Social networking sites are the most modern manifestations of these ancient needs.

Reputation is a common mechanism for raising the costs of defecting and increasing the benefits of cooperating. Buskers generally don't disrupt each other's acts because they don't want a bad reputation among their peers. Diamond merchants generally pay their debts promptly, don't pocket other people's diamonds, and don't substitute worthless stones for valuable ones, because they don't want to jeopardize their reputation within the community. And prisoners sometimes won't testify against each other because they don't want to be known as stool pigeons by the other criminals in town.

Here's how finely tuned we are to others watching our actions. The coffee room at the Division of Psychology at the University of Newcastle in Australia works on the honor system, just like Feldman's bagel business. Researchers found that if they put a sign above the pay box with a picture of a pair of eyes—not an entire face, just a pair of eyes—people put almost three times as much money in the box as they did when the sign had an image of flowers. Similarly, children who were told to take only one piece of Halloween candy but were left alone with a full bowl defected less when the bowl was placed in front of a mirror. And they defected even less when they were asked their names and addresses before being given the same opportunity. Along the same lines, religion often provides a universal observer. God is omniscient and the arbiter of one's final reputation, and a calculating believer behaves accordingly.[9]

Not only do we guard our reputation against blemishes, we also take pains to advertise our good reputation. This can be as grandiose as a company touting its customer satisfaction ratings or product quality awards, or as mundane as those small "I Voted" stickers that many polling places in the United States give to voters to wear for the rest of Election Day. The effect is both reputational and moral; voters can publicly demonstrate that they behaved in the group interest and voted, and simultaneously remind others of their civic responsibility. There's even a German expression, *"Tu Gutes und rede darüber"*: "Do good and talk about it."[10]

We need several more pieces to make a reputational pressure system work. We don't always have perfect information about what other people are doing. Maybe they cooperated when we thought they defected, or vice versa. Or they might have done the wrong thing accidentally or because they weren't thinking clearly. Our reputational systems have to work despite the occasional mistake. This requires two things: contrition and forgiveness. If you defect by accident, apologize, make amends, and then return to cooperating. And if someone does that to you, forgive and return to cooperating.

I'm glossing over a lot of subtleties here. Forgiveness is a complicated emotion, and there's a fine line between being forgiving and being a sucker, and between being contrite and being a doormat. There's a great word from the Tshiluba language, spoken in southeastern Democratic Republic of Congo, that regularly appears on impossible-to-translate word lists. *Ilunga* means someone who forgives any abuse the first time it occurs, tolerates it the second time, and neither forgives nor tolerates it the third time. The English saying is snappier: "Fool me once, shame on you; fool me twice, shame on me."

●   ●   ●

Throughout most of history, commerce was a local phenomenon. Reputation made it work, and reputation was local. The emergence of long-distance commerce in the Western world was aided in great part by the involvement of European Quakers, who earned a reputation for dealing honorably with their business partners. Prior to the mid-17th century, European traders ran a significant risk that trading partners from other countries would act in their own self-interest and renege on promises they had made; overseas contracts were often unenforceable, so the potential for profit often outweighed the likelihood of punishment. However, the Quakers' religious commitment to integrity and simple living, and their belief in the essential worth of every individual, informed all of their business dealings. Being upright with God was more important to them than making a fast buck. The moral benefit they experienced from acting in accord with their consciences, and the ensuing reputational benefits within both their religious and business communities, outweighed any short-term financial gains that might have come from shady dealing. A Quaker found to have dealt with others dishonestly ran the risk not only of losing business opportunities, but of being expelled from his religious community. As a result, Quakers would cooperate even if it went against their self-interest, and—as they consolidated their positions in industry—there was a gradual increase of trust in them among overseas traders.

The Quakers were an exception. The problem with reputation is that it doesn't naturally scale well. Recall Dunbar's numbers. We can recognize 1,500 faces, but the number of people we know enough about to know their reputation is much lower—maybe 500 or even 150. Once our societies get larger than that, we need other mechanisms by which to infer reputation than direct knowledge of the other person. And, as you'd expect, we have developed several of these.

One of the ways to scale reputation is to generalize based on group membership. So we might believe that people with a particular skin color, or who speak a particular language, or who worship a particular God, are untrustworthy. We might believe that a Quaker is trustworthy.

During the mid-17th century, being a Quaker meant something to the general community. In different periods of history, so did being a Freemason, or a member of the Medici family. In the 12th century, you could take a Templar letter of credit issued in England all the way to Jerusalem. In the 11th century, the Maghribi traders of the medieval Mediterranean had a reputation similar to the Quakers. A thousand years earlier, Roman letters of introduction were similarly trusted throughout the empire.

Political scientist Robert Putnam has argued that mistrust increases in a community as ethnic diversity increases. Evidence of this effect comes from sources as diverse as studies of carpooling, Peruvian micro-credit cooperatives, and Civil War deserters. Even worse, this inherent mistrust of those in other ethnic groups isn't offset by an increase in trust of those in one's own ethnic group; trust across the board weakens in more ethnically diverse communities.[11]

So it should come as no surprise that we have an enormous number of membership markers that we use to determine who is like us: language, dress, ethnicity, gang tags, haircuts, tattoos, jewelry, T-shirt slogans, food choices, gestures, secret handshakes, turns of phrase in speech, formal membership credentials, and so on. We generalize based on profession, city of residence, political affiliation, religious affiliation, sexual orientation, interests, and pretty much any other category you can think of. The theory is that all of these are vestigial remnants of prehistoric kin recognition mechanisms. But while these might have worked better in our evolutionary past than they do today, our brains are still stuck on them.

Take appearance, for example. Numerous experiments indicate that we are more likely to trust people who look like us. The phenomenon goes well beyond race; experimenters have digitally manipulated images of faces to more or less resemble those of their subjects and found that a variety of prosocial behaviors are correlated with facial similarity.

Dialect is a particularly interesting marker of group membership. With the nationalization and globalization of mass media, both accents and dialects are fading, but for most of human history, they were localized.[12] They're hard to fake, unless you're a rare gifted mimic, and they're generally set by adolescence. There is a lot of evidence, worldwide, that people are predisposed to cooperate with someone who speaks the same dialect they do. For instance, in one experiment, subjects were more likely to trust people with the same accent they had.[13] And we naturally change our patterns of speech and body language to mimic those around us, unconsciously trying to fit into the group.[14] Of course, the flip side of this is that we're less likely to trust people who don't sound like we do. Again, dialect preference seems to be a vestigial kin-recognition system.

It's worth noting that membership markers are harder to acquire and fake for groups that involve long-term—even inter-generational—cooperation and trust, than they are for groups involving more near-term cooperation and trust. It's much easier to learn the knowledge and skills to be a member of the community of football fans, or stamp collectors, or a particular church, than it is to acquire a new facial feature like an epicanthic fold or a dialect.

Gauging reputation by group membership is a lousy way to prejudge someone—another name for the practice is "stereotyping." But it's not an unreasonable cognitive shortcut, given our inability to interact meaningfully with more than 150 people, or even to put names to more than 1,500 faces. Historically, as the number of people we interacted with grew, we had to develop these shortcuts. Identifying someone as a member of a particular community, whether an ethnic community or a community of choice such as a professional association, gives us some indication about whether she is likely to cooperate with us or defect. If she's a member of the same community as us, we know she's likely to share the same set of ethical rules we do.

Recall the Golden Rule. It's not enough to want to cooperate. You also need to know how to cooperate according to your society's particular definition, so others can know you're reliably cooperative. One popular business-success book tried to "improve" on the Golden Rule, creating what it called the Platinum Rule: do unto others as they would want you to do unto them. That sounds even more altruistic, but it's not what has been encoded in our brains. Figuring out what someone else wants is easy to get wrong. It's much easier to assume that another person wants what you want. Of course, that works best if you only deal with people who are like you, and are likely to want the same things you want.

Social norms tell us how to cooperate. This is one of the reasons societies have tended to be homogeneous in their morals: it's advantageous. When people with different morals interact, they may have different default assumptions about what it means to cooperate. Remember the Machiguenga tribesmen in Chapter 7? They use a different definition of "fair" than Westerners do. Cooperation works better if we all agree on what it means to cooperate.[15]

Of course, just because our brains are hard-wired for this sort of in-group/out-group division doesn't mean it's the right thing to do.[16] There are all sorts of reasons why stereotyping is a bad system for judging individual people, and for those reasons we should strive to get beyond our more base instincts.

A substitute that can help reputation scale is commitment. By committing ourselves to an action in a way that we cannot undo, we can make up for a lack of reputation. Consider the coordination problem between a prostitute and a prospective client. The two have met in a bar and have agreed to meet upstairs in his hotel room later in exchange for $100. She wants him to pay her in advance, because she doesn't trust that he will pay her in his hotel room as promised. Similarly, he is concerned that, once having received the money, she won't follow through and meet him later. If the two could trust each other, this would be easy to solve. But they don't.

One solution is to tear the $100 bill in half, one piece for each of them. In the U.S. at least, half a $100 bill has no value, so neither party has the money. Now both parties have effectively committed to the rendezvous: so she can receive the other half of the $100 bill and he can receive the service. If either one of them defects and misses the meeting, neither gets the money.[17] eBay escrow services serve the same function; they facilitate trust by forcing the buyer and seller into a commitment they can't get out of easily.

A similar mechanism is to deliberately cut off your escape routes, so you have no choice but to follow through on your commitment. This could mean literally burning your bridges behind you. In 1519, when Hernán Cortés invaded what today is Veracruz, Mexico, he scuttled the ships he arrived on, signaling to both the Aztecs waiting for him and his own men that there would be no reneging on his commitment.

A second way to demonstrate commitment is to move in steps. When I hired a contractor to perform renovation work on my home, the contract stipulated several partial payments at different milestones during the project. This step-by-step approach—me paying the contractor partially, him doing some of the work, me paying some more, him doing some more work, etc.—helped both of us trust each other during the entire project because the severity of defection was lessened.

This was also the general idea behind the Cold War doctrine of mutually assured destruction. Both the U.S. and the USSR worked to convince the other that they were committed to massive retaliation in the event of a first strike. The result was that neither side was willing to use nuclear weapons; the two countries might not have trusted each other in general, but they both trusted that the other side was crazy enough to follow through on its commitment.

A third way to signal commitment is ritual. This could be a handshake to seal a commercial deal, a ceremony to seal a marriage, or an Eagle Scout induction ceremony. Rituals work because 1) reputation is at stake, and 2) society provides sanctions against anyone who reneges. Of course, these only work if everyone understands what the ritual is and what it means.

Zahavi's handicap signals from Chapter 3 are another way to scale reputation: costly and hard-to-fake demonstrations of our reputation. These include publicly attending religious services to demonstrate our morality,[18] ostentatiously spending money to demonstrate our social class, and engaging in particular activities to demonstrate our political or cultural proclivities.[19] Nobilities have complex displays of etiquette. Banks spend some of their money on imposing buildings to show off their financial health. Criminals have signals, too, to advertise their "good" reputation as a career criminal: prison time (that fellow criminals vouch for), tattoos, and deliberate physical self-harm.

Branding is yet another way to make reputation scale, similar to group membership. In many cases, we interact with organizations as groups rather than as individuals. That is, the corporate reputation of McDonald's is more important to our decision about whether or not to trust it than the individual reputation of any of the stores or the individual employees.

Branding isn't necessarily about quality; it's about sameness. Chain restaurants don't necessarily promise the best food, they promise consistency in all of their restaurants. So when you sit down at a McDonald's or a Cheesecake Factory, you know what you're going to get and how much you're going to pay for it. Their reputation reduces uncertainty.

Advertising can be about persuading consumers to associate a certain brand with a certain reputation. Shared brand names serve as means of aggregating individual reputations into an overarching group reputation, which—if it's maintained in good standing—benefits all members of the coalition. Companies call attention to their age, their size, and the quality of their products and services, all in an effort to enhance their reputation. Witness the ubiquity of advertising boasting about firms' positions on environmental and workplace issues or contributions to worthy causes. Or the effort the principals of the Saudi Binladin Group construction company have spent trying to differentiate themselves from their terrorist relative.

In ascertaining quality, consumers will often rely on the cognitive shortcut provided by a brand name, and will even pay a premium for products with brand names they associate with a reputation for quality. One study of Bordeaux wines found that customers will pay a premium for bottles from a more reputable producer, even if the wine is no better. Notions of branding have leaked into individual reputation as well. Career counselors now advise professionals to "cultivate their brand."

A final way to make reputation scale is to systemize it, so that instead of having to trust a person or company, we can trust the system. A professional police force and judiciary means that you don't have to trust individual policemen, you can trust the criminal justice system. A credit bureau means that lenders don't have to decide whether or not to trust individual borrowers, they can trust the credit rating system. A credit card relieves merchants from having to figure out whether a particular customer is able to pay later; the system does that work for them. Dunbar's number tells us there is a limit to the number of individuals we can know well enough to decide whether or not to trust; a single trust decision about a system can serve as a proxy for millions of individual trust decisions.

We have a lot of experience with this kind of thing online: ratings of sellers on eBay, reviews of restaurants on sites like Yelp, reviews of contractors on sites like Angie's List, reviews of doctors, accountants, travel agencies…pretty much everything you can think of. Social networking sites systemize reputation, showing us whom we might want to trust because we have friends in common.

This is an enormous development in societal pressure, one that has allowed society to scale globally. It used to be that companies could ignore the complaints of a smallish portion of their customers, because their advertising outweighed the word-of-mouth reputational harm. But on the Internet, this isn't necessarily true. A small complaint that goes viral can have an enormous effect on a company's reputation.

On the other hand, while these reputational systems have been an enormous success, they have brought with them a new type of trust failure. Because potential defectors can now attack the reputational systems, they have to be secured. We'll talk about this in Chapter 10.

●   ●   ●

Reputation isn't an effective societal pressure system unless it has consequences, and we both reward cooperators and punish defectors.

We reward cooperators all the time incidentally through our actions. We choose to do business with merchants who have proven to be trustworthy. We spend time with people who have demonstrated that they're trustworthy. We try to hire employees who have good reputations, and we promote and give bonuses to employees who cooperate. From a security perspective, friendships are mutual reward systems for cooperating.

The common thread in all of these rewards is participation. Humans are a social species, and we reward by allowing others to participate in the group: whatever it is doing, whatever benefits it is accruing, whatever status and credibility it has achieved. Our brains are hard-wired to need to participate; we crave the approval of the group.

We also punish defectors. And if participation is the canonical reward, exclusion is the corresponding punishment. In our evolutionary past, the most severe punishment was banishment from the group. As interdependent as humans were, this punishment was tantamount to death.

We still banish people today. We tell them we're no longer their friends and that they shouldn't come around anymore. We cut all ties with certain relatives, kick trolls out of online communities, and unfriend people on Facebook. On a different scale, someone with a destroyed credit rating is pretty much banished from the lending community.

Other punishments are less severe: physical violence, property damage, and so on. Sometimes we call this sort of thing "revenge." Here's how Maine lobstermen deal with one of their group violating traditional territories:

> Ordinarily, repeated violation of territorial boundaries will lead to destruction of the offender's gear. It is usual for one man operating completely on his own to first warn an interloper. In some places this is done by tying two half hitches around the spindle of the offending buoys; in other places by damaging the traps slightly. At this point, most intruders will move their traps. If they are not moved, they will be "cut off." This means cutting off the buoy and warp line from the trap, which then sinks to the bottom where the owner has no chance of finding it.... A man who violates a boundary is ordinarily never verbally confronted with the fact of his intrusion. And the man who destroys his gear will traditionally never admit to it.[20]

Most punishments are even less extreme. We may still hang around with some friends, but not rely on them as much or not tell them our intimate secrets. We may still invite *those* relatives to the family's holiday party, but not talk to them much.

Shame is a common reputational punishment, and—as a result—an important social emotion. Much of this is the informal kind of shaming we've all experienced amongst our friends and colleagues. More formal examples include police blotter reports, IRS quarterly listings of Americans who renounce their citizenship, public disclosure of excessive CEO pay, televised arrests, deadbeat dads in the media, and TV shows like *America's Most Wanted*. Of course, these all have a technological component, and some might be more properly put into the category of institutional pressure.

Informal punishments are so common we can miss them if we're not paying attention. An employee who has frequent conflicts with his colleagues may find himself shuffled into a dead-end position, or assigned the graveyard shift. A husband spied flirting with the housekeeper may be told by his friends and family that such behavior is unacceptable. An entertainer who espouses unpopular political positions may encounter a dip in his popularity at the box office as moviegoers boycott his films.

Informal punishments are common in our society. They're certainly prevalent through childhood, from early play amongst small children through social ostracism in school. Some groups define themselves through the exclusion of others.

Remember the Bad Apple Effect from the previous chapter? As you might expect, the effects of those bad apples diminishes if punishment is threatened.

There is an old idea that punishment can be transferred from one person to another. In many traditions, God punishes a person's relatives in addition to punishing the transgressor.[21] In some societies, if Alice kills Bob, one of Bob's relatives is allowed to kill one of Alice's relatives in retribution. The Nazis instituted this as government policy; it was called "*sippenhaft.*" This practice is a form of societal pressure. If Alice is considering defecting from some group norm—killing another person, committing adultery, whatever—she not only has to worry about human or divine retribution against her personally, but also retribution against members of her family. And threatening Alice's family should she defect both raises her perceived cost of defection and enlists her family members in persuading her not to defect in the first place. The Israeli government's current practice of bulldozing the homes of suicide bombers' families is an example. Of course, sometimes this goes very badly. Think of "honor killings" of rape victims, or blood feuds in various cultures throughout history, like the Hatfields versus the McCoys.

●   ●   ●

There's a variant of the Hawk-Dove game that demonstrates how reputation can solve a societal dilemma. It's designed so doves are more likely to interact with doves. When this happens, hawks can be isolated and their numbers reduced.

Compared with the basic Hawk-Dove game, cooperation turns out to be an even better strategy. Stable populations have even fewer hawks because doves, by preferring to interact with other doves, can effectively isolate them. Left to fight amongst themselves, hawks tend to kill each other off. Returning to human society, we are at our most cooperative when we seek out other cooperative people and avoid those who would take advantage of us. We learned this in Chapter 3 when we looked at the evolution of cooperation: cooperators do better when they can recognize each other. Reputation not only encourages cooperation, but also marginalizes defectors to the point where there ends up being fewer of them to deal with.

This is important. We've been talking about societal dilemmas as if they're always decisions to either cooperate or defect. In the real world, we often have a choice of people with whom to interact. We don't walk into stores randomly, wondering if the merchant will cheat us. We only walk into stores where we believe the merchant will not cheat us. Instead of defecting and cheating the merchant as punishment, we prefer to shop elsewhere.

●   ●   ●

In Chapter 3, we learned that two things are required for cooperation: reciprocal altruism and a calculating intelligence. Morals and reputation, the two things I've been calling our primitive toolbox of social pressures, provide that reciprocal altruism. Even so, reputational societal pressure can fail in many ways.

Defectors take steps to hide facts that can harm their reputation, or manipulate facts to help their reputation. Recall that in the mid-1970s, John Wayne Gacy managed to rape and kill 33 young men. All the while, his Chicago neighbors and colleagues on civic and charitable committees never suspected "Pogo the Clown" Gacy was involved in any work more diabolical than entertaining children for good causes. In the UK, Dr. Harold Shipman had a similar story. Described as "a pillar of the community" by his neighbors, he killed at least 250 people, mostly elderly widows, before he was caught. Most examples are less extreme. A politician might go to church and publicly pray, to encourage people to think he's honest: a whited sepulchre. An American trekking through Europe might sew a Canadian flag on his backpack.

Confidence tricksters spend a lot of time manipulating reputation signals. They employ all sorts of props, façades, and other actors—shills—to convince their victims that they have a good reputation by appearing authentic, building confidence, and encouraging trust. Corporations and political candidates both do similar things; they use paid supporters to deliberately spread artificial reputational information about them. This is becoming even more prevalent and effective on the Internet. Hired hands write fake blog posts, blog comments, tweets, Facebook comments, and so on. Scammers on eBay create fake feedback, giving themselves a better reputation. There are even companies that will give you fake Facebook friends, making you seem more popular with attractive people than you actually are.

Defectors try to minimize the effects of their bad reputation. People get new friends, move to another city, or—in extreme cases—change their names, get plastic surgery, or steal someone else's identity. Philip Morris renamed itself

Altria, because who would want to buy their Kraft Mac and Cheese from a cigarette company? ValuJet, its brand ruined after Flight 592 crashed in the Everglades in 1996, now operates as AirTran Airways. Blackwater, the defense contractor notorious for numerous Iraq war abuses, became Xe Services and then Academi. The School of the Americas, implicated in training many human rights–abusing military staff in Latin America, rebranded itself as the Western Hemisphere Institute for Security Cooperation.

Corporations work to minimize the effects of negative reputation on their brands through advertising and public relations. Multinational food and consumer product companies like Unilever and Procter & Gamble deliberately downplay their corporate brand and focus attention on their sub-brands. There are a lot of marketing reasons to engage in sub-branding, but the security thinking is that if there is a problem with one of their brands, the negative publicity won't spread across the company's entire product line.

Some people simply don't care about reputation. Like our individual morals, our individual concern about reputation varies—from person to person as well as from situation to situation. Some of us care a lot; others, not so much. Of course, this is contextual. We all have different reputations in different groups with respect to different personal attributes.

Some people end up with the wrong reputation. Even if someone does nothing wrong, there's no guarantee that his reputation is accurate. Untrue stories can circulate by mistake. Someone else might lie to give him a bad reputation. We all know people who have reputations they don't deserve, both good and bad.

Defectors band together in subgroups that have different reputational rules. Gang members thrive in groups. Sure, they have a terrible reputation in the broader community, but they care primarily about their reputation within their gangs. This dynamic is also true for defectors who have a different moral system from the dominant culture: a lone pot smoker in a pot-free community is going to have a lot harder time than one who finds other pot smokers in the vicinity. His friends will help him defect. In effect, he will choose to cooperate with the smaller society of defectors, rather than with the pot-abstaining majority. The same is true for those worshipping in secret out of fear: early Christians in the Roman Empire, pagans afterwards, Jews in post-expulsion Spain, devout Russian Orthodox in the former Soviet Union. We'll talk about this more in Chapters 11 and 12.

The value of defecting might be worth the reputational damage. Maybe it's a single large transaction, and the merchant is willing to sacrifice her reputation for the money. Or maybe it's a situation where the merchant can outrun his reputation.[22] We've all heard stories of home remodeling contractors that score a big contract, and then either don't do the work or do a quick, shoddy job, and disappear with the money. "Fly by night," it's called. They've made the risk trade-off and decided their reputation wasn't that valuable. If they're career scammers, a big payoff may even enhance their reputation among their fellow scammers. A restaurant owner in a tourist area could serve lousy food, confident that the reputational damage matters less when there's no repeat clientele. A corporate CEO might decide his company's ability to repair reputational damage allows it to get away with misdeeds he wouldn't have authorized if he didn't have such an effective public relations department.

The most important reason reputational pressure starts to fail is that groups get too large.[23] Assisted by technology, reputational pressure can scale globally. Think of the reputations of public figures and celebrities, companies and brands, or individuals on the Internet. Think of eBay's reputation system, review sites like Yelp, or how we can make friends on shared-interest websites. Think of the FBI's criminal databases, the information about you kept by credit bureaus, or Google's database of your interests. Think of passports, driver's licenses, or employee badges. These are all reputational systems, and all serve to apply reputational pressure in different risk trade-offs.

But these systems can have all sorts of inaccuracies. What we know about celebrities, corporations, and people in faraway places doesn't always match reality. It's not only the natural errors that creep into any large-scale process, it's that these systems can be manipulated and the technologies used to support them can be attacked. In order for reputation to scale, we need to trust these reputational systems, but sometimes that trust is not well-founded. We'll talk about this more in Chapter 10.

Reputational pressure works best within a group of people who know each other: a group of friends or coworkers in an office, compared to a bunch of strangers on a bus or a city full of people. Neighbors are good at settling disputes; people who don't live so close to each other are less good at it.

However, once the group size grows larger and the social ties between people weaken, reputation alone doesn't cut it.

Commenting on Hardin's original Tragedy of the Commons paper, psychologist Julian Edney wrote that "the upper limit for a simple, self-contained, sustaining, well-functioning commons may be as low as 150 people."[24]

Eleven years later, Dunbar wrote:

> The Hutterites, a group of contemporary North American religious funda-
> mentalists who live and farm communally, regard 150 as the maximum size
> for their communities. What is interesting is the reason they give for splitting
> communities at this size. They find that when there are more than about 150
> individuals, they cannot control the behaviour of members by peer pressure
> alone.

Commenting on the Hutterites, Hardin suggested, "Perhaps we should say a community below 150 really is managed—managed by conscience."

I read somewhere once that police officers represent a failure of the underlying social system.[25] The social system should be self-policing, and formal rules and rule enforcement should not be required. But it's not self-policing, and not just because we're wary of vigilantism. It's simply a natural effect of increasing the scale of the underlying social group.

Institutional Pressures

Store owners generally get to set their own hours. If their customers tend to shop early, the store opens early. If their customers tend to sleep in, the store doesn't open until late morning. Nights, weekends, holidays: a smart store owner is going to match his store's hours to his customers' needs.

This isn't true of stores in a shopping mall. Shopping malls have preset hours, and if you have a store in the mall, you have to adhere to those hours. It doesn't matter who your customers are. Called a "continuous operations clause," it's written into most mall leases.

This solves a societal dilemma: stores are individually better off if they can set their hours to suit their business, but the stores are collectively better off if everyone shares the same hours so customers know that everything will be open when they go. To ensure that stores follow the group interest, mall operators enforce continuous operations clauses through steep fines.

Societal Dilemma: Mall hours.	
Society: Group of merchants.	
Group interest: Mall stores all have uniform hours.	Competing interest: Maximize short-term profits.
Group norm: Stay open during agreed upon hours.	Corresponding defection: Open and close when it makes financial sense.
To encourage people to act in the group interest, society implements these societal pressures:	
Institutional: The group fines stores that close during common hours.	

As we saw in the previous chapter, solving a Prisoner's Dilemma involves changing the costs and benefits of acting in the person's selfish interest versus acting in the group interest. Shopping malls solve their Prisoner's Dilemma by using fines. A fine raises the cost of a store owner acting in his self-interest. Raise that cost high enough, and owners will open and close their stores in unison.

The common mall hours, and the fines for violating them, are an example of an institutional societal pressure. It's a rule established by the institution that owns the mall—it might even be a cooperative institution consisting of all the stores—that the society of store owners all agree to.

Political philosophers have long argued that informal societal pressures aren't enough for a successful human society. Thomas Hobbes, writing in the mid-17th century, believed individuals couldn't be trusted, and the opportunities to defect were simply too tempting. In this "state of nature"—that's anarchy, although he never used the word—our lives would be "solitary, poor, nasty, brutish, and short." Martin Luther said the same thing, a century earlier.

Immanuel Kant put it this way at the end of the 18th century:

> The problem of organizing a state, however hard it may seem, can be solved even for a race of devils, if only they are intelligent. The problem is: "Given a multitude of rational beings requiring universal laws for their preservation, but each of whom is secretly inclined to exempt himself from them, to establish a constitution in such a way that, although their private intentions conflict, they check each other, with the result that their public conduct is the same as if they had no such intentions."

The result is Social Contract Theory, which posits that people willingly grant government power that compels them to subordinate their immediate self-interest to the long-term group interest in order to protect themselves and their fellow citizens from harm. Thomas Hobbes, John Locke, Jean-Jacques Rousseau, and the 20th-century philosopher John Rawls all proposed different flavors of this idea. Their conclusions about the ideal way to achieve social order vary, but all maintain that it is both necessary and moral to forcibly limit individual freedoms, reasoning that without a government enforcing laws, defectors would take over, to the detriment of all.

At its basest form, it's an argument we've seen in the previous chapter: fear of punishment is what keeps the tempted honest. In Plato's *Republic*, Glaucon argues that if you remove that fear, the righteous will behave no differently than the wicked: "Mankind censure injustice, fearing that they may be the victims of it and not because they shrink from committing it." During the Italian

Renaissance, Niccolò Machiavelli built an entire political philosophy around this principle.

> Men never act well except through necessity: but where choice abounds and where license may be used, everything is quickly filled with confusion and disorder. It is said therefore that Hunger and Poverty make men industrious, and Laws make them good.

Of course, that's not precisely true. The righteous aren't really just calculating scoundrels behaving well only because they fear that someone else—or perhaps God—will punish them if they step out of line. Reciprocal altruism works, and most people are honest most of the time. It's the defectors that Machiavelli was talking about, and for them he got it mostly right.

Laws, regulations, and rules in general are all institutional societal pressures. They're similar to reputational pressure, but formalized. We all agree to comply with all sorts of institutional pressures as a precondition of being part of a group, the most common of which are the laws by which we agree to be bound as a condition of being part of whatever political units we're part of. (It's certainly debatable whether individuals "agree to be bound by" all of the rules that end up being applicable to them, but that's generally how political philosophers look at it.)

It's not always clear exactly when informal social mores become rules. The social pathologists make a distinction between codified and explicit norms established by the government and non-formal norms agreed upon by the group, but that leaves a large grey area for less-official groups. Still, codifying our reputational pressure into laws was a big step for the development of society, and it allowed larger and more complex social groupings—like cities.

Garrett Hardin, who created the phrase "the Tragedy of the Commons," later wished he'd called it "the tragedy of the unmanaged commons." The point of his paper was not that defectors will inevitably ruin things for the group, but that unless things are managed properly, they will. He was stressing the need for institutional pressure.

Institutional pressure requires an institution for implementation and enforcement; I mean the term very broadly. Institutions include governments of all sizes, but also religious institutions, corporations, criminal organizations, and so on. These institutions implement rules, laws, edicts—there are several terms—and sanctions for disobeying them and possibly incentives to obey them.

Burglary has costs that exceed the value of the goods stolen. Burglary costs in the time and effort to replace what's been stolen, the psychological effect of having one's home violated, the cost to the community of investigating the crime and prosecuting the accused, and even the cost of defending the suspect if he happens to be indigent. Sometimes the costs to the burglarized far exceed the value to the burglar: think of someone who steals copper wire out of a data center to sell as scrap metal, or destroys a building to get at valuables inside. But these costs are not borne by the burglar. They are externalities to him.

A well-written law combined with proper enforcement raises the costs to the burglar to the point where he is forced to bear the full costs of his actions. It could even raise the costs to the point where breaking, entering, and stealing is a worse trade-off than buying the same things legitimately.

Voting is another example. In the U.S., voter turnout is so low in part because there's no legal requirement to vote. In countries where voting is required by law—Australia, Belgium, Bolivia, etc.—turnout is much higher. This is also true in countries that don't have explicit voting laws, but have laws that raise the cost of not voting in other ways. For example, in Greece, it's harder for non-voters to get a passport or driver's license. If you don't vote in Singapore, you're removed from the electoral rolls and must provide a reason when you reapply. In Peru, your stamped voting card is necessary to obtain some government services. And in Mexico and Italy, there are informal consequences of not voting, harking back to the previous chapter. These "innocuous sanctions," as they're called in Italy, make it—for example—harder to get day care for your child.

Deacon's Paradox is another example. The societal dilemma looks like this:

Societal Dilemma: Respecting pair bonds.	
Society: Society as a whole.	
Group interest: Everyone trusts each other enough to go about daily tasks away from their long-term partners.	Competing interest: Maximize personal pleasure, maximize gene propagation.
Group norm: Respect each other's pair bonds.	Corresponding defection: Have sex with whomever you want.
To encourage people to act in the group interest, society implements these societal pressures:	
Moral: Teaching that adultery is wrong. The occasional commandment.	
Reputational: Public shaming of people who break their marriage vows.	
Institutional: Legal marriage contracts. Adultery laws.	

Initially, marriage rites were informal and reputational; both religious and civil institutions formalized them as we developed rules about property and inheritance. Of course, this isn't perfect. Philandering is as old as human society; rules are generally only selectively enforced, and friends of a philanderer will always be tempted to look the other way. But formalized marriage rules have been in effect throughout history, and they're largely effective.

Gridlock is another example. If you've ever driven in a crowded city center, you know the problem. Drivers stay as close as possible to the car in front of them, so no one will be able to cut in front of them and they will get where they're going as quickly as possible. The inevitable result of this strategy is that cars get stuck in the middle of an intersection when the light turns red, and cars going the other way can't pass. This is both inconvenient and a danger to public safety as emergency vehicles become unable to pass through the congestion. In extreme cases, gridlock can tie up traffic for hours. Everyone would do better if no one entered the intersection until the car was able to completely clear it on the other side, but unless everyone shows restraint, those who do are penalized. The solution: in many cities, it's now illegal to enter an intersection if you are unable to pass completely through without blocking cross-traffic.

Some societal dilemmas are particularly resistant to institutional pressure. Kidnapping and piracy are two examples. The dilemma is obvious. Kidnapping and piracy are bad for society, so paying ransom is bad because it makes these crimes profitable and emboldens those who commit them. Nonetheless, each and every one of us wants an exception to be made if we, our loved ones, or our cargo are held for ransom. So people follow their self-interest, their self-preservation interest, or their relational interest and pay up. This practice has made kidnapping profitable in many countries, most notably Mexico, Colombia, and Iraq, and has contributed to the escalation of piracy in Southeast Asia and off the coast of Somalia. All of these countries could pass laws making it illegal to pay kidnapping ransoms, but those would be hard to enforce. Both parties to these transactions want to hide them from the authorities. It's not enough to declare kidnapping illegal; enforcement matters, and most high-kidnapping and high-piracy countries have ineffective police forces at best, or corrupt police serving as accomplices at worst. Piracy has an additional externality; the costs are not borne by the country that hosts the pirates.[1] In countries like the United States, harsh enforcement has made kidnapping for ransom a very rare crime, and piracy nearly nonexistent. In other countries, like Somalia, paying ransoms is common, even though the government occasionally jails those who do so.

Compare this to bribery. Like kidnapping, bribery of public officials is a societal dilemma. Society is much better off without bribery, but when individuals are faced with a recalcitrant government official, they can be easily motivated to ignore that and pay up. Where bribery is illegal for both the giver and the receiver, both parties have an incentive to hide the bribe from the police, which makes enforcement of anti-bribery laws difficult. (The fact that it's sometimes the police who have to be bribed makes it even worse.) India's chief economic advisor recently argued that, for some classes of bribes, offering a bribe should be decriminalized. The rationale here is that if the bribe giver is not treated as a criminal, he will be more willing to help prosecute public employees who demand bribes. Of course, this only works for one-time bribes, where an official is demanding payment for a service that the recipient should normally receive. It doesn't work for bribes in which an official is being asked to do something he shouldn't normally do, or for a series of bribes over time. In all cases, the bribe payer would not want to make his actions public, regardless of the law. But in the more normal case of a government official trying to line his pockets through a one-off transaction, decriminalizing the bribe giver's actions would make it more likely for him to go public.[2]

Similarly, while it's bad policy to negotiate with terrorists, it's easy to make exceptions. At the height of the IRA's bombing campaign in the UK, Prime Minister Thatcher was publicly affirming that her government would never negotiate with terrorists while at the same time conducting secret back-channel negotiations with senior IRA figures. This was in addition to the negotiations the non-militarist wing of the IRA was conducting with the British government.

●   ●   ●

Just like reputational pressure, institutional pressure requires consequences to work. The difference is that while reputational consequences are informal, institutional consequences are formal, codified, and tangible. These can be punishments, more properly called sanctions, or rewards, better called incentives.

Think back to Bob and Alice in their respective prison cells, making their own risk trade-offs. Not implicating others enhances the reputation of a criminal; additionally, criminal organizations hunt down and punish those who don't keep silent.

Societal Dilemma: Criminals testifying against each other.	
Society: The criminal organization.	
Group interest: Minimize the amount of punishment for the society.	Competing interest: Minimize personal punishment.
Group norm: Don't testify against each other.	Corresponding defection: Testify against each other in exchange for reduced punishment.
To encourage people to act in the group interest, the society implements a variety of trust mechanisms.	
Moral: People feel good when they support other members of their group, and bad when they let them down.	
Reputational: Those who testify against their fellow criminals are shunned.	
Institutional: The criminal organization severely punishes stool pigeons.	

You could argue whether the criminal code of silence—and the practice of killing police informants—belongs in this chapter or the previous one. I suppose it depends on how formal the rules are. Certainly it goes far beyond shunning.

Sanctions serve several purposes. Modern penologists hold that prisons are primarily intended to reeducate and reform, minimizing recidivism. Financial sanctions serve as a penalty, raising the financial cost of defecting. And, unfortunately, both have an aspect of revenge about them—another formalization of reputational pressure.[3] But the part of it that matters most for societal pressure is the deterrent effect. A rule or law will encourage some people to cooperate simply based on their innate moral tendency to obey authority and follow the rules, but primarily—like reputational systems—laws rely on punishment as a deterrent to defection. Unlike reputational systems, though, imposing sanctions is more formalized.[4] This doesn't necessarily mean something that has been written down and agreed to like a legal code, although it generally is. Sanctions reduce the number of defections. And recalling the Bad Apple Effect from Chapter 7, they prevent further defections.

The general idea of such rewards is to formalize coercion. Even prohibitive laws have some aspect of this; they're prescriptive as well as punitive. They operate both before the decision about whether to cooperate or defect occurs, by providing guidelines for acceptable behavior and prior notification of any penalties, and afterwards, through enforcement.

Laws are only as good as society's ability to enforce them. It's not enough to pass a law requiring people to pay their taxes, or banning child labor, or limiting the amount of insect parts in your breakfast cereal; if you don't also sanction defectors, the laws will not act as much of a deterrent. Fines have to be assessed and collected. Jail time has to be served. And all of this has to be implemented with an eye towards solving the societal dilemma.

Alexander Hamilton said as much in *The Federalist 15*:

> It is essential to the idea of a law, that it be attended with a sanction; or, in other words, a penalty or punishment for disobedience. If there be no penalty annexed to disobedience, the resolutions or commands which pretend to be laws will, in fact, amount to nothing more than advice or recommendation.

Sanctions fall into three basic categories: confiscation of resources or possessions, shaming, or physical penalties. Fines and forced servitude fall into the first category, and the last category further breaks down into incarceration, physical harm, and execution. Shaming and physical harm were more common historically; the stocks are a good example of both, as people restrained by them could be abused by the community. Sex offender registries are a common modern shaming sanction, but others—such as requiring an offender to stand in a public place wearing a sign that broadcasts the nature of his offense—are slowly making a comeback, in spite of persuasive arguments that they are immoral, ineffective, and degrade the public as much as those subjected to them. House arrest, monitored by an electronic bracelet, has a shaming aspect too. So does community service, if it's obvious and in public.

Most modern sanctions consist of either incarceration or financial penalties. Incarceration removes the defector from society for a period of time, and prevents him from committing further defections. Done right, jail is a place to reform criminals. Done wrong, jail is a place where criminals learn how to be better criminals.

Financial penalties can be tricky to implement, and are therefore worthy of a longer discussion. Speeding is a risk trade-off. There are risks to speeding—accidents—but there are also rewards, such as getting to your destination sooner or the adrenaline rush that comes with driving faster. There are all sorts of pathologies in the trade-off—the rewards are immediate and constant, but the risks are nebulous and only happen occasionally—and one might think there's no reason society can't just let people make the trade-offs by themselves.

The problem is that when Alice speeds, she also increases the risk to everyone around her.[5] So there is a societal dilemma at work, and if you want Alice not to speed you're going to have to make it illegal and penalize her for doing it. Studies show that fines reduce speeding overall, even though they don't deter habitual speeders. Drunk driving laws and their enforcement are a similar example.

Societal Dilemma: Speeding.	
Society: Society as a whole.	
Group interest: Minimize automobile deaths.	Competing interest: Minimize travel time.
Group norm: Obey speed limits.	Corresponding defection: Speed.
To encourage people to act in the group interest, the society implements a variety of trust mechanisms.	
Moral: It's moral to drive in a way that doesn't endanger others. Also, it's moral to follow the rules.	
Reputational: There is some social pressure, in some circles, not to be known as a speeder or a reckless driver.	
Institutional: Speed limits.	

It's vital for the financial penalties to be high enough to make the behavior unprofitable. For example, if customs has a 10% chance of catching a smuggler, then the penalty for smuggling needs to be at least ten times the value of the goods—otherwise it would make financial sense to smuggle. One report demonstrated that uninsured drivers in the UK are capable of doing the math, and will remain uninsured if the expected penalty for doing so is less than the cost of insurance. This is even more important when dealing with corporations; there are many examples of fines being so small as to be viewed as an incidental cost of doing business. We'll talk about this more in Chapter 13.

Fixed financial penalties are regressive. Like everything else about the speeding trade-off, the cost of a speeding ticket is relative. If you're poor, a $100 speeding ticket is a lot of money. If you're rich, it's a minor cost of the trip.[6] Finland, Denmark, and Switzerland address the problem by basing traffic fines on the offender's income. Wealthy people in those countries have regularly been issued speeding tickets costing over $100,000. You might disagree with the system as a matter of policy, but it certainly is a more broadly effective societal pressure. Jail time for speeders accomplishes much the same thing.

There are two basic ways the law can prescribe financial penalties. It can pass a direct law, or it can institutionalize liabilities. If the affected individuals can sue the defectors and win sufficient punitive damages, that will also increase the cost of defecting. In both cases, laws remove the externality by making sure the defector pays the cost of defection. Watch how it works:

- *Overfishing.* Pass and enforce a law fining (or even jailing) those who overfish, and the dilemma goes away. Assuming the cost of the fine multiplied by the probability of getting caught—that's "cost" defined broadly, in terms of money, jail time, social stigma, whatever—is greater than the value of the additional fish, it changes Alice's risk trade-off.
- *Polluting the river.* Allow people living downstream from the polluter to sue. Assuming the court system works properly, the cost of the lawsuits to the polluter will be greater than the cost not to pollute the river.
- *Unsafe food handling.* Consumer protection laws raise the cost of ignoring food safety—presumably to save money—by imposing financial penalties on those who engage in it.

All this assumes a system where both the plaintiff and the defendant can afford the same quality of legal representation. The trade-off changes when the river polluters are corporations with deep pockets, and the people affected don't have the means to pay for lawyers. Or when the bad behavior occurs when foreign companies import food into another country, and the probability of getting caught is low. Again, we'll return to these considerations in Chapter 13.

Taxes can be another type of institutional pressure. It's weird, because it doesn't actually prohibit anything. But if the goal is to reduce the scope of defection, charging people for their marginal defection is one way to do it. Like fines, taxes increase the cost of defecting. But unlike fines, they operate during and not after the defection.[7] For example, a sanction for littering requires the authorities to detect the crime and then assess the penalty. This happens after the littering occurs, and there's always the chance of not getting caught. A tax on excess trash occurs at the time of trash pickup, although the person may pay the tax later.

The societal dilemma surrounding antibiotics mirrors the one surrounding vaccination: overuse vs. underuse. It's in everyone's immediate self-interest to use antibiotics to treat conditions that respond to them, but if they're overused, bacteria develop resistance, making them ineffective for everyone. A big part of the problem is the wholesale use of antibiotics in agriculture: administering antibiotics to livestock in order to produce faster growth, regardless of whether they are needed to treat disease. The problem of antibiotic-resistant supergerms is an externality. But doctors also contribute significantly to the problem; they frequently prescribe antibiotics in cases where they're not really necessary. But here again, use of antibiotics makes sense from the perspective of the doctor, who reasons that they won't hurt and might help the immediate patient, whose patients regularly ask for them, and to whom the larger social costs are an externality as well.

One solution, proposed by the Infectious Diseases Society of America, is to tax the use of antibiotics. This is a societal pressure, increasing the cost of using antibiotics as a way to remove the externality. We can debate the effectiveness of the measure: it'll definitely help in agricultural uses, but how much it will reduce superfluous doctor prescriptions will depend on who pays the tax and how. Not to mention how easy it would be to smuggle in untaxed antibiotics.

●   ●   ●

The converse of penalties are incentives: rewarding someone for cooperating. There is a whole class of institutional pressure systems designed to reward cooperative behavior. Examples include:

- Tax deductions or tax credits for certain behaviors.
- Faster tax refunds for people who file their returns electronically.[8]
- Time off a prison sentence for good behavior.
- Employee bonuses.
- Bounties and rewards for turning in wanted fugitives.
- Deferred or non-prosecution of SEC violations as an incentive to provide evidence against other, larger, violators.
- Certifications, both coercive ones (FDA approval for new drugs) and optional ones (LEED certifications for buildings).
- Whistle-blower statutes, where the whistle-blower gets a percentage of the fraud found.

The problem with rewarding cooperators via an institutional mechanism is that it's expensive. If we assume that the majority will cooperate regardless of the reward, then a lot of people will get a reward for doing what they were going to do already. Either the reward will have to be very small and not much of an additional incentive to cooperate, or the total cost of rewarding everyone will be very expensive. In general, it's more efficient to spend that money going after the minority of defectors.

Financial incentives and penalties interact weirdly with other categories of societal pressures. It's easy to regard societal pressures as cumulative—and to assume that moral plus institutional pressure will be more effective than morals alone—but our moral systems are more complicated than that.

In one experiment, participants were presented with a societal dilemma: they were in charge of a manufacturing plant that emitted toxic gas from its smoke-stacks. They could either spend more money to clean up a lot of the toxin, or spend less money to clean up a little bit of the toxin. The dilemma came from the fact that pending government legislation—a bad thing in the experiment's scenario—depended on how much cleaning up the manufacturing plants did collectively. It's a free-rider problem: a subject could either cooperate and clean up his share, or defect and hope enough others cleaned up enough to forestall legislation.

What makes this experiment particularly interesting is that half of the subjects were also told that the industry would be inspecting smokestacks to verify com-pliance and fining defectors. It wasn't a big risk; both the chance of inspection and the cost of noncompliance were low. Still, inspections are a societal pressure, and you'd expect they would have some positive effect on compliance rates. Unexpectedly, they had a negative effect: subjects were more likely to cooperate if there were no noncompliance fines than if there were. The addition of money made it a financial rather than a moral decision. Paradoxically, financial penalties intended to discourage harmful behavior can have the reverse effect.

For this reason, signs featuring anti-littering slogans like "Don't Mess with Texas" are more effective than signs that only warn, "Penalty for Littering: $100"; and "smoking in hotel rooms is prohibited" signs are more effective than signs that read "$250 cleaning penalty if you smoke." In one experiment with day care providers, researchers found that when they instituted a fine for parents picking their children up late, late pickups increased. The fine became a fee, which par-ents could decide to pay and assuage any moral resistance to defection.

More generally, the very existence of rules or laws can counter moral and reputational pressure. Some towns are experimenting with eliminating all traffic laws and signs. The idea is that drivers who must follow the rules pay less atten-tion to the world around them than drivers with no rules to follow.

Financial rewards have the same effect that financial penalties do; they engage the brain's greed system and disengage the moral system. A fascinating inci-dent in Switzerland illustrates this. Trying to figure out where to put a nuclear waste dump, researchers polled residents of several small towns about how they would feel about it being located near them. This was 1993, and a lot of fear surrounded the issue; nonetheless, slightly more than half of the residents agreed to take the risk, for the good of the country.

In order to motivate the other half, the researchers offered money in exchange for siting the nuclear dump near them: about $2,000 per person per year. Instead of enticing more residents to accept the dump, it reduced their number by half. The researchers doubled and then tripled the amount offered, but it didn't make a difference. When they simply asked nicely, the researchers stimulated the altruistic part of the residents' brains—and, in many cases, they decided it was the right thing to do. Again, the addition of money can increase the defection rate.[9]

Financial advisors exhibit this unconscious bias in favor of their clients. In one experiment, analysts gave different weights to the same information, depending on what the client wanted to hear. An obvious societal pressure system to address this problem would be to require advisors to disclose any conflicts of interest; but this can have the reverse effect of increasing the number of defectors. By disclosing their conflicts, financial advisors may feel they have been granted a moral license to pursue their own self-interest, and may feel partially absolved of their professional obligation to be objective.

●   ●   ●

Elinor Ostrom received a Nobel Prize in 2009 for studying how societies deal with Tragedies of the Commons: grazing rights in the Swiss Alps, fishing rights off the coast of Turkey, irrigation communities in the Philippines. She's studied commons around the world, and has a list of rules for successfully managing them.[10] Generalizing them to our broad spectrum of societal dilemmas, they serve as a primer for effective institutional pressure:

1. Everyone must understand the group interest and know what the group norm is.
2. The group norm must be something that the group actually wants.
3. The group must be able to modify the norm.
4. Any institution delegated with enforcing the group norm must be accountable to the group, so it's effectively self-regulated. We'll discuss these institutions in Chapter 14.
5. The penalties for defecting must be commensurate with the seriousness of the defection.

6. The system for assessing penalties must be consistent, fair, efficient, and relatively cheap.
7. The group must be able to develop its own institutional pressure and not have it imposed from outside the group.
8. If there are larger groups and larger group interests, then the groups need to be scaled properly and nested in multiple layers—each operating along these same lines.

Ostrom's rules may very well be the closest model we have to our species' first successful set of institutional pressures. They're not imposed from above; they grow organically from the group. Societies of resource users are able to self-regulate if they follow these rules, and that self-regulation is stable over the long term. It's generally when outsiders come in and institutionalize a resource-management system that things start to fail.

I mentioned institutional pressure as a formalization of reputational pressure. This works in several ways. Laws formalize reputation itself. In Chapter 8, we talked about group membership as a substitute for individual reputation. As societies grow, laws formalize some group memberships.

For example, doctors need a license to practice. So do architects, engineers, private investigators, plumbers, and real estate agents. Restaurants need licenses and regular inspections by health officials to operate. The basic idea is that these official certifications provide a basis for people to trust these doctors, private investigators, and restaurants without knowing anything about their reputations. Certification informs potential clients that a businessperson has at least the minimum formal education and skill required to safely and competently perform the service in question, and that the businessperson is accountable to someone other than the customer: a licensing body, a trade organization, and so on. Handicap license plates are another formalized reputational system. Not all certifications are controlled by the government; some come from private institutions, such as Underwriter's Laboratories' certifications, the Good Housekeeping Seal of Approval, Consumer Reports rankings, and a variety of computer standards.

Other formal memberships that serve as reputation substitutes include academic degrees, bar associations for lawyers, the Better Business Bureau, food products' labels of origin—*appellation d'origine contrôlée* in France, and U.S. counterparts like "Wisconsin cheese" and "Made in Vermont"—USDA Organic certification, consumer credit ratings and reports, bonding, accreditation of educational institutions. Negative reputation can also be institutionalized: public sex-offender registries, the DHS terrorist "no fly" list, blacklists for union organizers or suspected

Communists, and designations on driver's licenses of a felony conviction. The scarlet letter is an older example, and the yellow star the Nazis required Jews to wear is a particularly despicable one.

Laws also formalize commitment. Legal contracts are probably the best example. Marriage licenses, curfew laws, and laws that enforce parents' commitment to raise their children are others.

Societal Dilemma: Following contracts.	
Society: Society as a whole.	
Group interest: Effectively formalize agreements.	Competing interest: Maximize some self-interest.
Group norm: Follow contracts.	Corresponding defection: Break contracts.

To encourage people to act in the group interest, the society implements a variety of trust mechanisms.

Moral: We feel good about keeping our word.

Reputational: No one does business with individuals and companies with a reputation for breaking contracts.

Institutional: There are all sorts of laws regarding the legality of contracts, and sanctions for breaking them.

Finally, laws formalize societal norms that reputation traditionally enforced: anti-incest laws and age-of-consent laws, minimum drinking ages, bans on false advertising, blue laws, public indecency/intoxication laws, city lawn and weed ordinances, noise ordinances, libel and slander laws, zoning regulations, laws against impersonating police officers, and—in a perverse way—laws prohibiting people from criticizing the government. Employment applications that ask if you have ever been convicted of a felony are a formalization of reputation.

All of these institutional pressures allow reputation to scale, by giving people a system to trust so they don't have to necessarily trust individuals. If I trust the system of government-issued identification cards and driver's licenses, I don't have to wonder whether to trust each and every a person when he tells me he's old enough to drink in my bar.

There are many ways institutional pressure fails:

There is too little or too much of it. We've seen how institutional pressure is required to augment moral and reputational pressures in large and complex societies. Too little institutional pressure and the scope of defection is too great. For example, there's more tax evasion if the crime goes unpunished.

But more institutional pressure isn't always better. Gary Becker won a Nobel Prize in economics in part for his work in criminology. He asked the obvious question, what's the optimal level of crime? The naïve answer is zero, but that is unattainable and requires so much institutional pressure that society falls apart. Too much institutional pressure, and you get a country that looks like North Korea or the former East Germany: police states with a good part of the population working for the police. The other extreme—no police—doesn't work, either. You get lawless countries like Afghanistan and Somalia. Somewhere in the middle is the optimal scope of defection and the optimal level of enforcement.

In a lot of ways, this is similar to how evolution solves security problems. Antelopes don't need perfect protection against lions, and such protection would be too expensive in evolutionary terms. Instead, they accept the cost of losing the occasional antelope from the herd and increase their reproductive efficiency to compensate.

Similarly, we can never ensure perfect security against terrorism. All this talk of terrorism as an existential threat to society is nonsense. As long as terrorism is rare enough, and most people survive, society will survive. Unfortunately, it's not politically viable to come out and say that. We're collectively in a pathological state where people expect perfect protection against a host of problems—not just terrorism—and are unwilling to accept that that is not a reasonable goal.

Laws don't always have their intended effect. They can be a blunt tool, especially when it comes to violent crime and disaffected populations. There isn't a clean cause-and-effect relationship between incentives and behavior; more often than not, incentives are emotional, and are far more compelling than a rational consideration of even the most severe sanction.[11] There's a lot of research in this area, with many counterintuitive—and sometimes contradictory—results. We know that, in general, spending more money on police reduces crime somewhat. On the other hand, there are studies that demonstrate that the death penalty reduces murders as well as studies that demonstrate it doesn't. While it's easy for politicians to be "tough on crime," it's not always obvious that that's the best solution. An increase in the severity of punishment often doesn't translate into a drop in crime; an increase in the probability of punishment often does.[12] Often the societal causes of crime are what's important, and changes in the law do very little to help.

Laws have a clearer effect on more calculating crimes. Increasing penalties against tax fraud reduces tax fraud, at least for a little while. Increasing penalties on corporate crimes reduces those crimes. In those instances, potential defectors have plenty of time to make a rational risk trade-off.[13]

It's not always possible to enforce a law. International law, for example, only matters to the extent that the countries are willing to observe it or are able to enforce it on each other. Viktor Bout was an international arms dealer for about twenty years before his arrest in 2008. He was able to ship weapons to every conflict region imaginable, even those under UN embargo. He benefited from the lack of international law addressing transnational criminal activity, deliberately slack customs enforcement in countries seeking to attract business, and nations that found it convenient to let him do their dirty work.

Laws are open to interpretation, and that interpretation process can be expensive. Earlier I talked about solving the societal dilemma of pollution with a legal security measure: allowing people downstream from the polluter to sue. This is good in theory, but can be problematic in practice. The polluter can hire a team of lawyers skilled in the art of legal delay. If the cost of the lawyers is less than the cost of cleaning up the pollution, or if the polluter can outspend his legal opponents, he can neutralize their ability to raise the cost of defecting. This kind of expensive legal defense can also work against government regulations, tying the case up in the courts until the government gives up. In the state anti-trust suits against Microsoft, almost all states settled before trial.

Laws can have loopholes. This can happen by accident, when laws are linguistically ambiguous, contain simple errors, or fail to anticipate some new technological development. It can also happen deliberately, when laws are miswritten to enable the skillful few to evade them.

Examples of accidental loopholes are the "Double Irish" and "Dutch Sandwich" loopholes that allow multinational corporations to avoid U.S.—and other—taxes.[14] It's how Google pays only 2.8% of profits in tax. One estimate claims the U.S. loses $60 billion per year in taxes this way. Another loophole allows large paper mills to claim $6 billion in tax credits per year for mixing diesel fuel in with a wood byproduct they already burn; the law with the loophole was intended to reduce the consumption of fossil fuels.[15] A variety of loopholes make video games one of the most highly subsidized industries in the U.S. And, so as not to entirely pick on the U.S., the International Whaling Commission's loophole for research that Japan exploits to hunt whales commercially is another example.

Although it's hard to prove, there are many examples of laws believed to be deliberately written with loopholes to benefit someone. The UN Convention on the Law of the Sea provisions on international fisheries are deliberately ambiguous, making much of it impossible to enforce. Also at the UN, Security Council Resolution 1441—used to justify invading Iraq—seems to have been designed to be ambiguous enough to both support and oppose the use of force.

More generally, loopholes are ways institutional pressure is subverted by defectors to do things it wasn't originally intended to do. Think of patent law, originally intended to protect inventors but now used by corporations to attack other corporations, or by patent trolls to extort money out of corporations. Or the legal profession, originally intended to serve justice but now used as an offensive weapon. Or stocks, originally intended to provide capital for companies but now used for all sorts of unintended purposes: weird derivatives, indexes, short-term trading, and so on. These are all defections. Either the law should be effective, or it shouldn't exist. A law with a loophole is the worst of both.

Laws can be applied inconsistently. If laws aren't objective, common, and universally applied, they are seen as unfair; and unfairness can exacerbate the Bad Apple Effect.

Judge Gordon Hewart put it best:

> There is no doubt, as has been said in a long line of cases, that it is not merely of some importance, but of fundamental importance, that justice should both be done and be manifestly seen to be done.

Laws try to outlaw legitimate and moral behavior. Sometimes it's perfectly legitimate for someone to follow her individual self-interest, regardless of the group interest. There's no inherent dividing line, and different people—and societies—will draw it differently.

Invasive species are at best a serious problem, and at worst an ecological disaster. They also pose a societal dilemma in which even a single defector can cause the group severe harm. All it took was one farmer releasing silver carp into the natural waterways of North America for it to invade everywhere, one flight accidentally carrying a pregnant brown tree snake to decimate the ecosystem of Guam, and one boat with zebra mussel larvae in its ballast water or milfoil clinging to its hull to overwhelm a previously pristine lake. As such, there need to be some pretty strong societal pressures in place to deal with this problem.

Some invasive species are easy to define as pests, but others are not. Monk parakeets are an invasive species in the U.S., thought to have been first released by pet owners either accidentally or as an easy way to get rid of them. The main harm they cause is crop damage, although they also cause fires and blackouts by building massive, elevated nests in electrical equipment, and they outcompete indigenous birds. On the other hand, they make cute pets and a lot of people like them. This results in a legal mess: the Wild Bird Conservation Act of 1992 prohibits importing them into the U.S., but state laws vary wildly, with some states banning them, while others have no laws whatsoever.

One of the most useful things a court system does is strike a balance between polarities of interest. How should society balance my individual right to play loud music with my neighbors' right to peace and quiet? Or my right to run a tannery versus my neighbors' right to an unsmelly environment? How should society balance my individual desire to keep a parakeet as a pet with the community's need to minimize the dangers posed by feral birds? Laws that try to outlaw legitimate and moral behavior are less likely to succeed.

Laws don't affect every type of defector equally. In addition to those who can afford to fight and those who can't, there are three broad types of defectors when it comes to laws. The first are the individuals who know the law, believe the law is good (or at least that they don't want these things happening to *them*), and choose to break it anyway: burglars, muggers, kidnappers, murderers, speeders, and people in desperate straits. The second are individuals who know the law, believe the law is wrong, and choose to break it: pot smokers, some parakeet and ferret owners, and members of the Underground Railway who helped escaped slaves from the American South flee to safety in Canada. There is also a third category: those who don't know they're breaking the law, or don't realize how their actions affect the group. People might speed because they legitimately didn't see the speed limit sign, or they might not realize that certain sexual practices are against the law. These three groups will react differently to different laws, sanctions, and incentives.

Sometimes and for some people, laws aren't enough. Sometimes the incentives to defect are worth the risk. That's where security technologies come in.

Security Systems

Security systems are all around us, filling in the gaps where moral, reputational, and institutional pressures aren't effective enough. They include the door locks and burglar alarms in our homes, the anti-counterfeiting technologies in major world currencies, and the system of registering handguns and taking ballistic prints. They can be high-tech, like automatic face recognition systems, or low-tech, like defensive berms and castle walls. They don't even have to be physical systems; they can be procedural systems like neighborhood watches, customs interviews, and police pat-downs.

Theft of hotel towels isn't high in the hierarchy of world problems, but it can be expensive for hotels. Moral prohibitions against stealing prevent most people from stealing towels. Many hotels put their name or logo on their towels. That works as a reputational pressure system; most people don't want their friends to see obviously stolen hotel towels in their bathrooms. Sometimes, though, this has the opposite effect: making towels souvenirs of the hotel and more desirable to steal. It's against the law to steal hotel towels, of course, but with the exception of large-scale thefts, the crime will never be prosecuted.[1] The result is that the scope of defection is higher than hotels want. And large, fluffy towels from better hotels are expensive to replace.

The only thing left for hotels to do is take security into their own hands. One system that has become increasingly common is to set prices for towels and other items, and automatically charge the guest for them if they disappear from the rooms. This works with things like bathrobes, but it's too easy for the hotel to lose track of how many towels a guest has in his room, especially if piles of them are available at the pool or can easily be taken from a housekeeper's cart in the hallway.

A newer system, still not widespread, is to embed washable computer chips into the towels and track their movement around the hotel electronically. One anonymous Hawaii hotel claims they've reduced towel theft from 4,000 a month to 750, saving $16,000 monthly in replacement costs. Assuming the RFID tags are inexpensive and don't wear out too quickly, that's a pretty good security system.

Let's go back to our two prisoners. They are morally inclined not to betray each other. Their reputation in the underworld depends on them not betraying their fellow criminal. And the criminal organization they're part of has unwritten but very real sanctions against betraying other criminals to the police. That's probably enough for most criminals, but not all. And—depending on the country—the police can be very persuasive.

What some organizations do—terrorists and spies come to mind—is add a security system. They organize themselves in cells so that each member of the criminal organization only knows a few other members: the members of his cell and maybe one or two others. There are a lot of ways to do this, and the organizational structure of the World War II French Resistance wasn't the same as Al Qaeda. If he's arrested or otherwise captured and interrogated, there's only so much damage he can do if he defects. This doesn't help the two captured prisoners, of course, but it does protect the rest of the criminal organization.

Societal Dilemma: Criminals testifying against each other.	
Society: The criminal organization.	
Group interest: Minimize the amount of jail time for the society.	Competing interest: Minimize personal jail time.
Group norm: Don't testify against each other.	Corresponding defection: Testify against each other in exchange for reduced jail time.
To encourage people to act in the group interest, the society implements a variety of trust mechanisms.	
Moral: People feel bad when they let members of their group down. Reputational: Those who testify against their fellow criminals are shunned. Institutional: The criminal organization punishes stool pigeons. Security: The criminal organization limits the amount of damage a defecting criminal can inflict.	

Of course, there are some good reasons not to run an organization like this. Imagine how much less effective a corporate worker would be if he only knew the five people in his department, and only communicated with his supervisor using dead drops and the occasional voice-disguised conversation from constantly changing pay phone locations. But sometimes security wins out over clean lines of communication and managerial open-door policies.

In Chapter 6's Figure 8, I broke out several different types of security systems:

- *Defenses.* This is what you normally think of as security: weapons, armor, door locks, bulletproof vests, guard dogs, anti-virus software, speed bumps, bicycle locks, prison walls, panic rooms, chastity belts, and traffic cones. The common aspect of all these things is they try to physically stop potential defectors from doing whatever they're trying to do.
- *Interventions.* These are other security measures that happen during the defection that either make defection harder or cooperation easier. To make defection harder, think of obfuscation and misdirection measures, security cameras in casinos, guard patrols, and authentication systems. To make cooperation easier, think of automatic face-recognition systems, uniforms, those automatic road-sign radar guns that tell you what speed you're going, and road signs that inform you of the rules.
- *Detection/response systems.* These include burglar alarms, sensors in smokestacks to detect pollutants, RFID tags attached to store merchandise—or hotel towels—and detectors at the doorways, intrusion-detection systems in computer networks, and a UV light to detect if your hotel's bed sheets are clean.
- *Audit/forensic systems.* These are primarily enhancements to institutional societal pressure. They include fingerprint- and DNA-matching technology and the expert systems that analyze credit card spending, looking for patterns of fraud.
- *Recovery systems.* These are security measures that make it easier for the victim to recover from an attack. Examples are a credit monitoring service or an insurance plan. What's interesting about these measures is that they don't directly influence the risk trade-off. If anything, they make someone more likely to defect, because he can more easily rationalize that the victim won't be hurt by his actions.
- *Preemptive interventions.* These operate before the attack, and directly affect the risk trade-off. Think of things like forced castration (chemical or otherwise), mandatory drug therapy to alter the personality of a career criminal, or a frontal lobotomy. Yes, these are often punishments after an attack, but they can prevent a future attack, too. Incarceration is also a preemptive intervention as well as a punishment; there are entire categories of crimes that someone in jail simply can't commit. So is execution, for the

same reason. Also in this category are predictive policing programs that increase police presence at times and places where crimes are likely to occur.

I'd be the first to admit this classification isn't perfect, and there are probably examples that don't fit neatly into my different boxes. That's okay; I'm less interested in precisely categorizing all possible security countermeasures, and more interested in looking at the breadth of security systems we use every day for societal pressures—many without even realizing it.

Security systems comprise a unique category of societal pressure. They're the last layer of defense—and the most scalable—against defection. You can view them as a way to technologically enhance natural defenses. Even if humans were complete loners and had never formed society, never worried about societal dilemmas, and never invented societal pressures, security systems could still protect individuals.

As a technological analog to natural defenses, they're the only societal pressure that actually puts physical constraints on behavior. Everything else we've discussed so far affects the risk trade-off, either directly, such as moral pressure, or through feedback, such as reputational pressure. Security can work this way as well, but it can also stop someone who decides to defect. A burglar might not have any moral qualms about breaking into a jewelry store, and he might not be worried about his reputation or getting caught—but he won't be able to steal anything unless he can pick the door lock and open the safe. Security might constrain him technically (the ability to pick the lock), financially (the cost to buy an oxyacetylene torch capable of cutting open the safe), or temporally (the time required to cut open the safe). Sometimes the constraints are relative, and sometimes they're absolute. This is what makes security systems so powerful and scalable. Security systems can work even if a defector doesn't realize that he's defecting. For example, a locked gate will stop someone who doesn't realize he's entering private property.

Also as an analog to natural defenses, security systems aren't always used as societal pressures. That distinction depends on who implements the security system and why. Think back to the sealed-bag exchange: the merchant could implement a variety of security systems to prevent his customers from shoplifting, cheating, or otherwise defrauding him. He could install security cameras and put anti-theft tags on his merchandise. He could buy a device that detects counterfeit money. He could use a service that verifies checks. All of this is the merchant's decision and the merchant's doing, and none of it is related to intra-group trust.

If a storeowner installs a camera behind his cash register, it's not societal pressure; if a city installs cameras on every street corner, it is. And if the police use all the individually installed cameras in the area to track a suspect—as was done with Timothy McVeigh's van—then it's societal pressure. If society decides to subsidize in-store cameras, that's also societal pressure.

If I carry a gun for self-defense, it's not societal pressure; if we as a society collectively arm our policemen, it is. You could argue there is no societal dilemma involved in the hotel's towel-security decision. This is certainly true, and illustrates that the boundary between individual security and security as societal pressure can be fuzzy. The same security measure—a camera, for example—might be individual in one instance and societal in another. There are also going to be security measures that are some of both. I'm less concerned with the hard-to-classify edge cases than I am with the general categories.

Even if a security system is implemented entirely by individuals, that doesn't mean it can't also serve as societal pressure. A security camera is more likely to displace crime than reduce it; a potential thief can just go to another store instead. But if enough stores install hidden cameras, potential burglars might decide that the overall risk is too great. Lojack, widely deployed, will reduce car theft (and will increase car theft in neighboring regions that don't have the same system). Various computer security systems can have a similar result. If a security system becomes prevalent enough, potential defectors might go elsewhere because the value of defection is reduced.

Of course, society often limits what sort of security systems someone can implement. It may be illegal for a store to install security cameras in dressing rooms, even if it would reduce shoplifting. And I'm not allowed to bury land mines in my front yard, even if I think it would deter burglars.

Our security systems are also limited by our own abilities. Carrying a gun for self-defense makes less sense if you don't know how to use one. And I don't have the time to test every piece of food I eat for poison, even if I wanted to. A more realistic example: a store might have a policy to test if large bills are counterfeit, but not bother with smaller bills. (Of course, defectors take advantage of this: it's why $20 bills are counterfeited more often than $100 bills.)

Security systems are both their own category of societal pressure and augment the other three categories, allowing them to scale better. Quite a lot of the societal pressures we've talked about in the previous three chapters have a security component. Examples include:

- *Security-augmented moral pressure.* Something as simple as a sign stating "Employees must wash hands after using the restroom" can be viewed as a security system. Measures that make compliance easier are another way to enhance morals, such as the electronic completion and filing of tax returns, photography to put a human face on victims and potential victims, and recycling bins in prominent locations. Other, more modern, technologies directly affect moral societal pressures: psychiatric therapies, personality-altering drugs, and brain-altering surgeries.

- *Security-augmented reputational pressure.* The eBay feedback mechanism is a reputational system that requires security to ensure the system can't be hacked and manipulated by unscrupulous merchants. Other examples are letters of introduction, tribal clothing, employee background checks, sex offender databases, diplomas posted on walls, and U.S. State Department travel advisories. Informal online reviews of doctors allow us to trust people we don't know anything about, with our health. Online reputational systems allow us to trust unknown products on Amazon, unknown commenters on Slashdot, and unknown "friends" on Facebook. Credit-rating systems codify reputation. In online games, security systems are less of an enhancement to, and more of a replacement of, moral and reputational pressures for ensuring game fairness.

- *Security-augmented institutional pressure.* A community might install cameras to help enforce speed limits. Or a government might use correlation software to analyze millions of tax returns, looking for evidence of cheating. Other examples include alarm systems that summon the police, surveillance systems that allow the police to track suspects, and forensic technologies that help prove guilt. Also time-lock safes, anti-shoplifting tags, cash register tapes, hard-to-forge currency, time cards and time clocks, credit card PIN pads, formal licensing of doctors, and the entire legal profession.

Let's put this all together. Think about an employee traveling for company business on an expense account. He can either live frugally, or enjoy the most expensive hotels, restaurants, and so on. It's a societal dilemma:

Here are some more societal dilemmas, and corresponding security systems that act as societal pressures.

- *Gridlock.* Security measures include traffic cops to keep cars moving, specially striped intersections to demarcate off-limits areas, and cameras to assist enforcement at gridlock-prone intersections.

- *Vaccines.* There is ongoing research on how to rebuild public confidence in vaccines and reduce defection. Tactics could include ad campaigns and other types of marketing. Also, inhalable vaccines make it easier to cooperate.

- *Cheating at games.* It's more fun for the group if everyone plays fairly, but it's sometimes more fun for the individual to cheat and win. To help combat cheating, the new version of Monopoly comes with an electronic gadget that keeps track of everyone's money and makes sure they go to the right square—no cheating.

Societal Dilemma: Corporate expenses.	
Society: The corporation.	
Group interest: Minimize corporate expenses.	Competing interest: More enjoyable corporate travel.
Group norm: Spend the corporation's money frugally.	Corresponding defection: Spend a lot on hotel, meals, and so on.

To encourage people to act in the group interest, the society implements a variety of trust mechanisms.

Moral: A company-wide belief that frivolous expenses are tantamount to stealing.

Reputational: Praising people who save the company money. Publicly chastising people who spend lavishly.

Institutional: Corporate travel policies, including per diem systems and daily spending limits.

Security: E-mail reminders that people should be parsimonious with the company's money (enhances moral pressure).

Requiring employees to submit for approval estimates of how much they'll spend beforehand, and making it difficult to get additional expenses reimbursed (enhances both moral and reputational pressure).

Putting everyone's travel expenses on a website that everyone in the company can see (enhances reputational pressure).

Requiring booking of airfare and hotels through a dedicated travel agent, who enforces the corporate policies (enhances institutional pressure).

Auditing of travel expenses, with overspenders being forced to reimburse the company (enhances institutional pressure).

A lot of those might not feel like security systems, but they are. The breadth of security systems is vast. This chart—from criminal justice professor Ronald V. Clarke—illustrates just how diverse security can be.

Crime Prevention Techniques

Increase the Effort	**1. Target harden** • Steering column locks and ignition immobilizers • Anti-robbery screens • Tamper-proof packaging	**2. Control access to facilities** • Entry phones • Electronic card access • Baggage screening	**3. Screen exits** • Ticket needed for exit • Export documents • Electronic merchandise tags	**4. Deflect offenders** • Street closures • Separate bathrooms for women • Disperse pubs	**5. Control tools/weapons** • "Smart" guns • Restrict spray paint sales to juveniles • Toughened beer glasses
Increase the Risks	**6. Extend guardianship** • Go out in a group at night • Leave signs of occupancy • Carry cell phone	**7. Assist natural surveillance** • Improved street lighting • Defensible space design • Support whistle-blowers	**8. Reduce anonymity** • Taxi driver IDs • "How's my driving?" decals • School uniforms	**9. Use place managers** • CCTV for double-deck buses • Two clerks for convenience stores • Reward vigilance	**10. Strengthen formal surveillance** • Red light cameras • Burglar alarms • Security guards
Reduce the Rewards	**11. Conceal targets** • Off-street parking • Gender-neutral phone directories • Unmarked armored trucks	**12. Remove targets** • Removable car radio • Women's shelters • Pre-paid cards for pay phones	**13. Identify property** • Property marking • Vehicle licensing and parts marking • Cattle branding	**14. Disrupt markets** • Monitor pawn shops • Controls on classified ads • License street vendors	**15. Deny benefits** • Ink merchandise tags • Graffiti cleaning • Disabling stolen cell phones
Reduce Provocations	**16. Reduce frustrations and stress** • Efficient lines • Polite service • Expanded seating • Soothing music/muted lights	**17. Avoid disputes** • Separate seating for rival soccer fans • Reduce crowding in bars • Fixed cab fares	**18. Reduce temptation and arousal** • Controls on violent pornography • Enforce good behavior on soccer field • Prohibit racial slurs	**19. Neutralize peer pressure** • "Idiots drink and drive" • "It's OK to say No" • Disperse trouble makers at school	**20. Discourage imitation** • Rapid repair of vandalism • V-chips in TVs • Censor details of modus operandi
Remove Excuses	**21. Set rules** • Rental agreements • Harassment codes • Hotel registration	**22. Post instructions** • "No Parking" • "Private Property" • "Extinguish camp fires"	**23. Alert conscience** • Roadside speed display boards • Signatures for customs declarations • "Shoplifting is stealing"	**24. Assist compliance** • Easy library checkout • Public lavatories • Litter receptacles	**25. Control drugs and alcohol** • Breathalyzers in bars • Server intervention programs • Alcohol-free events

In fact, one way to look at societal pressures is that *everything* I've written about in these past four chapters is a security system. Morals act as a preemptive intervention system. Reputation is a detection and response system; so are laws and sanctions. Taxes and incentives are interventions. And so on. While that may be true—and as a security guy that's really how I think of it all—it's more useful to think of security as its own thing.

I'm not going to talk more about specific security systems, both because such discussions can quickly get very technical, and because there are shelves full of books already written on the subject.

●   ●   ●

The use of performance-enhancing drugs in professional sports is a societal dilemma, and a good example of how security systems fail as a societal pressure.[2]

Societal Dilemma: Doping in professional sports.	
Society: All the athletes in the sport.	
Group interest: A safe and fair sport. Group norm: Don't take performance-enhancing drugs.	Competing interest: Winning and making a lot of money. Corresponding defection: Take performance-enhancing drugs.

To encourage people to act in the group interest, the society implements a variety of trust mechanisms.
 	
    Moral: Guilt at not winning fair and square. Reminders that athletes are role models, and appeals to "think of the children."
 	
    Reputational: Keep fans and endorsements by maintaining the reputation of a fair player.
 	
    Institutional: Bans on performance-enhancing drugs.
 	
    Security: Drug testing for specific performance-enhancing drugs.	

That's the idea, at least.[3] It turns out that enforcing anti-doping rules is very difficult. The problem is while the intent of the rules is to ban performance-enhancing drugs in general, the temptation to ignore the group interest and take these drugs is enormous. Here's a quote from professional cyclist Alex Zülle:

> I've been in this business for a long time. I know what goes on. And not just me, everyone knows. The riders, the team leaders, the organizers, the

officials, the journalists. As a rider you feel tied into this system. It's like being on the highway. The law says there's a speed limit of 65, but everyone is driving 70 or faster. Why should I be the one who obeys the speed limit? So I had two alternatives: either fit in and go along with the others or go back to being a house painter. And who in my situation would have done that?

Before the sport started paying attention, distance cyclists used stimulants such as caffeine, cocaine, nitroglycerine, amphetamines, and painkillers to improve their endurance. It's a classic arms race—everyone had to partake in order to keep up—and many athletes suffered catastrophic health effects from long-term use. Morals and reputation aren't going to work in situations like this, and the only effective measures are institutional rules enforced by security systems: tests for specific drugs. France passed the first anti-doping laws in 1965; testers found that almost a third of the participants in the Tour de France the next year tested positive for amphetamines. Over the decades, each new potentially performance-enhancing substance was countered with a ban and then a test.[4] Blacklists now encompass hundreds of substances.

Yet inconsistencies among various regulatory bodies' blacklists have led to the occasional sanction against athletes who never intended to break the rules.[5] At the 2000 Olympics, Romanian gymnast Andreea Răducan was stripped of her gold medal because she tested positive for pseudoephedrine; she had taken two pills of an over-the-counter cold medicine prescribed by her team doctor.

Security systems fail for several broad reasons.

They don't work as well as advertised. Technologies are often developed and sold by companies that tout their value, even if there's no real evidence to support it. So municipalities install security cameras in a mistaken belief that they prevent crime, the TSA buys full-body scanners in a mistaken belief that they prevent terrorism, and the military spends billions on weapons systems like the Sgt. York air defense gun that don't work. In previous centuries, physiognomy (facial features) and phrenology (skull measurements) were both believed to be useful in identifying criminal personalities.

Attackers develop ways around the technologies. Attackers are always trying to figure out ways around security systems, and some of them succeed. Every anti-counterfeiting measure is eventually successfully overcome by counterfeiters.[6] (Not just paper money; improvements in metallurgy result in better slugs.) No matter how many tax loopholes are closed, there is enough complexity in the tax code—and enough legislators willing to slip in provisions to benefit special interests—that unscrupulous companies can always find more. There are many ways to break the security of door locks and safes.

Major technologies change in ways that affect the security technologies. We'll talk about this extensively in Chapter 16. The Internet has given us an endless series of lessons in previously stable systems that failed when they moved online. For example, the security measures against impersonation fraud—identity theft—that worked in the world of face-to-face meetings and telephone conversations failed completely with online commerce. Computers make paper documents easier to forge, and fax machines make forgeries easier still. Electronic voting machines are considerably less secure than their predecessors. Modern electronics in cars bring with them new security risks. Networked medical devices can be hacked. There are hundreds of examples like this.

Sometimes the technological changes have absolutely nothing to do with the societal dilemma being secured. Between the ubiquity of keyboards and the tendency for teachers to focus on standardized tests, cursive is not being taught as much in schools. The result is that signatures are more likely to be either printed text or illegible scrawls, both easier to forge.

Security systems that augment other societal pressures, opening new avenues for attack. An example will illustrate.

In a small town, everyone knows each other, and lenders can make decisions about whom to loan money to, based on reputation (like in the movie *It's a Wonderful Life*). The system isn't perfect; there are ways for defectors to hide their reputations and cheat lenders. The real problem, though, is that the system doesn't scale. In order to enable lending on a larger scale, we enhanced reputation with technological security systems. For instance, credit reports and scores are a security-augmented reputational pressure. This system works well, and lending has exploded in our society in part because of it. But the new reputational pressure system can be attacked technologically. A defector could hack the credit bureau's database and enhance her reputation by boosting her credit score. Or she could steal someone else's reputation. All sorts of attacks that just weren't possible with a wholly personal reputational system become possible against a system that works on reputation plus a security system.

Even worse, many people don't realize that adding technological security to a reputational system makes such a difference, and continue to assume that it's a wholly reputational system. This adds to the risks. Some examples:

- Licensing is an institutional—formalized reputational—pressure system. When it is augmented with physical or electronic credentials, forging them becomes a way to attack it.

- Bank payment systems once had a combination of reputational and institutional pressure systems. Today it's primarily technological, and attackable through that technology.
- We traditionally used physical cues to assess the reputation of a business: the cleanliness of a restaurant, the impressiveness of a bank's building, and so on. Today we get a lot of those same cues from websites, where they are much easier to fake.[7] More generally, our learned abilities to read trust signals are continually being overtaken by technology.
- Universal ID systems can make impersonation fraud more profitable, because a single stolen ID can be used in many more places. Sometimes, a harder-to-forge ID is even riskier, because it is that much more profitable to forge.

There's a more general change afoot. We're moving a lot of our interactions with other people from evolved social systems into deliberately created sociotechnical systems. Instead of having a conversation face-to-face or voice-to-voice, we have it via text or e-mail. Instead of showing our friends our vacation pictures over drinks, we publish them on Flickr. Instead of sharing the intimacies of our life in person, we do it on Facebook. Instead of hanging out with our friends in bars or even street corners, we meet in massive multi-player games with a social component like World of Warcraft and Eve Online. This is an important change. In many of these systems, the technology fades to the background—that's the point, after all—and our brains primarily focus on the social aspects. As a result, we focus on the moral and reputational pressures endemic to the human interactions and ignore the technological part. So we forget that text conversations can be stored forever, retrieved later, and shared with other people. We forget there are people reading our Facebook comments who are not generally privy to the intimacies our life. We forget that Eve Online isn't the same as a face-to-face get-together. The technology changes how our social interactions work, but it's easy to forget that.

In this way, our traditional intuition of trust and security fails. There's a fundamental difference between handing a friend your photo album and allowing him to look through it and giving her access to your Flickr account. In the latter case, you're implicitly giving her permission to make copies of your photos that she can keep forever or give to other people.

Our intuitions about trust are contextual. We meet someone, possibly introduced by a mutual friend, and grow to trust her incrementally and over time. This sort of process happens very differently in online communities, and our intuitions aren't necessarily in synch with the new reality. Instead, we are often forced to set explicit rules about trust—whom we allow to see posts, what circles different "friends" are in, whether the whole world can see our photos or only selected people, and so on. Because this is unnatural for people, it's easy to get wrong.

Science is about to give us a completely new way security-augmented reputational pressure can fail. In the next ten years, there's going to be an explosion of results in genetic determinism. We are starting to learn which genes are correlated with which traits, and this will almost certainly be misreported and misunderstood. People may use these genetic markers as a form of reputation. Who knows how this will fall out—whether we'll live in a world like that of the movie *Gattaca*, where a person's genes determine his or her life, or a world where this sort of research is banned, or somewhere in-between. But it's going to be interesting to watch.

I don't mean to imply that it is somehow wrong to use technological security systems to scale societal pressures, or wrong to use security to protect those technological systems. These systems provide us with enormous value, and our society couldn't have grown to its present size or complexity without them. But we have to realize that, like any category of societal pressure, security systems are not perfect, and will allow for some scope of defection. We just need to watch our dependence on the various categories of societal pressure, and ensure that by scaling one particular system and implementing security to protect it, we don't accidentally make the scope of defection worse.

Expenditures on security systems can outweigh the benefits. Security systems can get very expensive, and there's a point of diminishing returns where you spend increasingly more money and effort on security and get less and less additional security in return.[8] Given a choice between a $20 lock and a $50 lock, the more expensive lock will probably be more secure, and in many cases worth the additional cost. A $100 lock will be even more secure, and might be worth it in some situations. But a $500 lock isn't going to be ten times more secure than a $50 lock. There's going to be a point where the more expensive lock will only be slightly more secure, and not worth the additional cost. There'll also be a point where the burglar will ignore the $500 lock and break the $50 window. But even if you increase the security of your windows and everything else in your house, there's a point where you start to get diminishing returns for your security dollar.

The same analysis works more generally. In the ten years since 9/11, the U.S. has spent about $1 trillion fighting terrorism. This doesn't count the wars in Iraq and Afghanistan, which total well over $3 trillion. For all of that money, we have not increased our security from terrorism proportionally. If we double our security budget, we won't reduce our terrorism risk by another 50%. And if we increase the budget by ten times, we won't get anywhere near ten times the security. Similarly, if we halve our counterterrorism budget, we won't double our risk. There's a point—and it'll be different for every one of us—where spending more money isn't worth the risk reduction. A cost-benefit analysis demonstrates that it's smart to allow a limited amount of criminal activity, just as we observed that you can never get to an all-dove population.

There can be too much security. Even if technologies were close to perfect, all they could do would be to raise the cost of defection in general. Note that this cost isn't just money, it's freedom, liberty, individualism, time, convenience, and so on. Too much security system pressure lands you in a police state.

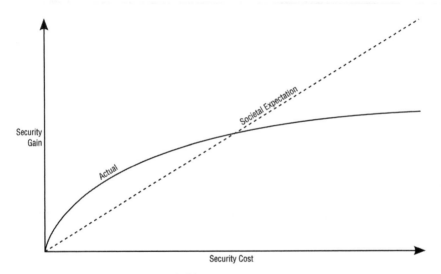

Figure 9: Security's Diminishing Returns

It's impossible to have enough security that every person in every circumstance will cooperate rather than defect. Everybody will make an individual risk trade-off. And since these trade-offs are subjective, and there is so much variation in both individuals and individual situations, the defection rate will never get down to zero. We might possibly, in some science-fiction future, raise the cost of defecting in every particular circumstance to be so high that the benefit of cooperating exceeds that of defecting for any rational actor, but we can never raise it high enough to dissuade all irrational actors. Crimes of passion, for example, are ones where the cost of the crime far outweighs the benefits, so they occur only when passion overrides rationality.

PART III
The Real World

Competing Interests

I n a societal dilemma, an individual makes a risk trade-off between the group interest and some competing interest. Until now, we've ignored those competing interests: it's been mostly selfish interests, with the occasional competing moral interest. It's time to fully explore those competing interests.

In general, there are a variety of competing interests that can cause someone to defect and not act according to the group norm:

- *Selfish self-interest.* This is the person who cheats, defrauds, steals, and otherwise puts his own selfish interest ahead of the group interest. In extreme cases, he might be a sociopath.
- *Self-preservation interest.* Someone who is motivated by self-preservation— fear, for example—is much more likely to behave according to her own interest than to adhere to the group norm. For instance, someone might defect because she's being blackmailed. Or she might have a drug addiction, or heavy debts. Jean Valjean from *Les Miserables*, stealing food to feed himself and his family, is a very sympathetic defector.
- *Ego-preservation interest.* There are a lot of things people do because they want to preserve a vision of who they are as a person. Someone might defect because he believes—rightly or wrongly—that others are already defecting at his expense and he can't stand being seen as a sucker. Broker Rhonda Breard embezzled $11.4 million from her clients, driven both by greed and the need to appear rich.
- *Other psychological motivations.* This is a catch-all category for personal interests that don't fit anywhere else. It includes fears, anxieties, poor impulse control, genuine laziness, and temporary—or permanent—insanity. Envy can motivate deception.[1] So can greed or sloth. People do things out

of anger that they wouldn't otherwise do. Some pretty heinous behavior can result from a chronic deprivation of basic human needs. And there's a lot we're still learning about how people make risk trade-offs, especially in extreme situations.

- *Relational interest.* Remaining true to another person is a powerful motivation. Someone might defect from a group in order to protect a friend, relative, lover, or partner.
- *Group interest of another group.* It's not uncommon for someone to be in two different groups, and for the groups' interests—and norms—to be in conflict. The person has to decide which group to cooperate with and which to defect from. We'll talk about this extensively later in this chapter.
- *Competing moral interest.* A person's individual morals don't always conform to those of the group, and a person might be morally opposed to the group norm; someone might defect because he believes it is the right thing to do. There are two basic categories here: those who consider a particular moral rule valid in general but believe they have some kind of special reason to override it, and those who believe the rule to be invalid per se. Robin Hood is an example of a defector with a competing moral interest. An extreme example of people with a competing moral interest are suicide bombers, who are convinced that their actions are serving some greater good—one paper calls them "lethal altruists."
- *Ignorance.* A person might not even realize he's defecting. He might take something, not knowing it is owned by someone. (This is somewhat of a special case, because the person isn't making a risk trade-off.)

An individual might have several simultaneous competing interests, some of them pressuring him towards the group norm and some away from it. In 1943, Abraham Maslow ordered human needs in a hierarchy, from the most fundamental to least fundamental: physiological needs, safety, love and belonging, self-esteem, self-actualization, and self-transcendence. Some of those needs advocate cooperation, and others advocate defection.

Figuring out whether to cooperate or defect—and then what norm to follow—means taking all of this into account. I'm not trying to say that people use some conscious calculus to decide when to cooperate and when to defect. This sort of idea is the basis for the Rational Choice Theory of economics, which holds that people make trade-offs that are somehow optimal. Their decisions are "rational" not in the sense that they are based solely on reason or profit maximization, but in the much more narrow sense that they minimize costs and maximize benefits, taking risks into account. For example, a burglar would trade off the prospective benefits of robbing a home against the prospective risks and costs of getting caught. A homeowner would likewise trade off the benefits of a burglar alarm system against the costs—both in money and in inconvenience—of installing one.

This mechanistic view of decision making is crumbling in the face of new psychological research into the psychology of decision making. It's being replaced by models of what's called Bounded Rationality, which provide a much more realistic picture of how people make these sorts of decisions. For example, we know that much of the trade-off process happens in the unconscious part of the brain; people decide in their gut and then construct a conscious rationalization for that decision. These gut decisions often have strong biases shaped by evolution, but we know that a lot of assessment goes into that gut decision and that there are all sorts of contextual effects.

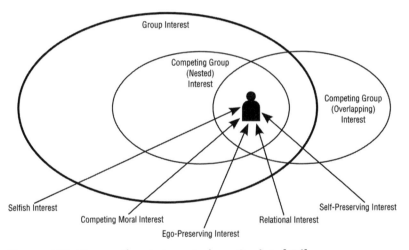

Figure 10: Competing Interests in a Societal Dilemma

This all gets very complicated very quickly. In 1958, psychologist Lawrence Kohlberg outlined six stages of moral development. Depending on which stage a person is reasoning from, he will make a different type of trade-off. The stage of moral reasoning won't determine whether a person will cooperate or defect, but instead will determine what moral arguments he is likely to use to decide.[2]

More generally, there are several counterbalancing pressures on a person as she makes her trade-off. We can organize pressures from the person outwards: self, kith and kin, less intimate friends, various larger and potentially overlapping groups, society as a whole (however we define that), all of humanity (a special case of society as a whole), and some higher moral system (religion, political or life philosophy, or whatever). Sometimes the pressures come entirely from a person's own head, as with the various self-interests. The rest of the time, they come from other people or groups.

Kohlberg's Stages of Morality[3]	
Level 1: Preconventional Morality Right and wrong determined by rewards/punishment.	Stage 1: Punishment-avoidance and obedience Makes moral decisions strictly on the basis of self-interest. Disobeys rules, if possible without getting caught.
	Stage 2: Exchange of favors Recognizes that others have needs, but makes satisfaction of own needs a higher priority.
Level 2: Conventional Morality Other's views matter. Avoidance of blame; seeking of approval.	Stage 3: Good boy/good girl Makes decisions on the basis of what will please others. Concerned about maintaining interpersonal relations.
	Stage 4: Law and order Looks to society as a whole for guidelines about behavior. Thinks of rules as inflexible, unchangeable.
Level 3: Postconventional Morality Abstract notions of justice. Rights of others can override obedience to laws/rules.	Stage 5: Social contract Recognizes that rules are social agreements that can be changed when necessary.
	Stage 6: Universal ethical principles Adheres to a small number of abstract principles that transcend specific, concrete rules. Answers to an inner moral compass.

This is important, because the stronger the competing pressure is, the easier it becomes to defect from the group interest. Self-preservation interests can be strong, as can relationship interests. Moral interests can be strong in some people and not in others. Psychological motivations like fears and phobias can be very strong. The group interests of other groups can also be strong, especially if those groups are smaller and more intimate.[4] Scale and emotional distance matter a lot. The diagram gives some feel for this, but—of course—it's very simplistic. Individuals might have different emotional distances to different levels, or a different ordering.

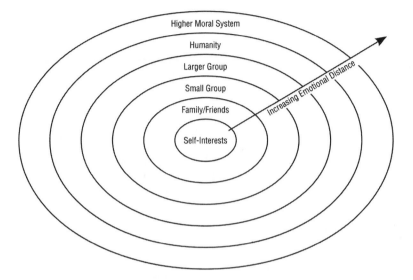

Figure 11: Scale of Competing Interests

Emily Dickinson wrote that people choose their own society, then "shut the door" on everyone else.

Competing interests, and therefore competing pressures, can get stronger once defectors start to organize in their own groups. It's one thing for Alice to refuse to cooperate with the police because she believes they're acting immorally. But it's far easier for her to defect once she joins a group of activists who feel the same way. The group provides her with moral arguments she can use to justify their actions, a smaller group she can personally identify with as fellow defectors, advice on how to properly and most effectively defect, and emotional support once she decides to defect. And scale matters here, too. Social pressures work better in small groups, so it's more likely that the morals of a small group trump those of a larger one than the other way round. In a sense, defectors are organizing in a smaller subgroup where cooperating with them means defecting from the larger group.

Depending on their competing interests, people may be more or less invested in the group norm. The selfish interests tend to come from people who are not invested in the group norm, and competing moral interests can come from people who are strongly invested in the group norm while also strongly invested in other norms. Because of these additional investments, they have to explicitly wrestle with the corresponding competing interests, and the trade-offs can become very complicated.

Someone with criminal tendencies might have a simple risk trade-off to make: should I steal or not? But someone who is both moral and invested in the group norm—Jean Valjean or Robin Hood—has a much harder choice. He has to weigh his self-preservation needs, the morality of his actions, the needs of others he's helping, the morality of those he's stealing from, and so on. Of course, there's a lot of individual variation. Some people consider their morality to be central to their self-identity, while others consider it to be more peripheral. René Girard uses the term "spiritual geniuses" to describe the most moral of people. We also describe many of them as martyrs; being differently moral can be dangerous.[5] Society, of course, wants the group interest to prevail.

Ralph Waldo Emerson wrote:

> Society is a joint-stock company, in which the members agree, for the better securing of his bread to each shareholder, to surrender the liberty and culture of the eater. The virtue in most request is conformity. Self-reliance is its aversion. It loves not realities and creators, but names and customs.

Henry David Thoreau talks about how he went along with the group norm, despite what his morals told him:

> The greater part of what my neighbors call good I believe in my soul to be bad, and if I repent of anything, it is very likely to be my good behavior. What demon possessed me that I behaved so well?

When historian Laurel Thatcher Ulrich wrote "Well-behaved women seldom make history," she was referring to defecting.

Socrates's morals pointed him in the other direction, choosing to cooperate and drink poison rather than defect and escape, even though he knew his sentence was unjust.

We accept that people absorb and live according to the morals of their culture—even to the point of absolution from culpability for actions we now consider immoral—because we examine culpability in light of the commonly available moral standards within the culture *at that* time.[6]

This all might seem unrelated to this book; however, it's anything but. Misunderstanding the defector is a common way societal pressures fail, something we'll talk about more in Chapter 15. Think of the risk trade-off as a balance. When Alice is deciding whether to cooperate or defect, she's weighing the costs and benefits of each side. Societal pressures are how the group puts its thumb on the scales and tries to make cooperating the more attractive option. If you think Alice is defecting because she's selfish (she's in it for the money) or concerned about her ego (she wants to look cool in front of her friends) when she actually has a competing moral interest, you're going to get societal pressures wrong. The details are different for every dilemma, but they're almost always important.

There's another important reason to understand the competing interests: you might get a different type of defection, depending on the competing interest. To illustrate this, let's use a more subtle societal dilemma: whether Alice should cooperate with the police.[7] This is important, because whether and to what extent members of society report crime and assist the police greatly influences how well laws against those crimes work. In the absence of 100% automated burglar alarms connected to the police station, a monitored security camera in every niche and nook, or police patrols tailing every citizen 24/7, the likelihood that a burglar is going to get caught depends mostly on the willingness of bystanders to take action: either by calling the police, or by tackling the burglar and then calling the police. The more people who report illegal activity—both crimes in progress and crimes after the fact—the better institutional pressure works.

That's the group interest. Competing interests for not reporting include:

- *Selfish self-interest.* Alice might simply not care enough about society to cooperate. She might be too busy with other things in her life, and not have the time to get involved. She might have concluded in a risk–reward calculation that her time and the hassle of reporting a theft outweighs her benefit from reporting it.
- *Self-preservation interest.* Alice might be scared to cooperate with the police for any of several reasons. 1) She might be a criminal herself, and would rather not have anything to do with the police. And even though the police often give protection to lesser criminals who help prosecute their more powerful bosses, that protection is irregularly applied, and there's no guarantee a particular criminal witness will be adequately protected. 2) The police might be a danger to her. It's not universally true that the police are benevolent and helpful. There are people who won't willingly interact with the police out of legitimate fear. 3) She might fear retaliation from the criminals or the criminals' compatriots. Criminal organizations stoke this fear of retribution to allow themselves to commit crimes in a community with relative impunity. There was even a "Stop

Snitching" campaign, including a DVD produced by the Baltimore underworld, designed to intimidate people into not reporting crimes.

- *Ego-preserving interest.* She might be invested in a self-image that emphasizes keeping one's head down and not borrowing trouble. She might, as a victim, be embarrassed and not want to admit it.
- *Other psychological motivation.* She might have an irrational fear of authority figures, severe anxiety, or pathological shyness.
- *Relational interest.* She might know the criminal in question, and would rather protect that person than assist the police.
- *Group interest of another group.* She might be part of, or sympathetic to, the group committing the crime, and decide to cooperate with the group rather than society as a whole.[8] For instance, she might notice her employer committing a crime and decide not to report it. Or she might be a cop watching another cop abusing a prisoner, and she feels loyalty to her fellow officers trumps her moral obligation to report crime.
- *Competing moral interest.* She might not believe in the law. Many people in our society would never even think of calling the police when they see an illegal alien ("that law is immoral"), or discover that someone downloads copyrighted music off the Internet ("that law is ridiculous"). She might think the police behave immorally, or that the victim of the crime deserved it.

Even when someone is the victim of a crime, he might choose not to report it. Examples include crimes like rape (which can be demeaning to the victim to prosecute), some kinds of fraud (which carry a social stigma with them), small-scale crimes where it is unlikely that the police can help, and instances where the victim has reason to fear the police. Would a prostitute call the police after being raped? When my wife's pocket was picked on the Budapest subway a decade ago, we didn't bother reporting it to the police because we didn't think they could do anything. Internet crimes can fall into this category, too. Quite a bit of credit card fraud isn't reported to the police because the amount is too small for the police to worry about. In fact, a fraudster can make a good living stealing small amounts of money from large numbers of people because it's not worth anyone's effort to pursue him.

As a side note, people have lots of reasons for not reporting crime. Sometimes crimes are simply too hard to report. International crimes, made easier by globalization and the Internet, fall into this category. Internet scam victims fleeced by criminals in Nigeria probably have no idea whom to call—and the unfortunate realization that no one can help. Con artists try to ensure that their victims don't call the police, because they thought they themselves did something illegal or because they're too embarrassed at being suckered.

Societal Dilemma: Cooperating with the police.	
Society: Society as a whole.	
Group interest: Effective law enforcement. Group norm: Cooperate with the police.	Competing interest: Laziness. Competing norm: Ignore the police.
	Competing interest: Self-preservation; that is, a legitimate fear of the police or criminals. Competing norm: Avoid the police.
	Competing interest: Ego-preservation as someone who doesn't get involved in others' affairs. Competing norm: Don't get involved.
	Competing interest: Friend or relative of the person the police are investigating. Competing norm: Mislead the police, either actively by lying or passively by remaining silent.
	Competing interest: Member of a group that opposes the police. Competing norm: Several possible, depending on the group norm of the group.
	Competing interest: Believes that the police are not morally justified in their actions. Competing norm: Avoid, obstruct, or mislead the police.

Not being aware of the crime is a problem with a lot of Internet fraud. Fake anti-virus software scams trick users into believing they have a virus, and charge them $25, or $50, or more for software to "remove" it. It's a multi-million-dollar industry, and most of the victims never realize they were scammed. There are Internet money laundering schemes that work the same way.

Competing interests are normal, and our society recognizes that people have them. Sometimes we even have mechanisms for dealing with these conflicts of interest. Judges are supposed to recuse themselves from cases in which they have a potential competing interest. Many governments exempt conscientious objectors from compulsory military service. Newspaper columnists, academic researchers, and others are supposed to declare any competing interests so their readers can understand their biases. Certain laws have religious exemptions.

Mostly, we're all better off because of these mechanisms: recusal makes it less likely that judges will issue decisions that reflect a personal bias; conscientious objector status makes it less likely that soldiers will have to rely on unwilling comrades to defend them in battle. But public health is *not* better off because there are religious exemptions to vaccination laws.

We even recognize the validity of certain competing interests in the law through the doctrine of necessity. Something as straightforward as prohibitions against murder have exceptions for things like self-defense, a self-preservation competing interest. But note that the onus is on the person to demonstrate the validity of that competing interest. If Alice shoots and kills Bob, the presumption—and by this I mean social presumption, not legal presumption—will be that she committed murder, unless she can demonstrate otherwise.

Another point: morals are complicated, and societal dilemmas can disappear because people don't recognize a particular moral claim and corresponding competing interest. Overfishing is not a societal dilemma if you're unconcerned about the long-term sustainability of the seas. You might not even notice as fishers deplete the oceans, because there will probably still be fish in the grocery store as long as you're alive.[9] Slavery isn't a problem if you don't believe the slave class has the same rights as the rest of the community. Even genocide isn't a societal dilemma if you have sufficiently dehumanized those you are slaughtering.

Of course, there's a lot more here that other books cover, and I recommend reading the literature on competing morals for some insights into how people should make trade-offs among a variety of competing interests. For our purposes, it's enough to recognize that people have many competing interests, the details of which affect the efficacy of societal pressures as well as the means of defection. And for societal pressures to work, we need mechanisms that address the motivation for defection as well as the means.

We're all members of many formal and informal groups. These are the societies in our societal dilemmas. For most people, humanity is the largest one.

Society as a whole—whether we define it as our town, our country, or all of humanity—is a group. The company we work for is a group. Our political party is a group. Our city of residence is a group. These groups might have subgroups: the particular department in our company, the particular local political organization of the national party, our neighborhood in our city. Extended families can also be considered groups, and they have lots of different subgroups. Large corporations have many levels of subgroups; so do militaries and some religious groups.

These groups and subgroups often come into conflict with each other. We regularly have to make risk trade-offs in societal dilemmas where the interest of one group is in opposition with the interest of another group, and where cooperating with one group means defecting from the other, and vice versa. The rest of this chapter and the next three chapters discuss group interests and competing group allegiances. This is essential to understand how cooperation and defection work in the real world.

Recall our prisoner, in a societal dilemma with the rest of his criminal organization. That's a fine story, but real life is more complicated.

For the early years of his life, Sean O'Callaghan was a domestic terrorist. He joined the Provisional IRA when he was fifteen, and over the next five years, participated in nearly seventy attacks against the British, including two murders. In 1976, he had a change of heart. For the next ten years, he was a police informant intent on sabotaging the IRA. He thwarted several bombing attempts, including one against the Prince and Princess of Wales, and disrupted the delivery of tons of weapons and explosives. He also publicly confessed to his own crimes, and testified against many other IRA members.

Defecting from the IRA was a very dangerous thing to do. He did so—and risked retribution—because of a competing moral interest, and also because of another group interest: that of his community. "I realised that there was only one way in which I could help damage the ruthless killing capacity of the IRA: by handing myself up to the RUC [Royal Ulster Constabulary] and giving evidence against as many people as possible." He was just as much cooperating with the larger group as he was defecting from the smaller group.

O'Callaghan faced a pair of societal dilemmas, both of which we've gone over in detail: criminals either cooperating with or defecting from their criminal organization and citizens assisting the police. These two societal dilemmas were in conflict. O'Callaghan had to make a choice: cooperate with the IRA and defect from society as a whole, or cooperate with society as a whole and defect from the IRA. The table below just lists the two competing societies and ignores the various other competing interests from previous tables.

Societal Dilemma: Cooperating with the police against the IRA.	
Society: Society as a whole.	Competing society: the IRA.
Group interest: A peaceful divided Ireland. Group norm: Cooperate with the police.	Competing group interest: A free united Ireland, and the well-being of the IRA. Corresponding group norm: Don't cooperate with the police.
To encourage people to act in the group interest, the society implements a variety of societal pressures.	To encourage people to act in the competing group interest, the society implements a variety of societal pressures.
Moral: Society teaches people to value peace over freedom and to help convict IRA terrorists. Reputational: Society praises people who help the police catch criminals. We give them awards, write articles about them, host them on television shows, and so on. Institutional: Laws against deliberately withholding evidence from the police, or actively misleading the police. Security: Hotlines that allow people to report crime anonymously. Witness protection programs.	Moral: IRA teaches people to value freedom over peace and not to let fellow IRA members down. Reputational: Those who testify against their fellow criminals are shunned, or worse. Institutional: The criminal organization punishes police informants. Security: The criminal organization limits the amount of damage a defecting criminal can inflict.

Competing societal dilemmas represent the normal state of affairs. Rarely is the real world so tidy as to isolate a single societal dilemma from everything else. Group interests are often in conflict, and cooperating in one necessitates defecting in another.

Nepotism is a problem in many organizations: companies, governments, and so on.[10] For example, President Ulysses S. Grant found jobs for many of his relatives. He appointed his brother-in-law as minister to Denmark, his cousin as minister to Guatemala. Another brother-in-law was made counsel to Leipzig, and a third became the White House usher.

It's a pair of societal dilemmas. Grant was a citizen of the United States, and bound by its laws and customs. He was also a member of his own family, and endeavored to further its interests.

Societal Dilemma: Nepotism	
Society: The organization.	Competing society: The family. (Other competing interests not listed.)
Group interest: Hiring the best people for the job. Group norm: Not showing any favoritism.	Competing group interest: Making sure your relatives do as well as they can. Corresponding group norm: Showing favoritism towards relatives.

To encourage people to act in the group interest, the society implements a variety of societal pressures.
 	
    Moral: It feels good to put the best interests of the organization ahead of personal interests.
 	
    Reputational: The rest of the organization will react badly to charges of nepotism.
 	
    Institutional: Anti-nepotism laws.
 	
    Security: A free press that exposes nepotism.
	To encourage people to act in the competing group interest, the society implements a variety of societal pressures.
	
	    Moral: It feels good to assist relatives. It's moral to take care of your family.
	
	    Reputational: The rest of the family will react well to showing favoritism and badly to not showing favoritism.
	
	    Institutional: You might be required to support your unemployed relatives.
	
	    Security: None.

Other examples of competing societal dilemmas include:

- A politician who is a member of a political party and also a resident of the district that elected him.
- An employee of a department who is also an employee of the whole corporation.
- A corporate employee who is also a member of a union of workers of that corporation.
- Someone who is an employee of Company A working as a contractor to Company B. Or, similarly, someone who is an employee of Defense Contractor A working for the military of Country B. Think of employees of private security firms working for the U.S. military in Iraq.
- A schoolteacher who is both a member of a teacher's union and a parent who sends her children to the school she teaches at.
- Married lawyers representing opposing parties,[11] or judges related to lawyers appearing before them.

- Legislators who have worked for companies they write laws to regulate, or who expect jobs with those companies after their legislative careers.
- Multiple people serving on the boards of directors of the same corporations, known as an interlocking directorate.

Some of these competing groups are nested, meaning that the members of the smaller group are all also members of the larger group. Others are overlapping, meaning that only some members of each group are also in the other group.

Most instances of competing interests are not societal dilemmas, and many are not relevant to security. That voter who lives in one district and votes in another will have to balance her competing interests when voting, but there are no security implications. That changes when the members of one group are expected to conform to some norm, and the members of the other group are expected to conform to some conflicting norm.

Another way to view moral interests is as a group interest. We are all part of the group of "everybody," whether we define it as society as a whole, the human race, all life on this planet, or whatever. Many people associate morals with the responsibilities arising from that group membership. Relational ethicists do this at all scales, but the moral concepts of "universal justice" and "human rights" are implicitly connected to membership in the human race. People differ on what those terms mean, of course.

When multiple groups have competing interests, it can feel like a battle to see which group has a stronger tie with the individual. Often it's the smaller, more intimate group. This is by no means definite—people don't blindly commit crimes just because their friends are doing so—but it is a tendency. In general, it takes more societal pressure to get someone to defect from a smaller group interest in favor of a larger group interest than it does to get someone to do the reverse.

Think of the societal dilemma that someone who is a member of society as a whole and also a member of a criminal gang might have about cooperating with the police. There are benefits to being a member of society, and there are also benefits to being a member of the criminal gang—especially for people who live in dangerous communities in which the police offer little protection, or even pose an additional threat. Defecting from the broader society is a whole lot easier than defecting from a tight-knit and violent gang. And as long as the criminal gang maintains social ties that are stronger than those of general society, members are more likely to cooperate with the gang than with society in general. This sort of dynamic plays out in organizations as diverse as corporations and terrorist organizations. Such organizations want their members to have a stronger loyalty to them than to society as a whole.

Benefits of group membership are important. In Chapter 12, we'll talk about instances where employees cooperate with their employers in breaking the law—defecting from society as a whole. It can be hard to go against your boss, even when you know that the company's actions are wrong. The benefits of being part of the group—things like the reputational approval of your colleagues and a continued paycheck—are powerful motivators to cooperate with the organization.

Over the millennia, we have developed a variety of measures that enhance group loyalty: initiation rites, rituals, shared markers of group membership, and so on. We talked about these in Chapter 8, as societal pressures to ensure commitment. When there are two groups in opposition, these measures become even more important.

It's not just formal organizations. When Larry Froistad confessed to killing his daughter on an online support group, Lisa DeCarlo alerted the authorities. She was vilified by the other members of the group.

Police solidarity provides another example. Called the "Blue Wall" or the "Blue Code of Silence," it can be very difficult to get police officers to incriminate each other. For example, during the Toronto G20 Summit meeting in 2010, several witnesses reported a policeman beating a protester. The officer was eventually identified. During the investigation, however, a pretty good photograph of the then-anonymous policeman was shown to his fellow officers, and no one admitted being able to identify him, including eight policemen who were in his immediate vicinity during the incident, and one who was his roommate during the summit.

A huge variety of informal groups can have competing interests in societal dilemmas: social groups, ethnic groups, class groups, and racial groups; and there are many societal dilemmas that involve protecting the rights of minorities.

Families are filled with competing interests. Do you save money for your child's college tuition, or do you help your aging parents with their medical expenses? Do you side with your spouse or your parents? After your parents divorce and one of them remarries, who do you spend holidays with? If you are close friends with both members of a couple and you find out one of them is having an affair, do you tell or remain silent? When your father's driving skills begin to deteriorate, do you take away his car keys? Sometimes security is at stake in family situations: if your parents abused you as a child, do you let your children sleep over at their house? In such cases, the societal pressures are primarily informal: morals and reputation. Only for extreme cases of abuse, or very dysfunctional families, is the legal system brought into play.

Since individuals are members of multiple competing groups, there are often redundant or conflicting societal pressures operating simultaneously. The societal pressures for one group don't always transfer to the other, and the pressures invoked at any time depend on the group that is being secured.

For example, the rules about what you can do in your family are different from the rules about what you can do out in the real world. We don't call the police if one of our children steals from the other, just as we don't call a burglar's parents if we catch him breaking into our house. Sometimes incidents of employee misconduct are dealt with by the corporation, but sometimes the police are called in. Groups of nations have their own organizations to call upon to deal with rogue nations. It all depends on scale.

When the scale changes, it can be confusing to know which rules to follow. We see this in schools, where some teachers and principals have begun calling the police for infractions that they previously would have called parents about. The scale has increased; the rules for dealing with these infractions are more often coming from the school district or larger community than from inside the classroom. This means the more informal moral and reputational systems stop working, and teachers feel the need to shift towards an institutional model. In general, as the size of the group grows, more formal societal pressures are required. And switching scales is messy, because the new systems are unfamiliar and often require new ways of thinking, and initially aren't good enough to work well.

●   ●   ●

In the next three chapters, we're going to talk about societal dilemmas surrounding organizations: both dilemmas facing groups and dilemmas within the groups. First, we'll talk about organizations in general, and then about specific types of organizations: corporations and (primarily government) institutions. We're going to see a lot of competing interests and societal dilemmas, and some pretty complicated societal pressures.

Organizations

So far, we've been talking primarily about how societal pressures affect individuals. Organizations—groups as small as several people and as large as hundreds of millions of people—also behave as individual actors. These organizations can be part of larger groups, just as individuals can, and those groups have group interests and corresponding group norms that affect those organizations. And just as Alice has to decide whether or not to steal, break a contract, or cooperate with the police, so do organizations.

It can be hard to think about organizations as a collective object. We often use individual metaphors when we talk about groups, and that results in us trying to use our understanding of individuals when we try to understand groups. We say things like "al Qaeda hates America," "Google is trying to control the Internet," and "China wants a strong dollar" as if those groups could have psychological states. It's metonymy, and while there's value to these generalizations, they also have their hazards. We're going to try to navigate those hazards.

Organizations are of course made up of individuals, who bring with them the sorts of societal dilemmas we've already discussed: both the dilemmas between the organizational interest and the individual's own competing interests, and the societal dilemmas that come from the individual being a member of the organization and a member of society as a whole. But we often treat organizations as if they actually were individuals, assuming that societal pressures work on them in the same way they do on individuals. This doesn't work, and results in some pretty bad trust failures, and high scopes of defection.

Organizations' competing interests include:

- *Selfish interest.* Organizations can have selfish interests, just like individuals. Depending on the organization, it might be profit, power, authority, influence, notoriety, or some combination of those things.
- *Self-preservation interest.* Organizations have strong self-preservation interests. They want to survive, just like individuals.
- *Ego-preserving interest.* Organizations have an analogue of self-image, and do things to preserve that image. For example, some organizations have a mission statement and go to great lengths to make sure their actions are consistent with their words. (Google's "don't be evil" motto is a good example.) Some organizations have particular reputations they want to preserve, for being honorable, ruthless, quick, and so on. Other organizations take pride in their geographic origins or in how long they've been in business. Still others have charitable foundations.
- *Other psychological motivations.* Organizations don't have psychologies, but they do have cultures. Examples are the not-invented-here syndrome, where companies become reluctant to adopt solutions from outside the organization; a "CYA," or "cover your ass" mentality, which predisposes an organization towards some solutions and away from others; dysfunctional communications, which lead to defection at one level that other levels don't know about; a caste system that can breed resentment in one group and lead to sabotaging behavior; or a skunk works dynamic, where a group inside the organization operates autonomously and in secret for a while.

Organizations also have competing group interests with other groups: rival organizations; groups of organizations, such as industry associations or geographical chambers of commerce; or society as a whole. Multinational organizations have potentially competing interests with a variety of countries.

An example of organizational interest is the March of Dimes. It started out as an organization to raise money to fight polio. After the polio vaccine was developed and polio almost eradicated, the March of Dimes didn't have a big party and wind up its accounts. Instead, it reconstituted itself as an organization to prevent birth defects in general, which should keep it going roughly forever.

Even though organizations have interests, the societal pressures we've already talked about work differently on organizations than they do on people.

- *Moral pressure.* Organizations are not people; they don't have brains, and they don't have morals. They can have group interests that are analogous to morals, though. Charities can have lofty mission statements, and a corporate mission statement like "don't be evil" is effectively a moral.

- *Reputational pressure.* For groups, reputation works differently than for individuals. Organizations care about their reputation just as individuals do: possibly more, due to size. They also have more control over it. Organizations can spend money to repair their reputations by undertaking advertising and public relations campaigns, making over their images, and so on—options that are simply unavailable to most individuals. On the other hand, because organizations are larger, their reputations are more valuable, and can be significantly harmed by the actions of a few of its members.

- *Institutional pressure.* Laws can be effective, but organizations cannot have sanctions imposed on them the way people can. They can't be put in jail or executed. In the U.S., there are occasional instances of physical-like punishments to corporations—the breakup of Standard Oil in 1911 comes to mind—and sometimes political parties are outlawed, such as Iraq's Ba'ath party in 2003. In extreme cases, individuals within organizations are jailed in punishment for organizational activity, but those are exceptions. Sometimes organizations are prohibited from certain actions by law as a punishment. For the most part, however, financial penalties are the only sanctions organizations face, which leads to all the issues of financial interests taking precedence over other moral interests we talked about in Chapter 9.

- *Security systems.* Security works differently against organizations than it does against people, primarily because they're *not* people. For the most part, security works against individuals inside the organizations rather than on the organization as a whole.

●   ●   ●

Organizations can be actors in all of the societal dilemmas discussed above. They have to decide whether to cooperate with the police and defraud people they do business with. They are affected by societal pressure. In addition, though, people within organizations have their own societal dilemmas with the organizations.

An example: Carol Braun was described as a "dedicated, dependable, competent and conscientious" 27-year employee of Goodwill Industries of North Central Wisconsin. She must have had some pretty good skills at reputation management, because over seven years, she used her position as comptroller to embezzle more than half a million dollars. Her actions were discovered when auditors found a $77,000 discrepancy and conducted a comprehensive fraud investigation. Braun pleaded no contest to a single charge of embezzlement in 2003, and was sentenced to five years in prison and another five years of extended supervision. Braun's actions resulted not only in significant financial loss to the Wisconsin Goodwill, but also in financial loss to her colleagues, whose pay had to be cut to make up the budget shortfall, and reputational damage to the agency.

That's a particularly egregious example, but organizations teem with societal dilemmas. We often don't notice them because we're intuitively adept at dealing with groups of people. We understand hierarchies and authority, and the difference among superiors, colleagues, and subordinates. We're facile at office politics because we've evolved to deal with social groups. But the societal dilemmas are still there, and sometimes it only takes a little nudge to bring them to the surface.

Every employee of an organization is faced with a societal dilemma: should he do what he wants, or should he do what the organization wants him to do? Stripped of context, it looks like this:

Societal Dilemma: Working within an organization.	
Society: The organization.	
Group interest: Maximize organizational interest.	Competing interest: Maximize personal interest.
Group norm: Do what the organization tells you to.	Corresponding defection: Do what you want.
To encourage people to act in the group interest, the society implements a variety of societal pressures.	
Moral: Work ethic, pride in a job well done, etc.	
Reputational: In some organizations, people who are perceived to work harder are treated better by their peers. In most organizations, they're treated better by their superiors.	
Institutional: Organizations have all sorts of rules about employee behavior. Employees are supervised. Firing, promotions, and raises are all tied to performance—at least in theory.	
Security: Time cards, auditing, employee monitoring, formal performance reviews, and so on.	

In economics, this is known as the *principal–agent problem:* the principal (in this case the organization) hires an agent (the employee) to pursue the principal's interests, but because the competing interests of the principal and the agent are different, it can be difficult to get the agent to cooperate.

Defection isn't all-or-nothing, either. Defections can be as diverse as coming in late, not working very hard, venting, whining, passive-aggressive behavior with coworkers, stealing paper clips from the office supply closet, or large-scale embezzlement. Remember the employee traveling for business from Chapter 10. He can cooperate with the organization and limit his expenses, or he can put his own self-interest first and spend wildly—or anything in-between.

We've all had experience with these sorts of defectors. Whether it's company employees, government employees, or members of any type of organization, there are always people who simply don't do the job they're supposed to.

There's another kind of defecting employee: someone who doesn't think of his employer's best interest while doing his job. Think of the officious employee who cares more about the minutiae of his procedures than the job he's actually supposed to do, or the employee who spends more time on office politics than actually working. The comic strip Dilbert is all about the dynamics of defecting employees and their defecting managers.

The fact that organizations almost never stop functioning because of defecting employees is a testament to how well societal pressures work in these situations. Organizations pay their employees, but there's a lot more than just salary keeping people doing their jobs. People feel good about what they do. They like being part of a team, and work to maintain their good reputation at work. They respond to authority, and generally do what their superiors want them to do. There's also a self-selection process going on; companies tend to hire and retain people who set aside their personal interests in favor of their employer's interests, and individuals tend to apply to work at companies that share their own balance between corporate and personal interests. And if those incentives aren't enough, corporations regularly fire employees who don't do what they're paid to do—or employees quit when they don't like their working conditions. There are also other financial incentives to cooperation in the workplace: commissions, profit sharing, stock options, efficiency wages, and rewards based on performance.

The poorer the job is—the less well-paying, the less personally satisfying, the more unpleasant, etc.—the more restrictive the security measures tend to be. Minimum-wage employees are often subject to rigorous supervision, and punitive penalties if they defect. Higher-level employees are often given more latitude and autonomy to do their job, which comes with a greater ability to defect.

This means that the ability to defect, and the stakes of defection, generally increase the higher up someone is within an organization. The overall trade-off is probably good for the organization, even though the occasional high-ranking defecting employee can do more damage before being discovered and realigned or fired than some misbehaving staff on the bottom rung. A senior executive can modify the organizational interest to be more in line with his own. And since he is in charge of implementing societal pressures to ensure that employees act in the organizational group interest, he can design solutions that make employees more likely to cooperate while still leaving him room to defect. He can build in loopholes. Additionally, because he can implement societal pressures to limit defections among the other employees, he can minimize the Bad Apple Effect that would magnify the adverse effects of his defection to the organization. In extreme cases, a CEO can run the company into bankruptcy for his personal profit, a ploy called "corporate looting" or "control fraud." His power makes it possible for him to impose his personal agenda on top of the organizational agenda, so the organization becomes—at least in part—his personal agent.

This kind of thing doesn't have to be as extreme as fraud. Think of a CEO whose salary depends on the company's stock price on a particular date. That CEO can either cooperate with the group interest by doing what's best for the company, or defect in favor of his self-interest and do whatever is necessary to drive the stock price as high as possible on that date—even if it hurts the company in the long run.[1]

Sambo's restaurants had an odd incentive scheme called "fraction of the action" that let managers buy a 10% interest in individual restaurants: not only the ones they worked at, but others as well. This enabled rapid early expansion for the chain, since it both helped finance new openings and gave managers a huge incentive to make restaurants prosper. But as the chain grew, people all over the hierarchy had individual financial interests that conflicted with their loyalty to the chain as a whole. People responsible for getting food to a whole region were able to favor specific restaurants, for instance.

On the other hand, executives have a lot of societal pressures focused on them that's supposed to limit this sort of behavior. In the U.S., Sarbanes-Oxley was passed precisely for this purpose. And the inherent restraints of their roles prevent most of them from being brazen about it. But there are exceptions, and some of those are what we read about in the newspapers.

We've mentioned organizations as individual actors in societal dilemmas, and we've talked about individuals in societal dilemmas inside organizations. Now let's put them together.

Think back to the overfishing societal dilemma from Chapter 5, but instead of Fisherman Bob deciding whether to cooperate and limit his catch or defect and overfish, it's the Robert Fish Corporation. Fisherman Bob and the Robert Fish Corporation face the same societal dilemma, but a corporation isn't actually a person; it's an organization of people in a hierarchy. Let's go through it step by step.

The Robert Fish Corporation has to decide whether or not to overfish. The scale is certainly different than the simpler example—the Robert Fish Corporation might have dozens of large fishing boats all over the world—but the idea is the same. The corporation will collect whatever information it needs via its employees, and some person or group within that corporation will decide whether to cooperate or defect. That trade-off will be made based on the corporation's competing interests and whatever societal pressures are in place.

For the moment, let's assume that the corporation decides to defect. For whatever reason, it is official policy of the Robert Fish Corporation to follow its short-term self-interest at the expense of the group interest of society as a whole. In this case, that means catching as much fish as possible, whenever possible, regardless of whether that depletes the stock.

Alice is the Vice President of Operations of the Robert Fish Corporation. Her job is to implement that corporate policy. Alice is in charge of over-fishing. As an employee, Alice has a societal dilemma to address. She can either cooperate and implement corporate policy to overfish, or defect and undermine her employer's goals. But in addition to her role as a Robert Fish Corporation employee, Alice is a member of society as a whole. And as a member of society, she has a second societal dilemma: she can either cooperate and ensure that her company fishes responsibly, or defect and allow it to overfish.

Those two societal dilemmas conflict, just like O'Callaghan's two societal dilemmas. Cooperating in one means defecting in the other. So when Alice decides whether or not her company is going to overfish, she is caught between two societal dilemmas. A whole gamut of corporate rules will pressure her to implement corporate policy, and laws against overfishing will pressure in the opposite direction.

Societal Dilemma: Overfishing	
Society: The Robert Fish Corporation.	Competing society: Society as a whole. (Other competing interests not listed.)
Group interest: Follow the corporate norms.	Competing group interest: Ensure long-term viability of fishing stocks.
Group norm: Overfish.	Corresponding group norm: Don't overfish.
To encourage people to act in the group interest, the society implements a variety of societal pressures.	To encourage people to act in the competing group interest, the society implements a variety of societal pressures.
Moral: It feels good to put the best interests of the organization ahead of personal interests.	Moral: Good stewardship of earth's resources, being a good global citizen are valorized.
Reputational: The rest of the organization will react badly to someone who doesn't act in the organizational interest.	Reputational: Environmental groups report on company behavior and organize letter writing campaigns or boycotts of defectors.
Institutional: Specific corporate overfishing policy regulating behavior. Raises and promotions tied to amount of fish caught.	Institutional: Laws prohibiting overfishing.
Security: Super-efficient fishing technology that is optimized to maximize the catch.	Security: Possibly government monitoring of fishing. Pesky protest boats.

There is also the normal gamut of competing interests that Alice might have. Alice might be morally predisposed to respect the authority of her bosses and go along with her group. She might believe that overfishing is morally wrong. She probably has some specialized knowledge of the life cycle of fish and the effects of overfishing. Concerns about her reputation as a good employee or a team player will make her more likely to cooperate with her employer. Her self-regard and her reputation as a moral individual might make her more likely to cooperate with society. Her self-preservation interest—she might be fired if she disobeys the corporate policy—comes into play as well. And remember that emotional distance is important: if Alice has stronger ties to her employer than to society, she's more likely to cooperate with her employer and defect from society. Organizations try to keep their employees loyal for this reason.[2]

Clearly Alice has a tough choice to make. Here are some examples of how that choice has played out in the real world. There is a lot of research in decision making within groups, especially corporations. We've already seen in Chapter 9 how financial considerations dampen moral considerations. There is considerable evidence, both observational and experimental, that the group dynamics of a hierarchical organizational structure, especially a corporate one, dampen moral considerations as well. There are many reasons for this, and it seems to increase as organizations grow in size.

From 1978 to 1982, the Beech-Nut Corporation sold millions of bottles labeled as apple juice, intended for babies, that contained no actual apple products. If you read the story of how this happened, and how it kept on happening for so long, you can watch as the senior executives wrestled with their two societal dilemmas. They could cooperate with society and not sell phony apple juice, but that would mean defecting from their corporation. Or they could cooperate with their corporation, first by not questioning how this "juice" supplier could be 25% cheaper than anyone else, and then by continuing to sell the product even after they knew it was phony; but that would mean defecting from society. In the end, the economic and social ties they had with their company won out over any ties with greater society, and it wasn't until an independent laboratory discovered their deception that they stopped the practice. In 1987, they were tried in federal court, and eventually agreed to pay a $2 million fine—at the time, the largest ever paid to the U.S. Food and Drug Administration. This is also one of the rare occasions that individuals within a corporation were jailed.

Since the mid-1980s, a growing docket of complaints, criminal prosecutions, and civil suits in the United States, Europe, and elsewhere has revealed that, since at least 1950, Roman Catholic bishops knowingly transferred thousands of priests accused of child molestation into unsuspecting parishes and dioceses, rather than diminish the ranks and reputation of the priesthood and expose the church to scandal. By 2011, allegations had been made against nearly 5,000 U.S. priests, and over 15,000 U.S. residents had testified to being victimized. (Estimates of the actual number of victims range as high as 280,000.) In a 2002 tally, approximately two-thirds of sitting U.S. bishops were alleged to have either retained accused priests in their then-current positions or moved them to new assignments. This was in keeping with the Vatican's exhortations to investigate cases of sexual abuse in secret, so they would remain bound only by canon law.

What happened inside the church can be explained as a pair of societal dilemmas. The larger one was within society as a whole: we are definitely all better off if people don't sexually molest minors, and we have implemented a variety of societal pressures—moral, reputational, and legal—to keep that particular defection down to a minimum. We even have a variety of security mechanisms to detect child porn on the Internet and determine who is taking and trading those pictures.

Meanwhile, a smaller societal dilemma unfolded within the Roman Catholic Church. Of course pedophilia and ephebophilia aren't the societal norm within the church; pedophile priests are just as much defectors from the church as they are from society as whole. But the church hierarchy (the bishops and the Vatican) decided that its ability to function as a trustworthy religious institution depended on reputation. This is known as the "doctrine of scandal," and means that its reputation was more important than justice—or preventing further transgressions. So the church systematically worked to keep secret the problem and the identities of the perpetrators.[3] The church has some pretty strong societal pressures at its disposal—primarily moral and reputational—which is why this scandal took decades to become public. In some cases, it even forced the victims to sign non-disclosure agreements (an institutional pressure).

Societal Dilemma: Protecting Pedophiles	
Society: The Roman Catholic Church.	Competing society: Society as a whole. (Other competing interests not listed.)
Group interest: A scandal-free church. Group norm: Protect pedophile priests from exposure and prosecution.	Competing group interest: Protecting minors. Corresponding group norm: Arrest, convict, and punish pedophiles.
To encourage people to act in the group interest, the society implements a variety of societal pressures.	To encourage people to act in the competing group interest, the society implements a variety of societal pressures.
Moral: Exposing the church is seen as a sin against it. Reputational: Praising people who kept quiet and punishing those who exposed the church. Institutional: Imposing sanctions against those who exposed the church. Non-disclosure agreements.	Moral: Child molestation is bad. Protecting minors, and punishing sex offenders, is paramount in our society. Reputational: People are rewarded, either emotionally or physically, for exposing pedophiles. Pedophiles are ostracized. Institutional: Laws against pedophilia. Rewards for turning in pedophiles.
Security: None.	Security: Chemical castration, actual castration.

In the end, this backfired massively. Unfortunately, cover-ups are not uncommon, as organizations try to protect their own reputation—and their profits from cheaper products. It happens within corporations. It happens within governments. It can happen within any type of organization.

On the other hand, there's a new trend that cuts in the opposite direction. One theory of corporate damage control advocates full disclosure, acknowledgement, and public displays of contrition, in hopes of a quick reputational resurrection. Lots of politicians have been taking this tactic with their tearful public confessions, resignations, treatment center visits, and then quick return to public life, problem supposedly solved.

● ● ●

Whistle-blowers are an extreme example of someone defecting from an organization to cooperate with society as a whole. When WorldCom's Vice President of Internal Audit, Cynthia Cooper, first expressed her concerns about bookkeeping anomalies she had discovered, she was met with hostility from her supervisor and apathy from the company's auditors. Despite this, she unilaterally conducted a full-scale financial audit of the company. What she discovered was that top WorldCom executives had routinely misidentified operating costs as capital expenditures, ultimately preventing $11 billion from being subtracted from the company's bottom line, and thereby misrepresenting the company's value to its board and investors. Cooper's discovery led to an SEC investigation, bankruptcy and reorganization of the company, and criminal convictions of WorldCom's top executives and accountants. It also brought into renewed focus the need for public companies to implement internal societal pressures to protect themselves and the public from defectors in their ranks.

Along similar—but not nearly as extreme—lines as Sean O'Callaghan, Cooper put herself at considerable personal risk by becoming a police informant.

This is a complicated risk trade-off, one that includes both the group interests of WorldCom and society as a whole, as well as Cooper's various self-interests.

Societal Dilemma: Whistle-blowing		
Society: The organization.	Competing society: Society as a whole.	Other competing interests.
Group interest: The best interest of the organization. Group norm: Organizational loyalty; do what the organization expects you to do, regardless of competing interests.	Competing group interest: Lawfulness. Competing group norm: Cooperate with the police and expose organizational wrongdoing.	Competing interest: Keep your job. Competing norm: Do what the organization wants. <hr>Competing interest: Do what's morally right. Competing norm: Expose and help prosecute crime. <hr>Competing interest: Don't get involved. Competing norm: Quit the job and don't say anything.
To encourage people to act in the group interest, the society implements a variety of societal pressures. Moral: Acting in the best interest of the organization is "the right thing to do." Reputational: People who act in the best interest of the organization are seen as good and loyal employees. Institutional: People who act in the best interest of the organization are rewarded, both financially and with advancement. Security: Employee monitoring, indoctrination procedures.	To encourage people to act in the competing group interest, the society implements a variety of societal pressures. Moral: Protecting the greater community is "the right thing to do." Reputational: People who protect the greater community are rewarded with the admiration of the media and the public. Institutional: Laws protecting whistle-blowers from retaliation. Security: Cameras, photocopies, and other recording devices make evidence gathering easier.	

I don't know the exact dimensions of the trade-off—likely the full range of competing interests includes everything related to cooperating with the police— but you get the general idea. And it's not just employees; corporate board members face a similar pair of societal dilemmas. Cooper had a variety of competing interests, and the full force of WorldCom's societal pressures fighting her.

Organizations can muster considerable societal pressures to prevent and punish whistle-blowing defections. Some extreme examples:

- National Security Agency analyst Thomas Drake, alarmed by the agency's initiation of warrantless domestic electronic surveillance after the September 11 attacks, first expressed his concerns to his superiors, then supplied classified information on the program to the House Permanent Select Committee on Intelligence and oversight committees investigating 9/11-related intelligence failures, and finally shared what he believed was unclassified information about the NSA with a reporter. A year and a half later, federal agents raided Drake's home, confiscated his computers, books, and papers, and accused him of participating in a conspiracy to violate the Espionage Act—a law originally aimed at those who aid the enemy and harm national security, rather than those whose disclosures serve the public interest.[4]
- The 1962 Vatican Instruction *"Crimen Sollicitationis"* prescribed excommunication of those who violated the oath of secrecy imposed on parties to investigations of sexual misconduct by priests, including pedophilia investigations.
- As a research physician, Nancy Fern Olivieri was part of a group conducting a clinical trial of a drug for the pharmaceutical company Apotex. When she came to believe that the drug was ineffective and possibly toxic, Apotex threatened all sorts of legal action against her if she took her concerns public.
- Detective Jeff Baird exposed misconduct in the New York City Police Department's Internal Affairs division. As a result, he was shunned and harassed by his fellow officers, gratuitously transferred to different units, and received anonymous death threats.

It's no wonder so few people become whistle-blowers, the consequences can be so devastating. Imagine you're in the middle of a Madoff-like pyramid scheme. Do you expose the scheme and risk prosecution or retaliation, feign naïveté and try to get out, or actively participate for greater rewards and greater risk?

An even more extreme example is military desertion in wartime. Militaries need strict hierarchies to function effectively. It's important that soldiers obey the orders of their superiors, and be able to give orders to their subordinates. But since these orders might be otherwise pretty abhorrent to individuals, the military implements a lot of societal pressure to make it all work. This is why military training uses substantial social pressures around strict obedience and group cohesion. In addition, militaries have strict rules about obeying orders, with serious sanctions for breaching them. Throughout much of history, desertion was punishable by death with less than due process, because it was just too important to the group preservation interest to allow for individual self-preservation.

This can change when the military is ordered to take action against the very people it believes it is protecting. In 2011, two high-ranking Libyan military pilots defected rather than carry out orders to bomb protesters in the Libyan city of Benghazi. The pilots realized that they were in a pair of societal dilemmas, and chose to cooperate with their fellow countrymen against the government rather than cooperate with their fellow soldiers against the protesters.

Societal Dilemma: Military Desertion		
Society: The military.	Competing society: Society as a whole.	Other competing interests.
Group interest: The best interest of the military. Group norm: Do whatever your superiors tell you to do.	Competing group interest: The best interest of the people in society. Competing group norm: Don't attack your fellow citizens.	Competing interest: Self-preservation. Competing norm: Don't put yourself in harm's way.
		Competing interest: Ego preservation. Competing norm: Don't let your fellow soldiers down.
		Competing interest: Do what's morally right. Competing norm: Don't kill people.
To encourage people to act in the group interest, the military implements a variety of societal pressures. Moral: Basic training instills a military morality. Reputational: Military units have strong group cohesion. Institutional: Disobeying orders is strictly punished. Security: A variety of security measures constrain soldiers.	To encourage people to act in the competing group interest, society implements a variety of societal pressures. Moral: Moral teaching not to harm others. Reputational: Society ostracizes those who turn against their own people. Institutional: Laws against war crimes. Security: None.	

In 2005, Captain Ian Fishback exposed the U.S.'s use of torture in Iraq because of his religious convictions. Similarly, Bradley Manning had to deal with two competing societal dilemmas in 2010 when he allegedly became a whistle-blower and sent 250,000 secret State Department cables to the anti-secrecy group WikiLeaks, which made them public.[5] Like the Libyan pilots, he chose to defect from the government and cooperate with what he perceived as the country as a whole. His subsequent treatment by the U.S. government—which incarcerated him, stripped him of due process, and tortured him—is in part a societal pressure by the government to prevent copycat defections. In previous eras, the king might have put his head on a pike for all to see.

Such anti-defection measures don't work perfectly, of course. Almost all corporate, government, and other institutional misdeeds become public eventually. All militaries have some level of insubordination and desertion. Historically, desertion was huge, mostly because there was no good way to enforce cooperation most of the time. These days, in most countries, it's generally kept at a low enough level that it doesn't harm the military organization as a whole.

●   ●   ●

It's not always the case that someone who defects from an organization hurts the organization. An individual member of the organization can defect against the desires of the organization but for the benefit of the organization.

This is easiest to explain with an example. Let's return to the Robert Fish Corporation. This time, the corporation decides it will not overfish. Alice, a fisher working for the corporation, has a societal dilemma as an employee: she can cooperate and implement the corporate policy, or she can defect and do what she wants. She also has the same dilemma as a member of society.

Like most employees, Alice generally cooperates and does what the corporation wants. The problem is that the corporation wants a lot of things, but only measures and pays attention to some of them. In our example, Alice's level of cooperation is measured by how much her actions affect the profitability of the corporation. She's rewarded for keeping revenues high and costs low, and penalized for doing the reverse.

Alice might overfish, even though the official corporate policy is not to. She defects in the societal dilemma with society as a whole, and also in the societal dilemma with the Robert Fish Corporation. But unless her management is specifically measuring her on overfishing, they're not going to realize that her increased revenues are coming from something that is against corporate policy.

And unless management penalizes her for doing so, she will be motivated to continue the practice.

This sort of dynamic is not uncommon in a corporate environment.

- In 2010, BP's Deepwater Horizon drilling rig exploded, killing 11 workers and injuring 17 others, then collapsed, and spilled 205 million gallons of oil and 225,000 tons of methane from the Macondo well into the Gulf of Mexico. Reading the reports on the Deepwater Horizon oil spill, it's obvious the company cut all sorts of safety corners and took undue risks. The employees of BP didn't do what was required by law. More importantly, BP's employees didn't do what was required by BP.[6]
- The "Big Dig," the massive highway project in downtown Boston from the 1990s, had a long list of defects resulting from shoddy business practices. Again, cutting costs and time was more important than doing the job right on a project already way over time and budget. And while in many cases the companies who did the substandard work were successfully sued, the individuals inside those companies who made the decisions were largely untouched.
- Before the 2008 financial crisis, there was an expression around Wall Street: "I'll be gone. You'll be gone." It was what self-interested investment bankers would say about worthless mortgage-backed securities, weird derivatives, or anything else that was more smoke and mirrors than real value. Yes, those who sold these financial instruments were going against the long-term interests of their employer by dealing in them. But by the time anyone would find out, they expected to be rich, retired, and beyond any reprisals from their bosses. It's only a small step removed from pump-and-dump stock scams.[7]

This isn't always a defection from the organization. Sometimes it's a defection in detail but not in spirit. Sometimes senior managers make sure they don't know the details of what's happening. Or they're perfectly aware corners are being cut and regulations violated, but make sure the facts never appear in a memo or e-mail. This gives them plausible deniability in the face of prosecution. In extreme cases, companies hire public relations people to lie to the public without realizing that they're lying. Of course, if someone gets caught doing this, the individual will be accused of not following company policy.

On the other hand, sometimes this is innocent and nothing more than the organization's failed societal pressure systems resulting in a too-high scope of defection. In either case, in corporations where this sort of thing is prone to happen, the individuals who do it are the ones who will most likely be rewarded. So if there are five fishers, and one of them breaks the rules and secretly overfishes, she will bring in the most revenue to the company and get promoted to manager. The fishers that cooperated and didn't overfish will be passed over. Investment managers who sold the toxic securities were the ones who got the big bonuses.

Sometimes this is incremental. If your colleagues are all overfishing 2%, then overfishing 3% isn't a big deal. But then it becomes 5%, 7%, 10%, and so on. As long as the incentive structure rewards doing slightly better than your colleagues, the incentive to defect remains. You get what you reward.

●   ●   ●

Larger organizations are naturally nested: departments within corporations, agencies within the government, units within a larger military structure, states within a country, and so on. This nested structure regularly leads to societal dilemmas. They're much like the employee societal dilemmas—should he work hard for the group interest of the company, or slack off for his own self-interest—but a subgroup inside the organization is the actor, rather than an individual. Should an airport screener act in the best interest of the TSA or in the best interest of the federal government? Should an employee act in the best interest of his department, his office, or his company as a whole?

I once worked for a company that had rigid rules about controlling costs. Those rules were implemented by department, not company-wide. The idea, of course, was that cost minimization at the smaller level would translate to cost minimization across the entire company. But sometimes it didn't work that way. I remember several instances where I had a choice between an action that would cost my department more, and an action that would cost my department less but would—because of costs to other departments—cost the company more. For example, I could fly a multi-city itinerary on several more expensive tickets, each allocated to the department that was responsible for that particular city. Or I could fly on a single cheaper ticket. Of course, my boss told me to choose the option that cost our department less, because that's how he was rewarded.

There are other competing interests within organizations: profits, perks (use of the corporate jet, for example), the corporate brand, an alternate idea of what the corporate brand should be, and so on. There are lots of these sorts of conflicts of interest in the investment banking world, such as the conflict between the group that takes companies public and the group that recommends stocks to investors.[8] A full discussion of that would take an entire book.

13   Corporations

Everything we discussed in the previous chapter applies to corporations, and some of the examples we used in the previous chapter were corporations. But because they are actors in so many societal dilemmas—they're legal persons in some countries—they warrant separate discussion. But before examining how societal dilemmas affect corporations, we need first to understand the basic supply-and-demand mechanics of a market economy as a pair of societal dilemmas.

Suppose a local market has a group of sandwich merchants, each of whom needs to set a sale price for its sandwiches. A sandwich costs $4 to make, and the minimum price a merchant can sell them at and stay in business is $5. At a price of $6 per sandwich, consumers will buy 100 of them—sales equally divided amongst the merchants. At a sale price of $5 per sandwich, consumers will buy 150—again, equally divided. If one merchant's prices are lower than the others', the undercutter will get all the business.

The merchants face a societal dilemma, an Arms Race akin to the advertise-or-not example in Chapter 5. It's in their collective group interest for prices to remain high; they collectively make a greater profit if they all charge $6 for a sandwich. But by keeping their prices high, each of them runs the risk of their competitors acting in their self-interest and undercutting them. And since they can't trust the others not to do that, they all preemptively lower their prices and all end up selling sandwiches at $5 each. In economics this is known as the "race to the bottom."

Societal Dilemma: Setting prices.	
Society: All the merchants.	
Group interest: Make the most money as a group. Group norm: Keep prices high.	Competing interest: Make the most money individually, and in the short term. Corresponding defection: Undercut the competition.
To encourage people to act in the group interest, the society implements a variety of societal pressures.	
Moral: The group encourages loyalty. Reputational: The group reacts negatively to those who break the cartel. Institutional: Various price-fixing schemes. Security: Internet price-comparison sites.	

This societal dilemma is in continuous force. Day after day, month after month, the merchants are under constant temptation to defect and lower their prices, not just down to $5, but even lower, if possible. The end result is that all of them end up selling sandwiches as cheaply as they possibly can, to the benefit of all the customers.

It's obvious how to solve this: the merchants need to trust each other. Like the mall stores at the beginning of Chapter 9, they can collectively agree to sell sandwiches at a minimum price of $6 because they know it benefits them as a group. This practice was common throughout history. The medieval guild system was a way for sellers to coerce each other into keeping prices high; it was illegal to engage in trade except through the guild, and the system was enforced by the king. Cartels are a more modern form of this; oligopolies are another. Another way is to convince the government to pass a law outlawing cheaper sandwiches. Whatever name you use, the result is price-fixing.

Merchants like doing this, because keeping prices high is profitable. As Adam Smith said, "People of the same trade seldom meet together, even for merriment and diversion, but the conversation ends in a conspiracy against the public, or in some contrivance to raise prices."

Price-fixing has had varying degrees of success throughout history.[1] Sometimes it lasts for a long time. De Beers has successfully controlled the diamond market and kept prices artificially high since the 1880s. And sometimes it collapses quickly—the global citric acid cartel lasted only four years and the DRAM computer-memory cartel just three. Sometimes buyers, such as Gateway and Dell in the DRAM price-fixing case, have a hand in breaking cartels, but it's usually government. Similarly, it's usually government that helps support them. Smuggling and other commerce often take place outside the cartel, but the cartel still works as long as they're kept to a minimum.

That's not good enough for a modern market economy. It is a basic tenet of capitalism that competition—sellers competing for buyers—rather than cartels are what should set prices. Capitalist society wants universal defection amongst sellers, because we recognize that a constant downward pressure on prices benefits the economy as a whole.

What we realize is that there's another societal dilemma functioning simultaneously and competing with the first.

Societal Dilemma: Setting prices.	
Society: Society as a whole.	
Group interest: Competition.	Competing interest: Make the most money as a group.
Group norm: Do not collude in setting prices.	Competing norm: Keep prices high.
To encourage people to act in the group interest, the society implements a variety of societal pressures.	

> Moral: The belief that price-fixing is wrong and that competition is good.
>
> Reputational: Being known as the merchant with the lowest price gives you an advantage, and being known as a price-fixer makes you look sleazy.
>
> Institutional: Anti-trust laws.
>
> Security: Various price-comparison websites.

Each merchant is in a societal dilemma with all of the other sandwich sellers; they're also in a larger societal dilemma with all the rest of society, including all the other sandwich sellers. Cooperating in one means defecting in the other, and in a modern market economy, the latter dilemma takes precedence.[2]

This works to the buyer's advantage, although more in theory than in practice. The previous societal dilemma pushes prices down only when there are more salable goods than there are buyers, and sellers are competing for buyers.

In some cases, the buyers can get stuck in a societal dilemma as well, pushing prices up. This is the other half of a market economy: buyers competing with each other. Imagine that a sandwich seller has twenty sandwiches left, and there are forty people who want to buy one—including customer Bob. The normal price for the sandwich is $5, but the seller has raised his price to $6.

Here's the new societal dilemma. Bob is actually willing to pay $6 for the sandwich, but he'd rather get it for $5. So would everyone else. If everyone cooperated and refused to pay $6 for a sandwich, the seller would eventually be forced to lower his prices. But there's always the incentive to defect—and be sure of getting a sandwich—rather than cooperate so that everyone who gets a sandwich pays only $5.

Societal Dilemma: Competing on to-buy prices.	
Society: All the customers.	
Group interest: Keep prices low.	Competing interest: Getting the item you want.
Group norm: Don't bid up the price of items.	Corresponding defection: Differing to pay more for an item.
To encourage people to act in the group interest, the society implements a variety of societal pressures.	
Moral: It's unfair to bid up merchandise.	
Reputational: There are negative reputational consequences for bidding up merchandise and for overpaying.	
Institutional: None.	
Security: None.	

Of course, this kind of thing never happens at sandwich shops. But it regularly happens in real estate markets, when buyers bid amounts higher than the asking price in order to out-compete other buyers for properties. It also happens with popular concerts and sporting events, where scalpers create a secondary market with higher prices as more buyers compete for a limited number of seats.

Auctions are fueled by this societal dilemma. As long as there are more bidders who want an item than there are items, they'll compete with each other to push prices as high as possible. And auctions implement societal pressures to prevent buyer collusion. For example, eBay makes it difficult for buyers to contact each other and collude.

A similar mechanism occurs with clothing in department stores. All department stores eventually mark down their seasonal inventory to get rid of it. Selling it cheap, or even at a loss, is better than keeping it on the shelves or in a storeroom somewhere. If Alice finds something she wants to buy early in the season, she is faced with a societal dilemma. If she cooperates with everyone else and refuses to buy the clothing at full price, eventually the entire inventory will be discounted—drastically. But she risks others defecting and buying the garments at full price, and there not being any left of what she wants at the end of the season for the store to discount. Some discount retailers such as Outnet .com explicitly make use of this societal dilemma in their sales techniques. A garment starts out at full price, and is discounted more each week, until it reaches a final—very large—discount. Shoppers are truly faced with a societal dilemma: buy now at the higher price, or wait for a lower price and potentially lose the garment to someone else.[3] Many antique shops and consignment stores use this strategy, too. As long as multiple buyers want the same item, it works.[4]

On the other hand, traditional buying clubs allow buyers to cooperate and push prices down. In addition to minimizing distribution and presentation costs, Costco and Sam's Club negotiate lower prices on behalf of their members.

Both of these pairs of societal dilemmas assume that, within each subgroup, buyers, sellers, and sandwiches are interchangeable. But of course that's not the case. Humans are a species of innovators, and we're always looking for ways to sell more profitable sandwiches and buy cheaper ones. The seller has two basic options:

- Merchant Alice can sell a cheaper sandwich. If Merchant Alice can substitute cheaper ingredients or use a cheaper sandwich-making process, she can either sell her sandwiches more cheaply than the competition or sell them at the same price with a greater profit margin—both options making her more money. It might not work. If the customers notice that Alice's sandwiches are of poorer quality than Bob's, they'll value them less. But if the customers don't notice that the sandwiches are any worse, then Alice deserves the increased business. She's figured out a way to make sandwiches cheaper in a way that makes no difference to the customer.[5]
- Merchant Alice can sell a better sandwich. Maybe she finds more expensive but tastier ingredients, or uses a more complicated sandwich-making process. Or she could make the sandwich-buying experience better by serving it with a smile and remembering her regular customers' names. She can either sell that better sandwich at the same price, bringing her more customers and more profit, or she can sell the better sandwiches at a more expensive price—whatever price the customers think those new sandwiches and the premium experience are worth. Of course, this requires that the customers value this better sandwich more. If they do, then Alice also deserves the increased business.

Both of these things happen all the time. Innovation is one of the important things a market economy fuels. On the buyer's side, the ways for customers to innovate are more limited.

Yes, this is all basic supply-and-demand economics; but it's economics from the perspective of societal pressures. You can look at a market economy as two different pairs of competing societal dilemmas: one preventing sellers from colluding, and the other preventing buyers from colluding. On a local scale, moral and reputational pressure largely enforces all of this. As long as buyers know the prices sellers are selling at and the sellers know what buyers are willing to pay—and this is generally true in local public markets—competition works as a price-setting mechanism. And if there are enough sellers, it's hard for them to collude and fix prices; someone is bound to defect and undercut the group. Sellers can try to differentiate their products from each other—either by selling less-desirable variants at a cheaper price or more-desirable variants at a higher price—and buyers will compete against each other to set new prices. The best way to succeed in this marketplace is to offer the best products at the lowest prices: that is, to have the best reputation for quality and price. There need to be enough buyers and sellers to make the market fluid, and enough transparency that the buyers know what they're buying; but if those things are true, then it all works.

It's only when you scale things up that these systems start failing. Societal pressures don't work the same when the sellers are large corporations as they do when they're sole proprietors in a public market. They don't work the same when the products are complicated—like cell phone plans—as they do when the products are simple. They don't work the same when commerce becomes global. They don't work the same when technology allows those corporations to defect at a scope larger than their own net worth.

●   ●   ●

During the early years of Prohibition, there was an epidemic of paralysis in the American South and Midwest, caused by "Jamaica Ginger," a popular patent medicine. It was mostly alcohol,[6] but about 500,000 bottles were laced with what turned out to be a nerve poison. It's hard to imagine a reputational pressure system being effective enough to prevent this kind of thing from happening. Sure, the company that sold this product was vilified, but not before tens of thousands of people were affected. (The "United Victims of Ginger Paralysis Association" had 35,000 members.) And, in fact, this incident led to the passage of the 1938 Food, Drug, and Cosmetic Act and the establishment of regulations requiring pre-market approval for drugs.

Corporations are organizations. They come in all sizes. The company that made all that Jamaican Ginger consisted of two guys and an office; many corporations employ more than 100,000 people; and Wal-Mart employs over 2,000,000. They have some of the same characteristics as individuals—they try to maximize their trade-offs, they have a self-preservation instinct, etc.—but they are not individuals. In some very important ways, they differ from individuals.

These differences may affect corporations' defection characteristics:

- *They have a single strong self-interest: the profit motive.* The case can be made that it's the only relevant interest a corporation has. A corporation is legally required to follow its charter, which for a for-profit corporation means maximizing shareholder value. Individuals have many more competing motivations.
- *They try to hire people who will maximize their selfish interest.* The people who run corporations, as well as the people promoted within them, tend to be willing to put the corporation's selfish interest (and sometimes their own selfish interest) ahead of any larger group interest. Individuals can't hire arms and feet selected to meet their needs.
- *They can be very large in several dimensions.* They can have a lot of assets, products, sales, stores, and employees. This increases their potential scope of defection: they can defect with greater frequency, and each defection can have greater intensity.
- *They can spread themselves over a large geographical area, so much so that they become unmoored from any physical location.* This reduces the effectiveness of institutional pressure that's tied to physical location: laws. It also reduces moral and reputational pressure against senior executives in those corporations, as they can remain socially isolated from those they harm.
- *They can be complex, especially if they're large.* This creates more internal subgroups at varying scales and intimacies, and the competing interests within them can change what they do. This gives them more options for evading accountability. It can also make it more difficult for people acting locally to determine what the competing interests actually are. Sometimes a single corporation can encompass different business units that compete directly with each other.

- *They can be powerful.* The combination of money and size can make corporations very powerful, both politically and socially. They can influence national and local legislation.[7]
- *Millions of people depend on corporations for their livelihood.* When a major corporation has problems—or even if it makes strategic decisions about automating, outsourcing, shutting down or starting up new product lines, and so on—many people and their families are affected. Whole communities can be affected. This means there are unintended consequences to many societal pressure systems.
- *They can be difficult to punish.* Corporate employees or owners are not the same as the corporation. Also, punishing a corporation can have ripple effects through society, hurting those who were in no way responsible for the corporation's misdoings.
- *They can live forever.* They are not tied to their founders, or to any particular people. They can live far longer than human lifespans.
- *They have more to lose than individuals do.* A damaged reputation can have much larger effects on corporations than on individuals, especially the big ones. This makes them more conservative.

Because of these differences, societal pressures work differently. Moral pressure is dampened in corporations. We've already seen in Chapter 9 that adding financial incentives tends to trump moral considerations. At the extreme, by telescoping the complexities of human morality into a wholly financial risk trade-off, corporations can largely relieve themselves of moral considerations. We also saw in Chapter 12 that morals are dampened in hierarchical group settings. The research is pretty clear on this point.

The upshot, to paint with a broad brush, is that corporations' risk trade-offs are much more focused on making a financial profit than individuals' are.[8] People are emotionally complicated, and will regularly forgo money in exchange for more subjective benefits. Corporations, because of their group nature, are simpler; they are far more likely to choose the more profitable trade-off. To take a familiar example, it's far easier for a chef/owner of a restaurant to forgo some profit to create the sort of restaurant that gives him the most creative satisfaction, while a corporate-owned restaurant chain will be more concerned about consistency and the bottom line.

Another example is a garment or shoe designer buying goods made in overseas sweatshops staffed with child labor. An individual might refuse to do that on moral grounds, recognizing that she is going to have to pay more for those goods made elsewhere and deliberately forgo the extra profits. A corporation is more likely to buy the goods, as long as it's legal to do so. And, as we've seen in Chapter 12, the person who is in charge of making this decision will do better personally if he ignores his own moral considerations and cooperates with his employer. Even worse, if the corporation doesn't maximize profits, it risks a shareholder lawsuit.

Additionally, market competition encourages sellers to ignore moral pressure as much as they can. Imagine if you were in a corporate boardroom, discussing the Double Irish tax loophole and how it could save your company millions. After it has been explained how the maneuver is perfectly legal, and how other companies are doing it, how far do you think a "but it's immoral" argument is going to go? Even if you don't want to do it, if you don't and your competitors do, you'll be uncompetitive in the marketplace—reminiscent of the sports doping example from Chapter 10. Morals have nothing to do with it; this is business. Likewise, on a smaller scale, hospitals tend to replace management teams who don't exploit Medicare billing loopholes, or engage in illegal upcoding, with teams that do.

Even when a corporation engages in seemingly altruistic behavior—investing in the community, engaging in charitable activities, pledging to follow fair labor guidelines, and so on—it is primarily doing so because of the value of increasing its reputation. It's only a bit over the top to call corporations "immortal sociopaths," as attorney and writer Joel Baken did. For corporations, the closest thing they have to morals is law. The analogy is pretty precise. Morals tell people what's right and what's wrong; the law tells corporations what's right and what's wrong. If corporations behave morally, it's generally because they believe it is good for their reputation, and to a lesser extent because it's good for employee morale. This is less likely to be true with smaller corporations run by individuals or small groups of individuals; there, the corporation is more likely an extension of the person.

Or as Baron Thurlow, a Lord Chancellor of England, put it sometime before 1792: "Corporations have neither bodies to be punished, nor souls to be condemned, they therefore do as they like." In more modern language, John Coffee wrote that corporations have "no soul to damn; no body to kick."[9]

Reputational pressure can also fail against corporations. There's a belief that the market's natural regulation systems are sufficient to provide societal pressure, and that institutional pressure—laws and regulations—are both unnecessary and have harmful side effects. From the perspective of this book, this is just another name for reputational pressure.

Let's take an example: toxins in bottled water. Assume there's no institutional pressures, only reputational. Consumers decide for themselves what sort of toxin levels they are willing to tolerate, and then either buy or don't buy the product. (The assumption here is that removing the toxins costs money, and will result in a more expensive bottle.) Companies that sell toxin-free water enjoy a good reputation. Companies that allow too much toxin in their bottled water face a diminished reputation, and as a result, will reduce those toxins in an attempt to repair their reputation. If this works, it effectively "regulates" the bottled water companies.

We already know how reputational pressures fail when arrayed against an individual, and those failures are even more likely in the case of corporate reputation.

- The corporation will try to manage its reputation. Just as a person tries to accentuate his good qualities and minimize his bad ones, corporations do the same. The difference is that corporations will employ people whose entire job is to do this. Corporate reputation management equals public relations, and corporations spend a lot of money on advertising—$130 billion annually in the U.S. alone. The science of advertising has completely changed over the past couple of decades. Today, it's more like psychological manipulation with a healthy dose of neuroscience.[10] As such, there can be a large difference between a corporation's behavior and what the public thinks is the corporation's behavior. It can be hard to remember the relative toxicity levels of different bottled water brands when the corporations are all engaged in advertising designed to make you believe you'll be more successful with the opposite sex if you would only drink their product.

- For reputation to work as a societal pressure system, there needs to be transparency. But consumers might not know enough about the relative toxicity levels to have it affect the reputation of the various companies. (They might not know what chemicals are in the water, they might not know at what concentrations those chemicals are toxic, and they might not know the toxic effects of those chemicals.) Corporations can be very private, especially about things that make them look bad. Sure, testing companies like Consumers Union can give consumers information about the various bottled water companies, but there seems to be very little demand for that sort of thing. Salience matters a lot, here. When you want a bottle of water, you're thinking about your thirst—not about independent third-party evaluations of water quality. To give a real example, corporations have successfully fought the labeling of genetically modified foods, so consumers aren't able to decide for themselves whether to eat them.

- Corporations might co-opt the testing and rating process. Those "independent third-party evaluations" aren't always so independent, and without transparency, consumers won't know.
- The damage resulting from the bad behavior might be so severe that no reputational consequences would be enough. Imagine that the bottled water is toxic enough that people start dying. Sure, the company will be out of business. But that seems like an inadequate penalty for killing people. And while this is an extreme story, there are lots of real-world examples of corporate decisions resulting in long-term disease and even death. In 2007 and 2008, at least ten Chinese companies produced contaminated batches of the blood-thinning drug heparin, substituting a cheap synthetic ingredient for a costlier natural one. At least 150 people died as a direct result of the contaminated drug; we may never know how many secondary deaths or related illnesses there were.
- There can be a long time lag between the bad behavior and the reputational consequences. If the toxin in the bottled water is slow-acting, people might not know about its effects for years or even decades. So a corporation could continue selling toxin-laced water for a long time before it suffered any reputational damage. Remember "I'll be gone, you'll be gone"? That's an economically rational self-interest strategy in that instance.
- Consumers might not be able to penalize the company that's making the bottled water. In an open-air market, customers know who their suppliers are. In the complex world of international outsourcing and subcontracting, it can be much harder. In 2011, Cargill recalled 36 million pounds of ground turkey because of salmonella risk. None of that turkey was sold under the Cargill name, making it difficult for customers to penalize Cargill. In 2005, the data broker ChoicePoint allowed a criminal group to steal the identifying information of 140,000 consumers. If consumers wanted to penalize the company by not doing business with them anymore, they couldn't—consumers aren't ChoicePoint's customers.
- The profit resulting from the bad behavior might be large enough that it'd be worth the reputational loss. If customers have no choice but to buy the bottled water—maybe there's no competition and the groundwater is even more toxic—then the corporation doesn't have to worry about what customers will think. Less-extreme versions of this scenario happen

all the time in the real world; many industries benefit from the difficulty customers have in switching to a competing product.[11]

All this is made worse by the various substitutes people use in place of direct reputation when it comes to brands. There's recognition: people buy what is familiar to them. There's social proof: people buy what others buy. There's even something called attribute substitution: people buy the red bottle because they like the color red and don't have any other way of choosing. These are some of the reasons consumers can be manipulated so easily.

Reputation relies on transparency to work, but for many modern products, the seller knows a lot more than the buyer. There's a general economic theory about this, called a lemons market. Both experiment and observation demonstrate that in a lemons market, bad products drive out good products. That is, if one company is selling cheap toxic water—or cheap unhealthy sandwiches—and the buyer doesn't know the difference between the good products and the cheap ones, he'll buy the cheap ones, and competitors will be pressured to make their products equally cheap and equally bad.

What we know about reputational pressures is that they work best in small groups where there are strong social ties among the individuals. A sandwich seller in a local public market probably doesn't need a whole lot of institutional pressure. He's part of a community, and if his sandwiches start making people sick fast enough that they notice the connection, no one will buy them anymore. But just as this sort of security system doesn't scale for individuals as the community gets larger, social ties weaken, and the value of the items being bought and sold increases, it doesn't scale for corporations, either. Globalization is making the effects of reputational pressure weaker. As a result, the effects of defection are greater. Three examples:

- In 2011, the pharmaceutical giant Glaxo Smith-Kline was fined $750 million for marketing drugs manufactured in a Puerto Rican plant whose managers ignored numerous FDA letters warning that products were likely contaminated.
- Hundreds of people in Haiti, Panama, and Nigeria died of kidney failure in the 1990s and 2000s after consuming medicinal syrups manufactured with toxic diethylene glycol—an industrial chemical used to make plastics. Economically minded manufacturers had secretly substituted the toxic chemical for the more expensive, but nontoxic, glycerin.
- Starting in the mid-1990s, the Ford Motor Company knew that its Explorer model was prone to rollover, but didn't do anything to fix the

problem until 2002. Until they did, there were 185 deaths and 700 injuries resulting from the problem.

Just as moral and reputational pressures can fail against corporations, so can institutional pressures. We've discussed some of the ways they fail against individuals in Chapter 9: interpretation, loopholes, lack of enforcement. These failures can be more severe in corporations, because corporations can afford more and better lawyers to figure out how to evade laws. And law enforcement is much more consumer-friendly when it comes to dealing with individual defectors. If someone steals your wallet, you know how to call the police. If a corporation breaks the law, whom do you call?

Fines can be an effective institutional penalty, but can fail if they're too small. The DeCoster family egg farms, responsible for the huge salmonella outbreak in 2010, had been repeatedly fined for health violations for over ten years. In 2011, the large pharmaceutical company Merck Serono agreed to pay a $44.5 million fine for illegally marketing the drug Rebif. That sounds like a lot, until you realize that the annual sales of the drug were $2.5 billion and the misconduct occurred over an eight-year period. It's no wonder the firm was a repeat offender; the fines were just a cost of doing business. Another example: the penalties for using child labor are so small in some countries—$59 to $147 in Egypt, $470 in India, $70 in Kenya, $47 to $470 in Nicaragua, $25 to $253 in the Philippines—that it makes financial sense for Western companies to defect. In Chapter 11, I mentioned the fake anti-virus industry. One company largely ignored the Federal Trade Commission prosecution because it was making more money than the fine was likely to be.[12]

We discussed other societal pressure failures inside corporations in the previous chapter: employees of a corporation defecting from that corporation, employee loyalty that encourages cooperation with the corporation and defection from society as a whole, and employees defecting from a corporation to benefit that corporation. Additionally, two of the differences between corporations and people listed above—that millions of people depend on them for their livelihood and that punishing them can have ripple effects through society—mean that sometimes it's in society's best interest to not punish defecting corporations: a fact a smart corporation can use to its advantage.

There is one more societal pressure failure that is unique to large and powerful corporations: the co-option of institutional pressure to further their own self-interest.

Imagine a societal dilemma, one that affects a rich and powerful interest: probably a corporation or an industry, but maybe a person or group of people. It could be the oil industry wanting government subsidies (in 2011, the U.S. effectively provided $4.4 billion in tax breaks to this industry alone, not even counting the military costs to protect their supply chains); or the Walt Disney Corporation wanting the government to extend the period of copyright so Mickey Mouse doesn't fall into the public domain. The group interest is to resolve the dilemma fairly. The self-interest for the corporation is to resolve the dilemma in its favor.

Societal Dilemma: Getting public money for projects.	
Society: Society as a whole.	
Group interest: Distribute government money fairly and maintain a level playing field.	Competing interest: Get as much money as you can for your pet projects.
Group norm: Play by the rules.	Corresponding defection: Manipulate the rules.
To encourage people to act in the group interest, the society implements a variety of societal pressures.	

> Moral: It can feel wrong to take too much from the government.
>
> Reputational: It can look bad to take too much from the government.
>
> Institutional: Laws determine what benefits different interests get, and prohibit any one interest from taking too much.
>
> Security: The Congressional Record provides evidence of some of this, assuming anyone actually reads it. There are now websites that try to track political donations.

If a company can convince the government to resolve the dilemma in its favor, then its self-interest becomes the group interest. In this way, companies can defect in spirit by deliberately changing the laws so they are not defecting in practice—thereby circumventing or subverting societal pressures. So, for example, companies that make car seats, airbags, full-body scanners, compact fluorescent bulbs, car insurance, surveillance cameras, vaccines, radon detectors, and Internet filters for schools have had laws passed mandating—or at least encouraging—their use. And the healthcare industry got a law passed limiting its liability for care improperly delayed or denied.

In a sense, what corporations are doing here is reversing the principal–agent relationship. They're deliberately manipulating institutional pressures so they can directly benefit from them. In economics, changing laws to suit your desires without adding any value is known as rent-seeking.

One way to manipulate laws is through licensing requirements. Over the past several years, there have been debates in several states about licensing interior designers. It's either a necessary measure to keep charlatans out of the business, or an onerous, pro-cartel, anti-competitive system. Another way is through public opinion. The political decision not to regulate the derivatives markets is a good example: not only did it involve lobbyists and campaign contributions to get laws changed, but also public relations to convince journalists and the public that keeping the markets unregulated was a good idea.

Here's another example. Hydraulic fracturing, or fracking, is a means of extracting oil and gas from subterranean reservoirs by forcing pressurized fluid into underground rock formations. The process was originally commercialized in 1949 and in its first few decades of use was primarily used to boost production of old wells. Recent advances in horizontal drilling technology, combined with hydraulic fracturing, have enabled the tapping of heretofore inaccessible reserves, and the recent rise in oil prices has made it economically viable. However, the procedure also poses environmental risks, most notably the risk that chemicals used in the process—including methanol, benzene, and diesel fuel—might contaminate ground water, degrade air quality, and migrate to the earth's surface; and that the resultant toxic wastewater might be impossible to decontaminate.[13] This societal dilemma sounds a lot like the monk parakeet example from Chapter 9, and you'd expect society to figure out whether this procedure is worth it. But the companies that use the procedure—Halliburton is a big player here—lobbied successfully for a provision in the 2005 Bush administration energy bill exempting fracking from regulation by the U.S. Environmental Protection Agency under the Safe Drinking Water Act.[14] That's the effect of reversing the principal–agent relationship: the government becomes the agent of the corporation.

One common way to do this is regulatory capture, which we'll talk about in the next chapter. Another way is to simply be unregulatable for political or economic reasons. Homebuilders have been sued repeatedly over the past decade for shoddy building practices, many of them illegal. "Too big to regulate" is how one source put it, making it impossible for homeowners to know they're getting a substandard house until it's too late. The banking industry is similarly trying very hard to be unregulatable, claiming that any regulations would damage the economy more than it would help it.

When it comes to organizations, size is proportional to power. Legislative bodies used to rule fewer people and smaller geographic areas. In the

United States, many laws that were passed by states in the 1800s became federal matters in the 1900s. There's nothing sinister about it; it's just that it now makes more sense to deal with these laws on that scale. Today, international legislative bodies have increasingly more power—simply because more things make sense to deal with on a multinational level.

This is especially true in corporations. Broadly speaking, there's a natural size of an organization based on the technology of its time. The average organization size used to be smaller, became larger, and now is even larger. Historically, there have only been a few very large organizations: the Roman Empire, the Catholic Church, and so on. These worked because they were organizations of organizations. That's how countries work; the U.S. has federal, state, and municipal governments. That's also how feudalism, militaries, franchise stores, and large multinational corporations work.

It still works this way, but we're better at it now. Organizational size is restricted by the limits of moving information around. Different people within, and different parts of, an organization need to communicate with each other; and the larger an organization, the harder that is to do. Most organizations are hierarchical, making communications easier. And militaries have generally been examples of the largest-sized organization a particular technological level can produce. But there's a limit where the costs of communications outweigh the value of being part of one organization. Economist Ronald Coase first pointed this out in 1937. Called "Coase's limit" or "Coase's ceiling," it's the point of diminishing returns for a company: where adding another person to an organization doesn't actually add any value to the organization. You can think of an employee inside of an organization having two parts to his job: coordinating with people inside the organization and doing actual work that makes the company money. Some people are wholly focused inside the organization: the HR department, for example. Others do the actual work, but still have internal coordination roles. There's a point where adding an additional person to the organization increases the internal coordination for everyone else to a point that's greater than the additional actual work he does. So, the company actually loses money overall by hiring him.[15] The ease of collecting, moving, compiling, analyzing, and disseminating information affects Coase's ceiling, and one of the effects of information technology is that it raises Coase's ceiling because the resultant efficiency increases.[16]

Larger size has several effects on societal dilemmas:

- Large corporations can do more damage by defecting. A single company, Enron, did $11 billion worth of financial damage to the U.S. economy.

That much damage might previously have required ten smaller companies to defect. This means that as large corporations grow, fewer defectors can do even more damage. So society needs more security, to further reduce the amount of defection, in order to keep the potential damage constant.

- Individuals within a large corporation can defect from the corporation to a greater degree, for greater personal gain and to the greater detriment of the corporation. Nick Leeson's unauthorized trading while he worked for Barings Bank destroyed the entire company in 1995. Kenneth Lay, Jeffrey Skilling, and other senior Enron executives destroyed that company. Kweku Adoboli lost $2.3 billion for the investment bank UBS in 2011.

- Large corporations have more power to deliberately manipulate societal pressures. This includes getting laws passed specifically to benefit them, and engaging in jurisdictional arbitrage by deliberately moving certain operations to certain countries in order to take advantage of local laws. Different countries have different, often conflicting, laws about price-fixing, and international companies have an easier time forming cartels. This sort of thing can be more local, too. Until recently, Amazon.com used its large national footprint and lack of physical stores to avoid having to charge sales tax in most states.

- Punishing a large corporation might result in so much cost or damage to society that it makes sense to let them get away with their wrongdoing. The ultimate expression of this is when a company is "too big to fail": when the government is so afraid of the secondary effects of a company going under that they will bail the company out in order to prevent it.[17]

- Individuals within large corporations can be emotionally further away from the individuals they're affecting when they make decisions about whether to cooperate or defect. Remember that moral pressure decreases in effectiveness with emotional distance. The larger the corporation, the larger the tendency towards emotional distance.

- Larger corporations have more to lose by defecting. Their reputation is more valuable, and damage to it will have greater effects on the corporation. This serves to restrict what they're willing to do.

Large corporations can also play one societal dilemma off another. Remember our sandwich seller in the market. He's stuck in a societal dilemma with all the other sandwich sellers, and has to set his prices accordingly. In order to prevent the market's sandwich sellers from cooperating, society as a whole—as part of a larger societal dilemma—passes laws to prevent collusion and price-fixing. But a larger sandwich seller has more options. He can expand his product offering across several dimensions:

- *Economies of scale.* He can buy his ingredients in bulk and streamline his production processes.
- *Depth.* More sandwich options.
- *Size.* Larger or smaller sandwiches.
- *Time.* Breakfast sandwiches or sandwiches for midnight snacks.
- *Scope.* Sandwich-like things, such as hot dogs, bagels, wraps, and muffins.
- *Accessories.* Chips and sodas, groceries.
- *Service.* Sandwich subscriptions, delivery, free wi-fi to go along with the sandwiches.

All this makes it much more difficult to enforce the basic societal dilemmas of a market economy. On the face of it, as a seller diversifies, he is now stuck in multiple different societal dilemmas: one with the other sandwich sellers in the market, and another with—for example—chip sellers. But by tying the two products together, perhaps selling a sandwich and chips together, or offering a once-a-week chip subscription with the purchase of a sandwich subscription, he is able to play the two societal dilemmas off each other, taking advantage of both.

We see this with various product schemes. Whether it's Citibank selling credit cards and consumer loans and anti-theft protection plans to go with those credit cards; or Apple selling computer hardware and software; or Verizon bundling telephone, cable, and Internet; product bundles and subscription services hide prices and make it harder for customers to make buying decisions. There's also a moral hazard here. The less Citibank spends on antifraud measures, the more protection plans it can sell; the higher its credit card interest rates, the more attractive its consumer loans are.

Large corporations can also use one revenue stream to subsidize another. So a big-box retail store can temporarily lower its prices so far that it's losing money, in order to drive out competition. Or an airline can do the same with airfares in certain markets to kill an upstart competitor.

Things get even more complicated when sellers have multiple revenue streams from different sources. Apple sells iPhones and iPads to customers, sells the ability to sell customer apps to app vendors, and sells the right to sell phone contracts to phone companies. Magazines sell both subscriptions and their subscription lists. This sort of thing is taken to the extreme by companies like Facebook, which don't even charge their users for their apps at all, and make all their money selling information about those users to third parties.[18] It turns out that offering a product or service for free is very different than offering it cheaply, and that "free" perturbs markets in ways no one fully understands. The optimal way to do business in an open-air market—offer the best products at the lowest prices—fails when there are other revenue streams available.

An additional complication arises with products and services that have high barriers to entry; it's hard for competitors to emerge. In an open-air market, if the sandwich vendors all sell their sandwiches at too-high prices, someone else can always come in and start selling cheaper sandwiches. This is much harder to do with cell phone networks, or computer operating systems, or airline tickets, because of the huge upfront costs. And industries can play the meta-game to prevent competition, as when the automobile industry bought and then dismantled cities' trolley networks, big agriculture lobbied government to impose draconian regulations on small farms, and so on.

There's one more problem with the technological corporations that doesn't really exist on the small scale of an open-air market: the risks of defection can be greater than the total value of the corporations themselves. An example will serve to explain.

Chemical plants are a terrorism risk. Toxins such as phosgene, chlorine, and ammonia could be dispersed in a terrorist attack against a chemical plant. And depending on whose numbers you believe, hundreds of plants threaten hundreds of thousands of people and some threaten millions. This isn't meant to scare you; there's a lot of debate on how realistic this sort of terrorist attack is right now.

In any case, the question remains of how best to secure chemical plants against this threat. Normally, we leave the security of something up to its owner. The basic idea is that the owner of each chemical plant best understands the risks, and is the one who loses out if security fails. Any outsider—in this case, a regulatory agency—is just going to get it wrong.

And chemical plants do have security. They have fences and guards. They have computer and network security. They have fail-safe mechanisms built into their operations.[19] There are regulations they have to follow. The problem is that might not be enough. Any rational chemical-plant owner will only secure the plant up to its value to him. That is, if the plant is worth $100 million, it makes no sense to spend $200 million on securing it. If the odds of it being attacked are less than 1%, it doesn't even make sense to spend $1 million on securing it. The math is more complicated than this, because you have to factor in such things as the reputational cost of having your name splashed all over the media after an incident, but that's the basic idea.

But to society, the cost of an actual attack could be much, much greater. If a terrorist blows up a particularly toxic plant in the middle of a densely populated area, deaths could be in the tens of thousands and damage could be in the hundreds of millions. Indirect economic damage could be in the billions. The owner of the chlorine plant would pay none of these costs; to him, they are externalities borne by society as a whole.

Sure, the owner could be sued. But he's not at risk for more than the value of his company, and the outcome of a lawsuit is by no means preordained. Expensive lawyers can work wonders, courts can be fickle, and the government could step in and bail him out (as it did with airlines after 9/11). And a smart company can often protect itself by spinning off the risky asset in a subsidiary company, or selling it off completely. Mining companies do this all the time.

The result of all this is that, by leaving the security to the owner, we don't get enough of it.

In general, the person responsible for a risk trade-off will make the trade-off that is most beneficial to *him*. So when society designates an agent to make a risk trade-off on its behest, society has to solve the principal–agent problem and ensure that the agent makes the same trade-off that society would. We'll see how this can fail with government institutions in the next chapter; in this case, it's failing with corporations.

Think back to the sandwich sellers in the local market. Merchant Alice is one of those sandwich sellers, and a dishonest, unscrupulous one at that. She has no moral—or reputational—issues with potentially poisoning her buyers. In fact, the only thing that's standing in the way of her doing so is the law. And she's going to do the math.

She has the opportunity of making her sandwiches using some substandard but cheaper process. Maybe she's buying ingredients that aren't as clean. Whatever she's doing, it's something that saves her money but is undetectable by her customers.

If her increased profit for selling potentially poisonous sandwiches is $10,000, and the chance of her getting caught and fined is 10%, then any fine over $100,000 will keep her cooperating (assuming she's rational and that losing $100,000 matters to her).

Now consider a large sandwich corporation, ALICE Foods. Because ALICE Foods sells so many more sandwiches, its increased profit from defecting is $1,000,000. With the same 10% probability of penalty, the fine has to be over $10,000,000 to keep it from defecting. But there's another issue. ALICE Foods only has $5,000,000 in assets. For it, the maximum possible fine is everything the corporation has. Any penalty greater than $5,000,000 can be treated as $5,000,000. So ALICE Foods will rationally defect for any increased profit greater than $500,000, regardless of what the fine is set at (again, assuming the same 10% chance of being fined and no semblance of conscience).

Think of it this way. Suppose ALICE Foods makes $10,000,000 a year, but has a 5% chance of killing lots of people (or of encountering some other event that would bankrupt the company). Over the long run, this is a guaranteed loss-making business. But in the short term, management can expect ten years of profit. There is considerable incentive for the CEO to take the risk.

Of course, that incentive is counteracted by any laws that ascribe personal liability for those decisions. And the difficulty of doing the math means that many companies won't make these sorts of conscious decisions. But there always will be some defectors that will.

This problem occurs more frequently as the value of defecting increases with respect to the total value to the company. It's much easier for a large corporation to make many millions of dollars through breaking the law. But as long as the maximum possible penalty to the corporation is bankruptcy, there will be illegal activities that are perfectly rational to undertake as long as the probability of penalty is small enough.[20]

Any company that is too big to fail—that the government will bail out rather than let fail—is the beneficiary of a free insurance policy underwritten by taxpayers. So while a normal-sized company would evaluate both the costs and benefits of defecting, a too-big-to-fail company knows that someone else will pick up the costs. This is a moral hazard that radically changes the risk trade-off, and limits the effectiveness of institutional pressure.

Of course, I'm not saying that all corporations will make these calculations and do whatever illegal activity is under consideration. There are still both moral and reputational pressures in place that keep both individuals and corporations from defecting. But the increasing power and scale of corporations is making this kind of failure more likely. If you assume that penalties are reasonably correlated with damages—and that a company can't buy insurance against this sort of malfeasance—then as companies can do more damaging things, the penalties against doing them become less effective as security measures. If a company can adversely affect the health of tens of millions of people, or cause large-scale environmental damage, the harm can easily dwarf the total value of the company. In a nutshell, the bigger the corporation, the greater the likelihood it could unleash a massive catastrophe on society.

Institutions

I n talking about group interests and group norms, I've mostly ignored the question of who determines the interests, sets the norms, and decides what scope of defection is acceptable and how much societal pressure is sufficient. It's easy to say "society decides," and from a broad enough viewpoint, it does. Society decides on its pair-bonding norms, and what sorts of societal requirements it needs to enforce them. Society decides how property works, and what sorts of societal pressures are required to enforce property rights. Society decides what "fair" means, and what the social norms are regarding taking more or doing less than your fair share. These aren't deliberate decisions; they're evolved social decisions. So just as our immune system "decides" which pathogens to defend the body against, societies decide what the group norms are and what constitutes defecting behavior. And just as our immune system implements defenses against those pathogens, society implements societal pressures against what it deems to be defection.

But many societal pressures are prescribed by those in power,[1] and while the informal group-consensus process I just described might explain most moral and reputational pressure, it certainly doesn't explain institutional pressure. Throughout most of our history, we have been ruled by autocrats—leaders of family groups, of tribes, or of people living in geographical boundaries ranging in size from very small to the Mongol Empire. These individuals had a lot of power—often absolute power—to decide what the group did. They might not have been able to dictate social norms, but they could make and enforce laws. And very often, those laws were immoral, unfair, and harmful to some, or even most, people in the group.

Throughout most of our history, people had no say in the laws that ruled them. Those who ruled did so by force, and imposed laws by force. If the monarch in power decided that the country went to war, that's what the people did. The group interest was defined by what the king wanted, and those who ignored it and followed some competing interest were punished. It didn't matter if the majority agreed with the king; his word defined the group norm. *"L'État, c'est moi"* and all.[2]

I'm eliding a lot of nuance here. Few rulers, from tribal leaders to emperors, had—or have—absolute power. They had councils of elders, powerful nobles, military generals, or other interests they had to appease in order to stay in power. They were limited by their roles and constrained by the societies they lived in. Sometimes a charismatic and powerful ruler could radically change society, but more often he was ruled by society just as much as he ruled it. Sometimes group norms are decided by privileged classes in society, or famous and influential people, or subgroups that happen to be in the right place at the right time.

In parts of our history, laws and policy were decided not by one person but by a cohort: the ancient Roman Senate, the *Maggior Consiglio* in medieval Venice, the British Parliament since the Magna Carta. Modern constitutional democracies take this even further, giving everybody—more or less—the right to decide who rules them, and under what rules those rulers rule.

This dynamic isn't limited to government; it also plays out in other groups. Someone in charge decides what the group's norms are, constrained by the "rules" of his office. A CEO can be removed from office by the board of directors. A Mafia head can be deposed by a rival; criminal gangs and terrorist groups have their own organizational structures.

The deciders generally don't decide the details of the norms and societal pressures. For example, while the king might decide that the country will go to war and all able-bodied men are to be drafted into the army, he won't decide what sorts of security measures will be put in place to limit defectors. Society delegates the implementation of societal pressures to some subgroup of society. Generally these are institutions, which I'll broadly define as an organization delegated with implementing societal pressure. We've already discussed delegation and the principal–agent problem. We're now going to look at how that plays out with institutions.

●   ●   ●

In 2010, full-body scanners were rushed into airports following the underwear bomber's failed attempt to blow himself up along with an airplane. There are a lot of reasons why the devices shouldn't be used, most notably because they can't directly detect the particular explosive the underwear bomber used, and probably wouldn't have detected his underwear bomb. There have been several court cases brought by people objecting to their use. One of them, filed by the Electronic Privacy Information Center, alleged the TSA didn't even follow its own rules when it fielded the devices. (Full disclosure: I was a plaintiff in that case.) I want to highlight an argument a Department of Homeland Security lawyer made in federal court. He contended that the agency has the legal authority to strip-search every air traveler, and that a mandatory strip-search rule could be instituted without any public comment or rulemaking. That is, he claimed that DHS was in charge of airline security in the U.S., and it could do anything—*anything*—it wanted to in that name.

After the September 11 attacks, people became much more scared of airplane terrorism. The data didn't back up their increased fears—airplane terrorism was actually a much larger risk in the 1980s—but 9/11 was a huge emotional event and it really knocked people's feeling of security out of whack. So society, in the form of the government, tried to improve airport security. George W. Bush signed the Aviation and Transportation Security Act on November 19, 2001, creating the Transportation Security Administration.

Societal Dilemma: Airplane terrorism.	
Society: Society as a whole.	
Group interest: Safe air travel.	Competing interest: Blowing up airplanes is believed to be an effective way to make a political point or advance a political agenda.[3]
Group norm: Not to blow up airplanes.	Corresponding defection: Blow up airplanes.

To encourage people to act in the group interest, society implements these societal pressures:

Moral: Our moral systems hold that murdering people and destroying property is wrong.

Reputational: Society punishes people who kill innocents, and even people who espouse doing that. In some cases, people are publicly vilified not because they themselves advocate violence, but because they aren't sufficiently critical of those who do.

Institutional: Nation states implement laws to fight airplane terrorism, including invasive passenger screening. We have severe punitive measures to deter terrorists, at least the non-suicide kind.

Security: Magnetometers, x-ray machines, swabs fed into machines that detect potential explosives, full-body scanners, shoe scanners, no-fly lists, behavioral profiling, and on and on.

The societal dilemma of airplane terrorism is a particularly dangerous one, because even a small number of defectors can cause thousands of deaths and billions of dollars in economic damage. People are legitimately concerned about this, and want strong societal pressures.[4] Moral and reputational pressures aren't nearly enough, both because the scale is too large and the competing group interest is so strong. Institutional pressure is required, and the institution in the U.S. that has been delegated with this responsibility is the Transportation Security Administration.

There are actually several levels of delegation going on. The people delegate security to their leaders—Congress and the president—who delegate to the Department of Homeland Security, which delegates to the TSA, which delegates to individual TSA agents staffing security checkpoints.

Figure 12 illustrates how institutional pressure is delegated. Ultimately, institutions are put in charge of enforcement. These aren't always governments; they can be any subgroup of society given the power to enforce institutional pressure at any level, such as:

- The police, who implement societal pressures against a broad array of competing norms. (Okay, I admit it. That's an odd way to describe arresting people who commit crimes against people and property.)
- The judicial system, which 1) punishes criminals and provides deterrence against future defections, and 2) adjudicates civil disputes, providing societal pressures based on both formal and informal societal norms.
- Government regulatory agencies, such as the U.S.'s TSA, the Occupational Safety and Health Administration, the Federal Communications Commission, and the Food and Drug Administration.
- Industry organizations, which implement industry self-regulation. (This is often agreed to in order to forestall government regulation.)
- Corporate security offices, which implement the physical and data-security policies of a corporation.
- Corporate auditors, who 1) verify the same, and 2) verify the corporation's books, providing societal pressures against corporate financial malfeasance.
- An independent security company, hired by an organization to guard its buildings.

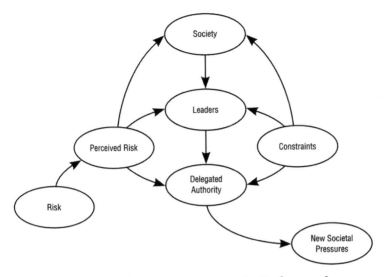

Figure 12: How Societal Pressures Are Delegated

The goal of delegation is for the institution to act as the group's agent. That is, to implement societal pressures on behalf of, and in the name of, the group. But because of the principal–agent problem, that institution doesn't have the same competing interests as the group as a whole—or even as any institution or subgroup above them. As a result, it won't necessarily implement societal pressures to the same degree or in the same way as the group would like. And that's an endless source of problems.

When it comes to terrorism and airplane security, those problems are legion. The TSA is a government institution with a mandate and funding from the U.S. government. It answers to the government. And the government has a mandate from, is funded by, and answers to, the people. Given all of that, you'd expect the people to have a lot of input into what the TSA does. Which is why it can seem so weird when it does things with absolutely no input from anyone. But it's a natural effect of the principal–agent problem.

The TSA's interests aren't the same as those of any of the groups it's an agent for: DHS, the government, or society as a whole.

For one, the TSA has a self-preservation interest. If it is seen as unnecessary—that is, if society as a whole believes there's a sufficiently diminished terrorist threat—it might be disbanded. Or perhaps its function would be taken over by some international security organization. In either case, like a person, the TSA is concerned about its own survival. (By the way, people working within the TSA are also concerned about their jobs, power, and reputation within the agency, and so on.)

For another, the TSA is concerned with its own reputation in the eyes of society. Yes, it wants to do a good job, but it also needs to be *seen* as doing a good job. If there's a terrorist attack, the TSA doesn't want to be blamed for not stopping the terrorists. So if a terrorist bombs a shopping mall instead of an airplane, it's a win for the TSA, even though the death toll might be the same.[5] Even without an actual terrorist attack, if it is seen as doing a bad job—even if it's actually doing a good job—it will be penalized with less public support, less funding, and less power.[6]

Finally, the TSA is concerned about its relative power within the government. The more funding it has, and the closer it is to the president, the better job it can do and the more likely it is to survive.

Societal Dilemma: Implementing airplane security.	
Society: Society as a whole.	
	Competing interest: Selfish interest—garner as much power and prestige as it can.
	Corresponding defection: Get as much money for its budget as possible.
Group interest: Airplane security whose benefits exceeds the costs.	Competing interest: Self-preservation—ensure that it won't be disbanded by the government.
Group norm: Implement airplane security at a reasonable level.	Corresponding defection: Become an indispensable part of airplane security.
	Competing interest: ego preservation - ensure that if there is a terrorist attack, it won't be blamed.
	Corresponding defection: implement a greater level of airplane security than the risk trade-off warrants.
To encourage people to act in the group interest, society implements these societal pressures:	
Moral: We teach people to do the right thing.	
Reputational: Institutions that put their own survival ahead of their nominal missions aren't thought of very well.	
Institutional: Legislators and courts rein institutions in.	
Security: Auditors, inspectors, cameras, and monitoring.	

The TSA's competing interests are common in government agencies. You can see it with the police and other law-enforcement bodies. These institutions have been delegated responsibility for implementing institutional pressure on behalf of society as a whole, but because their interests are different, they end up implementing security at a greater or lesser level than society would have.

Exaggerating the threat, and oversecuring—or at least overspending—as a result of that exaggeration, is by far the most common outcome. The TSA, for instance, would never suggest returning airport security to pre-9/11 levels and giving the rest of its budget back so it could be spent on broader anti-terrorism measures that might make more sense, such as intelligence, investigation, and emergency response. It's a solution that goes against the interests of the TSA as an institution.

This dynamic is hardly limited to government institutions. For example, corporate security officers exhibit the same behavior. In Chapter 10, I described the problem of corporate travel expenses, and explained that many large corporations implement societal pressures to ensure employee compliance. This generally involves approval—either beforehand for things like airfare and hotels, or after-the-fact verification of receipts and auditing—of travel expenses. To do this, the corporation delegates approval authority to some department or group of people, which determines what sort of pressures to implement. That group's motivation becomes some combination of keeping corporate travel expenses down and justifying its own existence as a department within the corporation, so it overspends.

Recall the professional athletes engaging in an arms race with drug testers. It might be in the athletes' group interest for the sport of cycling to be drug-free, but the actual implementation of that ideal is in the hands of the sport's regulatory bodies. The World Anti-Doping Agency takes the attitude of "ban everything, the hell with the consequences." It might better serve the athletes if the agency took more time and spent more money developing more accurate tests, was more transparent about its testing methodology, and had a straightforward redress procedure for athletes falsely accused—but it's not motivated to make that risk trade-off. And as long as it's in charge, it's going to do things its way.

Enforcing institutions have a number of other competing interests resulting from delegation. A common one has to do with how the enforcing institutions are measured and judged. We delegate to the police the enforcement of law, but individual policemen get reviewed and promoted based on their arrest and conviction rate. This can result in a variety of policing problems, including a police department's willingness to pursue an innocent person if it believes it can get a conviction, and pushing for an easy conviction on a lesser charge rather than a harder conviction on a more accurate charge.

There's one competing interest that's unique to enforcing institutions, and that's the interest of the group the institution is supposed to watch over. If a government agency exists only because of the industry, then it is in its self-preservation interest to keep that industry flourishing. And unless there's some other career path, pretty much everyone with the expertise necessary to become a regulator will be either a former or future employee of the industry, with the obvious implicit and explicit conflicts. As a result, there is a tendency for institutions delegated with regulating a particular industry to start advocating the commercial and special interests of that industry. This is known as regulatory capture, and there are many examples both in the U.S. and in other countries. U.S. examples include:

- The Minerals Management Service, whose former managers saw nothing wrong with steering contracts to ex-colleagues embarking on start-up private ventures, and having sexual relationships with and accepting gifts from oil and gas industry employees. In fact, the MMS was broken up in 2010 because this cozy relationship was blamed in part for the Deepwater Horizon oil spill.
- The Federal Aviation Administration, whose managers' willingness to overlook or delay action on crucial safety problems contributed to the 1996 crash of a ValuJet Airlines DC-9 in the Everglades, and the 2011 sudden in-flight failure of a section of fuselage on a Southwest Airlines 737.
- The Securities and Exchange Commission, whose lawyers routinely move to government employment from the banking industry, and back after their term of service is over. One of the effects of this revolving door was a poorly regulated banking industry that caused the financial crisis of 2008.

One way to think about all this is as a battle between diffuse interests and concentrated interests. If you assume that specific regulations are a trade-off between costs and benefits, a regulatory institution will attempt to strike a balance. On one side is the industry, which is both powerful and very motivated to influence the regulators. On the other side is everyone else, each of whom has many different concerns as they go about their day and none of whom are particularly motivated to try to influence the regulators. In this way, even if the interests of society as a whole are greater than the interests of the industry, they're not as well-represented because they're so diffuse. And to the extent that the institution is society's agent for implementing societal pressures, this becomes a colossal failure of societal interest. Moreover, each level of delegation introduces new competing interests, like a horribly conflicted game of telephone.

●   ●   ●

Institutions have power, and with that power comes the ability to defect. Throughout history, governments have acted in the self-interest of their rulers and not in the best interest of society. They can establish social norms and enforce those norms through laws and punishment. They can do this with or without the support of the people.

But there's a new type of potentially defecting institution, one that's made possible by the information age: corporations acting in the role of institutions. This can happen whenever public infrastructure moves into private hands. With the rise of the Internet as a communications system, and social networking sites in particular, corporations have become the designers, controllers, and arbiters of our social infrastructure. As such, they are assuming the role of institutions even though they really aren't. We talked in Chapter 10 about how combining reputational pressure with security systems gives defectors new avenues for bypassing societal pressures, like posting fake reviews on Yelp. Another effect is that the corporation that designs and owns the security mechanisms can facilitate defection at a much higher level.

Like an autocratic government, the company can set societal norms, determine what it means to cooperate, and enforce cooperation through the options on its site. It can take away legal and socially acceptable rights simply by not allowing them: think of how publishers have eroded fair use rights for music by not enabling copying options on digital players. And when the users of the site are not customers of the corporation, the competing interests are even stronger.

Take Facebook as an example. Facebook gets to decide what privacy options users have. It can allow users to keep certain things private if they want, and it can deny users the ability to keep other things private. It can grant users the ability to fine-tune their privacy settings, or it can only give users all-or-nothing options. It can make certain options easy to find and easy to use, and can make other options hard to find and even harder to use. And it will do or not do all of these things based on its business model of selling user information to other companies for marketing purposes. Facebook is the institution implicitly delegated by its users to implement societal pressures, but because it is a for-profit corporation and not a true agent for its users, it defects from society and acts in its own self-interest, effectively reversing the principal–agent relationship. Of course, users can refuse to participate in Facebook. But as Facebook and other social networking sites become embedded in our culture and our socialization, opting out becomes less of a realistic option. As long as the users either have no choice or don't care, it can act against its users' interests with impunity.

It's not easy to implement societal pressures against institutions that put their competing interests ahead of the group interest. Like any other organization, institutions don't respond to moral pressure in the same way individuals do. They can become impervious to reputational pressure. Since people are often forced to interact with institutions, it often doesn't matter what people think of them. Yes, in a democracy, people can vote for legislators who will better delegate societal pressures to these institutions, but this is a slow and indirect process. You could decide to not use a credit card or a cell phone and therefore not do business with the companies that provide them, but often that's not a realistic alternative.

Sometimes the authorities are just plain unwilling to punish defecting institutions. No one in the U.S. government is interested in taking the National Security Agency to task for illegally spying on American citizens (spy agencies make bad enemies). Or in punishing anyone for authorizing the torture of—often innocent—terrorist suspects. Similarly, there's little questioning legislatively about President Obama's self-claimed right to assassinate Americans abroad without due process.

The most effective societal pressures against institutions are themselves institutional. An example is the lawsuit I talked about at the start of this chapter. EPIC sued the TSA over full-body scanners, claiming the agency didn't even follow its own rules when it fielded the devices. And while the court rejected EPIC's Fourth Amendment arguments and allowed the TSA to keep screening, it ordered the TSA to conduct notice-and-comment rulemaking. Not a complete victory by any means, but a partial one.

And there are many examples of government institutions being reined in by the court system. In the U.S., this includes judicial review, desegregating schools, legalizing abortion, striking down laws prohibiting interracial and now same-sex couples from marrying, establishing judicial oversight for wiretapping, and punishing trust fund mismanagement at the Bureau of Indian Affairs.

What's important here is accountability. It is important that these mechanisms are seen publicly, and that people are held accountable. If we're going to keep government from overstepping its bounds, it will be through separation of powers: checks and balances. But it's not just government that needs to be watched; it's corporations, non-government institutions, and individuals. It's everyone's responsibility to keep everyone else in check.

PART IV
Conclusions

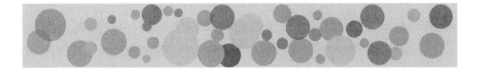

How Societal Pressures Fail

Let's start our discussion of societal pressure failures with an example: taxes. Paying taxes is a classic free-rider problem; if almost everyone cooperates by paying taxes, defectors get all the benefits of whatever those taxes are paying for without having to suffer the financial penalties of actually paying.[1] There are laws and enforcement, but at least in the U.S., with the exception of payroll taxes, income tax is almost entirely enforced by voluntary compliance. It's not just a financial risk trade-off; there are two pieces of moral pressure at work here: people paying taxes because it's the right thing to do, and people paying taxes because it's the law and following the law is the right thing to do.

Still, there's a lot of fraud in the U.S. According to the IRS, in 2001—the most recent year I could find comprehensive numbers for—the difference between total taxes owed and total taxes paid was $345 billion; about 19% of the total taxes due. A third-party estimate from 2008 tax returns also showed a 19% tax gap. Note that this gap is in the percentage of money owed, not the percentage of cheaters. By one estimate, 25% of individuals admit to cheating on their taxes. On the other hand, a single corporation avoiding billions in taxes costs taxpayers vastly more money than many thousands of waiters lying about their tip income.

There are many reasons people cheat on their taxes, and they all point to failures of societal pressure. First, there is very little enforcement. In 2007, for example, the IRS examined less than 1% of the 179 million tax returns filed, initiated criminal prosecutions in only 4,211 cases, and obtained indictments in only 2,322 cases. Corporate audits are down, too, both in number and thoroughness. And while there's debate about whether increasing the penalties against tax evaders increases compliance, we do know that increasing the number of audits increases compliance and—of course—collects more of the taxes owed.

Aside from low-level cheating that can be easily detected by computer matching, cheating on your taxes is easy and you're not likely to get caught.

Second, it's profitable. These days, if you're making a 5% return on your investments, you're doing really well. With the top federal tax rate at 35%, the money you can save by cheating is a pretty strong motivation. These are not people who can't afford to pay taxes; the typical tax cheat is a male under 50 in a high tax bracket and with a complex return. (Poorer users, with all their income covered by payroll taxes, have less opportunity to cheat.) The current situation creates an incentive to cheat.

Third, people think that lots of other people do it. Remember the Bad Apple Effect? There's a 1998 survey showing people believe that 38% of their fellow taxpayers are failing to declare all their income and listing false deductions. And the high-profile tax cheats that make the news reinforce this belief.

And fourth, recent political rhetoric has demonized taxes. Cries that taxation equals theft, that the tax system is unfair, and that the government just wastes any money you give it gives people a different morality, which they use to justify underpayment. This weakens the original moral pressure to pay up.

All of these reasons interact with each other. One study looked at tax evasion over about 50 years, and found that it increases with income tax rates, the unemployment rate, and public dissatisfaction with government. Another blamed income inequality.

Despite all of this, the U.S. government collects 81% of all taxes owed. That's actually pretty impressive compared to some countries.

There's another aspect to this. In addition to illegal tax evasion, there's what's called tax avoidance: technically legal measures to reduce taxes that run contrary to the tax code's policy goals. We discussed tax loopholes at length in Chapter 9. There are a lot of creative companies figuring out ways to follow the letter of the tax law while completely ignoring the spirit. This is how companies can make billions in profits yet pay little in taxes. And make no mistake, industries, professions, and groups of wealthy people deliberately manipulate the legislative system by lobbying Congress to get special tax exemptions to benefit themselves. One example is the carried-interest tax loophole: the taxation of private equity fund and hedge fund manager compensation at the 15% long-term capital gains tax rate rather than as regular income. Another is the investment tax credit, intended to help building contractors, that people used to subsidize expensive SUVs. There's also tax flight—companies moving profits out of the country to reduce taxes.

Estimates of lost federal revenue due to legal tax avoidance and tax flight are about $1 trillion. Adding tax evasion, the total amount of lost revenue is $1.5 trillion, or 41% of total taxes that should be collected. Collecting these taxes would more than eliminate the federal deficit.

Okay, so maybe that's not so good.

There are a lot of societal pressure failures in all of this. Morals differ: people tend to perceive tax evasion negatively, tax flight—companies moving profits out of the country to reduce taxes—neutrally, and tax avoidance positively: it's legal and clever. Even so, a reasonable case can be made that tax avoidance is just as immoral as tax evasion. The reputational effects of being a public tax cheat are few, and can be positive towards people who are clever enough to find legal loopholes. Institutional pressure depends on enforcement, which is spotty. Security systems are ineffective against the more complex fraud.

●   ●   ●

Remember the goal of societal pressures. We want a high level of trust in society. Society is too complex for the intimate form of trust—we have to interact with too many people to know all of their intentions—so we're settling for cooperation and compliance. In order for people to cooperate, they need to believe that almost everyone else will cooperate too. We solve this chicken-and-egg problem with societal pressures. By inducing people to comply with social norms, we naturally raise the level of trust and induce more people to cooperate. This is the positive feedback loop we're trying to get.

Societal pressures operate on society as a whole. They don't enforce cooperation in all people in all circumstances. Instead, they induce an overall level of cooperation. Returning to the immune system analogy, no defense works in all circumstances. As long as the system of societal pressures protects society as a whole, individual harm isn't a concern. It's not a failure of societal pressure if someone trusts too much and gets harmed because of it, or trusts too little and functions poorly in society as a result. What does matter is that the overall scope of defection is low enough that the overall level of trust is high enough for society to survive and hopefully thrive.

This sounds callous, but it's true. In the U.S., we tolerate 16,000–18,000 murders a year, and a tax gap of $1.5 trillion. By any of the mechanisms discussed in Chapter 14, society gets to decide what level of defection we're willing to tolerate, and those numbers have fluctuated over the years. These are only failures of societal pressure if society thinks these numbers are either too high or too low.

In Chapter 6, I talked about societal pressures as a series of knobs. Depending on the particular societal dilemma, society determines the scope of defection it can tolerate and then—if it's all working properly—dials the societal pressure knobs to achieve that balance. Recall the Hawk-Dove game from Chapter 3; a variety of different initial parameters result in stable societies. If we want less murder, we increase societal pressures. If that ends up being too expensive and we can tolerate a higher murder rate, we decrease societal pressures.

That metaphor is basically correct, but it's simplistic. We don't have that level of accuracy when we implement societal pressures. In the real world, the knobs are poorly marked and badly calibrated, there's a delay after you turn one of them before you notice any effects, and there's so much else going on that it's hard to figure out what the effect actually is. Think of a bathtub with leaky unmarked faucets, where you can't directly see the water coming out of the spout...outside, in the rain. You sit in the tub, oscillating back and forth between the water being too hot and too cold, and eventually you give up and take an uncomfortable bath. That's a more accurate metaphor for the degree of control we have with societal pressures.

Figure 13 tries to capture all of this.[2] On the left is the main feedback loop, between new societal pressures and the scope of defection. New societal pressures cause a change in the scope of defections, which causes a change in both risk and perceived risk. Then, the new perceived risk causes calls for changes in societal pressures.

Notice the delay between implementing new societal pressures and seeing corresponding changes in the scope of defection. The delay comes from several sources. One, moral and reputational pressures are inherently slow. Anything that affects risk trade-offs through a deterrence effect will require time before you see any effects from it. Depending on the form of government, new institutional pressures can also be slow. So can security systems: time to procure, time to implement, time before they're used effectively.

For example, the first people arrested for writing computer viruses in the pre-Internet era went unpunished because there weren't any applicable laws to charge them with. Internet e-mail was not designed to provide sender authentication; the result was the emergence of spam, a problem we're still trying to solve today. And in the U.S., the FBI regularly complains that the laws regulating surveillance aren't keeping up with the rapidly changing pace of communications technology.

Two, it can take time for a societal pressure change to propagate through society. All of this makes it harder to fine-tune the system, because you don't know when you're seeing the full effects of the societal pressures currently in place. And three, it takes time to measure any changes in the scope of defection. Sometimes you need months or even years of statistical data before you know if things are getting better or worse.

The feedback is also inexact. To use a communications theory term, it's noisy. Often you can't know the exact effects of your societal pressures because there are so many other things affecting the scope of defection at the same time; in Figure 13, those are the "other considerations." For instance, in the late 20th century, the drop in the U.S. crime rate has been linked to the legalization of abortion 20 years previously. Additionally, society's perceptions of risks are hard to quantify, and contain a cultural component. I'll talk more about this later in the chapter.

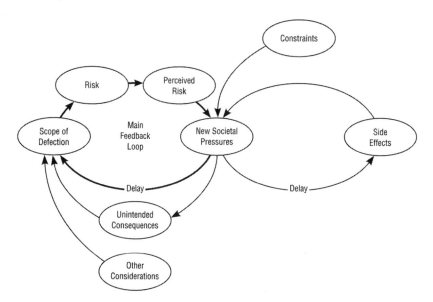

Figure 13: Societal Pressure's Feedback Loops

A related feedback loop, shown as the lower loop on the left in Figure 13, is also important. These are the unintended consequences of societal pressures that often directly affect the scope of defection. A large-scale example would be the effects on crime of Prohibition, or of incarcerating 16–25% of young black men in the U.S. A smaller-scale example is that hiring guards to prevent shoplifting may end up increasing shoplifting, because regular employees now believe that it's someone else's job to police the store and not theirs. Electronic sensor tags have a similar effect.

Security systems are complex, and will invariably have side effects on society. This is shown as the loop on the right side of Figure 13. For example, the U.S. incarceration rate has much broader social effects than simply locking up criminals. Prohibition did, too. A simple side effect is that some societal pressures, mostly security systems, cost money. More subtle side effects are fewer bicycle riders as a result of helmet laws, a chilling effect on computer-security research due to laws designed to prevent the digital copying of music and movies, and increased violence as a result of drug enforcement.

Decisions about whether to implement a new societal pressure require careful consideration of the trade-off between its costs and benefits—which are extremely difficult to predict.

Security systems are often what economists call an experiential good: something you don't understand the value of until you've already bought, installed, and experienced it.[3] This holds true for other forms of societal pressure as well. If you're knowledgeable and experienced and perform a good analysis, you can make some good guesses, but it can be impossible to know the actual effects—or unintended consequences—of a particular societal pressure until you've already implemented it. This means that implementing societal pressures is always an iterative process. We try something, see how well it works, then fine-tune.

Any society—a family, a business, a government—is constantly balancing its need for security with the side effects, unintended consequences, and other considerations. Can we afford this particular societal pressure system? Are our fundamental freedoms and liberties more important than more security?[4] More onerous ATM security will result in fewer ATM transactions, costing a bank more than the ATM fraud. A retail store that installs security cameras in its dressing rooms will probably have fewer customers as a result, with a greater loss of revenue than was saved by the decrease of shoplifting. Online retailers face similar choices, since complicated security measures reduce purchases. In Chapter 9, we talked specifically about how hard it is to get the security effects of laws right. It's hard for all categories of societal pressure.[5]

What all of this means is that it's easy to get societal pressures wrong. We implement more or less societal pressure than the risk warrants. We implement suboptimal, ineffective, or the wrong kind of security systems. Then, when we try to fix them, we get it wrong again. Many of the excesses in the War on Terror can be chalked up to overcompensation for the security failures that led to the terrorist attacks of 9/11.

●   ●   ●

In Chapters 7 through 10 we talked about how specific types of societal pressure fail. Here, I am going to talk more generally about societal pressure failures. These failures can be broken into several broad categories. These categories aren't hard and fast, and there's going to be some overlap. The goal here is just to give a feeling for how societal pressures can go wrong.

Misunderstanding the actor. Potential defectors have many competing interests, ranging from selfish to moral; if you misunderstand them, you're likely to get security wrong. Defectors also have different characteristics, such as motivation, skill, money, risk aversion, and so on.

It makes no sense to spend $2 to forge an ID card worth $1, right? That's true if the defector is in it for the money. But if he's a security researcher analyzing weaknesses in the production process, a competing company trying to damage the business, or a hacker just trying to understand how the stuff works, it might be. Similarly, if you think terrorists are all foreigners, you'll miss the homegrown ones.

We've also touched on the problem of organized defectors. Organization is common in crime—well-funded criminal organizations are far more effective than lone criminals—and in terrorism.[6] It's also common among reform-minded defectors: abolitionists, animal rights activists, and so on. When defectors organize, societal pressures that worked in the past might not work as well. We talked about both of these problems in Chapter 11. A common misunderstanding is to assume that defectors are unorganized when they are—this happens often with crime—or to assume that defectors are organized when they are not, as happened with al Qaeda.

Misunderstanding the security incentives. Sometimes societal pressure can fail because it creates an incentive for the wrong competing norm. An example will help make this clear.

Convincing people to reduce their trash is a societal dilemma. Moral pressure only goes so far, and reputational pressure against having a lot of trash is generally pretty weak. By far the easiest institutional pressure is to charge people by the amount of trash they generate: by the bag, by the bin, by the pound. The idea is to tax marginal defection and encourage people to reduce their trash.

Societal Dilemma: Limiting personal trash.	
Society: Society as a whole.	
Group interest: Limit the use of landfills. Group norm: Limit trash.	Competing interest: Laziness or apathy. Corresponding defection: Throw away as much trash as you want.
	Competing interest: Minimize cost. Corresponding defection: Overstuff the trash can.
To encourage people to act in the group interest, the society implements a variety of societal pressures.	
Moral: Awareness campaigns that emphasize the immorality of polluting. Reputational: Social pressure against people who put out a lot of trash. Institutional: Charge residents extra, based on how much trash they produce. Security: Garbage monitoring.[7]	

However, a resident who wants to avoid the extra charges has several other options. He can stuff his trash more tightly into his bin. He can burn his trash to reduce the volume. He can dump his trash on the side of the road, or in the bin of a neighbor down the block. These options were always available to him, but before the extra trash collection fee, there was no reason to bother. As soon as you add societal pressures, some people will look for ways to get around them without having to cooperate in the original dilemma.

This isn't just theoretical. A study of nine municipalities showed exactly this sort of behavior—increases in trash burning and dumping—when unit pricing was implemented. Stuffing more trash in the bins, known as the "Seattle stomp" after the municipality where it was first noticed, is very common.

The failure here is the assumption that there is only one competing norm. In this case, there are a variety of ways to defect. And if the societal pressures only raise the cost of one competing norm, it could make the others more attractive. In this example, the trash fee didn't increase the cost of generating more trash; it merely increased the cost of generating more trash *and* putting that trash in trash cans. Directly targeting trash creation would be a better institutional pressure, but I can't think of any way a municipality could possibly make that work. On a larger scale, a disposal tax could be assessed when someone purchases a product. This would motivate product manufacturers to reduce packaging, or otherwise make their products more disposal-friendly, depending on the particulars of the tax. Of course, administering that would be difficult, and society would have to balance that cost with the benefit.[8]

Misunderstanding the risk. We don't make risk trade-offs based on actual risk; as shown in Figure 13, we make them based on perceived risk. If we believe the scope of defection is higher or lower than it really is, we're not going to implement optimal societal pressures. And there are lots of ways we get risk wrong.

| Natural Biases in Risk Perception ||
We exaggerate risks that are...	We downplay risks that are...
Spectacular	Pedestrian
Rare	Common
Personified	Anonymous
Beyond our control	More under our control
Externally imposed	Taken willingly
Talked about	Not discussed
Intentional or man-made	Natural
Immediate	Long-term or diffuse
Sudden	Evolving slowly over time
Affecting us personally	Affecting others
New and unfamiliar	Familiar
Uncertain	Well understood
Directed against children	Directed against adults
Morally offensive	Morally desirable
Entirely without redeeming features	Associated with some ancillary benefit

This is all well-studied by psychologists. Current U.S. counterterrorism policy demonstrates these biases. Political scientist John Mueller wrote:

> Until 2001, far fewer Americans were killed in any grouping of years by all forms of international terrorism than were killed by lightning, and almost none of those terrorist deaths occurred within the United States itself. Even with the September 11 attacks included in the count, the number of Americans killed by international terrorism since the late 1960s (which is when the State Department began counting) is about the same as the number of Americans killed over the same period by lightning, accident-causing deer, or severe allergic reaction to peanuts.

But that's not the way people think. Terrorism is rare, spectacular, beyond our control, externally imposed, sudden, new and unfamiliar, uncertain, potentially directed against our children, offensive, and entirely without redeeming features. For these and other reasons, we exaggerate the risk and end up spending much too much on security to mitigate it.

Another example is computer crime. It's pedestrian, common, slowly evolving, affecting others, increasingly familiar, and (at least by techies) well-understood. So it makes sense that we understate the risks and underfund security.

There are cultural biases to risk as well. According to one study conducted in 23 countries, people have a higher risk tolerance in cultures that avoid uncertainty or are individualistic, and a lower risk tolerance in cultures that are egalitarian and harmonious. Also—and this is particularly interesting—the wealthier a country is, the lower its citizens' tolerance for risk. Along similar lines, the greater the income inequality a society has, the less trusting its citizens are.

Creating a dilemma that encourages deception. Think back to the two prisoners for a minute. Throughout this entire book, we've assumed that Alice and Bob are both actually guilty. What if they're not? Now, what is Alice's best strategy?

Disturbingly, it may still be in her best interest to confess and testify against Bob. Follow me here: if Bob lies and testifies against Alice, she is looking at either six or ten years in jail. Lying and testifying against Bob is the better choice for Alice: six years is better than ten. And if Bob remains silent, she's looking at either freedom or one year in jail. Again, lying is the better choice for Alice: freedom is better than one year in jail. By this analysis, both Alice and Bob fare best if they confess to crimes they did not commit in an attempt to get leniency for themselves while falsely accusing the other. To make matters worse, assume that Bob is innocent and Alice is guilty. It's still in Alice's interest to falsely testify against Bob.

Of course, the risk trade-off is more complicated than that. Alice and Bob have to assess the prosecutor's case, and weigh the trade-off between their false confession and the hope that justice will prevail in the end. But as soon as the police offer Alice and Bob this deal, they increase the likelihood that one or both of them will confess to a crime they didn't commit. This is the reason that plea bargaining is illegal in many countries: it sets up perverse incentives. This can only be exacerbated by the surprising tendency of people to make false confessions.[9] Generalizing, we find that all sorts of unsavory people try to align themselves with the police in exchange for leniency for their own actions. This kind of thing can happen whenever people cooperate with a norm they don't believe in.

Accidentally making the costs of cooperation too high. Recall Chapter 11, where we talked about people assisting the police. One of Alice's potential competing interests is that cooperating with the police is too difficult, time-consuming, or dangerous. So even if Alice wants to cooperate, the cost is too high and she's forced to defect. This is the reason laws requiring the police to enforce immigration laws are a bad idea. The last thing you want is for someone to be afraid to assist the police out of fear that he will be deported. Another example is rape; if the cost of reporting a rape and helping prosecute the rapist is too emotionally high, women will not come forward. In general, there is a cost associated with cooperating. If we want to limit defections, we need to limit the costs—and/or increase the benefits—of cooperation.

Accidentally increasing the incentive to defect. The point of societal pressure is to induce cooperation. Sometimes the results are backwards, and societal pressure induces defection. Again, an example will explain this. Currently in the United States, standardized student testing has incredible influence over the future fates of students, teachers, and schools. Under a law called the No Child Left Behind Act, students have to pass certain tests; if they don't pass, their schools are penalized. In the District of Columbia, the school system offered teachers $8,000 bonuses for improving test scores, and threatened them with termination for failing. Scores did increase significantly during the period, and the schools were held up as examples of how incentives affect teachers' behavior.

It turns out that a lot of those score increases were faked. In addition to teaching students, teachers cheated on their students' tests by changing wrong answers to correct ones.

There's a societal dilemma at work here. Teachers were always able to manipulate their students' test scores, but before the No Child Left Behind law, the competing interests were weak. People become teachers to teach, not to cheat... until their jobs depended on it. When the competing interests became stronger, the school districts should have increased societal pressures, probably security systems, to restore balance.[10]

Societal Dilemma: Cheating on students' tests.	
Society: Society as a whole.	
Group interest: Accurate testing of students. Group norm: Allow students to take their own tests.	Old competing interest: Selfish interest of having a star classroom.
	Old corresponding defection: Fake students' tests so they have a higher score.
	New competing interest: Financial reward, job retention.
	New corresponding defection: Fake students' tests so they have a higher score.
To encourage people to act in the group interest, society implements these societal pressures: Moral: Teacher integrity. Reputational: Loss of reputation if caught cheating. Institutional: Changing answers on students' tests is fraud, and there are laws against it. Security: Secure handling of tests makes it harder for teachers to change answers. Statistical analysis of test data can show evidence of cheating.	

There's a rule at work here. When you start measuring something and then judge people based on that measurement, you encourage people to game the measurement instead of doing whatever it is you wanted in the first place. If a company penalizes customer-support people for having long phone calls, they have an incentive to hang up on callers. If you reward software programmers for fixing bugs, they have an incentive to create buggy software to have bugs to fix instead of getting it right the first time.[11] If you pay CEOs based on stock price, they have an incentive to inflate the stock price at the expense of the company's long-term interest.

The incentive to defect can also be increased when the reason a thing is attacked changes. Driver's licenses are a great example. Originally, they were nothing more than proof that a person is legally allowed to drive a car. As such, there wasn't much of an incentive to forge them, and security around the licenses was minimal: they were made of paper, they didn't have photos, and so on. In the U.S., at least, it was only when they started being used for a completely different purpose—age verification as a condition of buying alcohol—that forgeries started being a problem. In response, state governments changed their licenses to include a variety of anti-forgery features: photographs, watermarks and holograms, microprinting, and the like. Recently, their use has changed again. Since

9/11, they have been increasingly used as proof that a person isn't on a terrorist watch list. And now the government wants even more security features associated with them, like computer chips and enhanced security around their issuance.

We saw this with pair-bonding. Informal pair-bonding was enough to deal with Deacon's Paradox with respect to infidelity, but when inheritance became an issue, more formal mechanisms were required. Another example is joyriding; because joyriders never intended to keep the cars they stole, they couldn't be charged with theft—so before specific joyriding laws were enacted, they got off relatively lightly.

The market can also increase the incentive to defect. When the price of glass eels—immature eels that are a delicacy in Japan and Europe—started rising, more people began to fish for them. The result was a Tragedy of the Commons: illegal overfishing and poaching in England, France, and the northeastern U.S. resulted in reduced yields, which resulted in higher prices. This resulted in even more overfishing, even further reduced yields, and even higher prices that rose from $25 to $950 per pound. Enforcement just couldn't keep up, and poachers have devastated the eel population. A technological advance might solve this societal dilemma; researchers are trying to breed and farm these eels, which will increase supply and reduce the incentive to overfish.

Technological advances can magnify societal dilemmas as well. We'll talk about this in the next chapter, but for now, think of the difference between banking in person and banking online, manual door locks and electronic locks, or paper ballots and touch-screen voting machines. In all cases, the addition of technology makes some attacks easier.

A final way the incentive to defect can increase is when the scale of the societal dilemma changes. We saw this in the difference between a single sandwich seller in a market and a large sandwich-producing corporation, and between Fisherman Bob and the Robert Fish Corporation. Large organizations can gain more, and inflict more damage on the group, by defecting. As organizations grow in size and power, societal pressures that might have worked in the past won't necessarily work as well any longer.

Misunderstanding how different societal dilemmas interact. Societal dilemmas don't exist in isolation, and societal pressures designed to decrease the scope of defection in one societal dilemma can, as a side effect, increase the scope of defection in another.

For example, we recognize that the police force is both a solution and a problem. It is our agent in institutional pressures against criminals in general, but as an institution with its own self-interests, it has to be dissuaded from defecting. So we have all sorts of societal pressures protecting society from the police: rules

limiting search and seizure, rules against self-incrimination, rules about interrogation, rules about evidence, and so on. These necessarily affect the defection
rate of criminals by making the police's job harder and more onerous, but we
have them because—on balance—the result is a better police force and a better society. Recently, this has been changing. In our efforts to protect ourselves
against terrorism, we have been dismantling many of the societal pressures we've
put in place to protect ourselves from abuse by the police.

Similarly, over the past couple of decades we have dismantled a variety of financial regulations that limited the behavior of banks and other financial institutions.[12] Yes, those regulations made it harder for institutions to make money, but
they also served to protect society from the effects of widespread bank defection.

Ignoring changing social norms. Sometimes societal norms change, and societal dilemmas start shifting to reflect the change. This often results in conflicting
societal dilemmas as the new norms work their way through society, and in conflicts between subgroups within society who are either clinging to the old norms
or embracing the new ones.

My favorite example is historical. In ancient Rome, it was important to worship the gods. It was also important that everyone in the community worship the
gods. The gods were angered if some people shirked their religious responsibilities, like participating in festivals. This is one reason the Romans didn't like the
early Christians. It's not that they worshipped their Christian god, it's that they
didn't *also* worship the Roman gods. This was not simply a disagreement with
Christians' personal choice; it was seen as a danger to the whole community.

Societal Dilemma: Worshipping Roman gods.	
Society: Society as a whole.	
Group interest: Making the Roman gods happy.	Competing interest: Making your own god happy.
Group norm: Worshipping the Roman gods.	Corresponding defection: Not worshipping the Roman gods as well.
To encourage people to act in the group interest, the society implements a variety of societal pressures.	
Moral: From birth, Romans were taught their religion.	
Reputational: Romans who didn't participate in public religious ceremonies were penalized by the community.	
Institutional: Serious offenders were thrown to the lions.	
Security: Lions.	

Eventually, social norms changed. Christians became a larger and larger minority. They were increasingly tolerated. Sometime in the early 300s AD, Emperor Constantine converted to Christianity. And slowly, what had been defection became cooperation.

Whether and when societal pressure failed depends on your point of view. If you believed in the Roman gods, then societal pressure failed when it didn't prevent Christians from offending the Roman gods. If you were an early Christian, then societal pressure failed when it didn't protect freedom of religion.

Another example is sexual harassment in the workplace. As long as those in power in the organization didn't enforce prohibitions against men harassing subordinate women, unwanted advances were relatively common and taken for granted. It wasn't until a larger society started enforcing sexual harassment rules that occurrences began to decline.

A similar dynamic is playing out with respect to gay marriage. It's a fundamentalist Christian belief that gay marriage isn't just a bad individual choice, but that its very existence threatens the traditional family: just like the Romans talking about Christianity. As such, it's a societal dilemma.

Societal Dilemma: Gay marriage.	
Society: Society as a whole.	
Group interest: Protecting the institution of marriage.	Competing interest: Allowing everyone free choice in whom they can marry.
Group norm: Only recognizing "approved" marriages.	Corresponding defection: Allowing gay couples to marry.
To encourage people to act in the group interest, the society implements a variety of societal pressures.	
Moral: Teach gay marriage is wrong.	
Reputational: Ostracize same-sex couples.	
Institutional: Refuse to give same-sex couples the same legal rights as different-sex couples. Pass laws making life especially difficult for same-sex couples.	
Security: None.	

Other people, though, don't see the dilemma. They don't accept that group defection would result in the social calamity the fundamentalists do. Not only do they defect, they don't even accept the dilemma as real.[13]

Norms can change quickly due to external threats. People are more willing to implement societal pressures—both the kinds that reward cooperators and the kinds that punish defectors—in times of war.

Most of the time, though, social norms change slowly. We've repeatedly talked about Deacon's Paradox, and how pair-bonding is a societal pressure. Enforcement of that has changed. There was a time when you could be stoned to death for adultery, or for fornication out of wedlock. Now, in most of the world, that doesn't happen. There are even parts of the world where it isn't even frowned upon very heavily. And on the technological side, defecting from pair-bonds has become safer. The "wages of sin" used to include pregnancy, which came with it significant health and financial risks, and venereal disease. Cheap and effective birth control changed that, so much so that the current societal dilemma for women is a very different risk trade-off. More recently, unsafe sex practices brought with them a different set of health risks, ones that could be effectively mitigated with technological security measures like condoms.

Our evolving definitions of "society" show how societal norms evolve. As Barbara Jordan famously noted, the original definition of "we the people" in the U.S. didn't include women or slaves. Over the centuries, our definitions of who is within the bounds of society have gradually become more inclusive.

You can see this evolution in the societal dilemma surrounding the current tone and integrity of political debates in the United States. The goal of politics—elections, policy debates, laws—is to govern the country by enacting the best policies for society and implementing the best laws to solve societal dilemmas. But there's a competing interest of getting laws passed that benefit us in particular. We're all better off if national policy debates are factual, honest, and civil, but it's easy to resort to spin, distortions, smears, and lies. But if enough people do that, you get the circus that characterizes far too much of current American politics.[14]

Societal Dilemma: Policy debates.	
Society: Society as a whole.	
Group interest: Make the best policy decisions. Group norm: Debate public policy fairly, whatever that might mean.	Competing interest: For your side to win. Corresponding defection: Debate by whatever means necessary.
To encourage people to act in the group interest, the society implements a variety of societal pressures.	
Moral: Shame, honesty, honorability, and so on.	
Reputational: Shame and ridicule heaped on dishonest politicians. Reputation for statesmanship bestowed on honest ones.	
Institutional: For particularly egregious lies, libel laws. Anti-gerrymandering laws.	
Security: The proper use of rhetoric. Fact checking.	

It's not clear that the level of dishonesty is new, but it seems to be carried out on a much broader scale today. Moral and reputational pressures used to work, but they are failing as the country bifurcates into two different groups with completely separate systems of values. Legal controls that impinge on free speech are a dangerous option. One solution is to stop gerrymandering safe legislative seats. By forcing these seats to be decided in the general election, as opposed to party-specific primaries or caucuses, candidates would have to appeal to swing centrist voters rather than their base. But potential legal societal pressures would be viewed as partisan, and untenable for that reason.

What's going on here is that the definition of "society" is changing. "Society as a whole" has less meaning in a polarized political climate such as the one in the U.S. in the early 21st century. People are defining their society as those who agree with them politically, and the other political side as "traitors," people who "hate America," or people who "want the terrorists to win." It's no surprise that there's widespread defection: with regard to the new, more restrictive, definition of "society," it's not defection at all.[15]

Technological Advances

Scale is one of the critical concepts necessary to understand societal pressures. The increasing scale of society is what forces us to shift from trust and trustworthiness based on personal relationships to impersonal trust—predictability and compliance—in both people and systems. Increasing scale is what forces us to augment our social pressures of morals and reputation with institutional pressure and security systems. Increasing scale is what's requiring more—and more complicated—security systems, making overall societal pressures more expensive and less effective. Increasing scale makes the failures more expensive and more onerous. And it makes our whole societal pressure system less flexible and adaptable.

This is all because increasing scale affects societal pressures from a number of different directions.

- *More people.* Having more people in society changes the effectiveness of different reputational pressures. It also increases the number of defectors, even if the percentage remains unchanged, giving them more opportunities to organize and grow stronger. Finally, more defectors makes it more likely that the defecting behavior is perceived as normal, which can result in a Bad Apple Effect.
- *Increased complexity.* More people means more interactions among people: more interactions, more often, over longer distances, about more things. This both causes new societal dilemmas to arise and causes interdependencies among dilemmas. Complex systems need to rely on technology more. This means that they have more flaws and can fail in surprising and catastrophic ways.
- *New systems.* As more and different technology permeates our lives and our societies, we find new areas of concern that need to be addressed, new

societal dilemmas, and new opportunities for defection. Airplane terrorism simply wasn't a problem before airplanes were invented; Internet fraud requires the Internet. The job of the defenders keeps getting bigger.

- *New security systems.* Technology gives certain societal pressure systems—specifically, reputational and institutional—the ability to scale. Those systems themselves require security, and that security can be attacked directly. So online reputation systems can be poisoned with fake data, or the computers that maintain them can be hacked and the data modified. Our webmail accounts can be hacked, and scammers can post messages asking for money in our name. Or our identities can be stolen from information taken from our home computers or centralized databases.

- *Increased technological intensity.* As society gets more technological, the amount of damage defectors can do grows. This means that even a very small defection rate can be as bad as a greater defection rate would have been when society was less technologically intense. This holds true for the sociopath intent on killing as many people as possible, and for a company intent on making as much profit as possible, regardless of the environmental damage. In both cases, technology increases the actor's potential harm. Think of how much damage a terrorist can do today versus what he could have done fifty years ago, and then try to extrapolate to what upcoming technologies might enable him to do fifty years from now.[1] Technology also allows defectors to better organize, potentially making their groups larger, more powerful, and more potent.

- *Increased frequency.* Frequency scales with technology as well. Think of the difference between someone robbing a bank with a gun and a getaway car versus someone stealing from a bank remotely over the Internet. The latter is much more efficient. If the hacker can automate his attack, he can steal from thousands of banks a day—even while he sleeps. This aspect of scale is becoming much more important as more aspects of our society are controlled not by people but by automatic systems.

- *Increased distance.* Defectors can act over both longer physical distances and greater time intervals. This matters because greater distances create the potential for more people, with weaker social ties, to be involved; this weakens moral and reputational pressure. And when physical distances cross national boundaries, institutional pressure becomes less effective as well.

- *Increased inertia and resistance to change.* Larger groups make slower decisions; and once made, those decisions persist and may be very difficult to reverse or revise. This can cause societal pressures to stagnate.

In prehistoric times, the scale was smaller, and our emergent social pressures—moral and reputational—worked well because they evolved for the small-scale societies of the day. As civilization emerged and technology advanced, we invented institutions to help deal with societal dilemmas on the larger scales of our growing societies. We also invented security technologies to further enhance societal pressures. We needed to trust both these institutions and the security systems that increasingly affected our lives.

We also developed less tolerance for risk. For much of our species' history, life was dangerous. I'm not just talking about losing 15–25% of males to warfare in primitive societies, but infant mortality, childhood diseases, adult diseases, natural and man-made accidents, and violence from both man and beast. As technology, especially medical technology, improved, life became safer and longer. Our tolerance for risk diminished because there were fewer hazards in our lives. (Large, long-term risks like nuclear weapons, genetic engineering, and global warming are much harder for us to comprehend, and we tend to minimize them as a result.)

Today, societal scale continues to grow as global trade increases, the world's economies link up, global interdependencies multiply, and international legal bodies gain more power. On a more personal level, the Internet continues to bring distant people closer. Our risk tolerance has become so low that we have a fetish for eliminating—or at least pretending to eliminate—as much risk as possible from our lives.

Let's get back to societal pressures as a series of knobs. Technology is continuously improving, making new things possible and existing things easier, cheaper, better, or more reliable. But these same technological advances result in the knobs being twiddled in unpredictable ways. Also, as scale increases, new knobs get created, more people have their hands on the knobs, and knobs regulating different dilemmas get interlinked.

New technologies, new innovations, and new ideas increase the scope of defection in several dimensions. Defectors innovate. Attacks become easier, cheaper, more reliable. New attacks become possible. More people may defect because it's easier to do so, or their defections become more frequent or more intense.

This results in a security imbalance; the knob settings that society had deemed acceptable no longer are. In response, society innovates. It implements new societal pressures. Perhaps they're based on new laws or new technology, perhaps there is some new group norm that gets reflected in society's reputational pressure, or perhaps it's more of what used to work. It's hard to get right at first, because of all the feedback loops we discussed, but eventually society settles on some new knob settings, and the scope of defection is reduced to whatever new level society deems tolerable. And then society is stable until the next technological innovation.

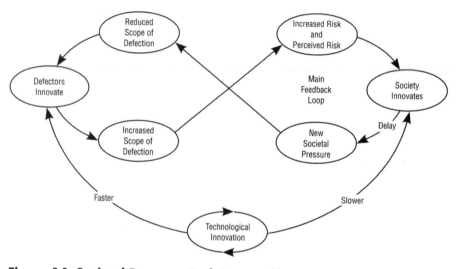

Figure 14: Societal Pressure Red Queen Effect

If Figure 14 looks familiar, it's because it's almost the same as Figure 3 from Chapter 2. This is a Red Queen Effect, fueled not just by natural selection but also by technological innovation. Think of airport security, counterfeiting, or software systems. The attackers improve, so the defenders improve, so the attackers improve, and so on. Both sides must continuously improve just to keep pace.

But it's not a normal Red Queen Effect; this one isn't fair. Defectors have a natural advantage, because they can make use of innovations to attack systems faster than society can use those innovations to defend itself. One of society's disadvantages is the delay between new societal pressures, and a corresponding change in the scope of defection, which we talked about in the previous chapter. In fact, the right half of Figure 14 is the same as the main feedback loop of Figure 13, but with less detail.

More generally, defectors are quicker to use technological innovations. Society has to implement any new security technology as a group, which implies agreement and coordination and—in some instances—a lengthy bureaucratic procurement process. Unfamiliarity is also an issue. Meanwhile, a defector can just use the new technology. For example, it's easier for a bank robber to use his new motorcar as a getaway vehicle than it is for the police department to decide it needs one, get the budget to buy one, choose which one to buy, buy it, and then develop training and policies for it. And if only one police department does this, the bank robber can just move to another town. Corporations can make use of new technologies of influence and persuasion faster than society can develop resistance to them. It's easier for hackers to find security flaws in phone switches than it is for the phone companies to upgrade them. Criminals can form international partnerships faster than governments can. Defectors are more agile and more adaptable, making them much better at being early adopters of new technology.

We saw it in law enforcement's initial inability to deal with Internet crime. Criminals were simply more flexible. Traditional criminal organizations like the Mafia didn't move immediately onto the Internet; instead, new Internet-savvy criminals sprung up. They established websites like CardersMarket and DarkMarket, and established new crime organizations within a decade or so of the Internet's commercialization. Meanwhile, law enforcement simply didn't have the organizational fluidity to adapt as quickly. They couldn't fire their old-school detectives and replace them with people who understood the Internet. Their natural inertia and their tendency to sweep problems under the rug slowed things even more. They had to spend the better part of a decade playing catch-up.

There's one more problem. Defenders are in what the 19th-century military strategist Carl von Clausewitz called "the position of the interior." They have to defend against every possible attack, while the defector just has to find one flaw and one way through the defenses. As systems get more complicated due to technology, more attacks become possible. This means defectors have a first-mover advantage; they get to try the new attack first. As a result, society is constantly responding: shoe scanners in response to the shoe bomber, harder-to-counterfeit money in response to better counterfeiting technologies, better anti-virus software to combat the new computer viruses, and so on. The attacker's clear advantage increases the scope of defection further.

Of course, there are exceptions. Sometimes societal pressures improve without it being a reaction to an increase in the scope of defection. There are technologies that immediately benefit the defender and are of no use at all to the attacker. Fingerprint technology allowed police to identify suspects after they left the scene of the crime, and didn't provide any corresponding benefit to criminals, for example. The same thing happened with immobilizing technology for cars, alarm systems for houses, and computer authentication technologies. Some technologies benefit both, but still give more advantage to the defenders. The radio allowed street policemen to communicate remotely, which makes us safer than criminals communicating remotely endangers us.

Still, we tend to be reactive in security, and only implement new measures in response to an increased scope of defection.

Because the attackers generally innovate faster than the defenders, society needs time to get societal pressures right. The result of this is a security gap: the difference between the scope of defection that society is willing to tolerate and the scope of defection that exists. Generally, this gap hasn't been an insurmountable problem. Sure, some defectors are able to get away with whatever it is they're doing—sometimes for years or even decades—but society generally figures it out in the end. Technology has progressed slowly enough for the Red Queen Effect to work properly. And the slowness has even helped in some situations by minimizing overreactions.

The problem gets worse as technology improves, though. Look at Figure 15. On the top, you can see the difference between the defectors' use of technological innovation to attack systems and the defenders' use of technological innovations in security systems and other types of societal pressures. The security gap arising from the fact that the attackers are faster than the defenders is represented by the area under the technology curve between the two lines.

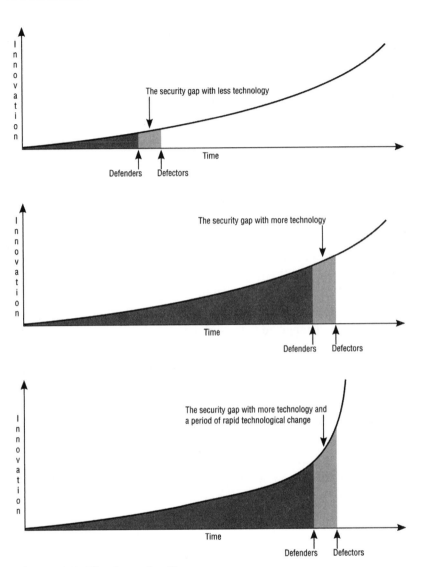

Figure 15: The Security Gap

Comparing the top picture with the middle one shows the difference between less and more technology. In the middle, the gap between attacker and defender is the same width, but because there's more technology, the area is greater. There are actually two dimensions to innovation: technological advancement and technological prevalence. In either dimension, the more technology there is, the greater the security gap. In other words, if there are more innovations to exploit, there will be more damage resulting from society's inability to keep up with exploiters of all of them.

Think about it this way. Technology is available to both the attackers and the defenders, and it's pretty much all there is until moral, reputational, and institutional pressures catch up. When there's more technology out there, the attackers have more opportunity to increase the scope of defection before the defenders catch up. Technology can affect the scope of defection in many ways, but in general, it gives the attackers more leverage. So the more technological a society is, the greater the security gap is.

This is an intrinsic condition of the problem, for all the reasons we just talked about. The security gap cannot be eliminated.

The security gap is also greater in periods of rapid technological change, as society struggles to manage the broader social changes as well as quickly adapting defectors do. In 1970, futurist Alvin Toffler wrote about *future shock*, the psychological and social problems that result from people being forced to absorb too much technological change too quickly. His estimates about how much technological change people could deal with were way too low—the rate of technological change in the second decade of the 21st century is much faster than the seventh decade of the 20th—but his basic ideas are sound. People learn how to cope with new technologies at their own pace, some more easily than others. And groups of people move more slowly than some of their members. Defectors are not inherently less susceptible to future shock than society at large, but the more successful ones are. Successful defectors are always going to be able to outpace the average capability of society.

Again, look at Figure 15, the bottom this time. In a period of rapid change, technology increases faster, so the curve climbs higher in the same period of time than in the earlier figures. This faster growth rate makes for a larger area under the curve in the same period of time—a greater security gap.

This has happened before, notably in the 19th century. That's when we got railroads, steamships, the widespread use of paper mail, the telegraph, and then the telephone—all allowing people to communicate at greater distances and with greater speed. But perhaps even more important than any of that, there were significant changes in attitudes about people and the world. Society came to expect economic growth, along with universal education and universal betterment. The world changed, and that affected security.

The ease of rapid travel meant more people traveled. On one hand, this meant that you could no longer distrust people just because they came from "out of town." On the other, this allowed for a new type of grifter, conning people out of their money and moving on before he could be caught. At the same time, cities got larger. Policing in 18th-century London was a hodge-podge of unpaid and unorganized constables and a draconian court system (160 different crimes carried the death penalty). This sort of community policing didn't scale to a large modern city, so Sir Robert Peel organized the first modern police force and criminal justice system. Other cities followed suit.

Technology directly changed society as well. The telegraph meant that money could be transferred instantaneously, but the open nature of the system meant conversations could be eavesdropped on and spoofed. So operators developed codes to prevent that. Other examples were the mass production of timepieces, making it easier to manage employees; the rise of unions, giving employees more power with respect to their employers; and the telegraph and then the telephone, an enormous change in communication that affected everyone. It was an age where defectors adapted to a changing society, and society had to adapt to changing defectors.

Today, we're seeing the effects of both more technology than ever before *and* a faster rate of technological change than ever before.[2] In particular, the revolutionary social and political changes brought about by information technology are causing security and trust problems to a whole new degree. We've already seen several manifestations of this: the global financial crisis, international terrorism, and cyberspace fraud. We've seen music and movie piracy grow from a minor annoyance to an international problem due to the ease of distributing pirated content on the Internet. We've seen Internet worms progress from minor annoyances to criminal tools to military-grade weapons that cause real-world damage, like the Internet worm Stuxnet, the first military-grade cyberweapon the public has seen. All this has come about because information technology increases the scope of defection in several ways:

- *Migration of all data onto the Internet.* As data moves onto computer networks, there are more—and, more importantly, different—risks. The security that worked when the systems were manual, or housed on computers not attached to a global network, no longer works.[3]
- *Technological mediation of social systems.* Similarly, social systems—including systems of reputational pressure—are vulnerable to technological attacks as they become technologically enabled. For example, e-mail has security risks that paper mail does not. Electronic voting has security

risks that paper voting does not. Internet telephony has security risks that conventional telephony does not.

- *Migration of evolved social systems into deliberately created socio-technical systems.* In Chapter 14, we discussed the problem of delegating societal pressures to institutions, specifically government institutions. More and more, we are delegating societal pressures to corporations: the security of our conversations, our photographs, and our data. This trend of corporations acting as institutions gives those corporations more ability and incentive to defect.

- *Class breaks.* A product, or line of products, may have common vulnerabilities that impact every copy of the product that has ever been made. As globalization allows a single product to be used worldwide, the discovery of such a vulnerability can have a global impact. This is not new, but information systems are particularly prone to this type of problem. Information systems have common vulnerabilities that can be exploited *en masse.* Someone who finds, for example, a vulnerability in an operating system that allows him to steal data can steal data from the entire class of computers using that operating system.

- *Automation.* Information system attacks can be automated. Instead of manually having to break into computer systems, an attacker can write a program to do it automatically. This not only drastically increases the frequency of defection, it also has two other effects. One, it makes attacks whose probability of success is very small viable. And two, it makes attacks whose profitability is very small—so-called salami attacks because of how thinly sliced each instance of fraud is—viable.

- *Action at a distance.* Attacks that used to require the attacker to get up close and personal to his victims can now be done remotely, from anywhere on the planet. It used to be that a store in Los Angeles didn't have to worry about burglars living in London or Lagos; those places were simply too far away for it to be worth the burglar's time or expense to fly to Los Angeles. But on the Internet, every web store has to worry about every cyber burglar in the world. There are no natural defenses against distance. Similarly, 20 years ago, few Americans had to worry about encountering Ukrainian or Nigerian criminals. On the Internet, it happens constantly.

- *Technique propagation.* Because information system attacks can be automated and encapsulated in software, the capability to launch these attacks can propagate. No longer does a criminal have to learn how to attack a security system: pick a lock, defraud a bank, or whatever. On the Internet, only the first attacker has to be skilled. Everyone else can just use software.

- *Technique iteration and improvement.* Because attacks can be so efficient, it's easier for attackers to learn from their mistakes and improve their attacks. They can create ten varieties of a computer worm and test which one works best, or a hundred varieties of spam to see which one fools recipients best. Because so many Internet attack tools become public, it's easy for one attacker to learn from another's work.

- *Defector aggregation.* One thing that makes it easier to defect from society is finding a subgroup of defectors. This both makes it easier to overcome moral and reputational pressures, and allows defectors to trade tips on overcoming the legal pressure and security systems. The Internet itself lets defectors easily find and communicate with like-minded individuals. There's a whole online community of people who think childhood immunization is evil. There are terrorist-sympathetic websites, which might—it's hard to separate reality from media hype—also act as terrorist-recruiting websites. There are a gazillion places on the Internet where you can learn to hack computer systems and commit fraud.

There are two more changes that belong on this, too, but they won't fit neatly into bullet points: changes in organizational structure and changes in organizational behavior.

Let's start with organizational structure. The Internet reduces the cost of organization dramatically, enabling ad hoc and loosely connected organizations of individuals who contribute tiny amounts of effort towards a large goal.[4] Linux and Wikipedia are both informally produced and freely available "products" created by legions of unpaid volunteers; and both are viable competition to corporate, traditionally created, alternatives. Crowdsourcing can produce results superior to more traditional mechanisms of delegating work.

From a societal pressure perspective, the normal competing interests we've come to expect from traditional organizations don't apply in the same way to these ad hoc organizations. For example, Microsoft can be—and in the past has been—pressured by the U.S. government to deliberately weaken encryption software in its products, so the government could better spy on people. This works because Microsoft is an American corporation, and in at least some ways beholden to American interests. Its operating system competitor, Linux, is not. Linux is an open-source operating system, not controlled by a business. The Linux team, even the few individuals at the core, are not motivated by profit. They're not in any one country. They are probably unlikely to agree to a confidential meeting with government officials of any nationality. They are a different sort of actor. On the other hand, Microsoft probably has better systems in place to prevent infiltration by rogue programmers.

WikiLeaks is another stateless organization. WikiLeaks sits somewhere between a loose organization of activists and the personal mission of a single individual named Julian Assange. It exposes information that governments and powerful corporations would rather keep secret. In this way it is very much like an organization of journalists. But because it is not a commercial enterprise, and because it is not moored within a country, it's much more difficult to corral. And this scares countries like the United States.

Compare WikiLeaks to a traditional newspaper. That newspaper is in a societal dilemma with all the other newspapers in that country.

Societal Dilemma: Newspapers publishing government secrets.	
Society: All the newspapers in the country and the government.	
Group interest: Government not clamping down on freedom of the press. Group norm: Self-censor.	Competing interest: Increase market share. Corresponding defection: Publish any juicy secrets you discover.
To encourage people to act in the group interest, the society implements a variety of societal pressures. Moral: It's unpatriotic, or otherwise wrong, to publish government secrets. Reputational: Newspapers want good reputations because it keeps their readers, advertisers, and sources all happy. Institutional: Often, none. In fact, the U.S. Supreme Court has held that it is legal to publish secrets, even though it is illegal to leak them. Security: Potentially, espionage that lets the government know when a story is about to leak.	

This doesn't look like effective societal pressure, but it largely works. It works because, even in the absence of any laws, the pressure to cooperate—to self-censor—is surprisingly powerful. No press organization wants to be labeled as unpatriotic or traitorous, or jeopardize its advertisers.

The result is that newspapers sometimes publish embarrassing government secrets, and sometimes they don't. In 1971, the *New York Times* published the Pentagon Papers, a secret and damning history of U.S. military involvement in Vietnam. In mid-2004, the *New York Times* learned about the NSA's illegal wiretapping of American citizens without a warrant, but delayed publishing the information for over a year—until well after the presidential election. Presumably there are things the *New York Times* has learned about and decided not to publish, period.

WikiLeaks changes that dynamic. It's not an American company. It's not even a for-profit company. It's not a company at all. And it's not really located in any legal jurisdiction. It simply isn't subject to the same pressures that the *New York Times* is. This means the government can't rely on the partial cooperation of WikiLeaks in the same way it can rely on that of traditional newspapers.[5]

In a blog post about the topic, Clay Shirky referred to the Supreme Court ruling in the Pentagon Papers case that said it's illegal to leak secrets but not illegal to publish leaks:

> The legal bargain from 1971 simply does not and cannot produce the outcome it used to. This is one of the things freaking people in the US government out about the long-term change in the media environment—not that the law has changed, but that the world has. Industrial era law, applied to internet-era publishing, might allow for media outlets which exhibit no self-restraint around national sensitivities, because they are run by people without any loyalty to—or, more importantly, need of—national affiliation to do their jobs.

Foreign journalists pose a similar problem. The U.S. government has much less leverage to pressure *El Pais* or Al Jazeera to change its coverage than it does with the *New York Times*. That mattered less before the Internet could bring all those news sources to everyone so easily.

This unmooring of institutions from nationality is upending many societal pressures; things that used to work no longer do. We saw the same dynamic in international corporations, which can more easily skirt national laws by moving between different countries.

Now to the final change, which is organization behavior. In addition to allowing organizations to grow in size, and therefore power, and facilitating new types of organizational structures, information technology is also changing how organizations act.

There have been many books and articles discussing how corporations today are putting short-term stock prices above all other business considerations, including company health and long-term shareholder value. I've read lots of explanations for this change. That executives' bonuses are based on short-term numbers. That stocks are used more for short-term "bets" than for long-term investments. That mutual funds and complex index options further remove investors from the companies they invest in. And that investors have access to more information faster—and can act on that information faster.

You get what you measure,[6] and things like short-term profitability are much easier to measure than abstract concepts like long-term viability, or intangibles like customer satisfaction or reputation. An important facilitator for this dynamic—I don't know whether it's a cause or not—is information technology. Improved information technology makes the short-term numbers easier to monitor, so investors monitor them much more closely than ever before. This continuous monitoring makes them easier to optimize. We are better able to predict what a company's balance sheet will look like next week, and because we're so quick to trade one company for another, we care much less what it will look like in five years. This necessarily changes how investing works and how organizations behave: and the two are locked in a positive-feedback loop.

All these effects of ever-faster information technology affect other organizations at every scale, from the smallest groups to the entire world.

●   ●   ●

Modern large and technological trade-offs between group interest and competing interest are what social planners call wicked problems. These are problems that are difficult (or impossible) to solve because of incomplete, poorly understood, contradictory, or changing requirements; because of complex interdependencies; and because of their uniqueness and novelty. Examples include global climate change, AIDS and pandemics in general, nuclear waste, terrorism and homeland security, drug trafficking and other international smuggling, and national healthcare. All of those problems involve societal pressures, and all of their solutions involve coercing people into following group norms ahead of other competing interests.

But—and this is important—all of the big societal pressure problems are about more than trust and security. They're interdependent with other societal dilemmas. They're interdependent with other societal systems. They have moral, social, economic, and political dimensions. Their solutions involve answering questions about how society organizes itself, the role of national and international government, the extent of individual liberties, and what sort of outcomes are optimal and desirable. And these aspects of the problems are far more important, and difficult, than the trust aspects. It's not simply a matter of implementing the best societal pressures to induce broad cooperation; everything else matters more. The geopolitics that results in terrorism matter much more than any particular security measure against terrorists. The politics in which multinational corporations thrive matter much more than the societal pressures to ensure those corporations cooperate. The politics surrounding drug laws, tax laws, laws protecting civil liberties, and our social safety net matter much more than the societal pressures to ensure that those laws are followed. Look back to the figure in Chapter 15; the "constraints" and the "other considerations" are more important than the primary loop.

Here's one example. In 2011, science fiction author Charles Stross gave a talk on the ubiquity of data that's coming in the near future, from technologies like genetic mapping, "lifeblogging"—the audio and video recording of everything that happens to you—sensors on everyone and everything. Nothing he said required anything more than mild extrapolation. And then he talked about the issues that society is going to have to wrestle with once this data exists:

> Is losing your genomic privacy an excessive price to pay for surviving cancer and evading plagues? (Broad analysis of everyone's genetic data will result in significant new understanding about disease, and a flurry of medical results that will significantly benefit everyone. At the same time, an individual's genetic data is both personal and private—even more so when companies start using it to prejudge people.)

> Is compromising your sensory privacy through lifeblogging a reasonable price to pay for preventing malicious impersonation and apprehending criminals? (Lifeblogs have the potential to be a valuable police tool, not just by allowing victims to record crimes, but in the incidental recording of events in the background that later could be instrumental in identifying criminals.)

> Is letting your insurance company know exactly how you steer and hit the gas and brake pedals, and where you drive, an acceptable price to pay for cheaper insurance? (Once insurance companies have all of this data, they could more easily offer differing insurance policy to different types of drivers.)

These are all societal dilemmas about how to balance group interest with self-interest. But before figuring out what kind of societal pressures to deploy to solve the problem, society first has to agree what the group interest is. We can't start talking about what kind of societal pressures to set up to prevent people from keeping their genome secret, or protecting the privacy of their lifeblog, or limiting access to their car's "black box" data, until we agree on what it means to cooperate and what it means to defect in these situations. It's difficult to solve societal dilemmas while society itself is changing so quickly.

This isn't the first time technological change has caused social changes that forced us to rethink society, and it won't be the last. The trick will be getting societal pressure right in a society that's moving so fast that getting it wrong is an increasingly dangerous option. This means getting faster and better at setting societal pressure knobs. It means setting them right the first time, and then correcting them quickly in response to feedback, delays, and technological changes. To that end, here is a list of principles for designing effective societal pressures:

- *Understand the societal dilemma.* Not just what the group interest is, but what the group norm is, what the competing norms are, how the societal dilemma relates to other societal dilemmas, what the acceptable scope of defection is, and so on. A lot of ineffective societal pressures come from not understanding the true problem.

- *Consider all four societal pressures.* It's common to believe that one is enough: that reputation obviates the need for laws, or that a good security system is sufficient to enforce compliance. It's rare that this is true, and effective societal pressure usually involves all four categories, though not necessarily in equal measure. Considering all four will indicate how resources might be most effectively spent.

- *Pay attention to scale.* The scale of the societal dilemma influences how effective each of the four societal pressures will be. Noticing the scale, and noticing when the scale changes, is vital.

- *Foster empathy and community, increasing moral and reputational pressures.* In our large, anonymous society, it's easy to forget moral and reputational pressures and concentrate on legal pressure and security systems. This is a mistake; even though our informal social pressures fade into the background, they're still responsible for most of the cooperation in society.

- *Use security systems to scale moral and reputational pressures.* The two social pressures work best on the small scale, but security systems can enhance them to work at much larger scales. They don't work the same way, and the security systems are themselves open to attack. Still, we can't simply replace moral and reputational pressures with institutional pressures, so it is important to use technology in this way.

- *Harmonize institutional pressures across related technologies.* There shouldn't be one law for paper mail and another for e-mail, or one law for telephone conversations and another for Internet telephony. This sort of thing used to work back when technology changed slowly. Now, by the time the legal system grinds through the process of creating a law, it may already be technologically obsolete. We need to make laws technologically invariant. This won't be easy, but we need to try.

- *Ensure that financial penalties account for the likelihood that a defection will be detected.* As I discussed in Chapter 13, a financial penalty that is too low can easily become a cost of doing business. If we expect a fine to be an effective societal pressure, it needs to be more expensive than the risk of defecting and paying it.

- *Choose general and reactive security systems.* Just as we need to make laws technologically invariant, we need to make security systems defector-invariant. That is, we need to concentrate on the broad motivations for defection, rather than on blocking specific tactics, to prevent defectors from working around security systems. One example is counterterrorism, where society is much better off spending money on intelligence, investigation, and emergency response than on preventing specific terrorist threats, like bombs hidden in shoes or underwear.

- *Reduce concentrations of power.* Power, whether it's concentrated in government, corporations, or non-government organizations, brings with it the ability to defect. The greater the power, the greater the scope of defection.[7] One of the most important things society can do to reduce the risk of catastrophic defection is to reduce the amount of power held by individual actors in key positions.

- *Require transparency—especially in corporations and government institutions.* Transparency minimizes the principal–agent problem and ensures the maximum effect of reputational pressures. In our complex society, we can't monitor most societal dilemmas directly. We need to rely on others—proxies—to do the work for us. Checks and balances are the most powerful tool we have to facilitate this, and transparency is the best way to ensure that checks and balances work. A corollary of this is that society should not suppress information about defectors, their tactics, and the overall scope of defection.

We're currently in a period of history where technology is changing faster than it ever has. The worry is that if technology changes too fast, the defectors will be able to innovate so much faster than society can that the imbalances become even greater—increased scope of defection leading to an even more increased scope of defection—which can cause large societal failures. Think of what would happen to the Red Queen Effect if the stoats evolved faster than the rabbits: they would become significantly faster than the rabbits, then eat all the rabbits, and then all starve (assume there's no other prey). Defectors in societal dilemmas can have the same effect if they evolve too quickly: they overwhelm the cooperators, which means there are no more cooperators, and the defectors themselves lose. Remember, parasites need society to be there in order to benefit from defecting; and being a parasite is a successful strategy only if you don't take too many resources from your host.

On the other hand, we're also in a period of history where the ability for large-scale cooperation is greater than it ever has been before. In 2011, law professor Yochai Benkler published a book that is in many ways a companion volume to this one: *The Penguin and The Leviathan: How Cooperation Triumphs Over Self-Interest*. Benkler writes that the Internet can and has enabled cooperation on a scale never seen before, and that politics—backed by science—is ready to embrace this new cooperation:

> I am optimistic in thinking that we are not ripe to take on the task of using human cooperation to its fullest potential—to make our businesses more profitable, our economy more efficient, our scientific breakthroughs more radical, and our society safer, happier and more stable....
>
> For decades we have been designing systems tailored to harness selfish tendencies, without regard to potential negative effects on the enormous potential for cooperation that pervades society. We can do better. We can design systems—be they legal or technical; corporate or civic; administrative or commercial—that let our humanity find a fuller expression; systems that tap into a far greater promise and potential of human endeavor than we have generally allowed in the past.

The lesson of this book isn't that defectors will inevitably ruin everything for everyone, but that we need to manage societal pressures to ensure they don't. We've seen how our prehistoric toolbox of social pressures—moral and reputational systems—does that on a small scale, how institutions enhance that on a larger scale, and how technology helps all three systems scale even more.

Over a decade ago, I wrote that "security is a process, not a product." That's true for all societal pressures. The interplay of all the feedback loops means that both the scope of defection and the scope of defection society is willing to tolerate are constantly moving targets. There is no "getting it right"; this process never ends.

The Future

Society can't function without trust, and our complex, interconnected, and global society needs a lot of it. We need to be able to trust the people we interact with directly: as we sit next to them on airplanes, eat the food they serve us in the cabin, and get into their taxis when we land. We need to be able to trust the organizations and institutions that make modern society possible: that the airplanes we fly and the cars we ride in are well-made and well-maintained, that the food we buy is safe and their labels truthful, that the laws in the places we live and the places we travel will be enforced fairly. We need to be able to trust all sorts of technological systems: that the ATM network, the phone system, and the Internet will work wherever we are. We need to be able to trust strangers, singly and in organizations, all over the world all the time. We also need to be able to trust indirectly; we need to trust the trust people we don't already know and systems we don't yet understand. We need to trust trust.

Making this all work ourselves is impossible. We can't even begin to personally verify, and then deliberately decide whether or not to trust, the hundreds—thousands?—of people we interact with directly, and the millions of others we interact with indirectly, as we go about our daily lives. That's just too many, and we'll never meet them all. And even if we could magically decide to trust the people, we don't have the expertise to make technical and scientific decisions about trusting things like airplane safety, modern banking, and pharmacology.

Writing about trust, economist Bart Nooteboom said: "Trust in things or people entails the willingness to submit to the risk that they may fail us, with the expectation that they will not, or the neglect of lack of awareness of that possibility that they might." Those three are all intertwined: we aren't willing to risk unless we're sure in our expectation that the risk is minor, so minor that most of the time we don't even have to think about it.

That's the value of societal pressures. They induce compliance with the group norms—that is, cooperation—so we're able to approximate the intimate trust we have in our friends on a much larger scale. It's not perfect, of course. The trust we have in actions and systems isn't as broad or deep as personal trust, but it's good enough. Societal pressures reduce the scope of defection. In a sense, by trusting societal pressures, we don't have to do the work of figuring out whether or not to trust individuals.

By inducing cooperation throughout society, societal pressures allow us to relax our guard a little bit. It's less stressful to live in a world where you trust people. Once you assume people can, in general and with qualifications, be trusted to be fair, nice, altruistic, cooperative, and trustworthy, you can stop expending energy constantly worrying about security. Then, even though you get burned by the occasional exception, your life is still more comfortable if you continue to believe.[1]

We intuitively know this, even if we've never analyzed the mechanisms before. But the mechanisms of societal pressure are important. Societal pressures enable society's doves to thrive, even though there's a minority of hawks. Societal pressures enable society.

And despite the largest trust gap in our history, it largely works. It's easy to focus on defection—the crime, the rudeness, the complete mess of the political system in several countries around the world—but the evidence is all around you. Society is still here, alive and ticking. Trust is common, as is fairness, altruism, cooperation, and kindness. People don't automatically attack strangers or cheat each other. Murders, burglaries, fraud, and so on are rare.

We have a plethora of security systems to deal with the risks that remain. We know how to walk through the streets of our communities. We know how to shop on the Internet. We know how to interact with friends and strangers, whether—and how—to lock our doors at night, and what precautions to take against crime. The very fact that I was able to write and publish this book, and you were able to buy and read it, is a testament to all of our societal pressure systems. We might get it wrong sometimes, but we largely get it right.

At the same time, defection abounds. Defectors in our society have become more powerful, and they've learned to evade and sometimes manipulate societal pressures to enable their continued defection. They've used the rapid pace of technological change to increase their scope of defection, while society remains unable to implement new societal pressures fast enough in response. Societal pressures fail regularly.

The important thing to remember is this: no security system is perfect. It's hard to admit in our technologically advanced society that we can't do something, but in security there are a lot of things we can't do. This isn't a reason to live in fear, or even necessarily a cause for concern. This is the normal state of life. It might even be a good thing. Being alive entails risk, and there always will be outliers. Even if you reduced the murder rate to one in a million, three hundred unlucky people in the U.S. would be murdered every year.

These are not technical problems, though societal pressures are filled with those. No, the biggest and most important problems are at the policy level: global climate change, regulation and governance, political process, civil liberties, the social safety net. Historically, group interests either coalesced organically around the people concerned, or were dictated by a government. Today, understanding group interests increasingly involves scientific expertise, or new social constructs stemming from new technologies, or different problems resulting from yet another increase in scale.

Philosopher Sissela Bok wrote: "...trust is a social good to be protected just as much as the air we breathe or the water we drink. When it is damaged the community as a whole suffers; and when it is destroyed, societies falter and collapse." More generally, trust is the key component of social capital, and high-trust societies are better off in many dimensions than low-trust societies. And in the world today, levels of trust vary all over the map—although never down to the level of baboons.[2]

We're now at a critical juncture in society: we need to implement new societal systems to deal with the new world created by today's globalizing technologies. It is critical that we understand what societal pressures do and don't do, why they work and fail, and how scale affects them. If we do, we can continue building trust into our society. If we don't, the parasites will kill the host.

In closing, there are several points I want to make.

No matter how much societal pressure you deploy, there always will be defectors. All complex ecosystems contain parasites, and all human systems of cooperation and trust include people who try to take advantage of them. This will not change as long as societies are made up of humans. The possibility of perfect trust, or unbreakable security, is a science-fiction future that won't happen in the lifetime of anyone we know.

Increasing societal pressure isn't always worth it. It's not just the problem of diminishing returns discussed in Chapter 10. Looking back through history, the societies that enforce cooperation and conformance to the group norm, that ruthlessly clamp down and punish defectors, and that monitor every aspect of their citizens' lives are not societies we think of as free. This is true whether the norms accurately reflect the desires of the group or are imposed from the top down.[3] Security always has side effects and unwanted consequences.

This is okay. We've repeatedly talked about societal pressures as being necessary to sustain trust.[4] This doesn't mean absolute trust, and it doesn't imply 100% cooperation. As long as the murder rate is low enough, speeders are few enough, and policemen on the take are rare enough, society flourishes.

Societal pressures can prevent cooperation, too. Not only do we sometimes fail to punish the guilty, we sometimes punish the innocent. People get reputations they don't deserve; people get convicted of crimes they didn't commit. And if the scope of defection is low enough, these false positives can be greater than the defection attempts thwarted. That's when you know it's time to dial back the knob.

We all defect at some times regarding some things. Sometimes we're simply being selfish. Sometimes we have another, stronger, self-interest. Sometimes we're just not paying attention. Sometimes our morality just doesn't permit us to cooperate with the group norm. And sometimes we feel a stronger attachment to another group, and its associated interests and norms. This is also okay.

Sometimes we defect honestly and innocently. Group norms can be too rigid for the way we live our lives. The white lies of our normal social interactions make relationships better, not worse. Sometimes assistants need to sign documents for their bosses, and sometimes attorneys and accountants need to innocently backdate documents. Sometimes defecting is a form of social lubricant: small social dishonesties that make life easier for everyone.

There are good defectors and there are bad defectors, and we can't always tell the difference—even though we think we can. We know that murderers are always bad and that pro-democracy demonstrators are always good, but even those truisms fray at the edges. Was the U.S.'s assassination of Osama bin Ladin good or bad? Is it okay that pro-democracy protesters in Egypt and other countries are anti-U.S. and anti-Israel? U.S. troops in Iraq may be either good or bad, depending on whether you're safely in the U.S., whether your daughter was just killed by one of them, or whether you own an oil company. Many defectors believe they are morally right: animal-rights activists who free animals from testing laboratories, the Sandinistas in Nicaragua, and the Nazis in Germany, just to name a few. And so did the Tiananmen Square protesters in China, and the United States' founding fathers.

I stumbled on this parable on the Internet as I was writing this book:

> There was this kid who came from a poor family. He had no good options in life so he signed up for the military. After a few years he was deployed to a conflict infested, god-forsaken desert outpost. It was the worst tour of duty he could have been assigned. It was going to be hot and dangerous. Every day he had to live with a hostile populace who hated his presence and the very sight of his uniform. Plus, the place was swarming with insurgents and terrorists.
>
> Anyhow, one morning the soldier goes to work and finds that he's been assigned that day to a detail that is supposed to oversee the execution of three convicted insurgents. The soldier shakes his head. He didn't sign up for this. His life just totally sucks. "They don't pay me enough," he thinks, "for the shit I have to do."
>
> He doesn't know he's going to be executing the Son of God that day. He's just going to work, punching the time clock, keeping his head down. He's just trying to stay alive, get through the day, and send some money back home to Rome.

Systems of societal pressure can't tell the difference between good or bad defectors. Societal pressures are the mechanism by which societies impose rules upon themselves, even as the societies overlap and conflict. Those rules could be good, like a respect for human rights or a system for enforcing contracts. Those rules could be bad, like slavery, totalitarianism, persecution, or ritual murder. Or those rules could be perceived as good by some societies and bad by others: arranged marriages; heavy taxation; and prohibitions against drinking, dancing, pot smoking, or sharing music files via BitTorrent. Societal pressures simply enforce cooperation, without much consideration as to why the defector chose some competing interest. This is a good thing when it protects individuals from harm, loss, or social injustice, and a bad thing when it protects a regime that is not good to its people or prevents positive social change.

Society needs defectors. Groups benefit from the fact that some members do not follow the group norms. These are the outliers: the people who resist popular opinion for moral or other reasons. These are the people who invent new business models by copying and distributing music, movies, and books on the Internet. These are people like Copernicus and Galileo, who challenged official Church dogma on astronomy. These are the people who—to take a recent example—disrupt energy auctions to protest government responsibility for climate change. They're also people living on the edge of society: squatters, survivalists, artists, cults, communes, hermits, and those who live off the grid or off the land. In 2011, U.S. Marine Dakota Meyer received the Medal of Honor for saving three dozen of his comrades who were under enemy fire. The thing is, he disobeyed orders in order to do so.

Defection represents an engine for innovation, an immunological challenge to ensure the health of the majority, a defense against the risk of monoculture, a reservoir of diversity, and a catalyst for social change. It's through defection from bad or merely outdated social norms that our society improves. In the stoat vs. rabbit Red Queen Effect from Chapter 2, it's the stoats that drive the change. Left to themselves, the rabbits will not improve.

This is important. The societies that societal pressures protect are not necessarily moral or desirable. In fact, they can protect some pretty awful ones. And because societal pressures necessarily become institutionalized—in police forces, in government agencies, in corporate security departments—they can be co-opted to justify and maintain those awful societies' awful institutions.

Sometimes a whistle-blower needs to publish documents proving his government has been waging an illegal bombing campaign in Laos and Cambodia. Sometimes a plutonium processing plant worker needs to contact a reporter to discuss her employer's inadequate safety practices. And sometimes a black woman needs to sit down at the front of a bus and not get up. Without defectors, social change would be impossible; stagnation would set in.

It's a tough balancing act, but I think we're up to it. Maybe not in the near term, but in the long term. History teaches how often we get it right. As Martin Luther King, Jr., said: "The arc of history is long, but it bends toward justice."[5]

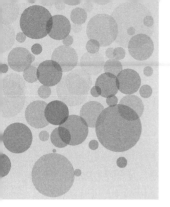

Acknowledgments

I consider writing a book to be a social as well as a solitary activity. As such, I have a great number of people to thank.

First, thank you to all the participants of the four Security and Human Behavior Workshops, for sparking many of the ideas that went into this book. Thank you to my primary researcher, Kathleen Seidel, for her ability to find just what I need whether I know it exists or not, and also to Deborah Pursch for additional research. Thank you to the Hennepin County Library, which already had many of the books I needed, and got me absolutely everything else I asked for via interlibrary loan...even if I could only keep any one thing for three weeks.

Thank you to all the people who read this book in varying stages of completion. Steve Bass, Charles Faulkner, Greg Guerin, Victoria Gaile Laidler, Stephen Leigh, and David Prentiss read an early draft of the book, and were especially helpful in organizing my initial ideas. Dorothy Denning and Jay Walker read a later draft, and both suggested a reframing—on the same day, coincidentally—that turned out to be particularly useful. Rebecca Kessler gave the book a badly needed final edit. Andrew Acquisti, Andrew Adams, Michael Albaugh, Ross Anderson, Marcia Ballinger, Jason Becker, David Brown, Steve Brust, Tyler Burns, Jon Callas, David Campbell, Raphael Carter, Cody Charette, Dave Clark, Ron Clarke, Chris Cocking, Karen Cooper, David Cowan, Tammy Coxen, Cory Doctorow, John Douceur, Kevin Drum, Nicole Emery, Oisin Feeley, Eric Forste, Amy Forsyth, Peter Fraser-Mackenzie, J. Carl Ganter, Edward Goldstick, Sarah Green, Rachael Greenstadt, Jim Harper, Bill Herdle, Cormac Herley, Chris Hoofnagle, Leif Huhn, Owen Imholte, David Kahn, Jerry Kang, Arlene Katz, John Kelsey, Lori Kingerly, David Leach, David Mandel, Chris Manning, Petréa Mitchell, David Modic, Josh More, Doug Morgenstern, John Mueller, Peter Neumann, Andrew Odlyzko, Evan Oslick, Gerrit Padgham, Cirsten Paine,

Ross Patty, David Perry, Daniele Raffo, Coe Roberts, Peter Robinson, Dave Romm, David Ropeik, Marc Rotenberg, Stuart Schechter, Jeff Schmidt, Martin Schneier, David Schroth, Eric Seppanen, Susan Shapiro, Adam Shostack, Daniel Solove, Thomas Sprinkmeier, Nisheeth Srivastava, Frank Stajano, Mark Stewart, Steven L. Victor, Alan Wagner-Krankel, Paul Wallich, Chris Walsh, Rick Wash, Skyler White, and Jeff Yan also commented on all or part of the book.

Thank you to all the readers of my blog, who read my intermittent posts on the book's progress and regularly left insightful comments. Thank you to Carol Kennedy, who suggested the title in one of those comments. Thank you to Luke Fretwell, who designed a cover because he didn't like any of the candidates I posted. His idea ended up being the inspiration for the final cover.

Thank you to Josh More, for creating all the diagrams and putting up with my endless changes and tweaks. Thank you to Kee Nethery for proofreading the galleys. Thank you to Beth Friedman, for copyediting the book before it even got to my publisher, for dealing with all the MS-Word style issues, and for inserting herself between me and the copyeditor.

Thank you to Carol Long, Ashley Zurcher, Ellen Gerstein, and Tom Dinse at Wiley for helping turn the manuscript into an actual book.

Finally, thank you to the Suiboku Museum of Toyama, Japan, for the ink painting of a bulbul that adorned the manuscript cover during the writing process.

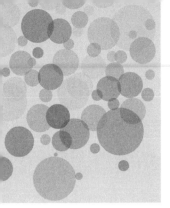

Notes

Chapter 1

Numbers preceding the notes refer to endnote numbers.

(1) In his book, *The Speed of Trust*, Stephen Covey talks about five levels of trust, which he calls "waves": self-trust, relationship trust, organizational trust, market trust, and societal trust.

(2) Piero Ferrucci wrote:

> To trust is to bet. Each time we trust, we put ourselves on the line. If we confide in a friend, we can be betrayed. If we put faith in a partner, we can be abandoned. If we trust in the world, we can be crushed. Far too often it ends that way. But the alternative is worse still, because if we do not put ourselves on the line, nothing will happen.

(3) Diego Gambetta: "When we say we trust someone or that someone is trustworthy, we implicitly mean that the probability that he will perform an action that is beneficial or at least not detrimental to us is high enough for us to consider engaging in some form of cooperation with him."

(4) David Messick and Roderick Kramer: "We will define trust in these situations as making the decision *as if* the other person or persons will abide by ordinary ethical rules that are involved in the situation."

(5) Sociologist Anthony Giddens proposed a similar three-level progression of trust:

> Trust in persons...is built upon mutuality of response and involvement: faith in the integrity of another is a prime source of a feeling of integrity and authenticity of the self. Trust in abstract systems provides for the security of day-to-day reliability, but by its very nature cannot supply either the mutuality or intimacy which personal trust relations offer....

In pre-modern settings, basic trust is slotted into personalised trust relations in the community, kinship ties, and friendships. Although any of these social connections can involve emotional intimacy, this is not a condition of the maintaining of personal trust. Institutionalised personal ties and informal or informalised codes of sincerity and honour provide (potential, by no means always actual) frameworks of trust....

With the development of abstract systems, trust in impersonal principles, as well as in anonymous others, becomes indispensable to social existence.

(6)   Piotr Cofta covered similar ground in his book *Trust, Complexity, and Control*.

(7)   Not coincidentally, I, along with colleagues Ross Anderson and Alessandro Acquisti, founded the annual Interdisciplinary Workshop on Security and Human Behavior in 2008.

(8)   Coming from mathematical security—cryptography—where research results are facts, it can be unsettling to research fields where there are theories, competing theories, overturned theories, and long-standing debates about theories. It sometimes seems that nothing is ever settled in the social sciences, and that for every explanation, there's a counter-explanation. Even worse, a reasonable case can be made that most research findings are false and there is sloppy methodology in the social sciences, primarily because of the pressure to produce newsworthy results. Also, that many results are based on experiments on a narrow and unrepresentative slice of humanity. The only way I can see to navigate this is to look at both the individual research results and the broader directions and meta-results.

(9)   Adam Smith wrote:

If there is any society among robbers and murderers, they must at least, according to the trite observation, abstain from robbing and murdering one another. Beneficence, therefore, is less essential to the existence of society than justice. Society may subsist, tho' not in the most comfortable state, without beneficence; but the prevalence of injustice must utterly destroy it.

Chapter 2

(1)   Chimpanzees have been observed using sticks as weapons, and wrasses have been observed using rocks to open up shells.

(2)   Some of this can be pretty complex; a single Brants's whistling rat builds a burrow with dozens or hundreds of entrances, so there's always one close by to retreat to. There's even an African rat that applies a tree poison to its fur to make itself deadly.

(3) Just recently, an entirely separate, probably older, immune system was discovered in bacteria and archaea, called *Clustered Regularly Interspaced Short Palindromic Repeats* or CRISPRs.

(4) In an earlier book, I mistakenly called this the "establishing reflex."

(5) In one experiment, children were faster at picking out a picture of a snake than pictures of more benign objects.

(6) Stephen Jay Gould used to call these "Just So Stories" because they rarely have any proof other than plausibility (and the fact that they make a good story). So while these seem like possible evolutionary explanations, there is still controversy in evolutionary biology over the levels of selection at work in any given instance. Certainly not all evolutionary biologists would accept these necessarily simple descriptions, although they would concur with the general outline that there was some evolutionary advantage to the possession of certain genes manifesting certain phenotypes in certain populations.

(7) Among other things, human intelligence is unique in the complexity of its expression, and its ability to comprehend the passage of time. More related to security, humans are vastly ahead of even chimpanzees in their ability to understand cause and effect in the physical world.

(8) No other creature on the planet does this. To use the words of philosopher Alfred Korzybski, humans are the only time binding species: we are the only species that can pass information and knowledge between generations at an accelerating rate. Other animals can pass knowledge between generations, but we're the only animal that does it at observable rates.

(9) All 5,600 or so species of mammals are at least minimally social, if only in mating and child-rearing.

(10) To use the words of philosopher Daniel Dennett, we need to adopt an *intentional stance* in order to understand each other. That is, instead of looking at people as physical objects or even biological systems, we have to look at them in terms of beliefs, intents, and thoughts.

(11) There's evidence from rodents that social group size is directly correlated with individuality.

(12) There's even a theory that reasoning evolved not because we needed to make better decisions, but because we needed to win arguments and convince other humans.

(13) Of course, this does not necessarily mean that the sole purpose of the neocortex is to deceive.

(14) It's actually a range between 100 and 230; 150 is the most common value. Dunbar has often said "150, plus or minus 50." Others posit the number is 200-ish. Groups that are more focused on survival tend to be larger, because "there's safety in numbers."

(15)   Larger group sizes aren't as stable because their members don't know each other well enough. We interact with people outside this circle more as categories or roles: the mailman, the emergency room nurse, that guy in the accounting department. We might recognize them as individuals, but we tend not to know a lot about them. A modern human might have a virtual network of 2,000 Facebook friends, but it's unlikely that he'll have more than a casual acquaintance with even a tenth of them.

(16)   Modern data from primitive peoples validates this number. In the primitive tribes of the New Guinea highlands, who lived apart from the rest of the world until the 1930s, about 25% of men and 5% of women died in warfare. The Yanomamö live in the upper reaches of the Orinoco River in Venezuela and Brazil. While they once had only sporadic contact with other cultures, they still lived apart in their traditional manner. They lost 24% of men and 7% of women to warfare.

(17)   Big-game hunting is inefficient because: 1) big game's low density means fewer encounters, 2) it's harder to catch, 3) it can hurt you when you hunt it, 4) it requires a lot of people to catch, 5) it takes a lot of work to butcher and preserve, and 6) it's perishable, and must be eaten quickly or preserved before it spoils.

(18)   Chimpanzees' aggression rates are two to three orders of magnitude higher than humans', although their lethal aggression rates are about the same as those of human subsistence societies.

Chapter 3

(1)   There is evidence that increased specialization is a function of group size. To be fair, there are researchers who maintain that division of labor is not what makes leafcutter ants so successful.

(2)   To some extent, this is also true of other social insects that don't have polymorphism. Bees, for instance, tend to change specializations as they age, but they can change early if some task is going undone. Leafcutter ants can't do this; they're physiologically distinct according to role.

(3)   This startling statistic comes from the fact that there are a lot of other organisms in our digestive tract: "The adult human organism is said to be composed of approximately 10^{13} eukaryotic animal cells. That statement is only an expression of a particular point of view. The various body surfaces and the gastrointestinal canals of humans may be colonized by as many as 10^{14} indigenous prokaryotic and eukaryotic microbial cells." Note that the percentage is by number, not by volume or weight. All those digestive organisms are much, much smaller than our own cells.

(4)   The initial paper is actually more complicated. In addition to hawks and doves, there are bullies who only pick on doves, retaliators who respond as hawks against hawks

and as doves against doves, and so on. And many other game theorists wrote papers analyzing this or that variant of the Hawk-Dove game, looking at other strategies or more complications in the simulation. But this simple representation is sufficient for our needs. Adding some sort of "fighting skill" parameter is a complexity that doesn't add to our understanding, either.

(5)   Researchers have also conducted Hawk-Dove games with more fluid strategies. Instead of being 100% hawk or 100% dove, individuals could be a combination of both. That is, one individual might behave as a dove 80% of the time and as a hawk 20% of the time. What that individual does in any given situation might be random, or depend on circumstance. This complication better mirrors the behavior of real people.

Another way to make strategies more fluid is to allow individuals to use some mixture of hawk and dove strategies in a *single* encounter. So instead of either being all hawk or all dove, an individual might be 20% hawk/80% dove. That is, she might cooperate a lot but not fully or exclusively. This is definitely a more realistic model; we cooperate to different degrees with different people at different times.

In this more complicated model, it's much harder for cooperative behavior to appear. If everyone is constantly switching from the dove camp to the hawk camp and vice versa—as happens in most species—a genetic mutation that enables a small amount of cooperation doesn't confer enough benefit to take hold in the broader population before it gets stamped out by the defectors taking advantage of it.

(6)   Of course this is simplistic. The effects of laws on crime isn't nearly as direct and linear as this example. We'll talk about this more in Chapter 9. But the basic idea is correct.

(7)   The costs and benefits of being a hawk also depend on population density. In simulations, dense populations have more doves, and sparse populations more hawks.

(8)   South African meerkats raise their young communally; even distantly related non-breeders will pitch in to protect newborn pups in their burrows, deliver them beetles, scorpions, and lizards to eat, and even pass along new foods mouth-to-mouth to help them become accustomed to unfamiliar flavors. Red ruffed lemurs engage in extensive alloparenting.

(9)   It's much less common in the wild. It's also slow; there is evidence that mutualism appears to evolve more slowly than other traits.

(10)   Between species, mutualism is more commonly known as symbiosis. Wrasse cleaner fish are the canonical example; they eat parasites and dead skin off larger fish. This feeds the wrasses and provides a health benefit to the larger fish. Similarly, clownfish tend to stay within the tentacles of Ritteri sea anemones; each protects the other from predators. Pollination, too: the bees get food, and the plants get pollinated. It is easy for mutualistic relationships to evolve, which is why they are common throughout the natural world.

(11)   Sometimes, the benefit of fighting and winning is so great that most individuals will be hawks. Male elephant seals are an example; the winner gets to mate with all the

females on the beach. Sometimes, the risk of injury is so low that most individuals will be hawks: some bullfrogs function that way, because they can't really injure each other. Sometimes, the risk of injury is so high that almost everyone is a dove: oryx and other hoofed animals with nasty horns, rattlesnakes, and so on. Most often, though, there is a mixture of hawks and doves within a population. Sometimes it's the more aggressive individuals that are hawks. Sometimes an animal is a hawk within its own territory and a dove outside it.

(12) Economist Kaushik Basu described the problem in the introduction to his book *The Less Developed Economy*. Paraphrasing: Imagine that you are in a strange city, and you've hired a taxi to take you from the airport to your hotel. You and the taxi driver have never previously met, and you'll never meet again. Why do you pay him at the end? If you were just calculating, you might not bother. After all, the taxi driver has already driven you to your destination. Still, you might realize that if you didn't pay, the driver would make a huge fuss, embarrass you in public, perhaps resort to violence, and perhaps call the police. It's just not worth the risk for such a small amount of money. But here's the problem: even if you do pay, the taxi driver could still do all of that. If the taxi driver is just as calculating as you are, why doesn't he accuse you of nonpayment regardless? Double money for him, and he'll never see you again. So if he were going to do that, you might as well not pay. You can take the analysis even further. Maybe you both calculate that if the police got involved, the courts would figure out who wronged the other—maybe there was a camera in the taxi that recorded the whole thing—so it makes sense to be honest. But that doesn't help, either. If the police and the judges are just as calculating as you and the taxi driver, why should they attempt to resolve the dispute fairly, rather than in favor of the side that gave them the biggest bribe? They might fear they would get caught and punished, but that fear assumes those doing the catching and punishing aren't calculating and will attempt to be fair and honest.

(13) Neuroscience is starting to make inroads into that question, too.

(14) The Ultimatum game was first developed in 1982, and has been replicated repeatedly by different researchers using different variants in different cultures; there are hundreds of academic papers about the Ultimatum game.

Here's how the game works. Two strangers are put in separate rooms and told they will divide a pot of money between them. They can't meet each other, and they can't communicate in any way. Instead, one of the subjects gets to divide the money any way he wants. That division is shown to the second subject, who gets to either accept or reject the division. If he accepts it, both subjects get their shares. If he rejects the division, neither subject gets a share. After this single division task, the experiment ends, and the two subjects leave via separate doors, never to meet.

Game theory predicts, and a rational economic analysis agrees, that the first player will make the most unfair division possible, and that the second player will accept that unfair division. Here's the logic. The second player is smart to accept any division, even the most lopsided one, because some money is better than no money. And the first player, knowing that the second player will accept any division, is smart to offer him the most lopsided division possible. So if there's $20 to divide, the first player will propose a $19/$1 split and the second player will accept it.

That makes sense on paper, but people aren't like that. Different experiments with this game found that first players generally offer between a third and a half of the money, and that the most frequent offer is a 50–50 split. That's right: they give money to strangers out of their own pocket, even though they are penalizing themselves economically for doing so, in an effort to be fair. Second players tend to reject divisions that are not at least reasonably fair; about half of the players turn down offers of less than 30%.

This experiment has been conducted with subjects from a wide variety of cultural backgrounds. It has been conducted with large amounts of money, and in places where small amounts of money make a big difference. Results are consistent.

(15) The Dictator game is like the Ultimatum game, but with one critical difference: the second player is completely passive. The first player gets to divide the money, and both players receive their share. If the first player wants to keep all of it, he does. The second player has no say in the division or whether or not it is accepted.

In the Ultimatum game, the first player had to worry if the second player would penalize him. The Dictator game removes all of that second-guessing. The first player gets a pile of money, and hands the second player some, then keeps the rest. He is in complete control. Even in this game, people aren't as selfish as rational economic theory predicts. In one experiment, first players split the money evenly three-quarters of the time. Other experimental results are more lopsided than that, and the first player's division tends to be less fair than in the Ultimatum game, but not as unfair as it could be.

(16) In the Trust game, the first player gets a pile of money. He can either keep it all or give a portion to the second player. Any money he gives to the second player is increased by some amount (generally 60%) by the researchers, then the second player can divide the increased result between the two players.

Assume $10 is at stake here. If the first player is entirely selfish, he keeps his $10. If he is entirely trusting, he gives it all to the second player, who ends up with $16. If the second player is entirely selfish, he keeps the $16. If he is completely fair, he gives the first player $8 and keeps $8.

Rational economic behavior predicts a very lopsided result. As in the Dictator game, the second player would be smart to give no money to the first player. And the first player, knowing this would be the second player's rational decision, would be smart to not give any money to the second player. Of course, that's not what happens. First players give, on average, 40% of the money to the second player. And second players, on average, give the first player back a third of the multiplied amount.

(17)   In a Public Goods game, each player gets a small pile of money. It's his to keep, but he can choose to pool some portion of it together with everyone else's. The researchers multiply this pool by a predetermined amount, then evenly divide it among all players.

A rational economic analysis of the game—that is, an analysis that assumes all players will be solely motivated by selfish interest or the bottom line—predicts that no one will contribute anything to the common pool; it's a smarter strategy to keep everything you have and get a portion of what everyone else contributes than it is to contribute to the common pool. But that's not what people do. Contrary to this prediction, people generally contribute 40–60% into the common pool. That is, people are generally not prepared to cooperate 100% and put themselves at the mercy of those who defect. But they're also generally not willing to be entirely selfish and not contribute anything. Stuck between those opposing poles, they more-or-less split the difference and contribute half.

(18)   One of the theories originally advanced to explain the first player's behavior in the Ultimatum game was fear of rejection. According to that theory, he is motivated to offer the second player a decent percentage of the total because he doesn't want the second player to penalize him by rejecting the offer. There's no rational reason for the second player to do that, but we—and presumably the first player—know he will. That explanation was proven wrong by the Dictator game.

Some researchers claim these experiments show that humans are naturally altruistic: they seek not only to maximize their own personal benefit but also the benefit of others, even strangers. Others claim that the human tendency at work in the different games is an aversion to being seen as greedy, which implies that reputation is the primary motivator.

Still other researchers try to explain results in terms of evolutionary psychology: individuals who cooperate with each other have a better chance of survival than those who don't. Today, we regularly interact with people we will never see again: fellow passengers on an airplane, members of the audience at public events, everyone we meet on our vacations, almost everyone we interact with if we live in a large city. But that didn't hold true in our evolutionary history. So while the Ultimatum, Dictator, and Trust games are one-time-only, our brains function as if we have a social network of not much more than 150 people, whom we are certain to meet again and again, often enough that the quality of our interactions matters in the long run.

(19)   We naturally gravitate toward fair solutions, and we naturally implement them: even when dealing with strangers, and even when being fair penalizes us financially. As one paper put it, "concerns for a fair distribution originate from personal and social rules that effectively constrain self-interested behavior."

Joseph Henrich interviewed his subjects after Ultimatum game experiments and found that they thought a lot about fairness. First players wanted to do what was fair. Second players accepted offers they thought were fair, and rejected offers they thought were unfair. They would rather receive no money at all than reward unfairness.

In variants of the Ultimatum and Dictator games where the first player won his position by an act of skill—doing better on a quiz, for example—he tended to offer less to the second player. It worked the other way, too; if the second player won his position in an act of skill, the first player tended to give him more.

(20) There's a variant of the Public Goods game where subjects are allowed to spend their own money to punish other players; typically, it's something like $3 deducted from the punished for every $1 spent by the punisher. In one experiment, two-thirds of the subjects punished someone at least once, with the severity of the punishment rising with the severity of the non-cooperation. They did this even if they would never interact with the punished player again.

What's interesting is that the punishment works. Stingy players who have been punished are less stingy in future rounds of a Public Goods game—even if the punishers themselves aren't involved in those future rounds—and that behavior cascades to other players as well.

There's other research, with rewards as well as punishment, but the results are mixed; rewards seem to be less effective than punishment in modifying players' behavior.

(21) A variant of the Dictator game illustrates this. Instead of giving, the first player can take money from the second player. And in many cases, he does. The rationalization goes along the following lines. In the standard version of the Dictator game, first players understand that the game is about giving, so they figure out how much to give. In this variant, the game is about taking, so they think about how much to take. A variant of the Trust game, called the Distrust game, illustrates a similar result.

(22) Lots of fraud is based on feigning group identity.

(23) About three-quarters of people give half of the money away in the Ultimatum game, but a few keep as much as possible for themselves. The majority of us might be altruistic and cooperative, but the minority is definitely selfish and uncooperative.

(24) To be fair, there is a minority of researchers who are skeptical that mirror neurons are all that big a deal.

(25) This is called the prototype effect, and has ramifications far greater than this one example.

(26) In many societies, sharing when you have plenty obligates others to share with you when you're in need.

(27) Notice that the four work best in increasingly larger group sizes. Direct reciprocity works best in very small groups. Indirect reciprocity works well in slightly larger groups. Network reciprocity works well in even larger groups. Group reciprocity

works well in even larger groups: groups of groups. I don't know of any research that has tried to establish the different human group sizes in which these operate, and how those sizes compare to Dunbar's numbers.

(28)   The majority belief is that it was primarily kin selection that sparked the evolution of altruistic behavior in humans, although Martin Nowak and Edward O. Wilson have recently caused quite a stir in the evolutionary biology community by proposing group selection as the driving mechanism. One rebuttal to this hypothesis was signed by 137 scientists. I have no idea how this debate will turn out, but it is likely that all mechanisms have operated throughout human evolutionary history, and reinforced each other.

(29)   There's a lot here, and there have been many books published in the last few years on this general topic of neuropsychology: Michael Shermer's *The Science of Good and Evil*, Nigel Barber's *Kindness in a Cruel World*, Donald Pfaff's *The Neuroscience of Fair Play*, Martin Nowak's *SuperCooperators*, and Patricia Churchland's *Braintrust*. The last two are the best. There's also an older book on the topic by Matt Ridley.

Chapter 4

(1)   Very often, understanding how societal pressures work involves understanding human—and other animal—psychology in evolutionary terms, just as you might understand the function of the pelvis, the spleen, or male pattern baldness. This is evolutionary psychology, first proposed by Edward O. Wilson in 1975, and which has really taken off in the last couple of decades. This is a new way of looking at psychology: not as a collection of behaviors, but as a manifestation of our species' development. It has the very real potential to revolutionize psychology by providing a meta-theoretical framework by which to integrate the entire field, just as evolution did for biology over 150 years ago.

To be fair, the validity of evolutionary psychology research is not universally accepted. Geneticist Anne Innis Dagg argues both that the genetic science is flawed, and that the inability to perform experiments or collect prehistoric data render the conclusions nothing more than Gould's "Just So Stories."

However, evolutionary psychology is not only about genetic determinism. An evolutionary explanation for behavior does not equate to or imply the existence of a genetic explanation. Behaviors, especially human behaviors, are much more multifaceted than that. Certainly genes are involved in many of our psychological processes, especially those as deep-rooted as making security and trust trade-offs, but natural selection is possible with any characteristic that can be passed from parent to child. Learned characteristics, cultural characteristics, stories that illustrate model behavior, technical knowledge—all can be passed on. Evolutionary psychology is a mix of genetic and non-genetic inheritance.

(2)   It's called *ecological validity*. We are built for conditions of the past, when—for example—humans were worried about attack from large predators, not from small lead slugs from a gun 100 yards away in the dark. So the forehead protects us against blows from blunt objects, but is much less effective against bullets. Similarly, the skull is great protection for falls, but less effective against IEDs. The loss of ecological validity has meant the end of many species that could no longer adapt to changing conditions.

(3)   Of course, the cost of not paying that tax would be even more expensive. To take just one example, Douglass North wrote: "The inability of societies to develop effective, low-cost enforcement of contracts is the most important source of both historical stagnation and contemporary underdevelopment in the Third World."

(4)   There's a reasonable argument that no money would be necessary, either. Reciprocal altruism would be enough for angels. Money is only required when debt becomes formal.

(5)   This is named after anthropologist Terrence Deacon, who first described it.

(6)   Conservative estimates are that between 20% and 25% of all Americans have had sex with someone who is not their spouse while they are married.

(7)   A gaggle of recent animal studies across a variety of species demonstrate that there's far more philandering going on in the animal world than we previously thought. Of about 4,000 mammalian species, only a few are monogamous. Even birds, once regarded as the poster children of monogamy, aren't all that faithful to their mates. Once DNA fingerprinting became cheap in the 1990s, study after study showed that anything from 10% to 40% of chicks are not raised by their biological father.

(8)   There's a balance here. Archaeological evidence indicates that Neanderthals, while violent like any other primate, were more compassionate than early humans. Yet they died out while our ancestors survived. There is preliminary evidence that Neanderthals engaged in cannibalism.

(9)   These numbers are reflected in military organization throughout history: squads of 10 to 15, organized into platoons of three to four squads, organized into companies of three to four platoons, organized into battalions of three to four companies, organized into regiments of three to four battalions, organized into divisions of two to three regiments, and organized into corps of two to three divisions.

(10) There are several theories on the evolutionary origins of religion. While all talk about the ways it induces societal cohesion, they differ as to whether that's an essential aspect of religion or just a side effect.

(11) The combination of these three are what sociologists call *social controls*. I am not using that term because 1) it traditionally does not include coercive measures, and I need a term that encompasses both coercive and non-coercive measures, and 2) its definition has changed over the years and now is limited to crime and deviance. Also, the sociological term has never included physical security measures. Finally, I am

avoiding it for the same reason I am avoiding the game-theoretic term "social dilemmas"; I want to emphasize the societal aspect of these systems.

(12)   The research is by no means conclusive, but data from Facebook, Twitter, and elsewhere indicates that Dunbar's numbers are not growing due to information technology. Facebook claims the average user has 130 friends; if you ignore people who don't actually use their accounts, my guess is that the median is around 150. (http://www.facebook.com/press/info.php?statistics.) There's even evidence that links the number of Facebook friends to the size of certain brain regions. Such social networks are changing the definition of "friend." How else can you explain that so many of our Facebook pages include people we would never have even considered talking to in high school, and yet we help water their imaginary plants?

Chapter 5

(1)   The Prisoner's Dilemma was originally framed in the 1950s by Merrill Flood and Melvin Dresher at the RAND Corporation, and was named several years later by Albert Tucker. Many researchers have informed and analyzed this game, most famously John Nash and then Robert Axelrod, who used it to help explain the evolution of cooperation.

(2)   I should probably explain about Alice and Bob. Cryptographers—and I started as a cryptographer—name the two actors in any security discussion Alice and Bob. To us, anyone we don't know is either Alice or Bob. If you meet me, don't be surprised if I call you Alice or Bob.

(3)   As stylized as the story is, this sort of thing is not uncommon. It's basic plea bargaining.

(4)   I heard the story of someone who never stops at four-way stop signs, because he figures that the other person will stop. This hawkish strategy works great, as long as he only meets doves at intersections.

(5)   One database search yielded 73,000 academic papers with the phrase "Prisoner's Dilemma" in the title.

(6)   Hardin used an open grazing pasture as an example. From the paper:

> Picture a pasture open to all. It is to be expected that each herdsman will try to keep as many cattle as possible on the commons. Such an arrangement may work reasonably satisfactorily for centuries because tribal wars, poaching, and disease keep the numbers of both man and beast well below the carrying capacity of the land. Finally, however, comes the day of reckoning, that is, the day when the long-desired goal of social stability becomes a reality. At this point, the inherent logic of the commons remorselessly generates tragedy.

As a rational being, each herdsman seeks to maximize his gain. Explicitly or implicitly, more or less consciously, he asks, "What is the utility to me of adding one more animal to my herd?" This utility has one negative and one positive component.

1. The positive component is a function of the increment of one animal. Since the herdsman receives all the proceeds from the sale of the additional animal, the positive utility is nearly +1.

2. The negative component is a function of the additional overgrazing created by one more animal. Since, however, the effects of overgrazing are shared by all the herdsmen, the negative utility for any particular decision-making herdsman is only a fraction of -1.

Adding together the component partial utilities, the rational herdsman concludes that the only sensible course for him to pursue is to add another animal to his herd. And another.... But this is the conclusion reached by each and every rational herdsman sharing a commons. Therein is the tragedy. Each man is locked into a system that compels him to increase his herd without limit—in a world that is limited. Ruin is the destination toward which all men rush, each pursuing his own best interest in a society that believes in the freedom of the commons.

(7) Normal games are zero-sum: someone wins, and someone else loses. The sum of the win (+1) and the loss (-1) totals zero.

(8) Yes, these rules are sometimes made by autocratic rulers for their own benefit. We'll talk about this in Chapter 11.

Chapter 6

(1) One way to think about defectors is that they are less risk-averse than cooperators. As a result, the cooperators tend to obtain moderate benefits with few severe costs, whereas defectors might get much larger benefits, but in the long run tend to pay more severe costs.

(2) Dan Ariely's term, "predictably irrational," describes us pretty well.

(3) The name comes from the movie *Rebel Without a Cause*, in which the antihero, Jim Stark, and the local bully race stolen cars toward a cliff; the first to jump out earns the shame of being called "chicken." Of course, if no one defects, both cars fly over the edge and both players die. (If you don't have a convenient cliff, you can play the game by racing two cars directly at each other; the first person to swerve to avoid the oncoming car is the chicken.) In this game, cooperate–cooperate is the best solution, but cooperate–defect or defect–cooperate is much better than defect–defect. In foreign policy, this is known as brinkmanship, a strategy that almost led to disastrous

consequences during the Cuban Missile Crisis of 1962. There have been some fascinating experiments with Chicken that really seem to have brought out the worst in people.

(4)   For many interactions, the Snowdrift Dilemma is a better model of the real world than the Prisoner's Dilemma.

(5)   There's also the unfortunately named Battle of the Sexes. He wants to do a stereotypically male thing on Saturday night. She wants to do a stereotypically female thing. The dilemma comes from the fact that each would rather do either of the two things with the other than do the stereotypical thing alone.

(6)   In behavioral economics, Prospect Theory has tried to capture these complexities. Daniel Kahneman is the only psychologist to ever win a Nobel Prize, and he won it in economics.

(7)   Many of the criticisms of Hardin's original paper on the Tragedy of the Commons pointed out that, in the real world, systems of regulation were commonly established by users of commons.

(8)   Douglas Hofstadter calls this "superrationality." He assumes that smart people will behave this way, regardless of culture. In his construction, a superrational player assumes he is playing against another superrational player, someone who will think like he does and make the same decisions he does. By that analysis, cooperate–cooperate is much better than defect–defect. In so doing, players are being collectively rational, rather than individually rational. Collectively, cooperating is better.

(9)   In societies that prescribed a particular hand for eating and the other hand for wiping, this also made it impossible for the thief to eat in public without shaming himself.

(10) Law professor Lawrence Lessig proposed a theory of regulation that identified four different modalities by which society can modify individual behavior: norms, markets, laws, and architecture. To use one of his examples, society could reduce smoking through a public ad campaign, a tax, smoking bans, or regulations on what quantity of addictive chemicals cigarettes can contain. According to Lessig, a smart regulator uses them all—or, at least, is aware of them all.

My model is similar. I've broken Lessig's "norms" into moral and reputational because, from the point of view of societal pressure, they're very different. Lessig's "markets" can either be informal or formal; in my model, that corresponds to reputational and institutional. And I've combined institutional markets with laws because, from a security perspective, they're similar enough to be treated together. My security is roughly analogous to Lessig's "architecture."

In *Freakonomics*, Steven Levitt and Stephen Dubner write that "there are three basic flavors of incentive: economic, social, and moral." These correspond to my institutional, reputational, and moral pressures.

Chapter 7

(1) Voting by mail is much easier, which is why it is becoming increasingly common in jurisdictions that offer the option to everyone.

(2) Unfortunately, the same analysis shows that it's not worth people's trouble to be informed voters; their most logical course of action is to vote but remain politically ignorant.

(3) It's related to other, more general, moral rules. For example, altruism is a major factor in predicting whether someone will vote or not.

(4) I am not distinguishing between the terms "morals" and "ethics." Although many philosophers make distinctions between the two concepts, a debate about moral theory is far beyond the scope of this book. And my definition of "morals" is pretty inclusive.

(5) "National Voter Turnout in Federal Elections 1960–2008," Infoplease.com, 2008. Note that this isn't the same as registered voters. In the U.S., voting is generally a two-step process. First you have to register. Then you have to vote. In most states, you can't even do both on the same day.

(6) Here is how it's expressed in a variety of religions:

Judaism: "What is hateful to you, do not do to your fellow man. This is the entire Law; all the rest is commentary." —Talmud, Shabbat 3id.

Christianity: "So in everything, do to others what you would have them do to you, for this sums up the Law and the Prophets." —Matthew 7:12. Also "Do to others as you would have them do to you." —Luke 6:31.

Islam: "No one of you is a believer until he desires for his brother that which he desires for himself." —Forty Hadith of an-Nawawi 13.

Hinduism: "This is the sum of duty; do naught onto others what you would not have them do unto you." —Mahabharata 5,1517.

Confucianism: "Do not do to others what you would not like yourself. Then there will be no resentment against you, either in the family or in the state." — Analects 12:2.

Buddhism: "Hurt not others in ways that you yourself would find hurtful." —Udana-Varga 5,1.

Taoism: "Regard your neighbor's gain as your gain, and your neighbor's loss as your own loss." —Tai Shang Kan Yin P'ien, Chapter 49.

Jainism: "A man should wander about treating all creatures as he himself would be treated." —Sutrakritanga 1.11.33.

Zoroastrianism: "That nature alone is good which refrains from doing unto another whatsoever is not good for itself." —Dadisten-I-dinik, 94,5.

Bahá'í: "And if thine eyes be turned towards justice, choose thou for thy neighbour that which thou choosest for thyself." —Epistle to the Son of the Wolf, 30.

Philosophers and theologians see a significant difference in the positive and negative phrasing of this rule—"do unto others what you want..." versus "don't do unto others what you don't want..."—but that's too far into the details for our purposes. As a societal pressure system, the altruistic and reciprocal nature of the rule is enough. Treat others well, because we will all be better off if everyone does the same.

(7)   Here's a random sampling:

From the Chácobo of Bolivia: "If you are a human being, then you will share what you have with those who are in need."

From the Maori of New Zealand: "By many, by thousands is the object attained."

From the Yeyi of Botswana: "When staying in a happy community be happy: when staying in a sad community be sad," and "It's the termites which cause the tree to fall down"—basically, minor disputes undermine the strength of the community.

(8)   It's also been demonstrated that people who believe in free will are less likely to cheat on tests or slack off on the job than those who believe in predestination. No one is sure why: perhaps believing that you don't have a choice in what you do undermines a person's sense of integrity, or perhaps it just provides a convenient excuse for giving in to selfish temptations, as if they were an unavoidable destiny. Predictably, individuals who embrace the concept of free will are also more likely to hold other people responsible for their own actions, which in turn makes them more likely to punish defectors. I'm not saying that the concept of free will is innate, or that it evolved as a societal pressure system, but it seems to function as one.

(9)   Hauser is a discredited academic. Harvard recently found him guilty of scientific misconduct; a paper has been retracted, and he's currently on leave and is no longer allowed to teach. Even so, his book has a lot of interesting insights into human moral systems.

(10)   Inbreeding is likely to result in recessive genetic disorders, making individuals less viable. This is why cheetahs, being so inbred because of how close to extinction they came at some point in their history, have such a high disease rate: there's just not enough variety in the gene pool: Amish, too.

(11)   The game was the Ultimatum game (see note 14 in Chapter 3 for a full description). The goal was to find people isolated from modern society, and the Machiguenga tribe fit the bill. What Henrich found was that the first player tended to make what we would consider unfair divisions—85%/15% or so—and the second player would accept them. By contrast, people from modern societies playing the same game tend to reject such unbalanced

divisions. In post-game interviews, Machiguenga subjects told him they would accept any offer. It's not that they were more unwilling than their more urbane counterparts to either be unfair or to accept unfairness, but that they considered the unfairness to have occurred at the point where the first and second player were chosen. That is, first players considered themselves lucky to have been chosen as first players, and second players thought it bad luck to have been chosen as second players. Once they accepted their positions, the division wasn't tainted with notions of fairness. The minority of tribesmen who responded to the game in a manner more similar to players from industrialized societies were those who had spent the most time interacting with people beyond their tribe.

(12) Believe it or not, there are security systems to help ensure that employees wash their hands before leaving the restroom, mostly involving hand stains that don't come out without vigorous washing.

(13) The phrase "bad apple" has been misused recently. More and more, it's used to mean isolated wrongdoers whose actions don't affect anyone else in the group. The entire phrase is "one bad apple spoils the entire bunch," and is intended to explicitly highlight how the reputation of one person can taint the reputation of all people in the group. Incidentally, this is actually true for apples stored in a root cellar. A spoiled apple will cause the rest of the apples to spoil.

(14) The logical extreme of this idea is the "broken windows theory" of John Q. Wilson and George Kelling, that visible signs of criminal activity like broken windows and abandoned cars actually incite people to commit crimes. Wilson and Kelling believed that if you clean up these visible signs of lawlessness, a neighborhood will become safer overall; societal pressures against petty crime will cause a reduction in violent crime.

It sounds good, and Kelling used the theory to explain the dramatic drop in crime in New York City in the 1990s, but it turns out there's not much actual evidence that it's true. Researchers compared New York City and other cities, and found that New York's punitive measures against low-level visible lawlessness—a lot of which might be considered punitive measures against homelessness—didn't make much of a difference. It's not that this effect doesn't exist at all—there is evidence that it does. It's that other causes of crime are more important, and focusing societal pressure on low-level criminal activities in the expectation that it will prevent other crimes is much less effective than directly preventing those other crimes.

Economist Steven Levitt looked at the reduction of crime across the U.S. in the 1990s and concluded: "Most of the supposed explanations...actually played little direct role in the crime decline, including the strong economy of the 1990s, changing demographics, better policing strategies, gun control laws, concealed weapons laws and increased use of the death penalty. Four factors, however, can account for virtually all of the observed decline in crime: increases in the number of police, the rising prison population, the waning crack epidemic and the legalization of abortion."

(15) A recent study of 75,000 households served by the Sacramento Municipal Utility District and Puget Sound Energy found that customers who received peer comparison

charts reduced their energy usage by an average of 1.2% to 2.1%, a change that was sustained over time. Of course, this isn't absolute. There are people who don't care, or don't care enough to make changes in their behavior—and there is evidence that this system backfires with some conservatives. Even so, enough people are swayed into cooperation by the comparison charts to make them an effective societal pressure system.

(16) In Rwanda, marriages between members of the Hutu and Tutsi ethnic groups are common. But when extremist Hutus came to power in the early 1990s, they pushed an increased stigmatization of Rwandese in mixed marriages. In the new Hutu morality, Tutsi women were vilified as immoral temptresses, and the men who succumbed to their charms were viewed as traitors.

(17) We tend to empathize more with people suffering from acute problems than those with chronic need. Witness the outpouring of aid to the Indian Ocean tsunami victims of 2004 versus the aid given annually for things like malnutrition.

(18) The cash box was made of wood, with a slot for money. Initially Feldman used an open basket of money, but some people took the money. He then tried a coffee can with a lid, but people stole from that, too. A locked wooden box is enough of a deterrent. The only way to take the money is to steal the box itself, which only happened about once a year.

There are a host of unknowns in these data. Did everyone pay 90%, or did nine in ten pay full price and one in ten pay nothing? This sort of honor system offers many ways to partially defect. Still, it offers interesting insights into how moral pressure works. As prices rose, the payment rate fell. This makes sense: as the financial benefit of non-payment increased, some people who were just barely on the side of cooperation were willing to overcome the moral prohibition against theft. Data from the number of bagels eaten showed that price-sensitive customers were more likely to defect than more consistent consumers. This also makes sense. People who purchased donuts— he started bringing them in, too—were more likely to underpay than people who purchased bagels. Maybe this meant that donut eaters were less cooperative than bagel eaters, although it might have had something to do with the perceived price versus value of the two items, or the fact that donuts are considered junk food whereas bagels are not. And there was a sharp and persistent increase in payment following the 9/11 terrorist attacks, in line with the in-group loyalty effects I talked about earlier.

Chapter 8

(1) Researchers have used the Prisoner's Dilemma to study this. People who defect predict a 76% defection rate from other players, and people who cooperate predict a 68% cooperation rate. Put in layman's terms, people reflexively think others are like themselves. More interestingly, in one experiment, people were asked to predict the behavior of

other players after chatting with them for half an hour. Then, people were better at predicting who would cooperate and who would defect. In another experiment, players were asked to evaluate the intentions of their opponents at various points during a multi-round Prisoner's Dilemma game. Cooperative players were better at recognizing other cooperative players; defecting players regularly mischaracterized cooperative players as defecting. This isn't surprising since people tend to see themselves in others.

(2)   Reputation mattered in the various "game" experiments mentioned in Chapter 3: the Ultimatum game, the Dictator game, the Public Goods game, and so on. Subjects were more altruistic, more fair, and more cooperative when their actions were known to the researchers or when they met the other players, and less so when they were anonymous and alone in a room.

(3)   In 1984, political scientist Robert Axelrod studied an iterated Prisoner's Dilemma. He set up a computer tournament and invited academic colleagues from all over to compete against each other. What he found was interesting, and in hindsight fairly obvious. Successful strategies had four basic characteristics:

> They were altruistic—Axelrod used the word "nice"—in that they did not defect before their opponent did.
>
> They were retaliatory, and responded to defection with defection.
>
> They were forgiving, and would cooperate again at some later point.
>
> They were non-envious; their goal wasn't to outscore their opponent.

The most successful strategy—called "tit-for-tat"—was extremely simple. A tit-for-tat player would first cooperate, then mirror his opponent's previous move. If his counterpart cooperated in a round, then tit-for-tat would cooperate in the next. If his counterpart defected in a round, then tit-for-tat would defect in the next. If two tit-for-tats competed, they would both cooperate forever. Essentially, Axelrod discovered reputation.

(4)   The oft-quoted line is that the average dissatisfied customer will tell 9–10 of his friends, and that 13% will tell 20 or more people. On Facebook, they'll tell everyone they know; and on Yelp, they'll tell everyone they don't know. Of course, there's a difference between reputation learned firsthand and reputation learned secondhand, similar to the personal and impersonal trust discussed in Chapter 1.

(5)   Target stores used to go so far as to accept returns of items they knew weren't purchased at Target. They calculated it was better to accept the return than argue with the customer about where the item was purchased. They no longer do this; presumably too many defectors took advantage of the system.

(6)   Prisoner's Dilemma experiments confirm that when players know each other's reputations—instead of being anonymous—cooperation jumps from around 50% to around 80%.

(7)   Dueling isn't always irrational; an economic analysis of the practice demonstrates that it made sense, given the reputational realities of the day. Similarly, the deadly defense of reputations that occurs in the criminal underworld also makes economic sense.

(8)   Chimpanzees are able to learn about the reputation of others by eavesdropping on third-party interactions, but they do not directly communicate with each other about the reputation of other chimpanzees.

(9)   The Islamic notion of *ihsan*—that people should do right because God is always watching their thoughts and deeds—is relevant here. Pascal's Wager takes this view to a somewhat cynical conclusion: it's better to cooperate (believe in God, follow God's rules, and so on) than to defect, because the potential downside of defecting is so great.

(10) Better yet, do good and let someone find out about it surreptitiously, as British essayist Charles Lamb commented: "The greatest pleasure I know, is to do a good action by stealth, and to have it found out by accident."

(11) There is counter-evidence as well. In some circumstances, diversity seems to enhance cooperation. Eric Uslaner disputes Putnam's thesis, and argues that diverse communities can be more cooperative because people living in them are more likely to accept strangers into their "moral community." Clearly more research is required.

(12) Two people living on opposite sides of the same Norwegian fjord would have spoken different dialects. Until recently, and possibly even still, it has been possible to identify the birthplace of native Britons to within 30 miles solely by their English dialects.

(13) Anthropologist David Nettle ran an interesting simulation, along similar lines to the Hawk-Dove game. He set up an artificial world where cooperation was necessary for survival, and individuals could choose whom they wished to cooperate with. When he allowed individuals to cooperate only with others who spoke the same dialect, hawks were kept down to a much smaller percentage of the total population than when dialect wasn't a factor. None of this is very surprising; we already know that reciprocity based on proximity is one of the ways cooperation can evolve in a species. Most interestingly, Nettle found that this system of using dialects as societal pressure worked best when they changed rapidly from generation to generation. The simulation mirrored the manner in which these changes occur in life; historically, there are clear differences in human dialects over only a few generations.

(14) We also try to adopt other cultural norms, to seem less foreign to others. We hand our business cards carefully with two hands to Japanese colleagues, and drink beer with German colleagues even if we prefer wine.

(15) There's an alternate analysis of the Prisoner's Dilemma that bears this out. So far, we've been doing a fairly straightforward analysis of Alice's and Bob's options to determine which ones are better. One can extend that analysis by taking into account the probabilities that Alice and Bob will choose various options. If Alice and Bob are not

complete strangers, they may know something about each other and how the other is likely to proceed. If Alice is in a Prisoner's Dilemma with Bob, and knows that Bob is from the same culture, shares the same religion, and is a member of the same social class, Alice may reasonably anticipate that he will evaluate the situation the same way she does and—in the end—choose whatever option she does. Although she doesn't know Bob's decision beforehand, she knows that she and Bob are enough alike that they will probably choose the same option. Given that assumption, Alice is only choosing between cooperate–cooperate and defect–defect. That's no dilemma at all: cooperate–cooperate is better.

(16) In general, "is" does not imply "ought."

(17) The system isn't entirely symmetrical. Once the john tears the bill in half, it's sunk cost. But the prostitute isn't yet at risk. If she doesn't keep her appointment, she doesn't gain but the john still loses his money.

(18) There is a whole theory that costly religious rituals, such as expensive funerals or Bar Mitzvah parties, are a signaling mechanism to demonstrate a variety of prosocial behaviors.

(19) The more costly and hard-to-fake the signals are, the more likely they are to be trust-worthy. Similarly, the higher the stakes, the more likely signals are to be verified. If you're applying for a job as a surgeon, your résumé is likely to be checked more care-fully than if you're applying for a job as a waiter.

(20) As a side note, Maine lobstermen have a system where they notch a "V" into the tails of breeding females. Other lobstermen who catch those notched females are supposed to throw them back in the water. This is a societal dilemma that's primarily solved through morals and reputation; the "V" makes cooperation easier by making the females easier to spot and harder to sell.

(21) Some examples of proverbs that illustrate this:

> "The gods visit the sins of the fathers upon the children." —Euripides (c. 485–406 B.C.), Phrixus, fragment 970.

> "For the sins of your fathers you, though guiltless, must suffer." —Horace, "Odes," III, 6, l. 1.

> "The Lord is long-suffering, and of great mercy, forgiving iniquity and transgression, and by no means clearing the guilty, visiting the iniquity of the fathers upon the sons to the third and fourth generation." —Exodus 34:6–7.

> "The sins of the father are to be laid upon the children." —Shakespeare, The Merchant of Venice, Act III, Scene V, l. 1.

(22) I tend not to trust ticket scalpers outside of stadiums. I'll never see them again, so they have little incentive not to rip me off. It was better when tickets were

hard-to-forge pieces of paper; that was a security system. But now that they're mostly printed receipts of online transactions and verified by bar codes, what's to stop a scalper from reprinting and reselling the same ticket over and over again? I'm essentially buying a sealed bag, and won't know if it's a real ticket or a box of rocks until I get to the gate.

(23)   Reputation doesn't scale down, either. If you're having dinner with your family, no one probably cares how much food you take when. As long as there's trust in this intimate setting, people already know who eats how much and how quickly, and trust that they will get their share eventually. Sometimes this sort of thing happens with close friends or in an intimate business setting, but there's more potential for defection.

(24)   Edney listed several reasons why a small group size is more effective: there's better communication within the group, it's easier to see how individuals react to scarcity, it's more difficult for individuals to avoid their responsibilities, there's less alienation, and the role of money is reduced. Edney wrote: "The improved focus on the group itself, the greater ease of monitoring exploitive power, and the opportunities for trust to develop among individuals with face-to-face contact are also enhanced." He doesn't use the terms, but he's talking about moral and reputational pressure.

(25)   Michel Foucalt said something similar, when he was asked why he participated in student demonstrations when—as a tenured professor—he didn't need to get arrested and beaten up in order to show that he agreed with the student movement. He said: "I consider that it is a cop's job to use physical force. Anyone who opposes cops must not, therefore, let them maintain the hypocrisy of disguising this force behind orders that have to be immediately obeyed. They must carry out what they represent, see it through to the end."

Chapter 9

(1)   Historically, some countries, like England, France, the Netherlands, and the United States, have even sponsored pirates, giving them the designation of "privateers."

(2)   There's a similar system in Sweden to combat prostitution: the purchase of sex remains illegal, but the sale of sex has been decriminalized.

(3)   There's a lot more here that I am not going to get into. American prisons are nowhere near the forefront of penological science, and what penologists believe prisons are about isn't the same thing as what corrections officers believe prisons are about; and neither of these two things is what the public thinks prisons are about.

(4)   This is why I am using the word "sanction" instead of "punishment." Punishment implies an expectancy of felt guilt, an emotional satisfaction on the part of the punisher, some sort of existential balance restored. A sanction is a simple *quid pro quo* between the justice system and the accused.

(5) Moreover, like most drivers, Alice is probably sure her driving skill is better than average, so she underestimates the risk that her speeding imposes on others.

(6) I've always thought that the process of getting pulled over, and the wait while the policeman writes the ticket up, is a bigger incentive to obey the speed limit than the fine for a lot of people. The fine is only money, but getting pulled over directly counterbalances the incentive to speed: it results in you getting to your destination more slowly. The inequity of the same fines being assessed to people of all income levels is partly addressed through a points system, whereby states revoke a driver's license if he gets caught speeding too many times.

(7) Technically, some taxes operate before (airline tickets), some during (road tolls), and some after (capital gains tax). But for our purposes, what matters is not when the money is collected, but that the tax only applies when someone does a particular thing.

(8) Electronic filing makes it easier for the IRS to detect some types of fraud because all the data arrives digitally and can be automatically cross-checked.

(9) This sort of thing has been observed many times. Students perform better on tests when they're told to try their best than when they're paid for each correct answer. Friends are more likely to help you move if you ask as a favor than if you offer them money. Pizza and beer at the end of the move don't count; that's reciprocal altruism. And salary bonuses in altruistic jobs can decrease performance. In general, the altruistic portion of a person's brain only works when the thrill center isn't stimulated by the possibility of financial compensation. If you try to stimulate both simultaneously, the thrill center wins.

(10) Ostrom's original rules are:

1. The commons must be clearly defined, as must the list of individuals who can use it.

2. What can be taken out of the commons, and what sort of resources are needed to maintain it, must be suited to local conditions.

3. Those affected by the rules of the commons need to have a say in how those rules can be modified.

4. The group charged with monitoring or auditing use of the commons must be accountable to the individuals being monitored.

5. Individuals who overuse the commons must be assessed graduated penalties, in line with the seriousness of their offense.

6. Individuals must have access to quick and cheap mechanisms to resolve the inevitable conflicts that come up.

7. Individuals who use the commons must be able to come up with their own rules for managing it, without those rules being overruled by outside powers.

8. If the commons is part of a larger system, all of this needs to be nested in multiple layers operating along the same lines.

(11) Jeremy Bentham believed that crime could be abolished by using two knobs: making crimes harder to commit, and making punishments more draconian. However, he rightly pointed out that the punishment has to fit the crime. If, for example, both rape and murder are punishable by death, a calculating rapist will kill his victim so as to reduce the chance of his arrest. Similarly, if the fine is the same for driving three miles over the limit as it is for driving thirty miles over, you might as well drive faster— you'll get to your destination sooner, and the punishment for being caught is the same. Gary Becker expanded on this idea considerably.

(12) Also note that increasing the probability of punishment is often cheaper—and more humane—than increasing the severity of punishment.

(13) There's also conflicting evidence as to whether or not the probability of getting caught has a strong effect on breaking rules. One study measured how much people cheat on tests, given three different scenarios that changed their likelihood of getting caught. The rate of cheating did not increase with the probability that their cheating would remain undetected.

(14) The trick with this pair of loopholes is to establish two Irish subsidiaries: one based in a tax haven that holds the rights to its intellectual property outside the U.S., and another based in Ireland that receives the income gained from that property. In order to avoid Irish taxes, a third subsidiary—a Dutch corporation—serves as a transfer for royalties flowing from the subsidiary in Ireland to the tax haven. This byzantine arrangement is legal, even if those three corporations exist on paper only, and allows the parent company to avoid the IRS, even if it is entirely located in the United States.

(15) That loophole closed after a year, but a bigger one opened up—and it's retroactive.

Chapter 10

(1) This might be different in Third World countries. In 2010, someone was sentenced to three months in jail for stealing two towels from a Nigerian hotel.

(2) It's not just physical sports. There's doping in professional Scrabble. Some players take "smart drugs" like piracetam and modafinil.

(3) The reality is much more complicated. While I'm sure that all doctors realize that doping is not in the group interest, as do most athletes, the general public is primarily interested in the spectacle and doesn't really care one way or the other.

(4) In the 1970s, cyclists used corticosteroids and psychostimulants such as Ritalin, and newly developed norepinephrine-dopamine reuptake inhibitors such as Pemoline. They were banned, and by the end of the decade assays were developed to detect those substances. In the 1980s, athletes turned to newly developed analogues of endogenous

substances made possible through recombinant DNA technology, including human growth hormone, testosterone, anabolic steroids, and synthetic human erythropoietin (EPO). EPO, a glycoprotein hormone that controls red blood cell production, acts to increase oxygenation, an effect valued as highly by endurance athletes as it was by people suffering from anemia. EPO use became rampant in cycling and other sports, and continues to be rampant in spite of bans since the early 1990s and the development in the late 1990s of carbon-isotope ratio tests capable of determining whether substances are made naturally by the body or come from performance-enhancing drugs.

Next came analogues of analogues, such as darbepoetin alfa (Aranesp), a variation on the theme of EPO that became commercially available in 2001. It swiftly gained a following among bike racers and other endurance athletes; a test to detect it followed in 2003. A new EPO replacement, Mircera, found its way to both the medical and sports markets in 2007; assays to detect it were developed by 2008.

Norbolethone, first developed in 1966, was resurrected in the late 1990s and marketed as the first designer steroid by an entrepreneurial bodybuilder-turned-chemist intent on evading detection by the doping police. Its fingerprint was traceable by 2002. This scenario was replayed with tetrahydrogestrinone and madol, with assays developed within two years of their introduction into sports. The mid-to-late 2000s have seen an increase in blood doping: the use of blood transfusions to increase blood oxygen concentrations. This was soon followed by the development of flow cytofluorometry tests to detect it.

The as-yet-unrealized prospect of gene doping has led regulatory bodies to preemptively ban any non-therapeutic uses of genetic technology in sports. Presumably tests to detect athletes using them will follow.

(5)   In at least two instances, positive tests for norandrosterone, a steroid of which traces are found naturally in human urine, have been traced to adulterated supplements consumed by unsuspecting bicycle racers. Another athlete tested positive for benzo-diazepine after consuming a Chinese herbal product. The most widely used urine test for EPO has been found to result in false positives in urine collected after strenuous physical exercise, though this conclusion has been hotly contested by the test's developer and others. Rapid-screen immunoassays—the most widely used tests—all too frequently yield false positives in individuals taking routine over-the-counter and prescription pain relievers and allergy, and acid reflux medications. Alpine skier Alain Baxter won the first British medal in Alpine skiing at the 2002 Winter Games in Salt Lake City. Two days after his victory, he was forced to return the bronze medal due to a positive test for methamphetamine resulting from a Vicks Vapor Inhaler.

(6)   Counterfeiting is a particularly hard problem, simply because of the economics. Anti-counterfeiting technologies must be cheap to copy in bulk, yet very expensive to copy

individually. To put it in concrete terms, it is certainly worth $80 for a counterfeiter to make a passable forgery of a $100 bill. But the government can't spend more than a few dollars on printing the real bills, so any anti-counterfeiting technology has to be inexpensive.

(7)   Studies show that despite knowing how easy it is for a criminal to create or clone a legitimate-looking website, people often use the appearance of a website as a gauge of credibility. A better way to judge legitimacy is the URL.

(8)   For example, a study on reducing terrorism risks at shopping centers found that the least costly measure suspicious package reporting, reduced risk by 60%, but the costly and inconvenient searching of bags at entrances achieved only a 15% additional risk reduction. Overall, in fact, the cheapest six security measures reduced risk by 70%, and the remaining 12 more costly security measures reduced risks by only another 25%.

Chapter 11

(1)   On the other hand, he might not steal because of pride. This dialogue appears in Robert A. Heinlein's *To Sail Beyond the Sunset*:

> "Thou shalt not steal. I couldn't improve that one, Father."
>
> "Would you steal to feed a baby?"
>
> "Uh, yes."
>
> "Think about other exceptions; we'll discuss it in a year or two. But it is a good general rule. But why won't you steal? You're smart; you can probably get away with stealing all your life. Why won't you do it?"
>
> "Uh—"
>
> "Don't grunt."
>
> "Father, you're infuriating. I don't steal because I'm too stinkin' proud!"
>
> "Exactly! Perfect. For the same reason you don't cheat in school, or cheat in games. Pride. Your own concept of yourself. 'To thine own self be true, and it must follow, as the night the day—'"
>
> "'—thou canst not then be false to any man.' Yes, sir."
>
> "But you dropped the 'g' from the participle. Repeat it and this time pronounce it correctly: You don't steal because–"
>
> "I am too...*stinking*...proud!"

"Good. A proud self-image is the strongest incentive you can have towards correct behavior. Too proud to steal, too proud to cheat, too proud to take candy from babies or to push little ducks into water. Maureen, a moral code for the tribe must be based on survival for the tribe...but for the individual correct behavior in the tightest pinch is based on pride, nor on personal survival. This is why a captain goes down with his ship; this is why 'The Guard dies but does not surrender.' A person who has nothing to die for has nothing to live for."

(2) Moral philosophers cover similar territory using a different vocabulary. Theologians talk about three levels of moral meaning: the first is personal desire, the second is commitment to social order, and the third is "about the relations among extant order and the relations to past and future orders." I'm making a gross generalization here, but someone at the first level will choose his self-interest and defect, someone at the second level will choose the long-term group interest and cooperate, and someone at the third level will either cooperate or defect depending on some higher moral principles.

(3) William C. Crain provides a good summary of Kohlberg's six stages:

At stage 1 children think of what is right as that which authority says is right. Doing the right thing is obeying authority and avoiding punishment. At stage 2, children are no longer so impressed by any single authority; they see that there are different sides to any issue. Since everything is relative, one is free to pursue one's own interests, although it is often useful to make deals and exchange favors with others.

At stages 3 and 4, young people think as members of the conventional society with its values, norms, and expectations. At stage 3, they emphasize being a good person, which basically means having helpful motives toward people close to one. At stage 4, the concern shifts toward obeying laws to maintain society as a whole.

At stages 5 and 6 people are less concerned with maintaining society for its own sake, and more concerned with the principles and values that make for a good society. At stage 5 they emphasize basic rights and the democratic processes that give everyone a say, and at stage 6 they define the principles by which agreement will be most just.

(4) Social identity theory has a lot to say about the relative strength of different groups.

(5) Between 800 and 3,000 people worldwide immolated themselves in the 40 years between 1963 and 2002 in support of various political and social causes.

(6) Author and poet Brian Christian writes this about relative morals:

Thomas Jefferson owned slaves; Aristotle was sexist. Yet we consider them wise? Honorable? Enlightened? But to own slaves in a slave-owning society and to be sexist in a sexist society are low-entropy personality traits. In a compressed biography of people, we leave those out. But we also tend on the whole to pass *less judgment* on the low-entropy aspects of someone's personality compared to the high-entropy aspects. The *diffs* between them and their society are, one could argue, by and large wise and honorable. Does this suggest, then, a *moral* dimension to compression?

(7)   If you think back to the Prisoner's Dilemma, the police deliberately put the prisoners in that artificial and difficult situation to induce their cooperation. It turns out this is a useful mechanism for social control.

(8)   The Stop Snitching campaign can also be explained as a pair of societal dilemmas. The trade-off is between cooperating with society as a whole, and cooperating with the people in the local neighborhood.

(9)   On the other hand, there's a lot less cod in the stores now than there was in the 1970s. And what there is is a lot more expensive.

(10)   Nepotism is making a comeback in the United States, especially in politics. George W. Bush and Dick Cheney both brought relatives into the federal government while they were in the White House, as did many in their administration. When Republican Senator Frank Murkowski became governor of Alaska, he appointed his daughter as his Senate replacement. Republican Representative Richard Pombo might be the worst recent offender in the country; he used his office to funnel money to all sorts of family and friends. Not to pick only on Republicans, Democratic Representative Eddie Bernice Johnson awarded thousands of dollars in college scholarships to four of her relatives and two of her top aide's children. Even Bernie Sanders has paid family from campaign donations, and he's a socialist.

It's not all big government, either. One study of Detroit libraries found that one in six staffers had a relative who also worked in the library system. And Rupert Murdoch's News Corp. was sued in 2011 by shareholders for nepotism when it bought his daughter's company.

(11)   Many states have policies about this.

Chapter 12

(1)   One.Tel in Australia was an example of this. CEO compensation was based on the number of subscribers. As a result, CEOs initiated new-customer campaigns with very cheap contracts—so cheap that the company was losing money on each new subscriber. As a result, the CEOs got their bonuses and One.Tel went bankrupt.

(2)   I am not trying to imply that organizations encourage employee loyalty in order to make them more likely to defect from society as a whole, only that it's one effect of employee loyalty.

(3)   There's another complication. A bishop is not just an employer or supervisor of a priest. In the theological understanding of the church, a bishop is considered to have something of a paternal relationship to a priest. Therefore, the bishop has a responsibility to his priests that a bank supervisor would not have to one of his subordinates. The bishop legitimately is supposed to look out for his priests, especially since his priests have given up all their normal family social connections, and dedicated their lives to the church.

(4)   There was no evidence of a conspiracy, and the Bush Justice Department never followed through with prosecution. Although President Barack Obama had previously praised whistle-blowers as "often the best source of information about waste, fraud, and abuse in government," in April 2010—two and a half years after the original raid—the Obama Justice Department indicted Drake under the Espionage Act, putting him at risk of 35 years' imprisonment on charges of "wilfully retaining" copies of documents he had provided to Congressional investigators. The case was halted on the eve of trial; the government dropped all of the major charges, the financially devastated Drake pleaded guilty to a single misdemeanor, and he was sentenced to community service and a year of probation.

(5)   At the time of writing, Manning has not been convicted of being the source of the WikiLeaks cables, nor has he confessed to the crime.

(6)   Substandard safety by Massey Energy is a similar example. In 2010, its Upper Big Branch mine exploded and killed 25 people. Sacrificing safety to save money was one of the causes.

(7)   Here's one example, from investment banker Jonathan Knee:

> The bankers who pressed these questionable telecom credits at Morgan in their quest for market share, fees, and internal status coined an acronym that could well be a rallying cry for what the entire investment banking industry had become more broadly. "IBG YBG" stood for "I'll Be Gone, You'll Be Gone." When a particularly troubling fact came up in due diligence on one of these companies, a whispered "IBG YBG" among the banking team members would ensure that a way would be found to do the business, even if investors, or Morgan Stanley itself, would pay the price down the road. Don't sweat it, was the implication, we'll all be long gone by then.

(8)   Famously, Henry Blodget of Merrill-Lynch described dot.coms as "crap" while at the same time talking them up to investors.

Chapter 13

(1)   There's a theory about which industries will attempt to fix prices in a free-market economy: mature industries where there are only a few major companies that have been lobbying together for a long time. Those companies are likely to have executives who have worked for all the other companies during their careers, and are personally friendly with all the other executives. They are also likely to have former regulators working for them, and former employees as regulators. At this point, there's enough trust amongst them for them to band together into a cartel. Another researcher wrote that the two features that are necessary for successful cartels are high seller market sales concentration and product homogeneity. High barriers to entry help ensure that a cartel is long-lived.

(2)   The only markets where we have routinely allowed for monopolies are utilities: power, gas, telephone, etc. The idea is that the cost of infrastructure is so high, and the potential for profit is so slim, that market economics will simply drive sellers out of business. Given that, society has given companies monopolies and then heavily regulated them. If technology changes the cost of infrastructure, it makes sense to deregulate those industries.

(3)   I am ignoring any effects from the garment going out of season, or out of style, as it hangs unsold on the rack.

(4)   The same societal dilemma exists in the labor market. Individual sellers—potential employees—are competing for buyers: jobs. And just as competition in the sandwich market results in the cheapest possible sandwiches, competition in the labor market results in the lowest possible wages. But in this case, society recognizes there is an inherent value to higher labor prices. So we allow sellers to organize themselves into cooperative groups: unions.

(5)   Of course, by this I mean the average customer. There will be customers who notice that the sandwiches are worse, and they'll either find it impossible to buy better sandwiches or they'll have to go to special "high quality" sandwich shops for their now-more-expensive sandwiches. Today, we now have to buy organic food, at higher prices, sometimes in high-end grocery stores, to get the same quality of food that was commonly available 50 years ago.

(6)   Calling it "medicine" allowed the company to exploit a loophole in the Prohibition laws.

(7)   Two examples: Rupert Murdoch and his News Corp. founded Fox News; and David and Charles Koch and their immense manufacturing and investment company Koch Industries were among the founders of the Tea Party.

(8) There are exceptions. The Patagonia clothing company is an example of socialist capitalism at its finest.

(9) There was a big debate in the UK in the 19th century about whether limited companies should be easy to set up, or if an Act of Parliament should be required for each separate company. Much of the debate focused on the fact that companies don't have souls and thus cannot be guilty of treason. It's the same "immortal sociopath" argument.

(10) Advertising can actually implant false memories.

(11) The economic term for this is *lock-in*. Think about your cell phone and cell plan, your computer and operating system, your game console, and so on. It's hard to switch to a competitor, because it involves things like losing months on a subscription service, buying new applications and having to learn how to use them, giving up your already-purchased stock of peripherals, and so on. Industries with low switching costs are very susceptible to changes in reputation. If you drink a Coke today and don't like it, you can easily switch to Pepsi tomorrow. Industries with high switching costs are more robust; if your cell phone company provides lousy service, you're much less likely to switch, because switching is hard and expensive. Raising switching costs is one of the ways corporations artificially limit the effects of a bad reputation on their sales—and another way a modern corporate economy tries to break the fundamental societal dilemmas of a market economy.

(12) The company, Innovative Marketing, and its CEO James M. Reno, were eventually able to bargain down their $1.8 million judgment to a measly $17,000 in back taxes and $100,000 in forfeitures. Given that their scam was alleged to be in the vicinity of $100 million, they definitely came out ahead.

(13) In April 2011, a Congressional committee report revealed that between 2005 and 2009, the 14 leading hydraulic fracturing companies in the United States used over 2,500 hydraulic fracturing products containing 750 compounds, more than 650 of which were known or possible human carcinogens, substances regulated under the Safe Drinking Water Act, or hazardous air pollutants.

(14) The company's arguments were basically 1) we think it's safe, and 2) those chemicals are trade secrets.

(15) The same dynamic explains why many large projects fail when management adds more people to them.

(16) There are two basic ways to increase Coase's ceiling. The first is to decrease the cost of internal organizational tasks. The second is to decrease the cost of building a hierarchical organization of organizations. Technology aids in both of those: travel technology to allow people to move around, communications technology to allow better coordination and cooperation, and information technology to allow information

to move around the organization. The fact that all of these technologies have vastly improved in the past few decades is why organizations are growing in size.

(17)   Senator Bernie Sanders actually had a reasonable point when he said that any company that is too big to fail is also too big to exist.

(18)   The people who use sites like Google and Facebook are not those companies' customers. They are the products that those companies sell to their customers. In general: if you're not paying for it, then you're the product. Sometimes you're the product even if you are paying for it. This isn't new with the Internet. Radio and television programs were traditionally distributed for free, and the audience was the product sold to advertisers. Newspapers are priced far below production costs, with the difference made up by readers being sold to advertisers.

(19)   For example, many large chemical companies use hazardous substances like phosgene, methyl isocyanate, and ethylene oxide in their plants, but don't ship them between locations. They minimize the amounts that are stored as process intermediates. In rare cases of extremely hazardous materials, no significant amounts are stored; instead, they are only present in pipes connecting the reactors that make them with the reactors that consume them.

(20)   For individuals, this is called being judgment-proof, and generally involves minimizing assets. Corporations can achieve the same thing with subsidiaries, so that liability falls on a corporate shell with no assets.

Chapter 14

(1)   And by those no longer in power. Some systems of societal pressures can be hard to get rid of once they're in place.

(2)   This quote, attributed to Louis XIV of France, translates as "The state, it's me." More colloquially, "I am the state." Or in the terms of this book: "As ruler of this country, what is in my interest is necessarily in society's interest."

(3)   In general, terrorism is an ineffective tactic to advance a political agenda. Political scientist Max Abrams analyzed the political motivations of 28 terrorist groups—the complete list of "foreign terrorist organizations" designated by the U.S. Department of State since 2001. He listed 42 policy objectives of those groups, and found that they only achieved them 7% of the time.

(4)   This isn't to say that we have a good intuition about what level of security is reasonable. A strict cost/benefit analysis of most airline security measures demonstrates that they don't make much sense. But of course, security trade-offs are subjective and have a strong psychological component. There are several aspects of terrorism that cause us

to exaggerate the threat. I'll talk about them in Chapter 15, but basically, we feel less secure than we actually are. So we want more societal pressure than would make strict economic sense.

(5)   If you do the math, more people have died because they chose to drive instead of fly than the terrorists killed on 9/11.

(6)   This isn't just theoretical. There is evidence that these considerations affect policy.

Chapter 15

(1)   Of course, there's a lot more to the trade-off of paying taxes than free riding. The tax rates might be so high that it is impossible for someone to survive if he pays his taxes. The taxes might be used to fund an immoral government. And it's possible for the system to collapse even if everyone pays their taxes; the government might allocate the money badly. The former Soviet Union serves as a nice example of this.

(2)   Those of you who have studied systems dynamics will recognize this diagram as a combination of two systems archetypes: Fixes that Fail, and Limits to Success.

(3)   Traditional examples of experiential goods include vacations, college educations, therapists, and management consulting. This is opposed to something like a desk chair or a can of Coke, where you pretty much know what you're getting before you buy it. Other experiential goods are restaurant dinners, fine art, home improvements, and a move to a new city. Even things that are pretty much commoditized have aspects of experience: a new car, a big-screen television, or a pet gerbil. We know from psychology that people tend to overestimate how much happier they expect a big purchase to make them. Security systems suffer from this same psychological problem; even if people knew exactly how much security a system would give them, they couldn't predict how much safer that additional security would make them feel.

(4)   Ben Franklin said: "Those who would give up essential liberty to purchase a little safety deserve neither liberty nor safety."

(5)   It's also human nature to not consider, or at least not consider with sufficient weight, the possibility of unintended consequences.

(6)   To take one example, criminals can threaten store owners and steal money from them. Lone criminals generally use guns for this purpose, although they have other ways. Criminal organizations are far more efficient. They can run protection rackets, where they extort money from store owners by threat of violence. They can make far more money this way, often without ever brandishing weapons or even making overt threats. "Nice store you have here" can go a long way if you have a good enough reputation.

(7)   There was a major political backlash in the UK against trash monitoring technologies.

(8)   In Europe, life-cycle management laws are beginning to reduce the amount of trash generated by forcing manufacturers of automobiles to pay for disposal of their products when they are eventually junked.

(9)   The Innocence Project, which works to exonerate convicted felons using DNA evidence, has found that approximately 25% of the 273 people they exonerated in the past 20 years confessed to crimes they didn't commit.

(10)   Cheating on test scores in response to the No Child Left Behind Act also happened in Chicago, Atlanta, across Pennsylvania, and probably elsewhere in the U.S. as well. One teacher described the societal pressure to ensure cooperation with the group of teachers: "It's easy to lose your moral compass when you are constantly being bullied."

(11)   In *The Dilbert Principle*, Scott Adams wrote:

> A manager wants to find and fix software bugs more quickly. He offers an incentive plan: $20 for each bug the Quality Assurance people find and $20 for each bug the programmers fix. (These are the same programmers who create the bugs.) Result: An underground economy in "bugs" springs up instantly. The plan is rethought after one employee nets $1,700 the first week.

(12)   It's 18 years if you count from 1994, when banks were first allowed to engage in interstate banking (yes, no banks operated in multiple states before then); 15, if you count from the Fed's relaxation of Glass-Steagall restrictions; 12, if you count from the repeal of Glass-Steagall.

(13)   Not accepting the dilemma as claimed is common among many defectors, including pot smokers, music pirates, and people who count cards at casinos.

(14)   The potential failure from widespread defection is great. Alexis de Tocqueville said: "The American Republic will endure until the day Congress discovers that it can bribe the public with the public's money."

(15)   I believe that the modern representative democracy is outdated as a political institution. I like to say that it's the best form of government that the mid-18th century could produce. Think about it: because both travel and communications were hard, local groups had to pick one of their own to go all the way to the capital and help make laws in the group's name. Now that travel and communications are easy, there's probably a better system.

Chapter 16

(1)   ~~It would be interesting to chart, as a function of historical time, how much damage an~~ armed group of ten men could do in society before they were subdued. The amount would be pretty stable until the invention of gunpowder, and then would grow continuously

until today. Future advances in chemical, nuclear, and biological weapon capabilities will increase that number even more in the future.

(2) I don't mean to compare now with ten years ago, or even thirty years ago. I mean to compare it with 100 years ago, 500 years ago, and 1,000 years ago. If you drew a graph, it would be jagged, but over the long term, the rate of technological change has been steadily increasing.

What might be different today is that the rate of change might never again slow down. Not only is the rate of change increasing, but the rate of the rate of change is accelerating as well. Future shock is affecting more of us and more aspects of our lives. The endgame may be the singularity—which plenty of other people have written and spoken about—but what do we do between now and then? The singularity does answer the question of what comes next for societal pressure. After moral, reputational, institutional, and security pressures comes group mind—technologically-enhanced moral pressure—à la the Borg on *Star Trek*. I don't advocate this as a research direction, but it would give us a huge advantage over the leafcutter ants.

(3) I don't just mean security against criminals and spies, I also mean security against the government. Over the decades, countries have developed social security systems that prevent law enforcement from abusing the power society delegates to them. In the U.S., these include the warrant process, rules of evidence, search and seizure rules, rules of interrogation, rules prohibiting self-incrimination, and so on. When our communications and writings were on paper, the police would need to demonstrate probable cause and receive a warrant from a judge. Today, our communications and writings are on commercial networks: Facebook, Google Docs, our e-mail providers, and so on. In many cases, the police can simply ask the companies for that data: with no probable cause, without a warrant, and without you even knowing.

(4) Clay Shirky writes extensively about these types of organizations.

(5) The difference is obvious when you look at SafeHouse, a copycat version of WikiLeaks run by the *Wall Street Journal*. Its terms of service state that SafeHouse "reserve[s] the right to disclose any information about you to law enforcement authorities or to a requesting third party, without notice, in order to comply with any applicable laws and/or requests under legal process...." The *Wall Street Journal* can't do otherwise; the costs of defecting are just too great.

(6) This is a simplification of something Lord Kelvin said:

I often say that when you can measure what you are speaking about, and express it in numbers, you know something about it; but when you cannot measure it, when you cannot express it in numbers, your knowledge is of a meagre and unsatisfactory kind; it may be the beginning of knowledge, but you have scarcely in your thoughts advanced to the state of Science, whatever the matter may be.

(7) Or, as Lord Acton said over 100 years ago: "Power tends to corrupt, and absolute power corrupts absolutely."

Chapter 17

(1)   In some ways, this is similar to Kierkegaard's leap of faith, the non-logical acceptance of belief required for most religions.

(2)   The World Values Survey measures impersonal trust in about 70 different countries by asking the question: "Generally speaking, would you say that most people can be trusted or that you need to be very careful in dealing with people?" The Scandinavian countries reported the highest level of trust (60% in Norway, Sweden, and Denmark believe most people can be trusted), while countries like Peru, Turkey, Rwanda, and Trinidad and Tobago reported the lowest. The United States ranked towards the higher end. The Gallup World Poll also measures trust by asking three questions: whether it was likely that a neighbor, a stranger, or the police would return to the owner a lost wallet with the money and valuables intact. Again, the results differ widely by country, and the perceived trustworthiness of neighbors, strangers, and the police differ as well.

All of these surveys collect data on what people say, not what they do. I have not found any study that actually tested these wallet numbers, but *Reader's Digest* tried something similar with cell phones. Researchers left cell phones unattended in conspicuous places in cities around the world. They then called the phones to see if anyone would answer and return them to their owners. Return rates varied wildly in different cities: Ljubljana won with a 97% return rate, while New York had an 80% return rate, Sydney a 60% return rate, and Singapore a 53% return rate. Hong Kong placed last with a 42% return rate. In a more controlled laboratory experiment with people from six different world cultures, researchers found significant differences in the level of trust displayed, especially when there was the potential for punishment.

(3)   It's commonly asserted that countries with authoritarian governments have low crime rates: that in these countries, both good and bad defectors are stamped out. And if we want to live in a free country where dissent is tolerated, we necessarily need to tolerate some level of crime. It's a good story, and it may be true, but there's not much in the way of supporting data. The problems are twofold. One: in authoritarian regimes, government-generated data pertaining to crime rates is vulnerable to distortion and manipulation, especially since the regime is motivated to flatter and defend itself. And two: crime statistics provided by authoritarian regimes are likely to be skewed by the absence of figures for crimes condoned or carried out by the state or against marginalized groups. So while rates of reported street crime like muggings, burglaries, and murders are often said to be lower under authoritarian regimes such as the former USSR, former East Germany, and Nazi Germany than in democratic countries, it might be that stamping out dissent doesn't actually make the streets safer. Mussolini didn't make the trains run on time; he just made it illegal to complain about them.

(4) There's an interesting analogy between protecting against defectors and vaccinating to achieve herd immunity. Society doesn't have to completely fix the problem of defections; it just has to fix it well enough that individuals are not likely to run into the problem. Doing so is much more cost-effective than trying to bring the scope of defection down to zero.

(5) This quote, widely attributed to King, is actually his paraphrase of an older quote by the abolitionist Theodore Parker from 1853: "I do not pretend to understand the moral universe. The arc is a long one. My eye reaches but little ways. I cannot calculate the curve and complete the figure by experience of sight. I can divine it by conscience. And from what I see I am sure it bends toward justice."

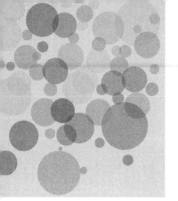

References

Chapter 1

Numbers preceding the references are page numbers.

2   *contain parasites*   Cory Doctorow (2005), "All Complex Ecosystems Have Parasites," O'Reilly Emerging Technology Conference, San Diego, California. Christopher Langton, ed. (1994), *Artificial Life III*, Westview Press.

3   *their own privacy*   Bruce Schneier (15 Jul 2009), "Facebook Should Compete On Privacy, Not Hide It Away," *The Guardian*.

4   *effectively looted*   Jeff Gottlieb (22 Jul 2010), "Bell Council Found Loophole in Law to Allow Big Salaries," *Los Angeles Times*. Jeff Gottlieb and Ruben Vives (8 Aug 2010), "Bell Councilman 'Ashamed,' 'Disgusted' that Rizzo Earned $1.5 Million," *Los Angeles Times*.

4   *internal cheating*   Greg Hoglund and Gary McGraw (2007), *Exploiting Online Games: Cheating Massively Distributed Systems*, Addison-Wesley Professional.

5   *trust is a bet*   Piotr Sztompka (1999), *Trust: A Sociological Theory*, Cambridge University Press, 25.

5   *Trust involves*   Russell Hardin (1992), "The Street-Level Epistemology of Trust," *Analyse & Kritik*, 14:152–76.

5   *impersonal trust*   Susan P. Shapiro (1987), "The Social Control of Impersonal Trust," *American Journal of Sociology*, 93:623–58.

5   *described trust*   Don Tapscott and David Ticoll (2003), *The Naked Corporation: How the Age of Transparency Will Revolutionize Business*, Free Press.

6   *Trust is the expectation*   Francis Fukuyama (1995), *Trust: The Social Virtues and the Creation of Prosperity*, Simon & Schuster, 26.

6   *three critical functions*   Barbara Misztal (1996), *Trust in Modern Societies: The Search for the Bases of Social Order*, Cambridge Polity Press.

6   *recent example*   David Remmick (1993), *Lenin's Tomb: The Last Days of the Soviet Empire*, Random House.

7   *value of trust*   Francis Fukuyama (1995), *Trust: The Social Virtues and the Creation of Prosperity*, Simon & Schuster. Barbara Misztal (1996), *Trust in Modern Societies: The Search for the Bases of Social Order*, Cambridge Polity Press. Adam B. Seligman (1997), *The Problem of Trust*, Princeton University Press. Piotr Sztompka (1999), *Trust: A Sociological Theory*, Cambridge University Press. Steven M.R. Covey (2006), *The Speed of Trust: The One Thing That Changes Everything*, Free Press.

7   *trust is the atmosphere*   Sissela Bok (1978), *Lying: Moral Choice in Private and Public Life*, Pantheon Books, 31.

Chapter 1 Notes

249   *five levels of trust*   Steven M.R. Covey (2006), *The Speed of Trust: The One Thing That Changes Everything*, Free Press.

249   *To trust is to bet*   Piero Ferrucci (2006), *The Power of Kindness: The Unexpected Benefits of Leading a Compassionate Life*, Tarcher, 80–1.

249   *When we say we trust*   Diego Gambetta (1988), "Can We Trust Trust?" in Diego Gambetta, ed., *Trust: Making and Breaking Cooperative Relations*, Blackwell Publishers, 213–37.

249   *We will define trust*   David M. Messick and Roderick M. Kramer (2001), "Trust as a Form of Shallow Morality," in Karen S. Cook, ed., *Trust in Society*, Russell Sage Foundation, 89–117.

249   *three-level progression*   Anthony Giddens (1990), *The Consequences of Modernity*, Stanford University Press, 114–24.

250   *Piotr Cofta covered*   Piotr Cofta (2007), *Trust, Complexity, and Control: Confidence in a Convergent World*, John Wiley & Sons.

250   *findings are false*   John P.A. Ioannidis (2005), "Why Most Published Research Findings Are False," *PLoS Medicine*, 2(8): e124.

250   *sloppy methodology*   Eric-Jan Wagenmakers, Rudd Wetzels, Denny Borsboom, and Han van der Maas (2011), "Why Psychologists Must Change the Way They Analyze Their Data: The Case of Psi," *Journal of Personality and Social Psychology*, 100:426–32. Joseph P. Simmons, Leif D. Nelson, and Uri Simonsohn (2011), "False Positive Psychology: Undisclosed Flexibility in Data Collection and Analaysis Allows Presenting Anything as Significant," *Psychological Science*, 22:1359–66.

250   *narrow and unrepresentative*   Joseph Henrich, Steven J. Heine, and Ara Norenzayan (2010), "The Weirdest People in the World?" *Behavioral & Brain Sciences*, 33:61–83.

250   *Adam Smith*   Adam Smith (1759), *The Theory of Moral Sentiments*.

Chapter 2

17 *territorial chorus*   Tim Clutton-Brock (2009), "Cooperation between Non-Kin in Animal Societies," *Nature*, 462:51–7.

17 *hornworms*   André Kessler, Rayko Halitschke, Celia Diezel, and Ian T. Baldwin (2006), "Priming of Plant Defense Responses in Nature by Airborne Signaling between *Artemisia tridentata* and *Nicotiana attenuate*," *Ocologia*, 148:280–92.

17 *plasmids secrete*   Michael B. Yarmolinsky (1995), "Programmed Cell Death in Bacterial Populations," *Science*, 267:836–7.

17 *Heat and light*   Henry Lutz Ehrlich and Dianne K. Newman (2009), *Geomicrobiology*, CRC Press. Smithsonian Institution (2009), "The Archean: The First Life on Earth," in *Geologic Time: The Story of a Changing Earth, Department of Paleobiology*, National Museum of Natural History, Smithsonian Institution.

18 *first animal predator*   Ben Harder (9 Apr 2002), "Was This the Earth's First Predator?" *National Geographic*.

18 *The Selfish Gene*   Richard Dawkins (1976), *The Selfish Gene*, Oxford University Press.

19 *defend against*   William D. Hamilton, Robert Axelrod, and Reiko Tanese (1990), "Sexual Reproduction as an Adaptation to Resist Parasites (A Review)," *Proceedings of the National Academy of Sciences of the United States of America*, 97:3566–73. Levi T. Morran, Olivia G. Schmidt, Ian A. Gelarden, Raymond C. Parrish II, and Curtis M. Lively (2011), "Running with the Red Queen: Host-Parasite Coevolution Selects for Biparental Sex," *Science*, 333:216–18.

19 *jawed fish*   Charles A. Janeway (2006), *Immunobiology: The Immune System in Health and Disease*, Sixth Edition, Taylor & Francis Group.

19 *orienting response*   Ivan P. Pavlov (1927), *Conditioned Reflexes: An Investigation of the Physiological Activity of the Cerebral Cortex*, tr. G.V. Anrep, Oxford University Press. Evgeni Nikolaevich Sokolov (1963), "Higher Nervous Functions: The Orienting Reflex," *Annual Review of Physiology*, 25:545-80.

19 *particularly good*   Joshua New, Leda Cosmides, and John Tooby (2007), "Category-Specific Attention for Animals Reflects Ancestral Priorities, Not Expertise," *Proceedings of the National Academy of Sciences of the United States of America*, 104:16598–603. Lynn Isabell (2009), *The Fruit, the Tree, and the Serpent: Why We See So Well*, Harvard University Press.

19 *throw things*   Justin. N. Wood, David D. Glynn, and Marc D. Hauser (2007), "The Uniquely Human Capacity to Throw Evolved from a Non-Throwing Primate: An Evolutionary Dissociation between Action and Perception," *Biology Letters*, 3:360–5.

19 *size-weight misperception*   Qin Zhu and Geoffrey P. Bingham (2011), "Human Readiness to Throw: The Size-Weight Illusion Is Not an Illusion When Picking the Best Objects to Throw," *Evolution & Human Behavior*, 32:288–93.

19 *Similar stories*   Stephen Jay Gould (Oct 1985), "Not Necessarily a Wing," *Natural History*, 94:12–25.

20   *weird security*   Randolph M. Nesse (2001), "The Smoke Detector Principle: Natural Selection and the Regulation of Defensive Responses," *Annals of the New York Academy of Sciences*, 935:75–85.

21   *Red Queen Effect*   Leigh Van Valen (1973), "A New Evolutionary Law," *Evolutionary Theory*, 1:1–30. Leigh Van Valen (1977), "The Red Queen," *The American Naturalist*, 111:809–10. Matt Ridley (1994), *The Red Queen: Sex and the Evolution of Human Nature*, MacMillan Publishing Co.

21   *continuously improve*   Seth Finnegan, Jonathan L. Payne, and Steve C. Wang (2008), "The Red Queen Revisited: Reevaluating the Age Selectivity of Phanerozoic Marine Genus Extinctions," *Paleobiology*, 34:318–41. Michael J. Benton (2009), "The Red Queen and the Court Jester: Species Diversity and the Role of Biotic and Abiotic Factors Through Time," *Science*, 323:728–32. Michael J. Benton (2010), "Evolutionary Biology: New Take On the Red Queen," *Nature*, 463:306–7.

22   *other animals*   Edward A. Wasserman, Thomas R. Zentall (2006), *Comparative Cognition: Experimental Explorations of Animal Intelligence*, Oxford University Press. Zhanna Reznikova (2007), *Animal Intelligence: From Individual to Social Cognition*, Cambridge University Press. Jeremy Taylor (2009), *Not a Chimp: The Hunt to Find the Genes That Make Us Human*, Oxford University Press.

22   *supply our brains*   Adam D. Pfefferle, Lisa R. Warner, Catrina W. Wang, William J. Nielsen, Courtney C. Babbbitt, Olivier Fedrigo, and Gregory A. Wray (2011), "Comparative Expression Analysis of the Phosphocreatine Circuit in Extant Primates: Implications for Human Brain Evolution," *Journal of Human Evolution*, 60:205–12.

22   *cultural evolution*   Gregory Cochran and Henry Harpending (2009), *The 10,000 Year Explosion: How Civilization Accelerated Human Evolution*, Basic Books.

22   *Nicholas Humphrey*   Nicholas Humphrey (1976), "The Social Function of Intellect," in Paul Patrick Gordon Bateson and Robert A. Hinde, eds., *Growing Points in Ethology*, Cambridge University Press, 303–17.

23   *Daniel Gilbert*   Daniel Gilbert (2 Jul 2006), "If Only Gay Sex Caused Global Warming," *Los Angeles Times*.

23   *capacity for deception*   Richard W. Byrne and Nadia Corp (2004), "Neocortex Size Predicts Deception Rate in Primates," *Proceedings of the Royal Society B: Biological Sciences*, 271:1693–9.

23   *non-primate mammals*   James K. Rilling and Thomas R. Insel (1999), "The Primate Neocortex in Comparative Perspective Using Magnetic Resonance Imaging," *Journal of Human Evolution*, 37:191–223.

24   *neocortex correlates*   Robin I.M. Dunbar (1992), "Neocortex Size as a Constraint on Group Size in Primates," *Journal of Human Evolution*, 20:469–93.

24   *mean human group*   Robin I.M. Dunbar (2003), "The Social Brain: Mind, Language, and Society in Evolutionary Perspective," *Annual Review of Anthropology*, 32:163–81. Alberto Hernando, Diego Villuendas, Cristina Vesperinas, Marta Abad, and Ángel Plastino (2010), "Unravelling the Size Distribution of Social Groups with Information Theory on Complex Networks," *The European Physical Journal B: Condensed Matter & Complex Systems*, 76:87–97.

24 *number appears regularly*   R.A. Hill and Robin I.M. Dunbar (2003), "Social Network Size in Humans," *Human Nature*, 14:53–72.

24 *mean group size*   Robin I.M. Dunbar (2003), "The Social Brain: Mind, Language, and Society in Evolutionary Perspective," *Annual Review of Anthropology*, 32:163–81.

24 *died in warfare*   Steven A. LeBlanc and Katherine E. Register (2003), *Constant Battles: Why We Fight*, St. Martin's Press. Samuel Bowles (2009), "Did Warfare Among Ancestral Hunter-Gatherers Affect the Evolution of Human Social Behaviors?" *Science*, 324:1293–8.

24 *Paul Seabright*   Paul Seabright (2004), *The Company of Strangers: A Natural History of Economic Life*, Princeton University Press.

24 *other species*   J. Maynard Smith and George R. Price (1973), "The Logic of Animal Conflict," *Nature*, 246:15–8.

24 *should primarily hunt*   Craig B. Stanford (2001), "A Comparison of Social Meat-Foraging by Chimpanzees and Human Foragers," in Craig B. Stanford and H. Bunn, eds., *Meat-Eating and Human Evolution*, Oxford University Press. Gottfried Hohmann (2009), "The Diets of Non-Human Primates: Frugivory, Food Processing, and Food Sharing," in Jean-Jacques Hublin, Michael P. Richards, eds. (2009), *The Evolution of Hominin Diets: Integrating Approaches to the Study of Palaeolithic Subsistence*, Springer.

24 *all primitive societies*   Steven A. LeBlanc and Katherine E. Register (2003), *Constant Battles: Why We Fight*, St. Martin's Press.

25 *David Buss*   David M. Buss (2006), *The Murderer Next Door: Why the Mind Is Designed to Kill*, Penguin, 40.

25 *quite violent*   Steven A. LeBlanc and Katherine E. Register (2003), *Constant Battles: Why We Fight*, St. Martin's Press. David M. Buss (2006), *The Murderer Next Door: Why the Mind Is Designed to Kill*, Penguin. Bureau of Justice Statistics (1994), "Violent Crime," U.S. Department of Justice.

25 *some argue*   Steven Pinker (2011), *The Better Angels of Our Nature: Why Violence Has Declined*, Viking.

25 *kill in war*   Dave Grossman (1995), *On Killing: The Psychological Cost of Learning to Kill in War and Society*, Little, Brown & Co.

25 *with other primates*   Lars Rodseth, Richard W. Wrangham, Alisa M. Harrigan, and Barbara B. Smuts (1991), "The Human Community as a Primate Society," *Current Anthropology*, 32:221–54. Bruce M. Knauft (1991), "Violence and Sociality in Human Evolution," *Current Anthropology*, 32:391–428. Christoph P.E. Zollikofer, Marcia S. Ponce de Leon, Bernard Vandermeersch, and Francois Leveque (2002), "Evidence for Interpersonal Violence in the St. Cesaire Neanderthal,"*Proceedings of the National Academy of Sciences of the United States of America*, 99:6444–8. Margaret C. Crofoot and Richard W. Wrangham (2010), "Intergroup Aggression in Primates and Humans: The Case for a Unified Theory," in Peter M. Kappeler and Joan M. Silk, eds., *Mind the Gap: Tracing the Origins of Human Universals*, Springer.

Chapter 2 Notes

250 *sticks as weapons* Jill D. Pruetz and Paco Bertolani (2007), "Savanna Chimpanzees, Pan *troglodytes verus*, Hunt with Tools," *Current Biology*, 17:412–17.

250 *using rocks* Giacomo Bernardi (2011), "The Use of Tools by Wrasses (*Labridae*)," *Coral Reefs*, published online before print.

250 *Brants' whistling rat* Tim P. Jackson (2000), "Adaptation to Living in an Open Arid Environment: Lessons from the Burrow Structure of the Two Southern African Whistling Rats, *Parotomys brantsii* and *P. littledalei*," *Journal of Arid Environments*, 46:345–55.

250 *African rat* Jonathan Kingdon, Bernard Agwanda, Margaret Kinnaird, Timothy O'Brien, Christopher Holland, Thomas Gheysens, Maxime Boulet-Audet, and Fritz Vollrath (2011), "A Poisonous Surprise under the Coat of the African Crested Rat," *Proceedings of the Royal Society B: Biological Sciences*, published online before print.

251 *entirely separate* R. Jansen, J.D. Embden, W. Gaastra, L.M. Schouls (2002), "Identification of Genes That Are Associated with DNA Repeats in Prokaryotes," *Molecular Microbiology*, 43:1565–75.

251 *earlier book* Bruce Schneier (2006), *Beyond Fear: Thinking Sensibly About Security in an Uncertain World*, Copernicus.

251 *picture of a snake* Vanessa LoBue and Judy DeLoache (2008), "Detecting the Snake in the Grass: Attention to Fear-Relevant Stimuli by Adults and Young Children," *Psychological Science*, 19:284–9.

251 *cause and effect* Gema Martin-Ordas, Josep Call, and Fernando Colmenares (2007), "Tubes, Tables, and Traps: Great Apes Solve Two Functionally Equivalent Trap Tasks but Show No Evidence of Transfer Across Tasks," *Animal Cognition*, 11:423–30.

251 *time binding species* Alfred Korzybski (1933), *Science and Sanity: An Introduction to Non-Aristotelian Systems and General Semantics*, International Non-Aristotelian Library Publishing Corp.

251 *intentional stance* Daniel C. Dennett (1987), *The Intentional Stance*, MIT Press.

251 *social group size* Kimberly A. Pollard and Daniel T. Blumstein (2011), "Social Group Size Predicts the Evolution of Individuality," *Current Biology*, 21:413–7.

251 *win arguments* Hugo Mercier and Dan Sperber (2011), "Why Do Humans Reason? Arguments for an Argumentative Theory," *Behavioral & Brain Sciences*, 34:54–74.

251 *Others posit* Christopher McCarty, Peter D. Killworth, H. Russell Bernard, Eugene C. Johnsen, and Gene A. Shelley (2000), "Comparing Two Methods for Estimating Network Size," *Human Organization*, 60:28–39. H. Russell Bernard, Gene Ann Shelley, and Peter Killworth (1987), "How Much of a Network Does the GSS and RSW Dredge Up?" *Social Networks*, 9:49–63.

252 *primitive peoples* Mervyn J. Meggitt (1977), *Blood Is Their Argument*, Mayfield.

252 *Yanomamö* Napoleon A. Chagnon (1974), *Studying the Yanomamo*, Holt, Rinehart & Winston.

252 *Big-game hunting*   David A. Byers and Andrew Ugan (2005), "Should We Expect Large Game Specialization in the Late Pleistocene? An Optimal Foraging Perspective on Early Paleoindian Prey Choice," *Journal of Archaeological Science*, 32:1624–40. Kristen Hawkes, James F. O'Connell, and Nicholas G. Blurton-Jones (1991), "Hunting Income Patterns among the Hadza: Big Game, Common Goods, Foraging Goals and the Evolution of the Human Diet," *Philosophical Transactions of the Royal Society B: Biological Sciences*, 33:243–50. John D. Speth, Khori Newlander, Andrew A. White, Ashley K. Lemke, and Lars E. Anderson (2010), "Early Paleoindian Big-Game Hunting in North America: Provisioning or Politics?" *Quaternary International*, published online before print. Mary C. Stiner, Natalie D. Munro, and Todd A. Surovell (2000), "The Tortoise and the Hare: Small-Game Use, the Broad-Spectrum Revolution, and Paleolithic Demography," *Current Anthropology*, 41: 39–73.

252 *Chimpanzees' aggression rates*   Richard W. Wrangham, Michael L. Wilson, and Martin N. Muller (2006), "Comparative Rates of Violence in Chimpanzees and Humans," *Primates*, 47:14–26.

Chapter 3

27 *division of labor*   Edward O. Wilson (1987), "Causes of Ecological Success: The Case of the Ants," *Journal of Animal Ecology*, 56:1–9. Bert Holldobler and Edward O. Wilson (2009), *The Superorganism: The Beauty, Elegance, and Strangeness of Insect Societies*, W.W. Norton & Co. Bert Holldobler and Edward O. Wilson (2010), *The Leafcutter Ants: Civilization by Instinct*, W.W. Norton & Co.

28 *Hawk-Dove game*   John Maynard Smith and George R. Price (1973), "The Logic of Animal Conflict," *Nature*, 246:15–8.

31 *war of all against all*   Thomas Hobbes (1651), *Leviathan*, Printed for Andrew Crooke, at the Green Dragon in St. Paul's Churchyard.

33 *compassion extended*   Penny Spikins, Holly Rutherford, and Andy Needham (2010), "From Homininity to Humanity: Compassion from the Earliest Archaic to Modern Humans," *Time and Mind*, 3:303–25. Priyali Rajagopal and Nicole Votolato Montgomery (2011), "I Imagine, I Experience, I Like: The False Experience Effect," *The Journal of Consumer Research*, 38:578–94.

33 *invention of agriculture*   Robert Boyd and Peter Richerson (2004), *Not by Genes Alone: How Culture Transformed Human Evolution*, University of Chicago Press.

33 *Unrelated elephants*   Joshua M. Plotnik, Richard Lair, Wirot Suphachoksahakun, and Frans de Waal (2011), "Elephants Know When They Need a Helping Trunk in a Cooperative Task," *Proceedings of the National Academy of Sciences of the United States of America*, published online before print.

33 *ritualized battles*   Mark Briffa (2010), "Territoriality and Aggression," *Nature Education Knowledge*, 1:19. Craig Packer and Anne E. Pusey (1985), "Asymmetric Contests in Social Mammals Respect, Manipulation and Age-Specific Aspects," in Paul J.

Greenwood, Paul H. Harvey, and Montgomery Slatkin, eds., *Evolution: Essays in Honour of John Maynard Smith*, Cambridge University Press, 173–86. Tabitha M. Innocent and Stuart A. West (2006), "Social Evolution: Cooperation by Conflict," *Current Biology*, 16:365–67. Hanna Kokko, Andrés López-Sepulcre, and Lesley J. Morrell (2006), "From Hawks and Doves to Self-Consistent Games of Territorial Behavior," *The American Naturalist*, 167:901–12.

34 *Vampire bats*   Gerald S. Wilkinson (1984), "Reciprocal Food Sharing in the Vampire Bat," *Nature*, 308:181–4.

34 *large frontal lobes*   Kunwar P. Bhatnagar (2008), "The Brain of the Common Vampire Bat, *Desmodus rotundus murinus* (Wagner, 1840): A Cytoarchitectural Atlas," *Brazilian Journal of Biology*, 68:583–99.

34 *help each other*   Robert L. Trivers (1971), "The Evolution of Reciprocal Altruism," *Quarterly Review of Biology*, 46:35–7.

35 *transactional analysis*   Eric Berne (1996), "Principles of Transactional Analysis," *Indian Journal of Psychiatry*, 38:154–9.

35 *potential mate*   Amotz Zahavi (1975), "Mate Selection: A Selection for a Handicap," *Journal of Theoretical Biology*, 53:205–14. Amotz Zahavi (1977), "The Cost of Honesty (Further Remarks on the Handicap Principle)," *Journal of Theoretical Biology*, 67:603–5. Amotz Zahavi (1977), "Reliability in Communication Systems and the Evolution of Altruism," in Bernard Stonehouse and Christopher M. Perrins, eds., *Evolutionary Ecology*, Macmillan, 253–9. Rufus A. Johnstone (1995), "Sexual Selection, Honest Advertisement and the Handicap Principle: Reviewing the Evidence," *Biological Reviews*, 70:1–65. Amotz Zahavi and Avishag Zahavi (1997), *The Handicap Principle: A Missing Piece of Darwin's Puzzle*, Oxford University Press. Amotz Zahavi (2003), "Indirect Selection and Individual Selection in Sociobiology: My Personal Views on Theories of Social Behaviour," *Animal Behaviour*, 65:859–63.

35 *altruistic acts*   Randolph M. Nesse (2007), "Runaway Social Selection for Displays of Partner Value and Altruism," *Biological Theory*, 2:143–55.

35 *kind people*   Charlie L. Hardy and Mark Van Vugt (2006), "Nice Guys Finish First: The Competitive Altruism Hypothesis," *Personality & Social Psychology Bulletin*, 32:1402–13. Lauri A. Jensen-Campbell, Jennifer M. Knack, and Haylie L. Gomez (2010), "The Psychology of Nice People," *Social & Personality Psychology Compass*, 4:1042–56. Pat Barclay (2010), "Altruism as a Courtship Display: Some Effects of Third-Party Generosity on Audience Perceptions," *British Journal of Psychology*, 101:123–35. Timothy A. Judge, Beth A. Livingston, and Charlice Hurst (2011), "Do Nice Guys and Gals Really Finish Last? The Joint Effects of Sex and Agreeableness on Income," *Journal of Personality & Social Psychology*, in press.

35 *George Price*   Oren S. Harman (2010), *The Price of Altruism: George Price and the Search for the Origins of Kindness*, W.W. Norton & Co.

35 *bargaining games*   Gary E. Bolton (1998), "Bargaining and Dilemma Games: From Laboratory Data Towards Theoretical Synthesis," *Experimental Economics*, 1:257–81.

36 *found a coin* Paula F. Levin and Alice M. Isen (1972), "The Effect of Feeling Good on Helping: Cookies and Kindness," *Journal of Personality & Social Psychology*, 21:384–8.

36 *flying through clouds* Lawrence J. Sanna, Edward C. Chang, Paul M. Miceli, and Kristjen B. Lundberg (2011), "Rising Up to Higher Virtues: Experiencing Elevated Physical Heights Uplifts Prosocial Actions," *Journal of Experimental & Social Psychology*, 47:472–6.

36 *mirror neurons* Giuseppe di Pellegrino, Luciano Fadiga, Leonardo Fogassi, Vittorio Gallese, and Giacomo Rizzolati (1992), "Understanding Motor Events: A Neurophysiological Study," *Experimental Brain Research*, 91:176–80. Vittorio Gallese, Luciano Fadiga, Leonardo Fogassi, and Giacomo Rizzolatti (1996), "Action Recognition in the Premotor Cortex," *Brain*, 119:593–609. Vittorio Gallese and Alvin Goldman (1998), "Mirror Neurons and the Simulation Theory of Mind-Reading," *Trends in Cognitive Sciences*, 2:493–501.

36 *altruistic innately* Ernst Fehr and Simon Gächter (2002), "Altruistic Punishment in Humans," *Nature*, 415:137–40. Alan G. Sanfey, James K. Rilling, Jessica A. Aronson, Leigh E Nystrom, and Jonathan D. Cohen (2003), "The Neural Basis of Economic Decision-Making in the Ultimatum Game," *Science*, 300:1755–8. Tania Singer, Ben Seymour, John P. O'Doherty, Klass E. Stephan, Raymond J. Dolan, and Chris D. Frith (2006), "Empathic Neural Responses Are Modulated by the Perceived Fairness of Others," *Nature*, 439:466–9. Molly J. Crockett, Luke Clark, Golnaz Trabibnia, Mattthew D. Lieberman, and Trevor W. Robbins (2008), "Serotonin Modulates Behavioral Reactions to Unfairness," *Science*, 320:1739. Molly J. Crockett, Luke Clark, Marc D. Hauser, and Trevor W. Robbins (2010), "Serotonin Selectively Influences Moral Judgment and Behavior Through Effects on Harm Aversion," *Proceedings of the National Academy of Sciences of the United States of America*, 107:17433–8.

37 *fairness and justice* Katarina Gospic, Erik Mohlin, Peter Fransso, Predrag Petrovic, Magnus Johannesson, and Martin Ingvar (2011), "Limbic Justice: Amygdala Involvement in Immediate Rejection in the Ultimatum Game," *PLoS Biology*, 9 (5): e1001054.

37 *and attractive* Tania Singer, Ben Seymour, John P. O'Doherty, Klass E. Stephan, Raymond J. Dolan, and Chris D. Frith (2006), "Empathic Neural Responses Are Modulated by the Perceived Fairness of Others," *Nature*, 439:466–9.

37 *found that oxytocin* Paul J. Zak, Robert Kurzban, and William T. Matzner (2003), "Oxytocin Is Associated with Interpersonal Trust in Humans," *PLoS ONE*, 2:11, e1128. Zoe R. Donaldson and Larry J. Young (2008), "Oxytocin, Vasopressin, and the Neurogenetics of Sociality," *Science*, 322:900–4.

37 *someone's oxytocin* Michael Kosfield, Marcus Heinfichs, Paul J. Zak, Urs Fischbacher, and Ernst Fehr (2003), "Oxytocin Increases Trust in Humans," *Nature*, 435:673–6.

37 *Adam Smith* Adam Smith (1759), The Theory of Moral Sentiments.

38 *non-kin groups* Martin A. Nowak (2006), "Five Rules for the Evolution of Cooperation," *Science*, 314:1560–3. Martin A. Nowak and Roger Highfield (2011),

SuperCooperators: Altruism, Evolution, and Why We Need Each Other to Succeed, Free Press.

38   *Indirect reciprocity*   Martin A. Nowak and Karl Sigmund (1998), "Evolution of Indirect Reciprocity by Image Scoring," *Nature*, 393:573–7. Martin A. Nowak and Karl Sigmund (1998), "The Dynamics of Indirect Reciprocity," *Journal of Theoretical Biology*, 194:561–74. Manfred Milinski, Dirk Semmann, Theo C.M. Bakker, and Hans-Jürgen Krambeck (2001), "Cooperation Through Indirect Reciprocity: Image Scoring or Standing Strategy?" *Proceedings of the Royal Society B: Biological Sciences*, 268:2495–501.

38   *biological models*   Herbert Gintis (2003), "The Hitch-Hikers Guide to Altruism: Genes, Culture, and the Internalization of Norms," *Journal of Theoretical Biology*, 220:407–18.

38   *Patricia Churchland*   Patricia S. Churchland (2011), *Braintrust: What Neuroscience Tells Us About Morality*, Princeton University Press, 93.

38   *our murderousness*   Samuel Bowles (2006), "Group Competition, Reproductive Leveling, and the Evolution of Human Altruism," *Science,* 314:1569–72. Jung-Kyoo Choi and Samuel Bowles (2007), "The Coevolution of Parochial Altruism and War," *Science*, 318:636–40.

39   *And these processes*   Robert Boyd and Peter J. Richerson (1985), *Culture and the Evolutionary Process*, University of Chicago Press. Robert Bettinger, Peter J. Richerson, and Robert Boyd (1995), "Can Group Functional Behaviors Evolve by Cultural Group Selection?" *Current Anthropology*, 36:473–94.

Chapter 3 Notes

252   *increased specialization*   Raphaël Jeanson, Jennifer H. Fewell, Root Gorelick, and Susan M. Bertram (2007), "Emergence of Increased Division of Labor as a Function of Group Size," *Behavioral Ecology & Sociobiology*, 62:289–98.

252   *not what makes*   Anna Dornhaus (2008), "Specialization Does Not Predict Individual Efficiency in an Ant," *PLOS Biology*, 6:e285.

252   *startling statistic*   Dwayne C. Savage (1977), "Microbial Ecology of the Gastrointestinal Tract," *Annual Review of Microbiology*, 31:107–33.

253   *some mixture*   Stephen Le and Robert Boyd (2007), "Evolutionary Dynamics of the Continuous Iterated Prisoner's Dilemma," *Journal of Theoretical Biology*, 245:258–67.

253   *population density*   Pierre Auger and Dominique Pontier (1998), "Fast Game Theory Coupled to Slow Population Dynamics: The Case of Domestic Cat Populations," *Mathematical Biosciences*, 148:65–82.

253   *South African meerkats*   Tim H. Clutton-Brock, Peter N.M. Brotherton, M. Justin O'Riain, Ashleigh S. Griffin, David Gaynor, Ruth Kansky, Lynda Sharpe, and Grant M. McIlrath (2001), "Contributions to Cooperative Rearing in Meerkats," *Animal Behaviour*, 61:705–10. Alex Thornton (2008), "Social Learning about Novel Foods in Young Meerkats," *Animal Behaviour*, 76:1411–21.

253 *Red ruffed lemurs*   Natalie Vasey (2007), "The Breeding System of Wild Red Ruffed Lemurs (*Varecia rubra*): A Preliminary Report," *Primates*, 48:41–54.

253 *much less common*   Lee Alan Dugatkin (1997), *Cooperation Among Animals: An Evolutionary Perspective*, Oxford University Press.

253 *also slow*   Carl T. Bergstrom and Michael Lachmann (2003), "The Red King Effect: Evolutionary Rates and the Division of Surpluses in Mutualisms," in Peter Hammerstein, ed., *Genetic and Cultural Evolution of Cooperation*, MIT Press, 223–8.

253 *Wrasse cleaner fish*   Frans de Waal (Apr 2005), "How Animals Do Business," *Scientific American*, 72–79.

253 *Elephant seals*   Burney J. Le Boeuf (1974), "Male-Male Competition and Reproductive Success in Elephant Seals," *American Zoologist*, 14:163–76.

254 *some bullfrogs*   Richard D. Howard (1978), "The Evolution of Mating Strategies in Bullfrogs, *Rana catesbeiana*," *Evolution*, 32:850–71.

254 *everyone is a dove*   Valerius Geist (1974), "On the Relationship of Social Evolution and Ecology in Ungulates," *American Zoologist*, 14:205–20.

254 *there is a mixture*   John Maynard Smith and Geoffrey A. Parker (1976), "The Logic of Asymmetric Contests," *Animal Behaviour*, 24:159–75. Peter Hammerstein (1981), "The Role of Asymmetries in Animal Contests," *Animal Behaviour*, 29:193–205.

254 *Kaushik Basu*   Kaushik Basu (1984), *The Less-Developed Economy: A Critique of Contemporary Theory*, Oxford University Press, 5–6.

254 *Neuroscience is starting*   Kerri Smith (2011), "Neuroscience vs Philosophy: Taking Aim at Free Will," *Nature*, 477:23–5.

254 *Ultimatum game*   Charles A. Holt (2000), "Y2K Bibliography of Experimental Economics and Social Science: Ultimatum Game Experiments," University of Virginia. Hessel Oosterbeek, Randolph Sloof, and Gijs van de Kuilen (2004), "Cultural Differences in Ultimatum Game Experiments: Evidence From a Meta-Analysis," *Experimental Economics*, 7:171–88.

254 *how the game works*   Werner Güth, Rolf Schmittberger, and Bernd Schwarze (1982), "An Experimental Analysis of Ultimatum Bargaining," *Journal of Economic Behavior & Organization*, 3:267–88.

255 *turn down offers*   Hessel Oosterbeek, Randolph Sloof, and Gijs van de Kuilen (2004), "Differences in Ultimatum Game Experiments: Evidence from a Meta-Analysis," *Experimental Economics*, 7:171–88.

255 *cultural backgrounds*   Donna L. Bahry (2004), "Trust in Transitional Societies: Experimental Results from Russia," Paper presented at the American Political Science Association Meeting, Chicago. Michael Gurven and Jeffrey Winking (2008), "Collective Action in Action: Prosocial Behavior In and Out of the Laboratory," 110:179–90. Joseph Henrich (2000), "Does Culture Matter in Economic Behavior? Ultimatum Game Bargaining Among the Machiguenga of the Peruvian Amazon," *American Economic Review*, 90:973–9. Joseph Henrich, Robert Boyd, Samuel Bowles, Colin Camerer, Ernst Fehr, Herbert Gintis, Richard McElreath, Michael Alvard, Abigail Barr, Jean Ensminger, Kim Hill, Francisco Gil-White, Michael Gurven, Frank

Marlowe, John Q. Patton, Natalie Smith, and David Tracer (2005), "'Economic Man' in Cross-Cultural Perspective: Behavioral Experiments in 15 Small-Scale Societies," *Behavioral & Brain Sciences*, 28:795–855. Joseph Henrich, Richard McElreath, Abigail Barr, Jean Ensminger Clark Barrett, Alexander Bolyanatz, Juan Camilo Cardenas, Michael Gurven, Edwins Gwako, Natalie Henrich, Carolyn Lesorogol, Frank Marlowe, David Tracer, and John Ziker (2006), "Costly Punishment Across Human Societies," *Science*, 312:1767–70.

255 *large amounts of money* Juan Camilo Cardenas and Jeffrey P. Carpenter (2005), "Experiments and Economic Development: Lessons from Field Labs in the Developing World," Middlebury College Economics Discussion Paper No. 0505.

255 *more lopsided* Daniel Kahneman, John L. Knetsch, and Richard H. Thaler (1986), "Fairness and the Assumptions of Economics," *Journal of Business*, 59:S285–S300. Christoph Engel (2011), "Dictator Games: A Meta Study," *Experimental Economics*, 14:584–610.

255 *Trust game* Joyce Berg, John Dickhaut, and Kevin McCabe (1995), "Trust, Reciprocity, and Social History," *Games & Economic Behavior*, 10:122–42.

255 *not what happens* Colin Cramer (2003), *Behavioral Game Theory: Experiments in Strategic Interaction*, Russell Sage Foundation.

256 *Public Goods game* John O. Ledyard (1995), "Public Goods: A Survey of Experimental Research," in Alvin E. Roth and John H. Kagel, eds., *Handbook of Experimental Economics*, Princeton University Press.

256 *fear of rejection* Daniel Kahneman, John L. Knetsch, and Richard H Thaler (1986), "Fairness and the Assumptions of Economics," *Journal of Business*, 59:S285–S300. Joseph Henrich, Robert Boyd, Samuel Bowles, Colin Camerer, Ernst Fehr, Herbert Gintis, Richard McElreath, Michael Alvard, Abigail Barr, Jean Ensminger, Kim Hill, Francisco Gil-White, Michael Gurven, Frank Marlowe, John Q. Patton, Natalie Smith, and David Tracer (2005), "'Economic Man' in Cross-Cultural Perspective: Behavioral Experiments in 15 Small-Scale Societies," *Behavioral & Brain Sciences*, 28:795–855.

256 *Some researchers claim* Ernst Fehr and Urs Fischbacher (2005), "Human Altruism: Proximate Patterns and Evolutionary Origins," *Analyse & Kritik*, 27:6–47.

256 *Others claim* Roland Bénabou and Jean Tirole (2006), "Incentives and Prosocial Behavior," *American Economic Review*, 96:1652–78. Amihai Glazer and Kai A. Konrad (1996) "A Signaling Explanation for Charity," *American Economic Review*, 86:1019–28. Dan Ariely, Anat Bracha, and Stephan Meier (2008), "Doing Good or Doing Well? Image Motivation and Monetary Incentives in Behaving Prosocially," Federal Reserve Bank of Boston Working Paper No. 07–9.

256 *fair solutions* Gary E. Bolton, Elena Katok, and Rami Zwick (1998), "Dictator Game Giving: Rules of Fairness Versus Acts of Kindness," *International Journal of Game Theory*, 27:269–99.

256 *do what was fair* Joseph Henrich, Robert Boyd, Samuel Bowles, Colin Camerer, Ernst Fehr, Herbert Gintis, Richard McElreath, Michael Alvard, Abigail Barr, Jean

Ensminger, Kim Hill, Francisco Gil-White, Michael Gurven, Frank Marlowe, John Q. Patton, Natalie Smith, and David Tracer (2005), "'Economic Man' in Cross-Cultural Perspective: Behavioral Experiments in 15 Small-Scale Societies," *Behavioral & Brain Sciences*, 28:795–855.

257 *act of skill*   Elizabeth Hoffman, Kevin McCabe, Keith Shachat, and Vernon L. Smith (1994), "Preferences, Property Rights, and Anonymity in Bargaining Games," *Games & Economic Behavior*, 7:346–80.

257 *other way, too*   Bradley J. Ruffle (1998), "More Is Better, But Fair Is Fair: Tipping in Dictator and Ultimatum Games," *Games & Economic Behavior*, 23:247–76.

257 *punish other players*   Christopher T. Dawes, James H. Fowler, Tim Johnson, Richard McElreath, and Oleg Smirnov (2007), "Egalitarian Motivations in Humans," *Nature*, 446:794–6.

257 *the punishment works*   Ernst Fehr and Simon Gächter (2002), "Altruistic Punishment in Humans," *Nature*, 415:137–40. James H. Fowler and Nicholas A. Christakis (2010), "Cooperative Social Behavior Cascades in Human Social Networks," *PNAS Early Edition*.

257 *results are mixed*   David Rand, Anna Dreber, Tore Ellingsen, Drew Fundeberg, and Martin Nowak (2009), "Positive Interactions Promote Public Cooperation," *Science*, 325:1272–5. Christopher T. Dawes, James H. Fowler, Tim Johnson, Richard McElreath, and Oleg Smirnov (2007), "Egalitarian Motivations in Humans," *Nature*, 446:794–6. James Andreoni, William Harbaugh, and Lise Vesterlund (2003), "The Carrot or the Stick: Rewards, Punishments, and Cooperation," *The American Economic Review*, 93:893–902.

257 *game is about taking*   Nicholas Bardsley (2008), "Dictator Game Giving: Altruism or Artifact?" *Experimental Economics*, 11:122–33.

257 *Distrust game*   Iris Bohnet and Stephan Meier (2005), "Deciding to Distrust," Federal Reserve Bank of Boston Public Policy Discussion Paper 05-4.

257 *half of the money*   Ernst Fehr and Klaus M. Schmidt (1999), "A Theory of Fairness, Competition, and Cooperation," *The Quarterly Journal of Economics*, 114:817–68. Daniel Kahneman, John L. Knetsch, and Richard H Thaler (1986), "Fairness and the Assumptions of Economics," *Journal of Business*, 59:S285–S300.

257 *who are skeptical*   Ilan Dinstein, Cibu Thomas, Marlene Behrmann, and David J. Heeger (2008), "A Mirror Up to Nature," *Current Biology*, 18:R13–8. Kaspar Meyer and Antonio Damasio (2008), "Mirror Neurons: Behind the Looking Glass," *Nature*, 454:167–8. Gregory Hickok (2009), "Eight Problems for the Mirror Neuron Theory of Action Understanding in Monkeys and Humans," *Cognitive Neurosciences*, 21:1229–43.

257 *prototype effect*   Eleanor Rosch (1975), "Cognitive Representation of Semantic Categories," *Journal of Experimental Psychology*, 104:192–233. George Lakoff (1987), *Women, Fire and Dangerous Things: What Categories Reveal About the Mind*, University of Chicago Press.

257 *In many societies*   Rebecca L. Bliege Bird and Douglas W. Bird (1997), "Delayed Reciprocity and Tolerated Theft: The Behavioral Ecology of Food-Sharing Strategies,"

Current Anthropology, 38:49–78. Serge Bahuchet (1990), "Food Sharing Among the Pygmies of Central Africa," *African Study Monographs*, 11:27–53. Catherline Feeley (2011), "The Host's Dilemma: Game Theory and Homeric Hospitality," Classical Association of Canada Annual Meeting, Vancouver, Canada, 11 May 2002, unpublished conference paper.

258 *majority belief* Martin A. Nowak, Corina E. Tarnita, and Edward O. Wilson (2010), "The Evolution of Eusociality," *Nature*, 466:1057–62.

258 *One rebuttal* Patrick Abbot, Jun Abe, John Alcock, et al. (2011), "Inclusive Fitness Theory and Eusociality," *Nature*, 471:E1–4.

258 *reinforced each other* Robert Wright (1994), *The Moral Animal: The New Science of Evolutionary Psychology*, Pantheon Books, 201–2.

258 *many books published* Michael Shermer (2004), *The Science of Good and Evil: Why People Cheat, Gossip, Care, Share, and Follow the Golden Rule*, Times Books. Nigel Barber (2004), *Kindness in a Cruel World: The Evolution of Altruism*, Prometheus Books. Donald W. Pfaff (2007), *The Neuroscience of Fair Play: Why We (Usually) Follow the Golden Rule*, Dana Press. Martin A. Nowak and Roger Highfield (2011), *SuperCooperators: Altruism, Evolution, and Why We Need Each Other to Succeed*, Free Press. Patricia S. Churchland (2011), *Braintrust: What Neuroscience Tells Us About Morality*, Princeton University Press.

258 *older book* Matt Ridley (1996), *The Origins of Virtue*, Viking.

Chapter 4

41 *Robert Sapolsky* Robert Sapolsky (2003), "A Bozo of a Baboon: A Talk with Robert Sapolsky," *Edge*.

41 *Matt Ridley* Matt Ridley (1993), *The Red Queen: Sex and the Evolution of Human Nature*, HarperCollins Publishers, 9–10.

42 *hyperbolic discounting* Richard H. Thaler (1981), "Some Empirical Evidence on Dynamic Inconsistency," *Economics Letters*, 8:201–7. Shane Frederick, George Loewenstein, and Ted O'Donoghue (2002), "Time Discounting and Time Preference: A Critical Review," *Journal of Economic Literature*, 40:351–401.

43 *Francis Fukuyama* Francis Fukuyama (1995), *Trust: The Social Virtues and the Creation of Prosperity*, Simon & Schuster, 27–8.

43 *James Madison* James Madison (1788), *The Federalist*, 51.

46 *many distinct levels* Richard J. Smith (1996), "Biology and Body Size in Human Evolution: Statistical Inference Misapplied," *Current Anthropology*, 37:451–81.

46 *begin to fail* Bruce Schneier (Jul 2009), "Security, Group Size, and the Human Brain," *IEEE Security & Privacy*, 7:88.

50 *Code of Hammurabi* Martha T. Roth (1997), *Law Collections from Mesopotamia and Asia Minor*, Scholars Press.

Chapter 4 Notes

258   *evolutionary psychology*   Edward O. Wilson (1975), *Sociobiology: The New Synthesis*, Harvard University Press. Edward O. Wilson (1978), *On Human Nature*, Harvard University Press.

258   *genetic science is flawed*   Anne Innis Dagg (2004), *"Love of Shopping" Is Not a Gene: Problems with Darwinian Psychology*, Black Rose Books.

259   *Douglass North*   Douglass C. North (1990), *Institutions, Institutional Change, and Economic Performance*, Cambridge University Press, 54.

259   *no money would*   David Graeber (2011), *Debt: The First 5,000 Years*, Melville House.

259   *Terrence Deacon*   Terrence W. Deacon (1997), *The Symbolic Species: The Co-Evolution of Language and the Human Brain*, W.W. Norton & Co., 384–401.

259   *far more philandering*   Simon C. Griffith, Ian P. Owens, and Katherine A. Thuman (2002), "Extra Pair Paternity in Birds: A Review of Interspecific Variation and Adaptive Function," *Molecular Ecology*, 11:2195–212. Anna Dubiec (2009), "Avian Infidelity," *Research in Progress: Behavioral Ecology*, 3:32–4.

259   *There's a balance*   Thomas D. Berger and Erik Trinkaus (1995), "Patterns of Trauma Among the Neanderthals," *Journal of Archaeological Science*, 22:841–52. Daniel S. Adler, Guy Bar-Oz, Anna Belfer-Cohen, and Ofer Bar-Yosef (2006), "Ahead of the Game: Middle and Upper Palaeolithic Hunting Behaviors in the Southern Caucasus," *Current Anthropology*, 47:89–118. Penny Spikins, Holly Rutherford, and Andy Needham (2010), "From Homininity to Humanity: Compassion from the Earliest Archaic to Modern Humans," *Time & Mind*, 3:303–25.

259   *preliminary evidence*   Carles Lalueza-Fox, Antonio Rosas, Almudena Estalrrich, Elena Gigli, Paula F. Campos, Antonio García-Tabernero, Samuel García-Vargas, Federico Sánchez-Quinto, Oscar Ramírez, Sergi Civit, Markus Bastir, Rosa Huguet, David Santamaría, M. Thomas P. Gilbert, Eske Willerslev, and Marco de la Rasilla (2011), "Genetic Evidence for Patrilocal Mating Behavior Among Neanderthal Groups," *Proceedings of the National Academy of Sciences of the United States of America*, 108:250–3.

259   *military organization*   Wei-Xing Zhou, Didier Sornette, Russell A. Hill, and Robin I.M. Dunbar (2005), "Discrete Hierarchical Organization of Social Group Sizes," *Proceedings of the Royal Society B: Biological Sciences*, 272:439–44.

259   *origins of religion*   Scott Atran (2004), *In Gods We Trust: The Evolutionary Landscape of Religion*, Oxford. Pascal Boyer (2002), *Religion Explained: The Evolutionary Origins of Religious Thought*, Basic Books. David Sloan Wilson (2003), *Darwin's Cathedral: Evolution, Religion, and the Nature of Society*, University of Chicago Press. Lewis Wolpert (2007), *Six Impossible Things Before Breakfast: The Evolutionary Origins of Belief*, Norton.

259   *social controls*   Edward Alsworth Ross (1896), "Social Control," *The American Journal of Sociology*, 1:513–35.

259   *not using that term*   Mathieu Deflem (2007), "The Concept of Social Control: Theories and Applications," paper presented at the International Conference on Charities as Instruments of Social Control in Nineteenth-Century Britain, Université de Haute Bretagne (Rennes 2), Rennes, France, November 22–23.

260   *not growing*   Zeynep Tufekci (2008), "Grooming, Gossip, Facebook and Myspace," *Information, Communication & Society*, 11:544–64. Bruno Goncalves, Nicola Perra, and Alessandro Vespignani (2011), "Validation of Dunbar's Number in Twitter Conversations," *PLoS ONE*, 6:e22656. *The Economist* (26 Feb 2009), "Primates on Facebook: Even Online, the Neocortex Is the Limit."

260   *certain brain regions*   Ryota Kanai, Bahador Bahrami, Rebecca Roylance, and Geraint Rees (2011), "Online Social Network Size Is Reflected in Human Brain Structure," *Proceedings of the Royal Society B: Biological Sciences*, published online before print.

Chapter 5

53   *Douglas Hofstadter*   Douglas Hofstadter (1985), *Metamagical Themas*, Bantam Dell Publishing Group.

57   *free-rider problem*   Robert Albanese and David D. van Fleet (1985), "Rational Behavior in Groups: The Free-Riding Tendency," *The Academy of Management Review*, 10:244–55.

57   *Whooping cough*   Paul Offit (2011), *Deadly Choices: How the Anti-Vaccine Movement Threatens Us All*, Basic Books.

Chapter 5 Notes

260   *Prisoner's Dilemma*   Merrill M. Flood (1952), "Some Experimental Games," Research Memorandum RM 789–1, The RAND Corporation. Republished as: Merrill M. Flood (1958), "Some Experimental Games," *Management Science*, 5:5–26. Albert W. Tucker (1980), "A Two-Person Dilemma," *UMAP Journal*, 1:101–3. Albert W. Tucker (1983), "The Mathematics of Tucker: A Sampler," *The Two-Year College Mathematics Journal*, 14:228–32.

260   *Many researchers*   Sylvia Nasar (2001), *A Beautiful Mind: The Life of Mathematical Genius and Nobel Laureate John Nash*, Simon & Schuster. John Nash (2008), "The Agencies Method for Modeling Coalitions & Cooperations in Games," *International Game Theory Review*, 10:539–64. Robert Axelrod and William D. Hamilton (1981), "The Evolution of Cooperation," *Science*, 211:1390–6. Robert Axelrod (1984), *The Evolution of Cooperation*, Basic Books.

260   *open grazing pasture*   Garrett Hardin (1968), "The Tragedy of the Commons," *Science*, 162:1243–8.

Chapter 6

63 *don't overfish* Boris Worm, Ray Hilborn, Julia K. Baum, Trevor A. Branch, Jeremy S. Collie, Christopher Costello, Michael J. Fogarty, Elizabeth A. Fulton, Jeffrey A. Hutchings, Simon Jennings, Olaf P. Jensen, Heike K. Lotze, Pamela M. Mace, Tim R. McClanahan, Cóilín Minto, Stephen R. Palumbi, Ana M. Parma, Daniel Ricard, Andrew A. Rosenberg, Reg Watson, and Dirk Zeller (2009), "Rebuilding Global Fisheries," *Science*, 325:578–85. Ed Pilkington (17 May 2010), "Saving Global Fish Stocks Would Cost 20 Million Jobs, Says UN," *The Guardian*.

64 *Jean-Jacques Rousseau* Jean-Jacques Rousseau (1754), *A Discourse on a Subject Proposed by the Academy of Dijon: What Is the Origin of Inequality of Men, and Is it Authorized by Natural Law?*

64 *defections happen* Brian Skyrms (2004), *The Stag Hunt and the Evolution of Social Structure*, Cambridge University Press.

65 *Snowdrift Dilemma* Michael Doebeli and Christoph Hauert (2005), "Models of Cooperation Based on the Prisoner's Dilemma and the Snowdrift Game," *Ecology Letters*, 8:748–66.

65 *social dilemmas* Robyn M. Dawes (1980), "Social Dilemmas," *Annual Review of Psychology*, 31:169–93. Samuel S. Komorita and Craig D. Parks (1994), *Social Dilemmas*, Westview Press.

65 *much more complicated* Richard H. McAdams (2008), *"Beyond the Prisoners' Dilemma: Coordination, Game Theory and the Law,"* John M. Olin Law and Economics Working Paper No. 437, The Law School, University of Chicago.

68 *need to conform* Solomon Asch (Nov 1955), "Opinions and Social Pressure," *Scientific American*, 193:31–5.

Chapter 6 Notes

261 *predictably irrational* Dan Ariely (2008), *Predictably Irrational: The Hidden Forces That Shape our Decisions*, Harper Perennial.

261 *Cuban Missile Crisis* Steven J. Brams (24 Jan 2001), "Game Theory and the Cuban Missile Crisis," *Plus Magazine*.

262 *worst in people* Morton Deutsch and Robert M. Krauss (1960), "The Effect of Threat upon Interpersonal Bargaining," *Journal of Abnormal & Normal Social Psychology*, 61:181–9.

262 *better model* Rolf Kümmerli, Caroline Colliard, Nicolas Fiechter, Blaise Petitpierre, Flavien Russier, and Laurent Keller (2007), "Human Cooperation in Social Dilemmas: Comparing the Snowdrift Game with the Prisoner's Dilemma," *Proceedings of the Royal Society B: Biological Sciences*, 274:2965–70.

262   *Prospect Theory*   Daniel Kahneman and Amos Tversky (1979), "Prospect Theory: An Analysis of Decision under Risk," *Econometrica*, 47:263–92.

262   *systems of regulation*   Susan Jane Buck Cox (1985), "No Tragedy on the Commons," *Environmental Ethics*, 7:49–62.

262   *superrationality*   Douglas Hofstadter (1985), *Metamagical Themas*, Bantam Dell Publishing Group.

262   *collectively rational*   Anatol Rapoport, ed. (1974), *Game Theory as a Theory of Conflict Resolution*, Reidel Publishing Co.

262   *four different modalities*   Lawrence Lessig (1998), "The New Chicago School," *The Journal of Legal Studies*, 27:661–91. Lawrence Lessig (2000), *Code and Other Laws of Cyberspace*, Basic Books.

262   *three basic flavors*   Steven D. Levitt and Stephen J. Dubner (2006), *Freakonomics: A Rogue Economist Explores the Hidden Side of Everything*, Morrow, 17.

Chapter 7

75   *not to vote*   William Riker and Peter Ordeshook (1968), "A Theory of the Calculus of Voting." *American Political Science Review*, 62:25–42.

75   *people vote*   Derek Parfit (1984), *Reasons and Persons*, Oxford University Press.

75   *actual voters*   Aaron Edlin, Andrew Gelman, and Noah Kaplan (2007), "Voting as a Rational Choice: Why and How People Vote to Improve the Well-Being of Others," *Rationality and Society*, 19:293–314.

76   *modified our brains*   Patricia S. Churchland (2011), *Braintrust: What Neuroscience Tells Us About Morality*, Princeton University Press.

77   *the murder rate*   Criminal Justice Information Services Division (2010), "Crime in the United States by Volume and Rate per 100,000 Inhabitants, 1990–2009," U.S. Department of Justice, Federal Bureau of Investigation.

77   *Elsewhere in the*   United Nations Office on Drugs & Crime (2008), "The Tenth United Nations Survey of Crime Trends and Operations of Criminal Justice Systems (2005–2006)."

77   *Golden Rule*   Jeffrey Wattles (1996), *The Golden Rule*, Oxford University Press.

78   *associated with religion*   Azim F. Shariff and Ara Norenzayan, "God is Watching You: Priming God Concepts Increases Prosocial Behavior in an Anonymous Economic Game," *Psychological Science*, 18:803–9.

78   *Ten Commandments*   Nina Mazar and Dan Ariely (2006), "Dishonesty in Everyday Life and Its Policy Implications," *Journal of Public Policy & Marketing*, 25:117–26.

78   *harsh, punitive, vengeful*   Azim F. Shariff and Ara Norenzayan (2011), "Mean Gods Make Good People: Different Views of God Predict Cheating Behavior," *International Journal for the Psychology of Religion*, 21:85–96.

78   *pretty much useless*   Bernard Gert (1989), "Morality Versus Slogans," in Daryl Close and Nicholas Meier, eds. (1995), *Morality in Criminal Justice*, Wadsworth, 51–60.

78 *kill animals*   Jeff McMahan (2002), *The Ethics of Killing: Problems at the Margins of Life*, Oxford University Press.

78 *This is the stuff*   Alasdair MacIntyre (1981), *After Virtue: A Study in Moral Theology*, University of Notre Dame Press.

79 *moral instinct*   Stephen Pinker (13 Jan 2008), "The Moral Instinct," *New York Times Magazine.*

79 *Others relevant*   Donald E. Brown (1991), *Human Universals*, Temple University Press.

79 *specific brain functions*   Marc D. Hauser (2006), *Moral Minds: How Nature Designed our Universal Sense of Right and Wrong*, Ecco. John Mikhail (2007), "Universal Moral Grammar: Trends, Evidence, and the Future," *TRENDS in Cognitive Sciences*, 11:143–52.

79 *five fundamental systems*   Jonathan Haidt and Craig Joseph (2004), "Intuitive Ethics: How Innately Prepared Intuitions Generate Culturally Variable Virtues," *Daedalus*, 55–66. Jonathan Haidt and Jesse Graham (2009), "Planet of the Durkheimians, Where Community, Authority, and Sacredness Are Foundations of Morality," in John T. Jost, Aaron C. Kay, and Hulda Thorisdottir, eds., *Social and Psychological Bases of Ideology and System Justification*, Oxford University Press.

79 *strong tendency*   David Berreby (2005), *Us and Them: Understanding Your Tribal Mind*, Little, Brown and Co.

79 *defer to authority*   Stanley Milgram (1963). "Behavioral Study of Obedience," *Journal of Abnormal & Social Psychology*, 67:371–8. Neil Lutsky (1995), "When Is 'Obedience' Obedience? Conceptual and Historical Commentary," *Journal of Social Issues*, 51: 55–65. Thomas Blass (1999), "The Milgram Paradigm After 35 Years: Some Things We Now Know About Obedience to Authority," *Journal of Applied Social Psychology*, 29:955–78.

79 *purity and sanctity*   Mary Douglas (1978), *Purity and Danger: An Analysis of the Concepts of Pollution and Taboo*, Routledge & Kegan Paul.

79 *Spontaneous cooperation*   Rebecca Solnit (2009), *A Paradise Built in Hell: The Extraordinary Communities that Arise in Disaster*, Viking Adult.

79 *increase in solidarity*   Randall Collins (2004), "Rituals of Solidarity and Security in the Wake of Terrorist Attack," *Sociological Theory*, 22:58–87.

80 *increase in prosocial*   Kathryn S. Steinberg and Patrick M. Rooney (2005), "America Gives: A Survey of Americans' Generosity After September 11," Center on Philanthropy at Indiana University.

80 *Crime in New York*   Jason Bram (2003), "New York City's Economy Before and After September 11," *Federal Reserve Bank of New York Second District Highlights, Current Issues in Economics & Finance*, 9:1–6.

80 *in-group/out-group*   Colin Holbrook, Paolo Sousa, and Jennifer Hahn-Holbrook (2011), "Unconscious Vigilance: Worldview Defense Without Adaptations for Terror, Coalition, or Uncertainty Management," *Journal of Personality & Social Psychology*, 101:451–66

80 *increase in hate crimes* Tanya Schevitz (26 Nov 2002), "FBI Sees Leap in Anti-Muslim Hate Crimes, 9/11 Attacks Blamed for Bias—Blacks Still Most Frequent Victims," *San Francisco Chronicle.*

80 *Kin aversion* Mark Erickson (1989), "Incest Avoidance and Familial Bonding," *Journal of Anthropological Research,* 45:267–91. Debra Lieberman, John Tooby, and Leda Cosmides (2003), "Does Morality Have a Biological Basis? An Empirical Test of the Factors Governing Moral Sentiments Relating to Incest," *Proceedings of the Royal Society B: Biological Sciences,* 270:819–26. John M. Ingham and David H. Spain (2005), "Sensual Attachment and Incest Avoidance in Human Evolution and Child Development," *Journal of the Royal Anthropological Institute,* 11:677–701. Robin Fox (1984), *The Red Lamp of Incest: An Enquiry into the Origin of Mind and Society,* University of Notre Dame Press.

80 *protective impulses* Sarah Hall Sternglanz, James L. Gray, and Melvin Murakami (1977), "Adult Preferences for Infantile Facial Features: An Ethological Approach," *Animal Behaviour,* 25:108–15. Katherine A. Hildebrandt and Hiram E. Fitzgerald (1979), "Facial Feature Determinants of Perceived Infant Attractiveness," *Infant Behavior & Development,* 2:329–39. Morten L. Kringelbach, Annukka Lehtonen, Sarah Squire, Allison G. Harvey, Michelle G. Craske, Ian E. Holliday, Alexander L. Green, Tipu Z. Aziz, Peter C. Hansen, Piers L. Cornelissen, and Alan Stein (2008), "A Specific and Rapid Neural Signature for Parental Instinct," *PLoS ONE,* 3:e1664. Melanie L. Glocker, Daniel D. Langleben, Kosha Ruparel, James W. Loughead, Ruben C. Gur, and Norbert Sachser (2009), "Baby Schema in Infant Faces Induces Cuteness Perception and Motivation for Caretaking in Adults," *Ethology,* 115:257–63.

80 *small animals* Wakako Sanefuji, Hidehiro Ohgami, and Kazuhide Hashiya (2007), "Development of Preference for Baby Faces Across Species in Humans (*Homo sapiens*)," *Journal of Ethology,* 25:249–54.

80 *even dolls* Robert A. Hinde and L.A. Barden (1985), "The Evolution of the Teddy Bear," *Animal Behaviour,* 33:1371–3. Paul H. Morris, Vasudevi Reddy, and R.C. Bunting (1995), "The Survival of the Cutest: Who's Responsible for the Evolution of the Teddy Bear?" *Animal Behaviour,* 50:1697–700.

80 *notions of fairness* Joseph Henrich, Jean Ensminger, Richard McElreath, Abigail Barr, Clark Barrett, Alexander Bolyanatz, Juan Camilo Cardenas, Michael Gurven, Edwins Gwako, Natalie Henrich, Carolyn Lesorogol, Frank Marlowe, David Tracer, and John Ziker (2010), "Markets, Religion, Community Size, and the Evolution of Fairness and Punishment," *Science,* 327:1480–4.

81 *Don't mess with Texas* Lilli Rockwell (29 Sep 2006), "'Don't Mess With Texas' Named Top Ad," *Austin American-Statesman.*

81 *effective in changing* Robert B. Cialdini (2003), "Crafting Normative Messages to Protect the Environment," *Current Directions in Psychological Science,* 12:105–9.

81 *taking advantage* Jelena Grujić, Constanza Fosco, Lourdes Araujo, José A. Cuesta, and Angel Sánchez (2010), "Social Experiments in the Mesoscale: Humans Playing a Spatial Prisoner's Dilemma," *PLoS ONE,* 5:11, e13749.

82 *Andrew Colman*   Andrew M. Colman (1995), *Game Theory and Its Applications in the Social and Biological Sciences*, Second Edition, Routledge.

82 *how people evaluate*   Mark Grenovetter (1978), "Threshold Models of Collective Behavior," *American Journal of Sociology*, 83:1420–43.

82 *more likely to litter*   Robert B. Cialdini, Carl A. Kallgren, and Raymond R. Reno (1991), "A Focus Theory of Normative Conduct: A Theoretical Refinement and Reevaluation of the Role of Norms in Human Behavior," *Advances in Experimental Social Psychology*, 21:201–34. Susan M. Reiter and William Samuel (1980), "Littering as a Function of Prior Litter and the Presence or Absence of Prohibitive Signs," *Journal of Applied Social Psychology*, 10:45–55. E. Scott Geller, Jill F. Witmer, and Margaret A. Tuso (1977), "Environmental Interventions for Litter Control," *Journal of Applied Psychology*, 62:344–51.

82 *seeing someone*   Harold Grasmick, Robert Bursik, and Karyl Kinsey (1991), "Shame and Embarrassment as Deterrents to Noncompliance with the Law: The Case of an Antilittering Campaign," *Environment & Behavior*, 23:233–51. Carl A. Kallgren, Raymond R. Reno, and Robert B. Cialdini (2000), "A Focus Theory of Normative Conduct: When Norms Do and Do Not Affect Behavior," *Personality & Social Psychology Bulletin*, 26:1002–12.

82 *general breakdown*   James B. Stewart (2011), *Tangled Webs: How False Statements Are Undermining America: From Martha Stewart to Bernie Madoff*, Penguin Press.

82 *unpunished free rider*   Robert O. Kurzban and Daniel Houser (2001), "Individual Differences in Cooperation in a Circular Public Goods Game," *European Journal of Personality*, 15:S37–S52. David P. Myatt and Chris Wallace (2008), "When Does One Bad Apple Spoil the Barrel? An Evolutionary Analysis of Collective Action," *Review of Economic Studies*, 75:499–527.

82 *In Islam*   Sahih Muslim, Book 037, Hadith Number 6658.

83 *propaganda campaigns*   David Livingstone Smith (2011), *Less than Human: Why We Demean, Enslave, and Exterminate Others*, St. Martin's Press.

83 *failure or absence*   Simon Baron-Cohen (2011), *Zero Degrees of Empathy: A New Theory of Human Cruelty*, Penguin/Allen Lane; published in the U.S. as *The Science of Evil: On Empathy and the Origins of Human Cruelty*, Basic Books.

84 *food on the honor*   Stephen J. Dubner and Steven D. Levitt (6 Jun 2004), "What the Bagel Man Saw: An Accidental Glimpse at Human Nature," *New York Times Magazine*, 62–5.

84 *follow social norms*   Daniel Kahneman and Dale T. Miller (1986), "Norm Theory: Comparing Reality to Its Alternatives," *Psychological Review*, 93:136–53. Cass R. Sunstein (1996), "Social Norms and Social Roles," *Columbia Law Review*, 96:903–68. Helen Bernhard, Ernst Fehr, and Urs Fischbacher (2006), "Group Affiliation and Altruistic Norm Enforcement," *American Economic Review*, 96:217–21.

84 *Emmanuel Levinas*   Michael L. Morgan (2011), *The Cambridge Introduction to Emmanuel Levinas*, Cambridge University Press.

84 *people turned in*   Akiko Fujita (17 Aug 2011), "Honest Japanese Return $78 Million in Cash Found in Quake Rubble," *ABC News*.

85   *practice of religion*   David Kowalewski (1980), "Protest for Religious Rights in the USSR: Characteristics and Consequences," *Russian Review,* 39:426–41. Sabrina Petra Ramet, ed. (1993), *Religious Policy in the Soviet Union,* Cambridge University Press.

85   *Confidence tricksters*   Frank Stajano and Paul Wilson (Mar 2011), "Understanding Scam Victims: Seven Principles for Systems Security," *Communications of the ACM,* 54:70–5.

85   *we have trouble*   David McCullough (2003), *Truman,* Simon & Schuster, 510.

Chapter 7 Notes

263   *the same analysis*   Ilya Somin (2006), "Knowledge about Ignorance: New Directions in the Study of Political Information," *Critical Review,* 18:255–78.

263   *related to other*   James H. Fowler (2006), "Altruism and Turnout," *Journal of Politics,* 68:674–83. James H. Fowler and Cindy D. Kam (2007), "Beyond the Self: Altruism, Social Identity, and Political Participation," *Journal of Politics,* 69:811–25. James H. Fowler and Christopher T. Dawes (2008), "Two Genes Predict Voter Turnout," *Journal of Politics,* 70:579–94.

263   *not distinguishing*   Mark Johnson (1993), *Moral Imagination: Implications of Cognitive Science for Ethics,* University of Chicago Press.

263   *National Voter Turnout*   Demos (2009), "Demos Fact Sheet: Election Day Registration."

264   *significant difference*   Stephen Anderson (2009), "The Golden Rule: Not So Golden Anymore," *Philosophy Now,* 74:26–9.

264   *Chácobo of Bolivia*   Gilbert R. Prost (1983) "Chácobo: Society of Equality," unpublished manuscript, Department of Anthropology, University of Florida; quoted in Michael Gurven (2004), "To Give and to Give Not: The Behavioral Ecology of Human Food Transfers," *Behavioral & Brain Sciences,* 27:543–59.

264   *Maori of New Zealand*   Raymond Firth (1926), "Proverbs in Native Life, with Special Reference to Those of the Maori," *Folklore,* 37:134–53.

264   *Yeyi of Botswana*   Alistair J. Sutherland (1981), "Local Level Dispute Processes in Botswana: The Yeyi Moot Encapsulated," *Journal of African Law,* 25:94–114.

264   *believe in free will*   Kathleen D. Vohs and Jonathan W. Schooler (2008), "The Value of Believing in Free Will: Encouraging a Belief in Determinism Increases Cheating," *Psychological Science,* 19:49–54

264   *believe in predestination*   Tyler F. Stillman, Roy F. Baumeister, Kathleen D. Vohs, Nathaniel M. Lambert, Frank D. Fincham, and Lauren E. Brewer (2010), "Personal Philosophy and Personnel Achievement: Belief in Free Will Predicts Better Job Performance," *Social Psychological & Personality Science,* 1:43–50.

264   *concept of free will*   Shaun Nichols (2011), "Experimental Philosophy and the Problem of Free Will," *Science,* 331:1401–3.

264   *Inbreeding is likely*   M. Menotti-Raymond and S.J. O'Brien (1993), "Dating the Genetic Bottleneck of the African Cheetah," *Proceedings of the National Academy of Sciences of the United States of America,* 90:3172–6. William Amos and John Harwood (1998),

"Factors Affecting Levels of Genetic Diversity in Natural Populations," *Philosophical Transactions of the Royal Society B*, 353:177–86. Mary Jane McKay (11 Feb 2009), "Genetic Disorders Hit Amish Hard," *CBS News*.

264   *isolated from modern*   Joseph Henrich (2000), "Does Culture Matter in Economic Behavior? Ultimatum Game Bargaining Among the Machiguenga of the Peruvian Amazon," *American Economic Review*, 90:973–9.

265   *wash their hands*   John M. Lynn (2000), "Method and Apparatus for Helping to Ensure the Washing of Hands," U.S. Patent #6,031,461. John M. Lynn (2000), "Method and Apparatus for Helping to Ensure the Washing of Hands," U.S. Patent #6,147,607. Fiona A. Lynn and John M. Lynn (2001), "Method and Apparatus for Helping to Ensure the Washing of Hands," U.S. Patent #6,211,788.

265   *broken windows theory*   James Q. Wilson and George L. Kelling (Mar 1982), "Broken Windows," *Atlantic Monthly*, 127:29–38. George L. Kelling (17 Jul 2009), "How New York Became Safe: The Full Story," *City Journal*.

265   *Researchers compared*   Khaled Taqi-Eddin and Dan Macallair (1999), "Shattering Broken Windows: An Analysis of San Francisco's Alternative Crime Policies," Justice Policy Institute. Randall G. Shelden (2003), "Assessing 'Broken Windows': A Brief Critique," Center on Juvenile & Criminal Justice. Bernard E. Harcourt and Jens Ludwig (2006), "Broken Windows: New Evidence from New York City and a Five-City Social Experiment," *University of Chicago Law Review*, 73:271–320.

265   *evidence that it does*   Kees Keizer, Siegwart Lindenberg, and Linda Steg (2008), "The Spreading of Disorder," *Science*, 322:1681–5.

265   *Steven Levitt*   Steven D. Levitt (2004), "Understanding Why Crime Fell in 1990's: Four Factors that Explain the Decline and Six that Do Not," *Journal of Economic Perspectives*, 18:163–90.

266   *reduced their energy*   Ian Ayres, Sophie Raseman, and Alice Shih (2009), "Evidence from Two Large Field Experiments That Peer Comparison Feedback Can Reduce Residential Energy Usage," NBER Working Paper 15386, National Bureau of Economic Research.

266   *this system backfires*   Dora L. Costa and Matthew E. Kahn (2010), "Energy Conservation 'Nudges' and Environmentalist Ideology: Evidence from a Randomized Residential Electricity Field Experiment," NBER Working Paper No. 15939, National Bureau of Economic Research.

266   *people are swayed*   Matt Davis (2011), "Behavior and Energy Savings: Evidence from a Series of Experimental Interventions," Environmental Defense Fund.

266   *In Rwanda*   Heather B. Hamilton (2000), "Rwanda's Women: The Key to Reconstruction," *Journal of Humanitarian Assistance*.

266   *cash box was made*   Stephen J. Dubner and Steven D. Levitt (6 Jun 2004), "What the Bagel Man Saw: An Accidental Glimpse at Human Nature," *New York Times Magazine*, 62–5.

266   *a host of unknowns*   Steven D. Levitt (2006) "White-Collar Crime Writ Small: A Case Study of Bagels, Donuts, and the Honor System," *The American Economic Review*, 96:290–4.

Chapter 8

87   *ability to deceive*   David Livingstone Smith (2004), *Why We Lie: The Evolutionary Roots of Deception and the Unconscious Mind*, St. Martin's Press.

87   *Wason Selection Task*   Peter C. Wason (1966), "Reasoning," in B.M. Foss, *New Horizons in Psychology*, Penguin. Peter C. Wason and Diana Shapiro (1971), "Natural and Contrived Experience in a Reasoning Problem," *Quarterly Journal of Experimental Psychology*, 23:63–71.

87   *better at solving*   Leda Cosmides (1989), "The Logic of Social Exchange: Has Natural Selection Shaped How Humans Reason? Studies with the Wason Selection Task," *Cognition*, 31:187–276.

87   *scans of the brains*   Nicola Canessa, Alessandra Gorini, Stefano F. Cappa, Massimo Piattelli-Palmarini, Massimo Danna, Ferruccio Fazio, and Daniela Perani (2005), "The Effect of Social Context on Deductive Reasoning: An fMRI Study," *Human Brain Mapping*, 26:30–43.

88   *we cooperate primarily*   Natalie Henrich and Joseph Henrich (2007), "Evolutionary Theory and the Social Psychology of Human Cooperation," in Joseph Henrich and Natalie Henrich, eds., *Why Humans Cooperate: A Cultural and Evolutionary Explanation*, Oxford University Press: 35–74. Robert Boyd and Peter J. Richerson (1992), "Punishment Allows the Evolution of Cooperation (or Anything Else) in Sizable Groups," *Ethology & Sociobiology*, 13:171–95.

89   *reputation information*   Paul Resnick, Ko Kuwabara, Richard Zeckhauser, and Eric Friedman (2000), "Reputation Systems," *Communications of the ACM*, 43:45–8. Daniel Houser and John Wooders (2006), "Reputation in Auctions: Theory, and Evidence from eBay," *Journal of Economics & Management Strategy*, 15:353–69. Paul Resnick, Richard Zeckhauser, John Zwanson, and Kate Lockwood (2006), "The Value of Reputation on eBay: A Controlled Experiment," *Experimental Economics*, 9:79–101. Jian Yang, Xiaorhi Hu, and Han Zhang (2007), "Effects of a Reputation Feedback System on an Online Consumer-to-Consumer Auction Market," *Decision Support Systems*, 44:93–105.

89   *eBay changed this*   Max Sherry (30 Oct 2008), "eBay Feedback System Negative for Sellers," suite101.com. Greg Kusch (8 Jan 2010), "Leaving Buyer Feedback on eBay (I'll Scratch Your Back. Will You Scratch Mine?)," Ezinearticles.com.

89   *remember negative*   Felicia Pratto and Oliver P. John (1991), "Automatic Vigilance: The Attention-Grabbing Power of Negative Social Information," *Journal of Personality & Social Psychology*, 61:380–91. Roy F. Baumeister, Ellen Bratslavsky, Catrin Finkenauer, and Kathleen D. Vohs (2001), "Bad Is Stronger Than Good," *Review of General Psychology*, 5:323–70. Tiffany A. Ito, Jeff T. Larsen, N. Kyle Smith, and John T. Cacioppo (1998), "Negative Information Weighs More Heavily on the Brain: The Negativity Bias in Evaluative Categorizations," *Journal of Personality & Social Psychology*, 75:887–900. Elizabeth A. Kensinger (2007), "Negative Emotion Enhances

Memory Accuracy: Behavioral and Neuroimaging Evidence," *Current Directions in Psychological Science,* 16:213–18.

89 *theory that gossip* Peter J. Wilson (1974), "Filcher of Good Names: An Enquiry Into Anthropology and Gossip," *Man, New Series,* 9:93–102. Ronald S. Burt and Mark Knez (1995), "Kinds of Third-Party Effects on Trust," *Rationality & Society,* 7:255–92. Ralf D. Sommerfeld, Hans-Jurgen Krambeck, Dirk Semmann, and Manfred Milinski (2007), "Gossip as an Alternative for Direct Observation in Games of Indirect Reciprocity," *Proceedings of the National Academy of Sciences of the United States of America,* 104:17435–40. Robin I.M. Dunbar (22 Nov 1992), "Why Gossip Is Good for You," *New Scientist,* 28–31. Robin I.M. Dunbar (1996), *Grooming, Gossip and the Evolution of Language,* Harvard University Press.

89 *whom to interact* Robin I.M. Dunbar (2004), "Gossip in Evolutionary Perspective," *Review of General Psychology,* 8:100–10. Ralf D. Sommerfeld, Hans-Jurgen Krambeck, Dirk Semmann, and Manfred Milinski (2007), "Gossip as an Alternative for Direct Observation in Games of Indirect Reciprocity," *Proceedings of the National Academy of Sciences of the United States of America,* 104:17435–40.

89 *establish group interests* Richard H. McAdams (1997), "The Origin, Development, and Regulation of Norms," *Michigan Law Review,* 96:338–433. Roy F. Baumeister, Liqing Zhang, and Kathleen D. Vohs (2004), "Gossip as Cultural Learning," *Review of General Psychology,* 8:111–21.

89 *gossip helps keep* Richard McAdams (1996), "Group Norms, Gossip, and Blackmail," *University of Pennsylvania Law Review,* 144:2237–92. Dirk Semmann, Hans-Jürgen Krambeck, and Manfred Milinski (2005), "Reputation Is Valuable Within and Outside One's Own Social Group," *Behavioral Ecology & Sociobiology,* 57:611–6. Bianca Beersma and Gerben A. Van Kleef (2011), "How the Grapevine Keeps You in Line: Gossip Increases Contributions to the Group," *Social Psychological & Personality Science,* 2:642–9.

89 *Diamond merchants* Barak D. Richman (2002), "Community Enforcement of Informal Contracts: Jewish Diamond Merchants in New York," Harvard Law School John M. Olin Center for Law, Economics and Business Discussion Paper Series, Paper 384.

90 *a pair of eyes* Melissa Bateson, Daniel Nettle, and Gilbert Roberts (2006), "Cues of Being Watched Enhance Cooperation in a Real-World Setting," *Biology Letters,* 2:212–4.

90 *names and addresses* Arthur L. Beaman, Bonnel Kentz, Edward Diener, and Soren Svanum (1979), "Self-Awareness and Transgression in Children: Two Field Studies," *Journal of Personality & Social Psychology,* 37:1835–46.

90 *There's a great word* Oliver Conway (22 Jun 2004), "Congo Word 'Most Untranslatable,'" *BBC News.*

91 *Quakers would cooperate* Adrian Cadbury (2003), "Beliefs and Business: The Experience of Quaker Companies," The Foundation of Lady Katherine Leveson. James Surowiecki (2004), *The Wisdom of Crowds,* Anchor. Steven Davison (2011), "The Double-Culture Period: Factors in Quaker Success," unpublished manuscript.

92 *Maghribi traders*   Avner Greif (2008), "Contract Enforcement and Institutions among the Maghribi Traders: Refuting Edwards and Ogilvie," SIEPR Discussion Paper 08–018, Stanford Institute for Economic Policy Research.

92 *Robert Putnam*   Robert Putnam (2007), "*E Pluribus Unum:* Diversity and Community in the Twenty-First Century," *Scandinavian Political Studies,* 30:137–74. Robert Putnam (2001), *Bowling Alone: The Collapse and Revival of American Community,* Touchstone/Simon & Schuster.

92 *vestigial remnants*   David Sally (2000), "A General Theory of Sympathy, Mind-Reading, and Social Interaction, with an Application to the Prisoners' Dilemma," *Social Science Information,* 39:567–643.

92 *people who look like*   Lisa M. DeBruine (2004), "Facial Resemblance Increases the Attractiveness of Same-Sex Faces More Than Other-Sex Faces," *Proceedings of the Royal Society B: Biological Sciences,* 271:2085–90. Lisa M. DeBruine (2005), "Trustworthy but Not Lust-Worthy: Context-Specific Effects of Facial Resemblance," *Proceedings of the Royal Society B: Biological Sciences,* 272:919–22. Lisa M. DeBruine, Benedict C. Jones, Anthony C. Little, and David I. Perrett (2008), "Social Perception of Facial Resemblance in Humans," *Archives of Sexual Behavior,* 27:64–77. Alexandra Alvergne, Elise Huchard, Damien Caillaud, Marie J. E. Charpentier, Joanna M. Setchell, Charlène Ruppli, Delphine Féjan, Laura Martinez, Guy Cowlishaw, and Michel Raymond (2009), "Human Ability to Recognize Kin Visually Within Primates," *International Journal of Primatology,* 30:199–210.

92 *same accent*   Shirley Lev-Ari and Boaz Keysar (2010), "Why Don't We Believe Non-Native Speakers? The Influence of Accent on Credibility," *Journal of Experimental Social Psychology,* 46:1093–6.

92 *change our patterns*   Tanya L. Chartrand and John A. Bargh (1999), "The Chameleon Effect: The Perception-Behavior Link and Social Interaction," *Journal of Personality & Social Psychology,* 76:893–910. Jessica L. Lakin, Valerie E. Jefferis, Clara Michelle Cheng, and Tanya L. Chartrand (2003), "The Chameleon Effect As Social Glue: Evidence for the Evolutionary Significance of Nonconscious Mimicry," *Journal of Nonverbal Behavior,* 27:145–62. Tanya L. Chartrand and Rick van Baaren (2009), "Human Mimicry," *Advances in Experimental Social Psychology,* 41:219–74.

92 *don't sound like*   John Baugh (2010), "Linguistic Profiling," in Sinfree Makoni, Geneva Smitherman, and Arnetha Ball, eds., *Black Linguistics,* Routledge. Shiri Lev-Ari and Boaz Keysar (2010), "Why Don't We Believe Non-Native Speakers? The Influence of Accent on Credibility," *Journal of Experimental Social Psychology,* 46:1093–96.

93 *how to cooperate*   Ernst Fehr and Urst Fischbacher (2004), "Social Norms and Human Cooperation," *Trends in Cognitive Sciences,* 8:185–90.

93 *Platinum Rule*   Tony Alessandra and Michael J. O'Connor (1996), *The Platinum Rule: Discover the Four Basic Business Personalities—And How They Can Lead You to Success,* Warner Books.

93 *reputation scale*   Avinash Dixit and Barry Nalebuff (1991), *Thinking Strategically: The Competitive Edge in Business, Politics, and Everyday Life,* Norton, 144–61.

95 *Criminals have signals* Diego Gambetta (2009), *Codes of the Underworld: How Criminals Communicate,* Princeton University Press.

95 *Shared brand names* Jean Tirole (1996), "A Theory of Collective Reputations (with Applications to the Persistence of Corruption and to Firm Quality)," *Review of Economic Studies,* 63:1–22.

95 *Saudi Binladin Group* Holly Williams (20 Nov 2001), "Bin Laden Group Reputation Brief on Global Scale," *PR Week UK.*

95 *pay a premium* Stefano Castriota and Marco Delmastro (2009), "The Economics of Collective Reputation: Minimum Quality Standards, Vertical Differentiation, and Optimal Group Size," American Association of Wine Economists Working Paper 50.

95 *more reputable producer* Stuart Landon and Constance E. Smith (1998), "Quality Expectations, Reputation, and Price," *Southern Economic Journal,* 64:628–47. Olivier Gergaud and Florine Livat (2004), "Team versus Individual Reputations: A Model of Interaction and Some Empirical Evidence," Cahiers de la Maison des Sciences Economiques, No. bla04015.

95 *cultivate their brand* Smooch Reynolds (Dec 2002), "Career Branding: Is There Really Such a Concept?" *Public Relations Tactics,* 9:7,22.

96 *A small complaint* Daniel J. Solove (2007), *The Future of Reputation: Gossip, Rumor, and Privacy on the Internet,* Yale University Press.

96 *isn't an effective* Daniel Balliet, Laetitia B. Mulder, and Paul A.M. Van Lange (2011), "Reward, Punishment, and Cooperation: A Meta-Analysis," *Psychological Bulletin,* 137:594–615.

97 *Maine lobstermen* James M. Acheson (Apr 1972), "Territories of the Lobstermen," *Natural History Magazine,* 81 (4): 60–9.

97 *Shame is a common* Thomas J. Scheff (2000), "Shame and the Social Bond: A Sociological Theory," *Sociological Theory,* 18:84–99.

97 *excessive CEO pay* Sandeep Gopalan (2007), "Shame Sanctions and Excessive CEO Pay," *Delaware Journal of Corporate Law,* 32:757–97.

98 *Informal punishments* Marc Galanter and David Luban (1993), "Poetic Justice: Punitive Damages and Legal Pluralism," *The American University Law Review,* 42:1393–1463.

98 *bad apples diminishes* Jaap W. Ouwerkerk, Paul A.M. van Lange, Marcello Gallucci, and Norbert L. Kerr (2004), "Avoiding the Social Death Penalty: Ostracism and Cooperation in Social Dilemmas," Presentation at the 7th Annual Sydney Symposium of Social Psychology: "The Social Outcast: Ostracism, Social Exclusion, Rejection, and Bullying," 15–18 Mar, 2004. Norbert L. Kerr, Ann C. Rumble, Ernest S. Park, Jaap W. Ouwerkerk, Craig D. Parks, Marcello Gallucci, and Paul A.M. van Lange (2009), "'How Many Bad Apples Does It Take to Spoil the Whole Barrel?' Social Exclusion and Toleration for Bad Apples," *Journal of Experimental Social Psychology,* 45:603–13.

98 *if Alice kills Bob* Napoleon A. Chagnon (1988), "Life Histories, Blood Revenge, and Warfare in a Tribal Population," *Science, New Series,* 239:985–92. Jon Elster (1990), "Norms of Revenge," *Ethics,* 100:862–85.

98 *Nazis instituted this*   Robert Loeffel (2007), "Sippenhaft, Terror and Fear in Nazi Germany: Examining One Facet of Terror in the Aftermath of the Plot of 20 July 1944," *Contemporary European History*, 16:51–69.

98 *various cultures*   Jon Elster (1990), "Norms of Revenge," *Ethics*, 100:862–85. Stephen D. White (1986), "Feuding and Peace-Making in the Touraine Around the Year 1100," *Traditio*, 42:195–263. Trevor Dean (1997), "Marriage and Mutilation: Vendetta in Late Medieval Italy," *Past & Present*, 157:3–36. Joel T. Rosenthal (1966), "Marriage and the Blood Feud in 'Heroic' Europe," *The British Journal of Sociology*, 17:133–44.

98 *Hatfields versus the McCoys*   Otis K. Rice (1982), *The Hatfields and McCoys*, University of Kentucky Press.

98 *reputation can solve*   Brian Skyrms (1996), *The Evolution of the Social Contract*, Cambridge University Press, 56–8.

99 *John Wayne Gacy*   Clifford L. Linedecker (1980), *The Man Who Killed Boys: A True Story of Mass Murder in a Chicago Suburb*, St. Martin's Press.

99 *Dr. Harold Shipman*   Sarah Ramsay (2001), "Audit Further Exposes UK's Worst Serial Killer," *Lancet*, 357:123–4.

101 *settling disputes*   Robert C. Ellickson (1991), *Order without Law: How Neighbors Settle Disputes*, Harvard University Press.

102 *Dunbar wrote*   Robin I.M. Dunbar (Nov 1992), "Why Gossip Is Good For You," *New Scientist*, 28–31.

102 *Hardin: "Perhaps*   Garrett Hardin (1994), "The Tragedy of the Unmanaged Commons," *Trends in Ecology & Evolution*, 9:199.

Chapter 8 Notes

266 *People who defect*   James E. Alcock and Diana Mansell (1977), "Predisposition and Behaviour in a Collective Dilemma," *Journal of Conflict Resolution*, 21:443–57.

267 *better at predicting*   Robert H. Frank (1988), *Passions within Reason: The Strategic Role of the Emotions*, W.W. Norton & Co., 137–43.

267 *better at recognizing*   Harold H. Kelly and Anthony J. Stahelski (1970), "Errors in Perception of Intentions in a Mixed-Motive Game," *Journal of Experimental Social Psychology*, 6:279–400.

267 *Robert Axelrod*   Robert Axelrod (1984), *The Evolution of Cooperation*, Basic Books.

267 *oft-quoted line*   Pete Blackshaw (2008), *Satisfied Customers Tell Three Friends, Angry Customers Tell 3,000*, Crown Business.

267 *cooperation jumps*   Claus Wedekind and Manfred Milinski (1996), "Human Cooperation in the Simultaneous and the Alternating Prisoner's Dilemma: Pavlov Versus Generous Tit-for-Tat," *Proceedings of the National Academy of Sciences of the United States of America*, 93:2686–9.

268 *Dueling isn't always*   Christopher Kingston and Robert E. Wright (2009), "The Deadliest of Games: The Institution of Dueling," *Southern Economic Journal*, 76:1094–1106.

Diego Gambetta (2009), *Codes of the Underworld: How Criminals Communicate,* Princeton University Press.

268 *Chimpanzees are able* Francys Subaiul, Jennifer Vonk, Sanae Okamoto-Barth, and Jochen Barth (2008), "Do Chimpanzees Learn Reputation by Observation? Evidence from Direct and Indirect Experience with Generous and Selfish Strangers," *Animal Cognition,* 11:611–23.

268 *Charles Lamb* Charles Lamb (1833), "Table-Talk by the Late Elia," in Edward Verrall Lucas, ed. (1913), *The Works of Charles and Mary Lamb: Miscellaneous Prose, 1798–1834,* Macmillan, 400.

268 *counter-evidence* Francisco C. Santos, Marta D. Santos, Jorge M. Pacheco (2008), "Social Diversity Promotes the Emergence of Cooperation in Public Goods Games," *Nature,* 454:213–6. Sven Van Segbroeck, Francisco C. Santos, Tom Lenaerts, Jorge M. Pacheco (2009), "Reacting Differently to Adverse Ties Promotes Cooperation in Social Networks," *Physical Review Letters,* 102:058105–9.

268 *diverse communities* Eric M. Uslaner (2002), *The Moral Foundations of Trust,* Cambridge University Press. Eric M. Uslaner (2004), "Trust and Social Bonds: Faith in Others and Policy Outcomes Reconsidered," *Political Research Quarterly,* 57:501–7. Eric M. Uslaner (2011), "Trust, Diversity, and Segregation in the United States and the United Kingdom," *Comparative Sociology,* 10:221–47.

268 *different dialects* Ottar Tinglum (1929), "Landsmaal-Riksmaal: The Feud Between the Dialects and the Official Language of Norway," *American Journal of Sociology,* 34:686–92.

268 *English dialects* Sally Johnson, Tommaso M. Milani, and Clive Upton (2008), "Whose Voices? A Hypermodal Approach to Language Ideological Debates on the BBC 'Voices' Website," Working Paper No. 127, Lancaster University Department of Linguistics and English Language Centre for Language in Social Life. Clive Upton and John David Allison Widdowson (2006), *An Atlas of English Dialects,* Oxford University Press.

268 *David Nettle ran* David Nettle (1999), *Linguistic Diversity,* Oxford University Press.

268 *alternate analysis* Brian Skyrms (1996), *The Evolution of the Social Contract,* Cambridge University Press, 57–61.

269 *"is" does not imply* David Hume (1739), *A Treatise on Human Nature.*

269 *costly religious rituals* William Irons (1996), "Morality as an Evolved Adaptation," in J.P. Hurd, ed., *Investigating the Biological Foundations of Morality,"* Edwin Mellen Press, 1–34. William Irons (2001), "Religion as a Hard-to-Fake Sign of Commitment," in Randolph Nesse, ed., *The Evolution of Commitment,* Russell Sage Foundation, 155–78. Richard Sosis (2000), "Religion and Intra-Group Cooperation: Preliminary Results of a Comparative Analysis of Utopian Communities," *Cross-Cultural Research,* 37:211–39.

269 *breeding females* James Acheson and Roy Gardner (2011), "The Evolution of the Maine Lobster V-Notch Practice: Cooperation in a Prisoner's Dilemma Game," *Ecology & Society,* 16:41.

270   *Edney listed several*   Julian J. Edney (1981), "Paradoxes on the Commons: Scarcity and the Problem of Inequality," *Journal of Community Psychology*, 9:3–34.

270   *Michel Foucalt said*   Didier Eribon (1991), *Michel Foucault*, translated from French by Betsy Wing, Harvard University Press, 265.

Chapter 9

103   *continuous operation clause*   Marc C. Singer (2005), "'Going Dark' Provisions: Making Clients See the Light," *New Jersey Law Journal*, 179:1–3.

104   *solitary, poor, nasty*   Thomas Hobbes (1651), *Leviathan*, Printed for Andrew Crooke, at the Green Dragon in St. Paul's Churchyard.

104   *Martin Luther said*   Martin Luther (1524), *Von Kaufshandlung und Wucher*.

104   *Immanuel Kant*   Immanual Kant (1795), *First Supplement on the Guarantee for Perpetual Peace*.

104   *John Locke*   John Locke (1689), *Second Treatise of Government*.

104   *Jean-Jacques Rousseau*   Jean-Jacques Rousseau (1762), *Du Contrat Social (The Social Contract)*.

104   *John Rawls*   John Rawls (1971), *A Theory of Justice*, Belknap Press of Harvard University Press.

104   *In Plato's Republic*   Plato (c. 427–347 BC), *The Republic*.

105   *Niccolò Machiavelli*   Niccolò Machiavelli (1517), *Discourses Upon the First Ten Books of Titus Livy*.

105   *Garrett Hardin*   Garrett Hardin (1994). "The Tragedy of the Unmanaged Commons," *Trends in Ecology & Evolution*, 9:199.

106   *voting is required*   Elliot Frankal (4 Jul 2005), "Compulsory Voting Around the World," *The Guardian*.

107   *marriage rites were informal*   Stephanie Coontz (2005), *Marriage, a History: From Obedience to Intimacy, or How Love Conquered Marriage*, Viking.

107   *accomplices at worst*   Marla Dickerson and Cecilia Sanchez (5 Aug 2008), "Mexican Police Linked to Rising Kidnappings," *Los Angeles Times*.

107   *occasionally jails*   British Broadcasting Corporation (20 June 2011), "Somalia: Six Jailed for 'Pirate Ransom' Case," *BBC News*.

108   *offering a bribe*   Kaushik Basu (2011), "Why, for a Class of Bribes, the Act of Giving a Bribe Should Be Treated as Legal," Working Paper 1-2011-DEA, Ministry of Finance, Government of India.

108   *easy to make exceptions*   Ed Moloney (2002), *A Secret History of the IRA*, Viking Penguin.

110   *Alexander Hamilton*   Alexander Hamilton (1787), "The Federalist #15," in Alexander Hamilton, John Jay and James Madison; John C. Hamilton, ed. (1866), *The Federalist: A Commentary On the Constitution of the United States*, Lippincott, 143.

110   *immoral, ineffective*   Toni M. Massaro (1991), "Shame, Culture, and American Criminal Law," *Michigan Law Review*, 89:1880–1944. James Q. Whitman (1998), "What

Is Wrong with Inflicting Shame Sanctions?" *The Yale Law Journal,* 107:1055–92. Brian Netter (2005), "Avoiding the Shameful Backlash: Social Repercussions for the Increased Use of Alternative Sanctions," *The Journal of Criminal Law & Criminology,* 96:187–216. Dan M. Kahan (2006), "What's Really Wrong with Shaming Sanctions," *Texas Law Review,* 84:2075–95.

111 *fines reduce speeding*   Robert Beattie Crawford (1989), "Toward a Theory on Speeding and Penalties: Have the Increased Fines Reduced Speeding in Massachusetts?" Master's thesis, Massachusetts Institute of Technology. D.C. Webster and P.A. Wells (2000), "The Characteristics of Speeders," Road Safety Division, Department of the Environment, Transport and the Regions, TRL Report. Saranath Lawpoolsri, Jingyi Li, and Elisa R. Braver (2007), "Do Speeding Tickets Reduce the Likelihood of Receiving Subsequent Speeding Tickets? A Longitudinal Study of Speeding Violators in Maryland," *Traffic Injury Prevention,* 8:26–34.

111 *uninsured drivers*   Ray Massey (23 Nov 2010), "Uninsured Drivers Kill 160 People a Year but Face Inadequate Fines as Low as £50," *Daily Mail.*

111 *basing traffic fines*   British Broadcasting Corporation (14 Jan 2002), "Nokia Boss Gets Record Speeding Fine," *BBC News.* British Broadcasting Corporation (10 Feb 2004), "Finn's Speed Fine Is a Bit Rich," *BBC News.* Jason Paur (8 Jan 2010), "Swiss Slap Speeder With $290K Fine," *Wired.* British Broadcasting Corporation (12 Aug 2010), "Swede Faces World-Record $1m Speeding Penalty," *BBC News.*

113 *tax the use of antibiotics*   Infectious Diseases Society of America (2011), "Combating Antimicrobial Resistance: Policy Recommendations to Save Lives," *Clinical Infectious Diseases,* 52 (suppl. 5): S397–428.

114 *In one experiment*   Ann E. Tenbrunsel and David M. Messick (1999), "Sanctioning Systems: Decision Frames and Cooperation," *Administrative Science Quarterly,* 44:684–707.

114 *instituted a fine*   Uri Gneezy and Aldo Rustichini (2000), "A Fine is a Price," *Journal of Legal Studies,* 29:1–17.

114 *towns are experimenting*   Ben Hamilton-Baillie (2004), "Urban Design: Why Don't We Do It In The Road? Modifying Traffic Behavior Through Legible Urban Design," *Journal of Urban Technology,* 11:43–6. Peter Peters (2005), "Exchanging Travel Speed: Time Politics in Mobility Practices," *Configurations,* 13:395–419,436. Tom Vanderbilt (Summer 2008), "The Traffic Guru," *The Wilson Quarterly,* 26–32.

114 *incident in Switzerland*   Bruno S. Fray and Felix Oberhlozer-Gee (1997), "The Cost of Price Incentives: An Empirical Analysis of Motivation Crowding-Out," *American Economic Review,* 87:746–55.

115 *gave different weights*   Don A. More, Lloyd Tantu, and Max H. Bazerman (2010), "Conflict of Interest and the Intrusion of Bias," *Judgment & Decision Making,* 5:37–53.

115 *require advisors*   Daylian M. Cain, George Loewenstein, and Don A. More (2005), "The Dirt on Coming Clean: Perverse Effects of Disclosing Conflict of Interest," *The Journal of Legal Studies,* 34:1–25.

116 *able to self-regulate* Fikret Berkes, David Feeny, Bonnie J. McCay, and James M. Acheson (1989), "The Benefits of the Commons," *Nature*, 340:91–3. David Feeny, Fikret Berkes, Bonnie J. McCay, and James M. Acheson (1990), "The Tragedy of the Commons: Twenty-Two Years Later," *Human Ecology*, 18:1–19. Carl J. Dahlman (1992), "The Tragedy of the Commons that Wasn't: On Technical Solutions to the Institutions Game," *Population & Environment*, 12:285–96. Elinor Ostrom, Joanna Burger, Christopher B. Field, Richard B. Norgaard, and David Policansky (1999), "Revisiting the Commons: Local Lessons, Global Challenges," *Science*, 284:278–82.

116 *outsiders come in* Mansel G. Blackford (2009), "Fishers, Fishing, and Overfishing: American Experiences in Global Perspective, 1976–2006," *Business History Review*, 83:239–66.

117 *The scarlet letter* George Elliott Howard (1904), *A History of Matrimonial Institutions: Chiefly in England and the United States, with an Introductory Analysis of the Literature and the Theories of Primitive Marriage and the Family*, Fred B. Rothman & Co., 169–78.

118 *existential threat* John Mueller and Mark G. Stewart (2 Apr 2010), "Hardly Existential: Thinking Rationally About Terrorism," *Foreign Affairs*.

118 *death penalty reduces* Hashem Dezhbakhsh, Paul H. Rubin, and Joanna M. Shepherd (2003), "Does Capital Punishment Have a Deterrent Effect? New Evidence from Post-moratorium Panel Data," *American Law & Economics Review*, 5:344–76. Paul R. Zimmerman (2004), "State Executions, Deterrence, and the Incidence of Murder," *Journal of Applied Economics*, 7:163–93. Naci Mocan and Kaj Gittings (2010), "The Impact of Incentives on Human Behavior: Can We Make it Disappear? The Case of the Death Penalty," in Rafael Di Tella, Sebastian Edwards, and Ernesto Schargrodsky, eds., *The Economics of Crime: Lessons for and from Latin America*, University of Chicago Press. Steven S. Cuellar and Kyle Buehring (2010), "Does Capital Punishment Have a Deterrence Effect on the Murder Rate? Issues and Evidence," Sonoma State University.

118 *demonstrate it doesn't* Jeffrey Fagan (2005), "Deterrence and the Death Penalty: A Critical Review of New Evidence," Testimony to the New York State Assembly Standing Committee on Codes, Assembly Standing Committee on Judiciary and Assembly Standing Committee on Correction, Hearings on the Future of Capital Punishment in the State of New York, Jan 21, 2005. John J. Donahue and Justin Wolfers (2005), "Uses and Abuses of Empirical Evidence in the Death Penalty Debate," *Stanford Law Review*, 58:791–845. John J. Donahue and Justin Wolfers (2009), "Estimating the Impact of the Death Penalty on Murder," *American Law & Economics Review*, 11:249–309. Michael Radelet and Traci Lacock (2009), "Do Executions Lower Homicide Rates? The Views of Leading Criminologists," *The Journal of Criminal Law & Criminology*, 99:489–508.

118 *probability of punishment* Gary S. Becker (1968), "Crime and Punishment: An Economic Approach," *Journal of Political Economy*, 76:169–217. Jeffrey Grogger (1991), "Certainty vs. Severity of Punishment," *Economic Inquiry*, 29:297–309. Lixuan

Zhang, Wayne W. Smith, and William C. McDowell (2009), "Examining Digital Piracy: Self-Control, Punishment, and Self-Efficacy," *Information Resources Management Journal*, 22:24–44.

118   *societal causes of crime*   Peter W. English and Bruce D. Sales (2005), *More Than the Law: Behavioral and Social Facts in Legal Decision Making*, American Psychological Association.

119   *Laws can have loopholes*   Saul Levmore (2010), "Ambiguous Statutes," *The University of Chicago Law Review*, 77:1073–89.

119   *Google pays*   Jesse Drucker (21 Oct 2010), "Google 2.4% Rate Shows how $60 Billion Lost to Tax Loopholes," Bloomberg.

119   *large paper mills*   Steven Mufson (28 Mar 2009), "Papermakers Dig Deep in Highway Bill To Hit Gold," *The Washington Post*. Jad Mouawad and Clifford Krauss (19 Apr 2009), "Lawmakers May Limit Paper Mills' Windfall," *New York Times*. *Wall Street Journal* (30 Jun 2009), "The Black Liquor War."

119   *video games*   David Kochieniewski (10 Sep 2011), "Rich Tax Breaks Bolster Makers of Video Games," *New York Times*.

119   *Japan exploits*   Eldon V.C. Greenberg, Paul S. Hoff, and Michael I. Goulding (2002), "Japan's Whale Research Program and International Law," *California Western International Law Journal*, 32:151–209. Reuben B. Ackerman (2002), "Japanese Whaling in the Pacific Ocean: Defiance of International Whaling Norms in the Name of 'Scientific Research,' Culture, and Tradition," *Boston College International & Comparative Law Review*, 323–42.

120   *Law of the Sea*   Marcos A. Orellana (2004), "The Law on Highly Migratory Fish Stocks: ITLOS Jurisprudence in Context," *Golden Gate University Law Review*, 34:459–95.

120   *Security Council Resolution 1441*   Michael Byers (2004), "Agreeing to Disagree: Security Council Resolution 1441 and Intentional Ambiguity," *Global Governance*, 10:165–86.

120   *Judge Gordon Hewart*   Gordon Hewart (1923), Rex v. Sussex Justices, Ex parte McCarthy, King's Bench Division, *All England Law Reports*: 233.

120   *Invasive species*   Jason Van Driesche and Roy Van Driesche (2000), *Nature Out of Place: Biological Invasions in the Global Age*, Island Press.

120   *ecological disaster*   Daniel Simberloff (2001) "Biological Invasions: How Are They Affecting Us, and What Can We Do About Them?" *Western North American Naturalist*, 61:308–15.

120   *silver carp*   M. Freeze and S. Henderson (1982) "Distribution and Status of the Bighead Carp and Silver Carp in Arkansas," *North American Journal of Fisheries Management*, 2:197–200.

120   *pregnant brown tree snake*   Thomas H. Fritts and Gordon H. Rodda (1998), "The Role of Introduced Species in the Degradation of Island Ecosystems: A Cade History of Guam," *Annual Review of Ecology & Systematics*, 29:113–40.

120 *zebra mussel larvae*   David L. Strayer (2010), "Alien Species in Fresh Waters: Ecological Effects, Interactions With Other Stressors, and Prospects for the Future," *Freshwater Biology*, 55:152–74.

120 *Monk parakeets*   Michael A. Russello, Michael L. Avery, and Timothy F. Wright (2008), "Genetic Evidence Links Invasive Monk Parakeet Populations in the United States to the International Pet Trade," *BMC Evolutionary Biology*, 8:217.

120 *crop damage*   Eric A. Tillman (2000), "Bird Damage to Tropical Fruit in South Florida," *The Ninth Wildlife Damage Management Conference Proceedings*.

120 *also cause fires*   Michael L. Avery (2002), "Monk Parakeet Management at Electric Utility Facilities in South Florida," Internet Center for Wildlife Damage Management, USDA National Wildlife Research Center Staff Publications. Dan Mangan and Erin Calabrese (21 Apr 2009), "Fowl Play in Qns.: Blackout Parrots' Nests Cut Electricity," *New York Post*.

121 *state laws vary wildly*   Michael A. Russello, Michael L. Avery, and Timothy F. Wright (2008), "Genetic Evidence Links Invasive Monk Parakeet Populations in the United States to the International Pet Trade," *BMC Evolutionary Biology*, 8:217.

Chapter 9 Notes

270 *similar system in Sweden*   Heather Monasky (2011), "On Comprehensive Prostitution Reform: Criminalizing the Trafficker and the Trick, But Not the Victim—Sweden's Sexköpslagen in America," *William Mitchell Law Review*, 37:101–56.

271 *driving skill is better*   Justin Kruger and David Dunning (1999), "Unskilled and Unaware of It: How Difficulties in Recognizing One's Own Incompetence Lead to Inflated Self-Assessments," *Journal of Personality & Social Psychology*, 77:1121–34. Corey L. Guenther and Mark D. Alicke (2010), "Deconstructing the Better-Than-Average Effect," *Journal of Personality & Social Psychology*, 99:755–70.

271 *Electronic filing*   U.S. Internal Revenue Service (8 Jul 2009), "Update on Reducing the Federal Tax Gap and Improving Voluntary Compliance," Department of the Treasury. Barbara Weltman (24 Jan 2011), "Ten Ways to Avoid a Tax Audit," *Wall Street Journal*.

271 *Students perform better*   Uri Gneezy and Aldo Rustichini (2000), "Pay Enough or Don't Pay at All," *Quarterly Journal of Economics*, 115:791–810.

271 *salary bonuses*   Randall Eberts, Kevin Hollenbeck, and Joe Stone (2002), "Teacher Performance Incentives and Student Outcomes," *Journal of Human Resources*, 37:913–27.

271 *Ostrom's original rules are*   Elinor Ostrom (1980), *Governing the Commons: The Evolution of Institutions for Collective Action*, Cambridge University Press.

272 *Jeremy Bentham*   Jeremy Bentham (1789), *An Introduction to the Principles of Morals and Legislation*.

272 *Gary Becker*   Gary Becker (1996), "The Economic Way of Looking at Human Behavior: The Nobel Lecture," *Journal of Political Economy*, 101:385–409.

272   *increasing the probability*   Mark Kleinman (2009), *When Brute Force Fails: How to Have Less Crime and Less Punishment*, Princeton University Press.

272   *conflicting evidence*   Nina Mazar and Dan Ariely (2006), "Dishonesty in Everyday Life and Its Policy Implications," *Journal of Public Policy & Marketing*, 25:117–26.

272   *two Irish subsidiaries*   Joseph B. Darby III and Kelsey Lemaster (15 May 2007), "Double Irish More than Doubles the Tax Savings," *Practical US/International Tax Strategies*, 11:2,11–16.

272   *bigger one opened up*   Todd Neeley (28 Mar 2011), "Pulp, Paper Companies Amend Tax Returns Actions Could Cost Taxpayers Billions of Dollars," *DTN: The Progressive Farmer.*

Chapter 10

123   *making towels souvenirs*   Lynn Yaeger (2 Jun 2009), "Stealing Hotel Amenities: Right or Wrong?" *MSNBC*.

124   *reduced towel theft*   Sara J. Welch (2011), "Gee, How Did That Towel End Up in My Suitcase," *New York Times* blog.

125   *patterns of fraud*   Yufeng Kou, Chang-Tien Lu, Sirirat Sirwongwattana, and Yo-Ping Huang (2004), "Survey of Fraud Detection Techniques," *IEEE International Conference on Networking, Sensing and Control*, vol. 2, 749–54. Jon T.S. Quah and M. Sriganesh (2008), "Real-Time Credit Card Fraud Detection Using Computational Intelligence," *Expert Systems with Applications*, 35:1721–32. Edwin Raj Benson and A. Annie Portia (2011), "Analysis on Credit Card Fraud Detection Methods," *2011 International Conference on Computer, Communication and Electrical Technology*, 152–6. Arturo Elias, Alberto Ochoa-Zezzatti, Alejandro Padilla, and Julio Ponce (2011), "Outlier Analysis for Plastic Card Fraud Detection: A Hybridized and Multi-Objective Approach," *Hybrid Artificial Intelligence Systems, Lecture Notes in Computer Science*, Springer-Verlag, 6679:1–9. Amlan Kundu, Shamik Sural, and Arun K. Majumdar (2006), "Two-Stage Credit Card Fraud Detection Using Sequence Alignment," *Information Systems Security, Lecture Notes in Computer Science*, Springer-Verlag, 4332:260–75.

126   *predictive policing programs*   Martin B. Short, Maria R. D'Orsogna, Virginia B. Pasour, George E. Tita, P. Jeffrey Brantingham, Andrea L. Bertozzi, and Lincoln B. Chayes (2008), "A Statistical Model of Criminal Behavior," *Mathematical Models and Methods in Applied Sciences*, 18 (Supplement):1249–67. Beth Pearsall (2010), "Predictive Policing: The Future of Law Enforcement?" *NIJ Journal*, 266:16–9. Nancy Murray (2011), "Profiling in the Age of Total Information Awareness," *Race & Class*, 51:3–24.

127   *Timothy McVeigh's van*   Associated Press (28 Sep 2009), "Attorney: Oklahoma City Bombing Tapes Appear Edited," *Oklahoman*.

127   *reduce car theft*   Ian Ayres and Steven Levitt (1998), "Measuring Positive Externalities from Unobservable Victim Precaution: An Empirical Analysis of Lojack," *Quarterly*

Journal of Economics, 113:43–77. Marco Gonzalez-Navarro (2008), "Deterrence and Displacement in Auto Theft," Center for Economic Policy Studies Working Paper.

128   *confidence in vaccines*   Heidi Larson, Louis Z. Cooper, Juhani Eskola, Samuel L. Katz, and Scott Ratzan (6 Aug 2011), "Addressing the Vaccine Confidence Gap," *The Lancet,* 378:526–35.

129   *new version of Monopoly*   Stephanie Clifford (16 Feb 2011), "No Dice, No Money, No Cheating. Are You Sure This is Monopoly?" *New York Times.*

130   *Crime Prevention Techniques*   Ronald V. Clarke and John Eck (2003), *Become a Problem Solving Crime Analyst,* Willan Publishing. Derek B. Cornish and Ronald V. Clarke (2003) "Opportunities, Precipitators and Criminal Decisions," in *Theory for Practice in Situational Crime Prevention, Crime Prevention Studies, Vol. 16,* Criminal Justice Press.

131   *enforcing anti-doping*   David R. Mottram, ed. (2011), *Drugs in Sport, Fifth Edition,* Taylor & Francis.

131   *Alex Zülle*   John Hoberman (20 Sep 2007), "Dopers on Wheels: The Tour's Sorry History," MSNBC.

132   *almost a third*   Patrick Mignon (2003), "The Tour de France and the Doping Issue," *International Journal of the History of Sport,* 20:227–45.

132   *never intended*   Jamey Keaten (20 Jul 2007), "At Tour de France, Asthma Inhalers Can Be a Rider's Best Friend," *USA Today.*

132   *stripped of her gold medal*   *Sports Illustrated* (28 Sep 2000), "Arbitrators Uphold Decision to Strip Raducan of Gold," CNN.

132   *install security cameras*   Bruce Schneier (26 Jun 2008), "CCTV Doesn't Keep Us Safe, Yet the Cameras Are Everywhere," *The Guardian.*

132   *full-body scanners*   Bruce Schneier (2 Dec 2010), "Why the TSA Can't Back Down," *The Atlantic.*

132   *military spends billions*   New York Times (2 Oct 1984), "A Lemon the Size of the Pentagon," *New York Times.* Michael Ditton (Aug 1988), "The DIVAD Procurement: A Weapon System Case Study," *The Army Lawyer,* 3–9. Irene Willhite (Mar 2002), "40-mm Division Air Defense Gun: DIVAD (Sgt. York)," *Cold War Times,* 15–22.

132   *better slugs*   Ronald V. Clarke, Ronald P. Cody, and Mangai Natarajan (1994), "Subway Slugs: Tracking Displacement on the London Underground," *British Journal of Criminology,* 34:122–38.

132   *door locks and safes*   Mark Weber Thomas (2000), *Locks, Safes and Security,* Second Edition, Charles Thomas Publisher, Ltd. Matt Blaze (2003), "Cryptology and Physical Security: Rights Amplification in Master-Keyed Mechanical Locks," IEEE Security and Privacy. Matt Blaze (2004), "Safecracking for the Computer Scientist," *U. Penn CIS Department Technical Report.*

133   *fax machines*   Bruce Schneier (29 May 2008), "Why Do We Accept Signatures by Fax?" *Wired News.*

133   *Electronic voting machines*   Ariel J. Feldman, J. Alex Halderman, and Edward W. Felten (2006), "Security Analysis of the Diebold AccuVote-TS Voting Machine," Center for

Information Technology Policy, Princeton University. Adam Aviv, Pavol Cerny, Sandy Clark, Eric Cronin, Gaurav Shah, Micah Sherr, and Matt Blaze (2008), "Security Evaluation of ES&S Voting Machines and Election Management System," USENIX/ACCURATE Electronic Voting Technology Workshop (EVT '08), paper presented at "USENIX/ACCURATE. Hari K. Prasad, J. Alex Halderman, Rop Gonggrijp, Scott Wolchok, Eric Wustrow, Arun Kankipati, Sai Krishna Sakhamuri, and Vasavya Yagati (2010), "Security Analysis of India's Electronic Voting Machines," *Proceedings of the 17th ACM Conference on Computer and Communications Security,* Association of Computing Machinery. Doug Jones and Barbara Simons (2012), *Broken Ballots: Will Your Vote Count in the Electronic Age?* CSLI Publications.

133 *electronics in cars*   Stephen Checkoway, Damon McCoy, Brian Kantor, Danny Anderson, Hovav Shacham, Stefan Savage, Karl Koscher, Alexei Czeskis, Franziska Roesner, and Tadayoshi Kohno (2011), "Comprehensive Experimental Analyses of Automotive Attack Surfaces," USENIX Security.

133 *Networked medical devices*   William H. Maisel and Tadayoshi Kohno (2010), "Improving the Security and Privacy of Implantable Medical Devices," *New England Journal of Medicine,* 362:1164–6.

133 *cursive is not being taught*   Katie Zezima (28 Apr 2011), "The Case for Cursive," *New York Times.*

134 *read trust signals*   Jens Riegelsberger, M. Angela Sasse, and John D. McCarthy (2005), "The Mechanics of Trust: A Framework for Research and Design," *International Journal of Human-Computer Studies,* 62:381–422.

134 *harder-to-forge ID*   Bruce Schneier (2007), "Will REAL ID Actually Make Us Safer? An Examination of Privacy and Civil Liberties Concerns," testimony to the Senate Judiciary Committee.

135 *spent about $1 trillion*   John Mueller and Mark Stewart (2011), *Terrorism, Security, and Money: Balancing the Risks, Benefits, and Costs of Homeland Security,* Oxford University Press.

135 *doesn't count the wars*   Linda J. Bilmes and Joseph E. Stiglitz (2008), *The Three Trillion Dollar War: The True Cost of the Iraq Conflict,* W.W. Norton & Co.

136 *cost-benefit analysis*   Gary Becker (1968), "Crime and Punishment: An Economic Approach," *The Journal of Political Economy,* 76:169–217.

136 *passion overrides rationality*   Howard Engel (2001), *Crimes of Passion: An Unblinking Look at Murderous Love,* Firefly Books.

Chapter 10 Notes

272 *someone was sentenced*   Barbara de Lollis (15 Sep 2010), "Woman Faces Three Months in Jail for Stealing Hotel Towels," *USA Today.*

272 *doping in professional Scrabble*   Stefan Fatiss (2001), *Word Freak: Heartbreak, Triumph, Genius, and Obsession in the World of Competitive Scrabble Players,* Houghton Mifflin Harcourt.

272   *assays were developed*   John H. Lewis (1979), "A Routine Screening Method for the Major Metabolite of Methyl Phenidate in the Urine of Greyhounds," *Forensic Science International,* 14:221–7. Orisa J. Igwe and Jerry W. Blake (1981), "Gas/liquid Chromatographic Analysis of Pemoline in Biological Fluids Using Electron Capture Detection," *Journal of Chromatographic Science,* 19:617–24.

273   *EPO use became*   Robin Parisotto, Christopher J. Gore, Kerry R. Emslie, Michael J. Ashenden, Carlo Brugnara. Chris Howe, David T. Martin, Graham J. Trout, and Allan G. Hahn (2000), "A Novel Method Utilising Markers of Altered Erythropoiesis for the Detection of Recombinant Human Erythropoietin Abuse in Athletes," *Haematologica,* 85:564–72. Caroline K. Hatton (2007), "Beyond Sports Doping Headlines: The Science of Laboratory Tests for Performance-Enhancing Drugs," *Pediatric Clinics of North America,* 54:713–33. Rafael Maia de Almeida Bento, Lucia Menezes Pinto Damasceno, and Francisco Radler de Aquino Neto (2003), "Recombinant Human Erythropoietin in Sports: A Review," *Revista Brasileira de Medicina do Esporte,* 9:181–90.

273   *analogues of analogues*   Andreas Breidbach, Don H. Catlin, Gary A. Green, Inna Tregub, Henry Truong, and Jeffrey Gorzek (2003), "Detection of Recombinant Human Erythropoietin in Urine by Isoelectric Focusing," *Clinical Chemistry,* 49:901–7.

273   *new EPO replacement*   Don H. Catlin, George A. Maylin, Sabrina Benchaar, Sandra M. Neades, Miranda S. Timmons, and Kenneth H. McKeever (2009), "Detection of Pegylated Epoetin in Horse Plasma after Intravenous Administration," *Comparative Exercise Physiology,* 6:105–8.

273   *first designer steroid*   Henry K. Lee (4 Aug 2006), "Inventor of Clear Steroid Gets Three Months in Prison," *San Francisco Chronicle.*

273   *Its fingerprint*   Don H. Catlin, Brian D. Ahrens, and Yulia Kucherova (2002), "Detection of Norbolethone, an Anabolic Steroid Never Marketed, in Athletes' Urine," *Rapid Communications in Mass Spectrometry,* 16:1273–5.

273   *scenario was replayed*   Don H. Catlin, Michael H. Sekera, Brian D. Ahrens, Borislav Starcevic, Yu-Chen Chang, and Caroline K. Hatton (2004), "Tetrahydrogestrinone: Discovery, Synthesis, and Detection in Urine," *Rapid Communications in Mass Spectrometry,* 18:1245–9. Michael H. Sekera, Brian D. Ahrens, Yu-Chen Chang, Borislav Starcevic, Costas Georgakopoulos, and Don H. Catlin (2005), "Another Designer Steroid: Discovery, Synthesis, and Detection of Madol in Urine," *Rapid Communications in Mass Spectrometry,* 19:781–4.

273   *flow cytofluorometry*   Margaret Nelson, Michael Ashenden, Mark Langshaw, and Hazel Popp (2002), "Detection of Homologous Blood Transfusion by Flow Cytometry: A Deterrent against Blood Doping," *Haemetologica,* 87:881. Patricia A. Arndt and Belinda M. Kumpel (2008), "Blood Doping in Athletes: Detection of Allogeneic Blood Transfusions by Flow Cytofluorometry," *American Journal of Hematology,* 83:657–67.

273   *gene doping*   H. Lee Sweeney (Jul 2004), "Gene Doping," *Scientific American,* 291:63–9. Gary R. Gaffney and Robin Parisotto (2007), "Gene Doping: A Review of Performance-Enhancing Genetics," *Pediatric Clinics of North America,* 54:807–22.

273 *adulterated supplements*   Jeff Jones (4 Dec 2002), "Tainted Supplements: Positive or Not?" *Cycling News.*

273 *Chinese herbal product*   Patricia L. Eachus (1996), "Positive Drug Screen for Benzodiazepine Due to a Chinese Herbal Product," *Journal of Athletic Training,* 31:165–6.

273 *urine test for EPO*   Monique Beullens, Joris R. Delanghe, and Mathieu Bollen (2006), "False-Positive Detection of Recombinant Human Erythropoietin in Urine Following Strenuous Physical Exercise," *Blood,* 107:4711–13. Joris R. Delanghe, Mathieu Bollen, and Monique Beullens (2007), "Testing for Recombinant Erythropoietin," *American Journal of Hematology,* 83:237–41.

273 *hotly contested*   Don Catlin, Gary Green, Michael Sekera, Paul Scott, and Borislav Starcevic (2006), "False-Positive EPO Test Concerns Unfounded," *Blood,* 108:1778. Françoise Lasne (2006), "No Doubt About the Validity of the Urine Test for Detection of Recombinant Human Erythropoietin," *Blood,* 108:1778–9.

273 *Rapid-screen immunoassays*   Nancy C. Brahm, Lynn L. Yeager, Mark D. Fox, Kevin C. Farmer, and Tony A. Palmer (2010), "Commonly Prescribed Medications and Potential False-Positive Urine Drug Screens," *American Journal of Health Systems & Pharmacy,* 67:1344–50.

273 *Vicks Vapor Inhaler*   Telegraph (21 Mar 2002), "British Skier Stripped of Bronze."

274 *appearance of a website*   Rachna Dhamija, J.D. Tygar, and Marti Hearst (2006), "Why Phishing Works," *CHI '06 Proceedings of the SIGCHI Conference on Human Factors in Computing Systems.*

274 *least costly measures*   Tom LaTourette, David R. Howell, David E. Mosher, and John MacDonald (2006), *Reducing Terrorism Risk at Shopping Centers: An Analysis of Potential Security Options,* RAND Technical Report.

Chapter 11

139 *Rhonda Breard embezzled*   Kevin Opsahl (11 Aug 2010), "Kirkland Broker Rhonda Breard to Spend Nearly Seven Years in Prison for Fraud," *Seattle Post-Intelligencer.*

139 *Envy can motivate*   Simone Moran and Maurice E. Schweitzer (2008), "When Better is Worse: Envy and the Use of Deception," *Negotiation & Conflict Management Research,* 1:3–29.

139 *things out of anger*   Yang Wang, Saranga Komanduri, Pedro Giovanni Leon, Gregory Norcie, Alessandro Acquisti, and Lorrie Faith Cranor (2011), "'I Regretted the Minute I Pressed Share': A Qualitative Study of Regrets on Facebook," *Proceedings of the 7th Symposium on Usable Privacy and Security (SOUPS2011).*

140 *heinous behavior*   Ervin Staub (1992), *The Roots of Evil: The Origins of Genocide and Other Group Violence,* Cambridge University Press.

140 *extreme situations*   David DeSteno and Piercarlo Valdesolo (2011), *Out of Character: Surprising Truths About the Liar, Cheat, Sinner (and Saint) Lurking in All of Us,* Crown Archetype.

140 *lethal altruists*   Adolf Tobeña (2009), "Lethal Altruists: Itineraries along the Dark Outskirts of Moralistic Prosociality," *Annals of the New York Academy of Sciences,* 1167:5–15.

140 *Abraham Maslow*   Abraham H. Maslow (1943), "A Theory of Human Motivation," *Psychological Review,* 50:370–96.

140 *Rational Choice Theory*   Gary S. Becker (1976), *The Economic Approach to Human Behavior*, University of Chicago Press.

141 *Bounded Rationality*   Bryan D. Jones (1999), "Bounded Rationality," *Annual Review of Political Science,* 2:297–321. Daniel Kahneman (2003), "Maps of Bounded Rationality: Psychology for Behavioral Economics," *The American Economic Review,* 93:1449–75. Gerd Gigerenzer (2007), *Gut Feelings: The Intelligence of the Unconscious*, Viking Adult. Dan Ariely (2008), *Predictably Irrational: The Hidden Forces that Shape our Decisions*, Harper Perennial. Ori Brafman and Rom Brafman (2008), *Sway: The Irresistible Pull of Irrational Behavior*, Crown Business. Shankar Vedantam (2010), *The Hidden Brain: How Our Unconscious Minds Elect Presidents, Control Markets, Wage Wars, and Save our Lives*, Spiegel & Grau. Daniel Kahneman (2011), *Thinking Fast and Slow*, Farrar, Straus and Giroux. Duncan J. Watts (2011), *Everything is Obvious: *Once You Know the Answer*, Crown Business.

141 *trade-off process*   Bruce Schneier (2008), "The Psychology of Security," *AFRICACRYPT 2008,* Springer-Verlag, 50–79. Daniel Gardner (2008), *The Science of Fear: Why We Fear the Things We Shouldn't—and Put Ourselves in Greater Danger,* Dutton Adult. Paul Slovic (2000), *The Perception of Risk,* Earthscan Publications Ltd. Barry Glassner (1999), *The Culture of Fear: Why Americans Are Afraid of the Wrong Things,* Basic Books.

141 *different type of trade-off*   Lawrence Kohlberg (1981), *Essays on Moral Development, Vol. I: The Philosophy of Moral Development*, Harper & Row.

142 *Kohlberg's Stages*   University of Canberra Faculty of Education (2011), "University of Canberra Graduate Diploma of Education E-reserve Lecture Notes: Ed Foundations, Module B, Part 3."

143 *Emily Dickinson*   Emily Dickinson (1862), "The soul selects her own society," poem 303.

144 *morality to be central*   William Damon (1984), "Self-Understanding and Moral Development from Childhood to Adolescence, " in William M. Kurtines and Jacob L. Gewirtz, eds., *Morality, Moral Behavior, and Moral Development,* John Wiley & Sons.

144 *spiritual geniuses*   René Girard (1999), *Je Vois Satan Tomber Comme l'Éclair,* Grasset English translation (2001), *I See Satan Fall Like Lightning,* Orbis Books.

144 *Ralph Waldo Emerson*   Ralph Waldo Emerson (1841), "Self-Reliance," in *Essays: First Series.*

144 *Henry David Thoreau*   Henry David Thoreau (1852), *Walden.*

144 *Laurel Thatcher Ulrich*   Laurel T. Ulrich (2007), *Well-Behaved Women Seldom Make History,* Alfred A. Knopf.

144 *Socrates's morals*   Plato (360 BCE), *Crito,* tr. Benjamin Jowett, MIT Classics Archive. Plato (360 BCE), *Phaedo,* tr. Benjamin Jowett, MIT Classics Archive. Anthony D'Amato (1976), "Obligation to Obey the Law: A Study of the Death of Socrates," *California Law Review,* 49:1079–1108.

144 *Misunderstanding the defector* Bruce Schneier (2003), *Beyond Fear: Thinking Sensibly About Security in an Uncertain World*, Copernicus Books, Chapter 5.

145 *there's no guarantee* Laurie P. Cohen (29 Nov 2004), "Split Decisions: Federal Cases Show Big Gap in Reward For Cooperation," *Wall Street Journal*.

145 *"Stop Snitching" campaign* Rick Hampson (28 Mar 2006), "Anti-Snitch Campaign Riles Police, Prosecutors," *USA Today*. Rick Frei (2010), "Witness Intimidation and the Snitching Project," written testimony submitted to the Subcommittee on Drugs and Crime, U.S. Senate Committee on the Judiciary.

147 *Con artists try* David Maurer (1940), *The Big Con: The Story of the Confidence Man*, Bobbs Merrill.

147 *Fake anti-virus software* Brian Krebs (3 Aug 2011), "Fake Antivirus Industry Down, But Not Out," *Krebs on Security*.

147 *Internet money laundering* Mitchell Zuckoff (15 May 2005), "Annals of Crime: The Perfect Mark," *The New Yorker*, 36–42.

148 *doctrine of necessity* Leslie Wolf-Phillips (1979), "Constitutional Legitimacy: A Study of the Doctrine of Necessity." *Third World Quarterly*, 1:99–133.

148 *competing interests* H.E. Mason, ed. (1996), *Moral Dilemmas and Moral Theory*, Oxford University Press.

149 *publicly confessed* Sean O'Callaghan (27 Jan 1997), "The Lying: A Former Terrorist Describes His Life in the IRA," *National Review*.

149 *Defecting from the IRA* Sean O'Callaghan (1999), *The Informer: The Real Life Story of One Man's War Against Terrorism*, Corgi.

150 *Ulysses S. Grant* Louis A. Coolidge (1917), *Ulysses S. Grant*, Houghton Mifflin. Lawrence M. Salinger (2005), *Encyclopedia of White-Collar & Corporate Crime*, Sage Publications.

152 *interlocking directorate* Mark S. Mizruchi (1996), "What Do Interlocks Do? An Analysis, Critique, and Assessment of Research on Interlocking Directorates," *Annual Review of Sociology*, 22:271–98.

153 *Larry Froistad confessed* Debra J. Saunders (10 May 1998), "Spilled Milk," *San Francisco Chronicle*. Lisa DiCarlo (11 May 1998), "Murder, She Read," *New York Magazine*.

153 *Police solidarity* Jerome H. Skolnick (2002), "Corruption and the Blue Code of Silence," *Police Practice & Research*, 3:7–19. Louise Westmarland (2005), "Police Ethics and Integrity: Breaking the Blue Code of Silence," *Policing & Society*, 15:145–65. Gary R. Rothwell and J. Norman Baldwin, "Whistle-Blowing and the Code of Conduct in Police Agencies," *Crime & Delinquency*, 53:8–10. Barry Wright (2010), "Civilianising the 'Blue Code'? An Examination of Attitudes to Misconduct in the Police Extended Family," *International Journal of Police Science & Management*, 12:339–56.

153 *policeman beating* Jayme Poisson (10 Jun 2011), "Cop Unmasked: Meet Const. Glenn Weddell, the Officer ID'd in G20 Assault," *The Toronto Star*.

Chapter 11 Notes

274 *Robert A. Heinlein*   Robert A. Heinlein (1988), *To Sail Beyond the Sunset*, G.P. Putnam's Sons, 38–9.

275 *levels of moral meaning*   Kenneth R. Melchin (1998), *Living with Other People: An Introduction to the Christian Ethics Based on Bernard Longeran*, The Liturgical Press, 56–60.

275 *good summary*   William C. Crain (1985), "Kolhberg's Stages of Moral Development," Chapter 7 of *Theories of Development: Concepts and Applications*, Prentice-Hall, 118–36.

275 *Social identity theory*   Henri Tajfel (1974), "Social Identity and Intergroup Behaviour," *Social Science Information*, 13:65–93. Naomi Ellemers, Russell Spears, and Bertjan Doosje (2001), "Self and Social Identity," *Annual Review of Psychology*, 53:161–86.

275 *immolated themselves*   Michael Biggs (2005), "Dying Without Killing: Self-Immolations, 1963–2002," in Diego Gambetta, ed., *Making Sense of Suicide Missions*, Oxford University Press.

275 *Brian Christian*   Brian Christian (2011), *The Most Human Human: What Talking with Computers Teaches Us About What it Means to Be Alive*, Doubleday.

276 *useful mechanism*   Gordon Tullock (1967), "The Prisoner's Dilemma and Mutual Trust," *Ethics*, 77:229–30.

276 *Stop Snitching campaign*   Rachael Woldoff and Karen G. Weiss (2010), "Stop Snitchin': Exploring Definitions of the Snitch and Implications for Urban Black Communities," *Journal of Criminal Justice & Popular Culture*, 17:184–223. Bret D. Asbury (2011), "Anti-Snitching Norms and Community Loyalty," *Oregon Law Review*, 89:1257–312.

276 *Nepotism is making*   Helen Thomas (16 Aug 2001), "Bush Keeps It All in the Family," *Seattle Post-Intelligencer*.

276 *Senator Frank Murkowski*   Jonathan Turley (13 Jan 2003), "Public Payroll: A Family Affair," *Los Angeles Times*.

276 *Representative Richard Pombo*   League of Conservation Voters (2005), "Rep. Richard Pombo's Family & Friends Network."

276 *Representative Eddie Bernice Johnson*   Todd J. Gillman and Christy Hoppe (28 Aug 2010), "Rep. Eddie Bernice Johnson Violated Rules, Steered Scholarships to Relatives," *Dallas Morning News*.

276 *Even Bernie Sanders*   Vermont Guardian (21 Apr 2005), "Nepotism Crosses Party Lines," *Vermont Guardian*.

276 *one in six staffers*   Christine MacDonald (6 May 2011), "Nepotism Rampant at Detroit Libraries: 1 in 6 Staffers Have Relatives Who Work in Strapped Department," *The Detroit News*.

276 *Rupert Murdoch's News Corp*   Mark Sweney (17 Mar 2011), "Rupert Murdoch's News Corp Sued Over 'Nepotism' in Buying His Daughter's Firm: Investors Allege Group Is Overpaying in $675m Deal to Acquire Elisabeth Murdoch's TV Production Business Shine," *The Guardian*.

276 *Many states have policies* New York State Bar Association Committee on Professional Ethics (1975), "Topic: Conflict of Interests; Lawyer Spouses as Assistant District Attorney and Assistant Public Defender," Opinion #409—8/28/75 (69–75). State Bar of Montana (1988), "May Spouses Serve as Opposing Counsel, Actively Engaging in the Same Suit or Matter on Opposite Sides?" Ethics Opinion 950407. Sandra Carlin Guin (1985), "Marital Status as a Reason for Attorney-Spouse Disqualification," *Journal of the Legal Profession*, 9:181–8.

Chapter 12

158 *Carol Braun was* Jed Block (2004), *Betrayal*, Goodwill Industries of North Central Wisconsin, Inc.
159 *principal–agent problem* Kathleen M. Eisenhardt (1989), "Agency Theory: An Assessment and Review," *The Academy of Management Review*, 14:57–74. John M. Darley (2010), "Constructive and Destructive Obedience: A Taxonomy of Principal-Agent Relationships," *Journal of Social Issues*, 41:124–54.
160 *corporate looting* George A. Akerlof, Paul M. Romer, Robert E. Hall, and N. Gregory Mankiw (1993), "Looting: The Economic Underworld of Bankruptcy for Profit," *Brookings Papers on Economic Activity*, 1993(2): 1–73.
160 *Sambo's restaurants* Charles Bernstein (1984), *Sambo's: Only a Fraction of the Action: The Inside Story of a Restaurant Empire's Rise and Fall*, National Literary Guild.
163 *moral considerations* James A. Waters (1978), "Catch 205: Corporate Morality as an Organizational Phenomenon," *Organizational Dynamics*, 6:3–19. James Weber (1990), "Managers' Moral Reasoning: Assessing Their Responses to Three Moral Dilemmas," *Human Relations*, 43:687–702. Thomas M. Jones and Lori Verstegen Ryan (1998), "The Effect of Organizational Forces on Individual Morality: Judgment, Moral Approbation, and Behavior," *Business Ethics Quarterly*, 8:431–45. J. Stuart Bunderson (2001), "Normal Injustices and Morality in Complex Organizations," *Journal of Business Ethics*, 33:181–90. Linda K. Treviño, Gary R. Weaver, and Scott J. Reynolds (2006), "Behavioral Ethics in Organizations: A Review," *Journal of Management*, 32:951–90. Nicole Andreoli and Joel Lefkowitz (2009), "Individual and Organizational Antecedents of Misconduct in Organizations," *Journal of Business Ethics*, 85:309–32. William Carbonaro and Jessica L. Collett (2010), "Pushing the Man: Moral Judgments in Group Settings," Paper presented at the Annual Meeting of the American Sociological Association, San Francisco, California.
163 *many reasons for this* James Weber (1990), "Managers' Moral Reasoning: Assessing Their Responses to Three Moral Dilemmas," *Human Relations*, 43:687–702. Maurice Punch (2000), "Suite Violence: Why Managers Murder and Corporations Kill," *Crime, Law & Social Change*, 33:243–80. Yoav Vardi (2001), "The Effects of Organizational and Ethical Climates on Misconduct at Work," *Journal of Business Ethics*, 29:325–37.

163   *Beech-Nut Corporation*   Leonard Buder (14 Nov 1987), "Beech-Nut is Fined $2 Million for Sale of Fake Apple Juice," *New York Times*. James Traub (24 Jul 1988), "Into the Mouths of Babes," *New York Times Magazine*.

163   *being victimized*   BishopAccountability.org (2011), "What Percent of Priests Were Accused?"

163   *actual number of victims*   BishopAccountability.org (2011), "Data on the Crisis: The Human Toll." BishopAccountability.org (2011), "A Documentary History of the Crisis."

163   *retained accused priests*   Brooks Egerton and Reese Dunklin (12 Jun 2002), "Two-Thirds of Bishops Let Accused Priests Work," *Dallas Morning News*.

163   *Vatican's exhortations*   Office of the Holy See (1962), "Instruction on the Manner of Proceeding in Cases of Solicitation: The Decree Crimen Sollicitationis," Vatican Press. Catholics for a Free Choice (2002), "The Holy See and the Convention on the Rights of the Child: A Shadow Report," Catholics for a Free Choice. Antony Barnett (17 Aug 2003), "Vatican Told Bishops to Cover Up Sex Abuse: Expulsion Threat in Secret Documents," *The Guardian*. Associated Press (18 Jan 2011), "Vatican Letter Told Ireland's Catholic Bishops Not to Report Child Abuse," *The Guardian*.

164   *forced the victims*   Richard Nangle (1 Apr 2002), "Deal Mandated Silence: Accuser Not Allowed to Discuss Abuse Allegations," *Worcester Telegraph & Gazette*. Stephen Gillers (2002), "Speak No Evil: Settlement Agreements Conditioned on Noncooperation Are Illegal and Unethical," *Hofstra Law Review*, 31:1–22.

165   *top WorldCom executives*   Susan Pulliam and Deborah Soloman (8 Nov 2008), "How Three Unlikely Sleuths Exposed Fraud at WorldCom: Firm's Own Employees Sniffed Out Cryptic Clues and Followed Hunches," *Wall Street Journal*. Amanda Ripley (30 Dec 2002), "Cynthia Cooper: The Night Detective," *Time*. WorldCom (2003), "Report of Investigation by the Special Investigative Committee of the Board of Directors of WorldCom, Inc." Cynthia Cooper (2008), *Extraordinary Circumstances: The Journey of a Corporate Whistleblower*, John Wiley & Sons, Inc.

166   *corporate board members*   Peter J. Henning (2009), "Board Dysfunction: Dealing with the Threat of Corporate Criminal Liability," Wayne State University Law School Legal Studies Research Paper.

167   *analyst Thomas Drake*   Jane Mayer (23 May 2011), "The Secret Sharer: Is Thomas Drake an Enemy of the State?" *The New Yorker*. Glenn Greenwald (30 Jul 2011), "Obama's Whistleblower War Suffers Two Defeats," *Salon*. Thomas Drake and Jessalyn Radack (1 Aug 2011), "A Surprising War on Leaks Under Obama," *Philadelphia Inquirer*.

167   *1962 Vatican Instruction*   Office of the Holy See (1962), "Instruction on the Manner of Proceeding in Cases of Solicitation: The Decree Crimen Sollicitationis," Vatican Press.

167   *drug was ineffective*   Adrian Viens and Julian Savulescu (2004), "The Olivieri Symposium: Introduction to The Olivieri Symposium," *Journal of Medical Ethics*, 30:1–7. Rosamond Rhodes and J.J. Strain (2004), "The Olivieri Symposium: Whistleblowing

in Academic Medicine," *Journal of Medical Ethics*, 30:35–9. Thomas Faunce, Steve Bolsin, and Wei-Ping Chan (2004), "The Olivieri Symposium: Supporting Whistleblowers in Academic Medicine: Training and Respecting the Courage of Professional Conscience," *Journal of Medical Ethics*, 30:40–3.

167 *exposed misconduct* Jaime Adame (2 Jun 2004), "Police Whistleblowers," *Gotham Gazette*.

168 *military pilots defected* John Hooper and Ian Black (21 Feb 2011), "Libya Defectors: Pilots Told to Bomb Protesters Flee to Malta," *The Guardian*.

169 *U.S.'s use of torture* Ian Fishback (28 Sep 2005), "A Matter of Honor," *Washington Post*.

170 *Deepwater Horizon* Joe Nocera (18 Jun 2010), "BP Ignored the Omens of Disaster," *New York Times*.

170 *employees of BP* National Commission on the Deepwater Horizon Oil Spill and Offshore Drilling (2011), *Deep Water: The Gulf Oil Disaster and the Future of Offshore Drilling, Final Report*, Government Printing Office. National Commission on the Deepwater Horizon Oil Spill and Offshore Drilling (2011), *Macondo: The Gulf Oil Disaster, Chief Counsel's Report*, Government Printing Office.

170 *The "Big Dig,"* Andrea Estes (24 Jan 2008), "Big Dig Settlement Will Take Quick Hit," *Boston Globe*. Jonathan Saltzman (15 Nov 2008), "Companies to Settle for $26m in Tunnel Collapse," *Boston Globe*. Gregory W. Sullivan (2005), "A Big Dig Cost Recovery Referral: Waterproofing Mismanagement by Bechtel/Parsons Brinckerhoff in East Boston," Office of the Inspector General, Commonwealth of Massachusetts. David W. Fowler (2010), "The Big Dig: Lessons in Engineering and Ethics," CAEE Annual Alumni Ethics Seminar, Austin, Texas.

171 *conflict between the* Gregory M. Hebb (2002), "Conflict of Interest in Commercial Bank Equity Underwriting," *Financial Review*, 37:185–205. Dan R. Dalton, S. Trevis Certo, and Catherine M. Daily (2003), "Initial Public Offerings as a Web of Conflicts of Interest: An Empirical Assessment," *Business Ethics Quarterly*, 13:289–314. Lily Fang and Ayako Asuda (2009), "The Effectiveness of Reputation as a Disciplinary Mechanism in Sell-Side Research," *Review of Financial Studies*, 22:3735–77.

171 *A full discussion* Erik Sirri (2004), "Investment Banks, Scope, and Unavoidable Conflicts of Interest," *Federal Reserve Bank of Atlanta Economic Review*, Fourth Quarter 2004. Frederick S. Mishkin (2005), "Conflicts of Interest in the Financial Industry," in *The Economics of Money, Banking and Financial Markets, Alternate Edition*, Pearson Education. Frederick S. Mishkin (2005), "Policy Remedies for Conflicts of Interest in the Financial System," Bank of Canada. Cheolwoo Lee (2008), "Analyst Firm Parent-Subsidiary Relationship and Conflict of Interest: Evidence from IPO Recommendations," 2008 Financial Management Association Annual Meeting. Roni Michaely and Kent L. Womack (1999), "Conflict of Interest and the Credibility of Underwriter Analyst Recommendations," *Review of Financial Studies*, 12:653–86. Hamid Mehran and Rene M. Stulz (2007), "The Economics of Conflicts of Interest in Financial Institutions," *Journal of Financial Economics*, 85 (2007): 267–96.

Chapter 12 Notes

276   *One.Tel in Australia*   Elizabeth Sexton (27 Oct 2007), "Adler Settles In One.Tel Bonus Case," *Sydney Morning Herald.*

277   *Massey Energy*   U.S. Department of Labor Mine Safety and Health Administration (29 Jun 2011), "Upper Big Branch Mine, Mine ID: 46-08436, April 5, 2010 Accident, Public Briefing." J. Davitt McAteer, Katie Beall, James A. Beck, Jr., Patrick C. McGinley, Celeste Monforton, Deborah C. Roberts, Beth Spence, and Suzanne Weise (2011), "Upper Big Branch: The April 5, 2010, Explosion: A Failure of Basic Coal Mine Safety Practices," Governor's Independent Investigation Panel.

277   *questionable telecom credits*   Jonathan A. Knee (2006), *The Accidental Investment Banker: Inside the Decade that Transformed Wall Street,* Oxford University Press, xvii.

277   *described dot.coms*   In the matter of Merrill Lynch & Co. (2002), Decision and Order, Supreme Court of the State of New York.

Chapter 13

174   *result is price-fixing*   Robert Schuettinger and Eamonn F. Butler (1979), *Forty Centuries of Wage and Price Controls: How Not to Fight Inflation,* The Heritage Institute.

174   *Adam Smith*   Adam Smith (1776), *The Wealth of Nations.*

174   *global citric acid cartel*   John M. Connor (1998), "The Global Citric Acid Conspiracy," *Agribusiness,* 14:435–52.

175   *computer-memory cartel*   U.S. Department of Justice (5 Oct 2005), "Samsung Agrees to Plead Guilty and to Pay $300 Million Criminal Fine for Role in Price Fixing Conspiracy: Korean Company Pays Second Largest Criminal Antitrust Fine in U.S. History," press release.

178   *Ginger Paralysis Association*   John Parascandola (1995), "The Public Health Service and Jamaica Ginger Paralysis in the 1930s," *Public Health Reports,* 110:361–3. Cecil Munsey (Winter 2006), "Paralysis in a Bottle: The Jake Walk Story," *Bottles & Extras,* 7–12.

178   *this incident led*   Paul M. Wax (1995), "Elixirs, Diluents, and the Passage of the 1938 Federal Food, Drug and Cosmetic Act," *Annals of Internal Medicine,* 122:456–61.

179   *follow its charter*   Joel Baken (2004), *The Corporation: The Pathological Pursuit of Profit and Power,* Free Press.

180   *Moral pressure is*   Maurice Punch (2000), "Suite Violence: Why Managers Murder and Corporations Kill," *Crime, Law & Social Change,* 33:243–80. Jenny White, Albert Bandura, and Lisa A. Bero (2009), "Moral Disengagement in the Corporate World," *Accountability in Research,* 16:41–74. Jennifer J. Kish-Gephart, David A. Harrison, and Linda Klebe Trevino (2010), "Bad Apples, Bad Cases, and Bad Barrels: Meta-Analytic Evidence About Sources of Unethical Decisions at Work," *Journal of Applied Psychology,* 95:1–3.

180 *overseas sweatshops*   Dexter Roberts, Pete Engardio, Aaron Bernstein, Stanley Holmes, and Xiang Ji (27 Nov 2006), "Secrets, Lies, and Sweatshops," *Bloomberg Business Week*. Eric V. Edmonds and Nina Pavcnik (2005), "Child Labor in the Global Economy," *Journal of Economic Perspectives*, 19:199–220.

181 *replace management*   Leemore Dafny and David Dranove (2009), "Regulatory Exploitation and Management Changes: Upcoding in the Hospital Industry," *Journal of Law & Economics*, 52:223–50.

181 *immortal sociopaths*   Joel Baken (2004), *The Corporation: The Pathological Pursuit of Profit and Power*, Free Press.

181 *good for their reputation*   Charles J. Fombrun, Naomi A. Gardberg, and Michael L. Barnett (2000), "Opportunity Platforms and Safety Nets: Corporate Citizenship and Reputational Risk," *Business & Society Review*, 105:85–106. David M. Kreps (2000), "Corporate Culture and Economic Theory," in Nicolai J. Foss, ed., *The Theory of the Firm: Critical Perspectives on Business and Management*, Taylor & Francis. Einer Elhauge (2005), "Sacrificing Corporate Profits in the Public Interest," *New York University Law Review*, 80:733–869.

181 *Baron Thurlow*   John Poynder (1844), *Literary Extracts, Vol. 1*, J. Hatchard & Sons, 2.

181 *no soul to damn*   John C. Coffee (1981), "'No Soul to Damn, No Body to Kick': An Unscandalized Inquiry Into the Problem of Corporate Punishment," *Michigan Law Review*, 79:386–459.

182 *a lot of money*   Kantar Media (17 Mar 2011), "Kantar Media Reports U.S. Advertising Expenditures Increased 6.5 Percent In 2010," press release.

182 *psychological manipulation*   Robert B. Cialdini (1998), *Influence: The Psychology of Persuasion*, Collins.

182 *dose of neuroscience*   Samuel M. McClure, Jian Li, Damon Tomlin, Kim S. Cypert, Latané M. Montague, and P. Read Montague (2004). "Neural Correlates of Behavioral Preference for Culturally Familiar Drinks," *Neuron*, 44:379–87. Brian Knutson, Scott Rick, G. Eliot Wimmer, Drazen Prelec, and George Loewenstein (2007), "Neural Predictors of Purchases," *Neuron*, 53:147–56. Dan Ariely and Gregory S. Berns (2010), "Neuromarketing: The Hope and Hype of Neuroimaging in Business," *Nature Reviews Neuroscience*, 11:284–92. Douglas Rushkoff (2000), "Advertising," Chapter 5 of *Coercion: Why We Listen To What 'They' Say*, Putnam.

183 *150 people died*   U.S. Food and Drug Administration (2009), "Information on Adverse Event Reports and Heparin." Alan Coukell (2009), "Protecting Consumers from Adulterated Drugs," presentation at U.S. Food and Drug Administration, Public Meeting on Economically Motivated Adulteration, College Park, Maryland.

183 *Cargill recalled*   Tom Watkins (2011), "Cargill Recalls 36 Million Pounds of Ground Turkey," *CNN News*.

183 *ChoicePoint allowed*   Bob Sullivan (14 Feb 2005), "Database Giant Gives Access to Fake Firms," *MSNBC*. Jaikumar Vijayan (26 Jan 2006), "FTC Imposes $10M Fine Against ChoicePoint for Data Breach," *Computer World*.

184　*There's recognition*　Daniel G. Goldstein and Gerd Gigerenzer (2002), "Models of Ecological Rationality: The Recognition Heuristic," *Psychological Review*, 109:75–90.

184　*There's social proof*　Herbert C. Kelman (1958), "Compliance, Identification, and Internalization: Three Processes of Attitude Change," *Journal of Conflict Resolution*, 2:51–60.

184　*attribute substitution*　Daniel Kahneman and Shane Frederick (2002), "Representativeness Revisited: Attribute Substitution in Intuitive Judgment," in Thomas Gilovich, Dale Griffin, and Daniel Kahneman, eds., *Heuristics and Biases: The Psychology of Intuitive Judgment*, Cambridge University Press, 49–81.

184　*a lemons market*　George Akerlof (1970), "The Market for Lemons: Quality Uncertainty and the Market Mechanism," *Quarterly Journal of Economics*, 83:488–500. George E. Hoffer and Michael D. Pratt (1987), "Used Vehicles, Lemons Markets, and Used Car Rules: Some Empirical Evidence," *Journal of Consumer Policy*, 10:409–14. Steven E. Kaplan, Pamela B. Roush, and Linda Thorne (2007), "Andersen and the Market for Lemons in Audit Reports," *Journal of Business Ethics*, 70:363–73.

184　*Globalization is making*　Rick Mullin (2011), "Shock to the System: Big Questions About Drug Safety Arise in the Wake of Rampant Supply-Chain Globalization," *Chemical & Engineering News*, 89:11–20.

184　*Glaxo Smith-Kline*　Toni Clarke (26 Oct 2010), "Glaxo to Pay $750 Million in Adulterated Drugs Case," Reuters.

184　*died of kidney failure*　Walt Bogdanich and Jake Hooker (6 May 2007), "From China to Panama, a Trail of Poisoned Medicine," *New York Times*.

184　*prone to rollover*　Joan Claybrook (2001), "Criminal Penalties for Corporate Misbehavior," *Tort Source*, 3:1, 4.

185　*salmonella outbreak*　Mary Clare Jalonick (22 Aug 2010), "A Supplier in Egg Recall Has History of Violations, Including in Maine," *Portland Press Herald*. Brendan Flaherty (2010), "Salmonella Outbreak in Eggs: An Update," *Food & Drug Law Institute Update*, 6: 16–19.

185　*the drug Rebif*　U.S. Department of Justice (4 May 2011), "Pharmaceutical Giant, Serono, Agrees to Pay $44.3 Million to Settle False Claims Act Case," press release. *Wall Street Journal* (5 May 2011), "Settlement Reached In MS Drug Case."

185　*using child labor*　United States International Child Labor Program (1998), "By the Sweat and Toil of Children, Vol. V: Efforts to Eliminate Child Labor," Federal Publications, paper 144.

186　*oil industry wanting*　Jonathan Fahey (12 May 2011), "How the Oil Industry Saves $4.4 Billion in Taxes," *USA Today*.

186　*law passed limiting*　Fred J. Hellinger and Gary J. Young (2005), "Health Plan Liability and ERISA: The Expanding Scope of State Legislation," *American Journal of Public Health*, 95:217–23. Katherine L. Record (2010), "Wielding the Wand Without Facing the Music: Allowing Utilization Review Physicians to Trump Doctors' Orders, but Protecting Them from the Legal Risk Ordinarily Attached to the Medical Degree," *Duke Law Journal*, 59:955–1000.

186   *licensing interior designers*   Janet Zink (1 Apr 2011), "Real Knock-Down, Drag-Out Fight in Florida Is over Commercial Interior Design," *St. Petersburg Times*. George F. Will (22 Mar 2007), "Wallpapering with Red Tape," *The Washington Post*. Dick M. Carpenter II (2007), "Designing Cartels: How Industry Insiders Cut Out Competition," Institute for Justice.

187   *horizontal drilling technology*   Carl T. Montgomery and Michael B. Smith (2010), "Hydraulic Fracturing: History of an Enduring Technology," *Journal of Petroleum Technology*, 62:26–41.

187   *shoddy building practices*   Heather Timmons (25 Apr 2003), "Shoddy Building in the Housing Boom?" Bloomberg BusinessWeek.

188   *used to be smaller*   John Stopford (1998), "Multinational Corporations," *Foreign Policy*, 113:12–24. Gardiner C. Means (1931), "The Growth in the Relative Importance of the Large Corporation in American Economic Life," *The American Economic Review*, 21:10–42.

188   *Ronald Coase first*   Ronald Coase (1937), "The Nature of the Firm," *Economica*, 4:386–405.

189   *Nick Leeson's*   Richard W. Stevenson (28 Feb 1995), "The Collapse of Barings: The Overview: Young Trader's $29 Billion Bet Brings down a Venerable Firm," *New York Times*. Erik Ipsen (19 Jul 1995), "Bank of England Cites Fraud in Barings Collapse," *New York Times*. Peter Culshaw (8 Jan 2009), "Nick Leeson: How the Original Rogue Trader at Barings Bank Is Thriving in the Credit Crunch," *The Telegraph*.

189   *Kweku Adoboli*   Victoria Howley and Emma Thomasson (16 Sep 2011), "UBS $2 Billion Rogue Trade Suspect Held in London," Reuters. Haig Simonian (24 Sep 2011), "UBS Chief Resigns Over Rogue Trade Affair," *Financial Times*.

189   *Different countries*   John M. Connor and Darren Bush (2008), "How to Block Cartel Formation and Price Fixing: Using Extraterritorial Application of the Antitrust Laws as a Deterrence Mechanism," *Penn State Law Review*, 112:813–57. John M. Connor (2002), "The Food and Agricultural Global Cartels of the 1990s: Overview and Update," Purdue University Department of Agricultural Economics, Staff Paper 02–4.

189   *Amazon.com uses its*   Jeanine Poggi (2011), "Amazon Sales Tax: The Battle, State by State," TheStreet.com.

191   *free is very different*   Chris Anderson (2009), *Free: The Future of a Radical Price*, Hyperion. Dan Ariely (2008), *Predictably Irrational: The Hidden Forces That Shape Our Decisions*, HarperCollins.

191   *Chemical plants*   David Bollier, Frank Clemente, Laura MacCleery, Hugh Jackson, and Craig Aaron (2004), "Homeland Unsecured," Public Citizen. Linda-Jo Schierow (2006), "Chemical Facility Security," Congressional Research Service Report RL-31530.

191   *hundreds of plants*   Margaret E. Kosal (2006), "Terrorism Targeting Industrial Chemical Facilities: Strategic Motivation and the Implications for U.S. Security," *Studies in Conflict & Terrorism*, 29:719–51.

191   *The problem is*   Jeffrey Hahn, Donna Post Guillen, and Thomas Anderson (2005), "Process Control Systems in the Chemical Industry: Safety vs. Security," Paper presented at the 20th Annual CCPS International Conference, Idaho National Laboratory, April 2005.

Chapter 13 Notes

278   *band together into*   Tim Wu (2010), *The Master Switch: The Rise and Fall of Information Empires,* Alfred A. Knopf.

278   *High barriers to entry*   John M. Connor (2002), "The Food and Agricultural Global Cartels of the 1990s: Overview and Update," Purdue University Department of Agricultural Economics, Staff Paper 02-4.

279   *There are exceptions*   Yvonne Chouinard (2005), *Let My People Go Surfing: The Education of a Reluctant Businessman,* Penguin Press.

279   *implant false memories*   Priyali Rajagopal and Nicole Votolato Montgomery (2011), "I Imagine, I Experience, I Like: The False Experience Effect," *The Journal of Consumer Research,* 38:578–94.

279   *The economic term*   Paul A. David (1985), "Clio and the Economics of QWERTY," *The American Economic Review,* 75:332–7. W. Brian Arthur (1989), "Competing Technologies, Increasing Returns, and Lock-In by Historical Events," *The Economic Journal,* 99:116–31. Stan J. Liebowitz and Stephen E. Margolis (1995), "Path Dependence, Lock-In, and History," *Journal of Law, Economics & Organization,* 11:205–26. Begoña Garcia Mariñoso (2001), "Technological Incompatibility, Endogenous Switching Costs and Lock-In," *The Journal of Industrial Economics,* 49:281–98. Gal Zauberman (2003), "The Intertemporal Dynamics of Consumer Lock-In," *Journal of Consumer Research,* 30:405–19. William Barnes, Myles Gartland, and Martin Stack (2004), "Old Habits Die Hard: Path Dependency and Behavioral Lock-In," *Journal of Economic Issues,* 38:371–7. Joseph Farrell and Paul Klemperer (2007), "Coordination and Lock-In: Competition with Switching Costs and Network Effects," in Mark Armstrong and Robert Porter, eds., *Handbook of Industrial Organization, Volume 3,* North-Holland, 1967–2072.

279   *able to bargain down*   Tricia Bishop (13 Dec 2008), "Court Orders 'Scareware' Shut Down," *Baltimore Sun.* Lucian Constantin (16 Jun 2009), "ByteHosting Settles with the FTC in Scareware Advertising Lawsuit," *Softpedia.*

279   *hydraulic fracturing*   U.S. House of Representatives Committee on Energy and Commerce Minority Staff (2011), "Chemicals Used in Hydraulic Fracturing."

279   *company's arguments*   New York Times (3 Nov 2009), "The Halliburton Loophole (Editorial)," *New York Times.*

279   *The same dynamic*   Frederick P. Brooks, Jr. (1975), *The Mythical Man-Month,* Addison-Wesley.

280   *Senator Bernie Sanders*   Bernard Sanders (6 Nov 2009), "Too Big To Fail—Too Big To Exist," *Huffington Post.*

Chapter 14

196   *Full-body scanners*   Leon Kaufman and Joseph W. Carlson (2010), "An Evaluation of Airport X-Ray Backscatter Units Based on Image Characteristics," *Journal of Transportation Security*, 4:73–94. Andrew Welch (2010), "Full-Body Scanners: Full Protection from Terrorist Attacks or Full-On Violation of the Constitution," *Transportation Law Journal*, 37:167–98. David J. Brenner (2011), "Are X-Ray Backscatter Scanners Safe for Airport Passenger Screening?" *Radiology*, 259:6–10.

196   *the underwear bomber*   Steve Lord (17 Mar 2010), "Aviation Security: TSA Is Increasing Procurement and Deployment of the Advanced Imaging Technology, but Challenges to This Effort and Other Areas of Aviation Security Remain," Testimony of the Director, Homeland Security and Justice Issues, United States Government Accountability Office, before the Subcommittee on Transportation Security and Infrastructure Protection, Committee on Homeland Security, House of Representatives, Report GAO-10-484T.

197   *strip-search every*   Electronic Privacy Information Center (10 Mar 2011), "DHS: We Have the Authority to Routinely Strip-Search Air Travelers," press release. Electronic Privacy Information Center (15 Jul 2011), "Federal Appeals Court: TSA Violated Federal Law, Must Take Public Comment on Body Scanners," press release. *EPIC v. DHS* (15 Jul 2011), Opinion, Case No. 10N1157. DC Circuit Court of Appeals, filed November 1, 2010.

197   *September 11 attacks*   Nate Silver (4 Jan 2010), "The Skies Are as Friendly as Ever: 9/11, Al Qaeda Obscure Statistics on Airline Safety," *FiveThirtyEight.com*.

198   *scale is too large*   Bruce Schneier (2008), "Seven Habits of Highly Unsuccessful Terrorists," *Wired News*. Max Abrams (2008), "What Terrorists Really Want," *International Security*, 32:78–105.

202   *regulatory capture*   Jean J. Laffont and Jean Tirole (1991), "The Politics of Government Decision-Making: A Theory of Regulatory Capture," *The Quarterly Journal of Economics*, 106:1089–127. Mark Jickling (2004), "Barriers to Corporate Fraud: How They Work, Why They Fail," CRS Report for Congress RL32718, Congressional Research Service. Dieter Helm (2006), "Regulatory Reform, Capture, and the Regulatory Burden," *Oxford Review of Economic Policy*, 22:169–86. Ernesto Dal Bó (2006), "Regulatory Capture: A Review," *Oxford Review of Economic Policy*, 22:203–25.

202   *steering contracts to*   Charlie Savage (11 Sep 2008), "Sex, Drug Use and Graft Cited in Interior Department," *New York Times*. Earl E. Devaney (9 Sep 2008), "OIG Investigations of MMS Employees," memorandum to Secretary Dirk Kempthorne from the Office of the Inspector General, United States Department of the Interior.

202   *Federal Aviation Administration*   Mark C. Niles (2002), "On the Hijacking of Agencies (And Airplanes): The Federal Aviation Administration, 'Agency Capture,' and Airline Security," *Journal of Gender, Social Policy & the Law*, 10:381–442. John Downer

(2010), "Trust and Technology: The Social Foundations of Aviation Regulation," *The British Journal of Sociology*, 61:83–106. Johanna Neumann (3 Apr 2008), "FAA's 'Culture of Coziness' Targeted in Airline Safety Hearing," *Los Angeles Times*.

202 *Securities and Exchange*   Susan E. Woodward (1998), "Regulatory Capture at the Securities and Exchange Commission," prepared for the Milken Institute Conference on Capital Markets, March 16, 1998, Santa Monica, California. Mark Quintyn and Michael W. Taylor (2002), "Regulatory and Supervisory Independence and Financial Stability," International Monetary Fund Working Paper 02–46. Nicholas Dorn (2010), "The Governance of Securities: Ponzi Finance, Regulatory Convergence, Credit Crunch," *British Journal of Criminology*, 50:23–45.

204 *illegally spying*   James Risen and Eric Lichtblau (16 Dec 2005), "Bush Lets U.S. Spy on Callers without Courts," *New York Times*. *American Civil Liberties Union et al. v. National Security Agency et al.* (18 Aug 2006), Order, United States District Court for the Eastern District of Michigan, Case No. 06-CV-10204. *American Civil Liberties Union et al. v. National Security Agency et al.* (4 Oct 2006), Order, United States Court of Appeals for the Sixth Circuit, Case Nos. 06–2095/2140. Charlie Savage and James Risen (31 Mar 2010), "Federal Judge Finds N.S.A. Wiretaps Were Illegal," *New York Times*. *Al-Haramain Islamic Foundation, Inc., et al., v. Barack H. Obama, et al.* (31 Mar 2010), Opinion, United States Court of Appeals for the Ninth Circuit, Case No. C 07–0109 VRW.

204 *authorizing the torture*   Jane Mayer (13 Aug 2007), "The Black Sites," *The New Yorker*. Daniel Nasaw (24 Aug 2009), "Newly Released CIA Report Details Interrogation Techniques," *The Guardian*. Associated Press (14 Jun 2011), "New Scrutiny of CIA Torture, Botched Rendition," *CBS News*. Eric Lichtblau and Eric Schmitt (1 Jul 2011), "U.S. Widens Inquiries into 2 Jail Deaths," *New York Times*.

204 *right to assassinate*   John Griffing (5 Oct 2011), "Obama, the Hitman: Killing Due Process," *The American Thinker*.

204 *court rejected EPIC's*   Electronic Privacy Information Center (15 Jul 2011), "Federal Appeals Court: TSA Violated Federal Law, Must Take Public Comment on Body Scanners," press release. *EPIC v. DHS* (15 Jul 2011), Opinion, Case No. 10N1157 (filed Nov 1, 2010), DC Circuit Court of Appeals.

Chapter 14 Notes

280 *ineffective tactic*   Max Abrams (2006), "Why Terrorism Does Not Work," *International Security*, 31:42–78. Bruce Schneier (12 Jul 2007), "The Evolutionary Brain Glitch that Makes Terrorism Fail," *Wired News*.

281 *isn't just theoretical*   A. Peter McGraw, Alexander Todorov, and Howard Kunreuther (2011), "A Policy Makers Dilemma: Preventing Terrorism or Preventing Blame," *Organizational Behavior & Human Decision Processes*, 115:25–34.

Chapter 15

207 *people paying taxes* Luigi Bosco and Luigi Mittone (1997), "Tax Evasion and Moral Constraints: Some Experimental Evidence," *Kyklos*, 50:297–324.

207 *a lot of fraud* U.S. Department of the Treasury (2006), "IRS Updates Tax Gap Estimates," Informational release IR-2006–28.

207 *third-party estimate* Edgar L. Feige and Richard Cebula (2011), "America's Underground Economy: Measuring the Size, Growth and Determinants of Income Tax Evasion in the U.S.," Munich Personal RePEc Archive, MPRA Paper No. 29672.

207 *cheating on their taxes* James A. Tackett, Joe Antenucci, and Fran Wolf (2006), "A Criminological Perspective of Tax Evasion," *Tax Notes*, 110:654–8.

207 *reasons people cheat* Stuart P. Green (2009), "What Is Wrong With Tax Evasion?" *Houston Business & Tax Journal*, 9:220–33.

207 *very little enforcement* U.S. Department of the Treasury (2008), *IRS Oversight Board Annual Report 2007.*

207 *IRS examined less* Department of the Treasury (2008), Internal Revenue Service Data Book 2007.

207 *Corporate audits are down* Transactional Records Access Clearing House (2008), "Audits of Largest Corporations Slide to All Time Low."

207 *increasing the penalties* Mukhtar M. Ali, H. Wayne Cecil, and James A. Knoblett (2001), "The Effects of Tax Rates and Enforcement Policies on Taxpayer Compliance: A Study of Self-Employed Taxpayers," *Atlantic Economics Journal*, 29:186–202.

207 *increases compliance* Robert Halperin and Joseph Tzur (2002), "Tax Evasion and the Low Penalty, Low Audit Rate Phenomenon," *Journal of Accounting & Public Policy*, 9:179–96.

208 *Second, it's profitable* Patricia Sabatini (25 Mar 2007), "Tax Cheats Cost U.S. Hundreds of Billions," *Pittsburgh Post-Gazette*.

208 *failing to declare* Richard S. Dunham (15 Apr 1998), "Maybe Those Meanies at the IRS Aren't So Bad After All," *Business Week*.

208 *demonized taxes* Robert W. McGee (2004), *The Philosophy of Taxation and Public Finance*, Springer-Verlag.

208 *these reasons interact* Edgar L. Feige and Richard Cebula (2011), "America's Underground Economy: Measuring the Size, Growth and Determinants of Income Tax Evasion in the U.S.," Munich Personal RePEc Archive, MPRA Paper No. 29672 (Jan 2011).

208 *blamed income inequality* Kim M. Bloomquist (2003), "Tax Evasion, Income Inequality and Opportunity Costs of Compliance," Paper presented at the 96th Annual Conference of the National Tax Association.

208 *carried-interest tax* Nicholas Kristof (6 Jul 2011), "Taxes and Billionaires," *New York Times*. Laura Saunders (6 Aug 2011), "'Carried Interest' in the Cross Hairs," *Wall Street Journal*.

208 *investment tax credit* Don MacKenzie, Louise Bedsworth, and David Friedman (2005), "Fuel Economy Fraud: Closing the Loopholes That Increase U.S. Oil Dependence," Union of Concerned Scientists. Jim Hopkins (10 Feb 2004), "SUV Sales Climb on Tax Loophole," *USA Today*.

209 *lost federal revenue* Scott Horsley (30 Jun 2011), "What Tax 'Loopholes' Does Obama Want to Close?" National Public Radio.

209 *perceive tax evasion* Erich Kirchler, Boris Maciejovsky, and Friedrich Schneider (2003), "Everyday Representations of Tax Avoidance, Tax Evasion, and Tax Flight: Do Legal Differences Matter?" *Journal of Economic Psychology*, 24:535–53.

209 *just as immoral* Zoë Prebble and John M. Prebble (2010), "The Morality of Tax Avoidance," *Creighton Law Review*, 20:101–58.

210 *first people arrested* Bradley S. Davis (1994), "It's Virus Season Again, Has Your Computer Been Vaccinated? A Survey of Computer Crime Legislation as a Response to Malevolent Software," *Washington University Law Quarterly*, 72:410–40. Patrick J. Leahy (1992), "New Laws for New Technologies: Current Issues Facing the Subcommittee on Technology and the Law," *Harvard Journal of Law & Technology*, 5:1–23.

210 *laws regulating surveillance* Valerie Caproni (17 Feb 2011), "Going Dark: Lawful Electronic Surveillance in the Face of New Technologies," testimony before the House Judiciary Committee.

211 *legalization of abortion* John J. Donohue III and Steven D. Levitt, "The Impact of Legalized Abortion on Crime," *The Quarterly Journal of Economics*, 116:379–420.

211 *unintended consequences* Thomas P. Bonczar and Allen J. Beck (1997), "Lifetime Likelihood of Going to State or Federal Prison," Special Report NCJ-160092, U.S. Department of Justice, Office of Justice Programs, Bureau of Justice Statistics. Heather C. West, William J. Sabol, and Sarah J. Greenman (2010), "Prisoners in 2009," Report NCJ 231675, U.S. Department of Justice, Office of Justice Programs, Bureau of Justice Statistics. Bruce Western and Christopher Wildeman (2009), "The Black Family and Mass Incarceration," *The Annals of the American Academy of Political and Social Science*, 621:221–42.

211 *increasing shoplifting* Kerry Segrave (2001), *Shoplifting: A Social History*, Mcfarland & Co.

212 *fewer bicycle riders* Maxwell H. Cameron, A. Peter Vulcan, Caroline F. Finch, and Stuart V. Newstead (1994). "Mandatory Bicycle Helmet Use Following a Decade of Helmet Promotion in Victoria, Australia: An Evaluation," *Accident Analysis & Prevention*, 26:325–7. Dorothy L. Robinson (2007), "Bicycle Helmet Legislation: Can We Reach a Consensus?" *Accident Analysis & Prevention*, 39:86–93. Christopher S. Carpenter and Mark F. Stehr (2010), "Intended and Unintended Effects of Youth Bicycle Helmet Laws," NBER Working Paper No. 15658, National Bureau of Economic Research.

212 *chilling effect on* Electronic Frontier Foundation (2008), "Unintended Consequences: Ten Years Under DMCA."

212 *increased violence* Dan Werb, Greg Rowell, Gordon Guyatt, Thomas Kerr, Julio Montaner, and Evan Wood (2011), "Effect of Drug Law Enforcement on Drug Market Violence: A Systematic Review," *International Journal of Drug Policy*, 22:87–94.

References 343

212 *trade-off between* Bruce Schneier (2003), *Beyond Fear: Thinking Sensibly About Security in an Uncertain World*, Copernicus Books, Chapter 1.

213 *different characteristics* Bruce Schneier (2003), *Beyond Fear: Thinking Sensibly About Security in an Uncertain World*, Copernicus Books, Chapter 5.

214 *unit pricing was* Laetitia B. Mulder, Eric van Dijk, David De Cremer, and Henk A.M. Wilke (2006), "When Sanctions Fail to Increase Cooperation in Social Dilemmas: Considering the Presence of an Alternative Option to Defect," *Personality & Social Psychology Bulletin*, 32:1312–24. Marie Lynn Miranda and Joseph E. Aldy (1998), "Unit Pricing of Residential Municipal Waste: Lessons From Nine Case Studies," *Journal of Environmental Management*, 52:79–93.

214 *Stuffing more trash* Don Fullerton and Thomas C. Kinneman (1996), "Household Responses to Pricing Garbage by the Bag," *The American Economic Review*, 86:971–84.

215 *based on perceived* Bruce Schneier (3 Apr 2008), "The Difference Between Feeling and Reality in Security," *Wired News*.

215 *Natural Biases* Barry Glassner (1999), *The Culture of Fear: Why Americans Are Afraid of the Wrong Things*, Basic Books. Paul Slovic (2000), *The Perception of Risk*, Earthscan Publications. Daniel Gilbert (2 Jul 2006), "If Only Gay Sex Caused Global Warming," *Los Angeles Times*. Jeffrey Kluger (26 Nov 2006), "How Americans Are Living Dangerously," *Time*. Cass Sunstein and Richard Zeckhauser (2011), "Overreaction to Fearsome Risks," *Environmental & Resource Economics*, 48:435–49.

215 *John Mueller wrote* John Mueller (2004), "A False Sense of Insecurity?" *Regulation*, 27:42–6.

216 *exaggerate the risk* John Mueller (2006), *Overblown: How Politicians and the Terrorism Industry Inflate National Security Threats, and Why We Believe Them*, Free Press.

216 *tolerance for risk* Meir Statman (2010), "The Cultures of Risk Tolerance," *Social Sciences Research Network Behavioral & Experimental Finance eJournal*, 1–23.

216 *income inequality* Kate Pickett and Richard Wilkinson (2011), *The Spirit Level: Why Greater Equality Makes Societies Stronger*, Bloomsbury Press.

217 *false confessions* Saul M. Kassin, "False Confessions: Causes, Consequences, and Implications for Reform," *Current Directions in Psychological Science*, 17: 249–53. Jennifer T. Perillo and Saul M. Kassin (2011), "Inside Interrogation: The Lie, The Bluff, and False Confessions," *Law & Human Behavior*, 35:327–37.

217 *teachers cheated on* Jack Gillum and Marisol Bello (30 Mar 2011), "When Standardized Test Scores Soared in D.C., Were the Gains Real?" *USA Today*.

218 *analysis of test data* Brian A. Jacob and Steven D. Levitt (2003), "Rotten Apples: An Investigation of the Prevalence and Predictors of Teacher Cheating," *The Quarterly Journal of Economics*, 118:843–77. Brian A. Jacob and Steven D. Levitt (2003), "Catching Cheating Teachers: The Results of an Unusual Experiment in Implementing Theory," in William G. Gale and Janet Rothenberg Pack, eds., *Brookings-Wharton Papers on Urban Affairs*, Brookings Institution Press, 185–220.

218 *If you pay CEOs* Joel Spolsky (2001), "Measurement," *Joel on Software*.

219 *even more overfishing*   British Broadcasting Corporation (5 Apr 2006), "River Patrol
     to Halt Eel Poachers," *BBC News*. Steven Morris (28 May 2010), "Poachers Devas-
     tate Somerset's Elver Fisheries," *The Guardian*. Caroline Wyatt (11 Apr 2005), "Asia
     Demand Threatens French Eels," *BBC News*. Adam Sage (13 Dec 2007), "Eel Poach-
     ers Put 'White Gold' on Critical List," *Times*. Bob Ritchie and Dan McKiernan (1999),
     "Environmental Police Prepare for 'Glass Eel' Poaching Season," *Massachusetts Depart-
     ment of Marine Fisheries DMF News*, 19:6. Atlantic States Marine Fisheries Commis-
     sion, American Eel Plan Development Team (2000), "Interstate Fishery Management
     Plan for American Eel (*Anguilla rostrata*)," Fishery Management Report No. 36. Samuel
     J. Baldwin (11 May 2011), "Glass Eels Hit $950 Per Pound," *The Lincoln County News*.
219 *farm these eels*   Japan Times (10 Apr 2010), "Japan Succeeds in World's First Complete
     Cultivation of Eels."
220 *In ancient Rome*   Robert L. Wilken (1985), *The Christians as the Romans Saw Them*,
     Yale University Press. Peter Brown (1995), *Authority and the Sacred: Aspects of the
     Christianization of the Roman World*, Cambridge University Press.
221 *Norms can change quickly*   Ayelet Gneezy and Daniel M.T. Fessler (2011), "Conflict,
     Sticks, and Carrots: War Increases Prosocial Punishments and Rewards," *Proceed-
     ings of the Royal Society B: Biological Sciences*, published online before print, 8 Jun
     2011:1–5.
222 *women or slaves*   Barbara C. Jordan (24 Jul 1974), "Statement on House Judiciary
     Proceedings to Impeach President Richard Nixon," House Judiciary Committee.
222 *political debates*   Howard Fineman (2008), *The Thirteen American Arguments: Enduring
     Debates That Define and Inspire Our Country*, Random House.

Chapter 15 Notes

281 *studied systems dynamics*   Daniel H. Kim and Virginia Anderson (1989), *Systems Arche-
     type Basics*, Pegasus Communications. Peter Senge (1990), *The Fifth Discipline: The
     Art and Practice of the Learning Organization*, Currency.
281 *experiential goods*   Daniel Gilbert (2006), *Stumbling on Happiness*, Knopf.
281 *Ben Franklin said*   Richard Jackson (1759), *An Historical Review of the Constitution and
     Government of Pennsylvania*.
281 *also human nature*   Joyce Ehrlinger and Richard P. Eibach (2011), "Focalism and the
     Failure to Foresee Unintended Consequences," *Basic & Applied Social Psychology*,
     33:1, 59–68.
281 *major political backlash*   Sophie Goodchild (27 Aug 2006), "500,000 Wheelie Bins
     'Have a Spy In the Lid,'" *The Independent*. Louise Gray (21 Jul 2009), "Councils
     'Snooping' In Bins To See Who Is Recycling Properly," *The Telegraph*. Chris Gourlay
     and Maurice Chittenden (11 Oct 2009), "Bin Police Make You Save Every Scrap,"
     London Times. Philip Reynolds (30 Apr 2010), "Bin Sensor Technology Revolution-
     izes Waste Collection," *Materials Recycling Week*. British Broadcasting Corporation
     (5 Mar 2011), "Warning of Rise in Microchips in Council Bins," *BBC News*.

282 *life-cycle management*   U.S. Environmental Protection Agency (2010), "Recycling and Reuse: End-of-Life Vehicles and Producer Responsibility."

282 *The Innocence Project*   Innocence Project (2011), "Facts on Post-Conviction DNA Evidence."

282 *Cheating on test scores*   Heather Vogell (6 Jul 2011), "Investigation Into APS Cheating Finds Unethical Behavior Across Every Level," *Atlanta Journal-Constitution*. Jaime Sarrio (10 Jul 2011), "Cheating Scandal Adds Fuel to Debate Over High-Stakes Tests," *Atlanta Journal-Constitution*. Michael Winerip (31 Jul 2011), "Pa. Joins States Facing a School Cheating Scandal," *New York Times*.

282 *One teacher described*   Benjamin Herold (28 Jul 2011), "Confession of a Cheating Teacher," *The Notebook*.

282 *Scott Adams wrote*   Scott Adams (1996), *The Dilbert Principle: A Cubicle's-Eye View of Bosses, Meetings, Management Fads & Other Workplace Afflictions*, HarperBusiness, 12.

282 *18 years if*   Matthew Sherman (2009), "A Short History of Financial Deregulation in the United States," Center for Economic and Policy Research.

282 *potential failure*   Alexis de Tocqueville (1835), *Democracy in America*, Saunders and Otley.

Chapter 16

225 *have more flaws*   Bruce Schneier (Mar 2000), "Software Complexity and Security," *Crypto-Gram*.

225 *fail in surprising*   Charles Perrow (1984), *Normal Accidents: Living with High-Risk Technologies*, Basic Books. Dietrich Dörner (1996), *The Logic of Failure: Recognizing and Avoiding Error in Complex Situations*, Perseus Books.

226 *This aspect of scale*   Jane Wakefield (22 Aug 2011), "When Algorithms Control the World," *BBC News*.

227 *tend to minimize*   Daniel Gilbert (2 Jul 2006), "If Only Gay Sex Caused Global Warming," *Los Angeles Times*.

227 *pretending to eliminate*   Frank Furedi (1997), *The Culture of Fear*, Continuum International Publishing Group.

227 *knobs being twiddled*   Bruce Schneier (2003), *Beyond Fear: Thinking Sensibly About Security in an Uncertain World*, Copernicus Books, Chapter 7.

229 *hackers to find*   Ron Rosenbaum (Oct 1971), "Secrets of the Little Blue Box," *Esquire*, 117–25, 222–36. Gary D. Robson (Spring 2004), "The Origins of Phreaking," *Blacklisted 411*, 6:17–23.

229 *Criminals can form*   Allan Castle (1997), "Transnational Organized Crime and International Security," Institute of International Relations, The University of British Columbia Working Paper No. 19. Phil Williams (2001), "Transnational Criminal Networks," in John Arquilla and David F. Ronfeldt, eds., *Networks and Netwars: The Future of Terror, Crime, and Militancy*, RAND Corporation, 61–97. Oded Löwenheim

(2002), "Transnational Criminal Organizations and Security: The Case Against Inflating the Threat," *International Journal*, 57:513–36.

229   *Criminals were simply*   Warwick Ashford (6 Oct 2010), "ISSE 2010: Police Are Playing Catch-Up as Criminals Embrace IT," *Computer Weekly*. Stephen Pritchard (2 Jun 2011), "Vulnerabilities: Battle Is Joined on Two Fronts," *Financial Times*.

229   *position of the interior*   Carl von Clausewitz (1832), *On War*.

232   *Alvin Toffler wrote*   Alvin Toffler (1970), *Future Shock*, Random House.

232   *People learn how*   Michael Anissimov (2004), "Future Shock Level Analysis," *AcceleratingFuture.com*.

233   *new type of grifter*   David Maurer (1940), *The Big Con: The Story of the Confidence Man*, Bobbs Merrill.

233   *Other cities followed*   J.L. Lyman (1964), "The Metropolitan Police Act of 1829: An Analysis of Certain Events Influencing the Passage and Character of the Metropolitan Police Act in England," *The Journal of Criminal Law, Criminology, & Police Science*, 55:141–54.

233   *Internet worm Stuxnet*   Kim Zetter (2011), "How Digital Detectives Deciphered Stuxnet, the Most Menacing Malware in History," *Threat Level* blog, Wired.com.

234   *salami attacks*   Michael E. Kabay (24 Jul 2002), "Salami Fraud," *Network World*.

235   *just use software*   Bruce Schneier (2000), *Secrets & Lies: Digital Security in a Networked World*, John Wiley & Sons.

237   *delayed publishing*   Eric Lichtblau (26 Mar 2008), "The Education of a 9/11 Reporter: The Inside Drama Behind the Times' Warrantless Wiretapping Story," *Slate*.

237   *Clay Shirky referred*   Clay Shirky (31 Dec 2010), "Half-Formed Thought on WikiLeaks & Global Action," *Shirky.com*.

237   *other business considerations*   Alfred Rappaport (2005), "The Economics of Short-Term Performance Obsession," *Financial Analysts Journal*, 61:65–79. Thomas P. Byrne (2010), "False Profits: Reviving the Corporation's Public Purpose," *UCLA Law Review Discourse*, 25:25–49. Patrick Bolton, Jose Scheinkman, and Wei Xiong (2006), "Executive Compensation and Short-Termist Behaviour in Speculative Markets," *Review of Economic Studies*, 73:577–610. Lynne Dallas (2011), "Short-Termism, the Financial Crisis and Corporate Governance," San Diego Legal Studies Paper No. 11–052. Lawrence Mitchell (2011), *Corporate Irresponsibility: America's Newest Export*, Yale University Press. Alfred Rappaport (2011), *Saving Capitalism from Short-Termism*, McGraw-Hill.

238   *investors have access*   John C. Bogle (2005), *The Battle for the Soul of Capitalism*, Yale University Press.

238   *wicked problems*   C. West Churchman (1967), "Wicked Problems," *Management Science*, 14:141–2. Horst Rittel and Melvin Webber (1973), "Dilemmas in a General Theory of Planning," *Policy Sciences*, 4:155–69. E. Jeffrey Conklin (2006), *Dialog Mapping: Building a Shared Understanding of Wicked Problems*, John Wiley & Sons.

239   *ubiquity of data*   Charles Stross (2011), "Network Security in the Medium Term, 2061–2561 AD," paper presented at USENIX Security.

241 *better off spending* Bruce Schneier (2009), "Beyond Security Theater," *New Internationalist*, 427:10–13.

242 *Yochai Benkler* Yochai Benkler (2011), *The Penguin and the Leviathan: How Cooperation Trumphs Over Self-Interest*, Crown Business, 25–6.

242 *security is a process* Bruce Schneier (2000), *Secrets and Lies: Digital Security in a Networked World*, John Wiley & Sons, 273, 395.

Chapter 16 Notes

283 *the singularity* Vernor Vinge (1993), "Technological Singularity," paper presented at the VISION-21 Symposium sponsored by NASA Lewis Research Center and the Ohio Aerospace Institute, 30–31 March. Raymond Kurzweil (2005), *The Singularity is Near: When Humans Transcend Biology*, Penguin Press.

283 *against the government* Leonard Deutchman and Sean Morgan (2005), "The ECPA, ISPs and Obtaining E-mail: A Primer for Local Prosecutors," American Prosecutors Research Institute. U.S. Department of Justice, Computer Crime & Intellectual Property Section (2009), *Searching and Seizing Computers and Obtaining Electronic Evidence in Criminal Investigations*, Third Edition, Office of Legal Education Executive Office for United States Attorneys.

283 *Clay Shirky writes* Clay Shirky (2008), *Here Comes Everybody: The Power of Organizing Without Organizations*, Penguin Press.

283 *terms of service* Wall Street Journal (4 May 2011), "Terms of Use for SafeHouse," *Wall Street Journal*.

283 *Lord Kelvin said* Silvanus Phillips Thompson (2011), *The Life of William Thomson, Baron Kelvin of Largs*, Cambridge University Press.

Chapter 17

243 *Trust in things* Bart Nooteboom (2002), *Trust: Forms, Foundations, Functions, Failures and Figures*, Edward Elgar, 45.

245 *trust is a social good* Sissela Bok (1978), *Lying: Moral Choice in Private and Public Life*, Pantheon Books, 26–7.

245 *trust is the key* James Colman (1988), *Foundations of Social Theory*, Harvard University Press. Francis Fukuyama (1995), "Social Capital and the Global Economy: A Redrawn Map of the World," *Foreign Affairs*, 75:89–103. Luigi Guiso, Paola Sapienza, and Luigi Zingales (2004), "The Role of Social Capital in Financial Development," *American Economic Review*, 94:426–56.

247 *this parable* Richard Beck (2011), "Tales of the Demonic," *Experimental Theology*.

247 *do not follow* Tom Zeller, Jr. (26 Jul 2011), "Tim De Christopher: Is Civil Disobedience the Key to Climate Change Action?" *The Huffington Post*.

248 *Medal of Honor* Michael A. Memoli and Michael Muskal (15 Sep 2011), "Obama Awards Medal of Honor to Kentucky Marine," *Los Angeles Times*.

248 *contact a reporter* Richard L. Rashke (2000), *The Killing of Karen Silkwood: The Story Behind the Kerr-McGee Plutonium Case*, Second Edition, Cornell University Press.

Chapter 17 Notes

284 *leap of faith* Søren Kierkegaard (1844), *The Concept of Anxiety*. Alistair Hannay and Gordon Marino, eds. (1997), *The Cambridge Companion to Kierkegaard*, Cambridge University Press.

284 *World Values Survey* Jaime Diez Medrano (2011), "Interpersonal Trust," World Values Survey Archive and ASEP/JDS.

284 *results differ widely* Magali Rheault (5 Oct 2007), "Many World Citizens Trust Neighbors More Than Police: Trust in Neighbors and Police About Equal in 21 Countries," Gallup.

284 *tried something similar* *Reader's Digest* (Jul 2007), "The Reader's Digest Global Phone Test."

284 *laboratory experiment* Simon Gächter, Benedikt Herrmann, and Christian Thöni (2010), "Culture and Cooperation," CESifo Working Paper No. 3070.

285 *attributed to King* Jamie Stiehm (3 Sep 2010), "Oval Office Rug Gets History Wrong," *Washington Post*.

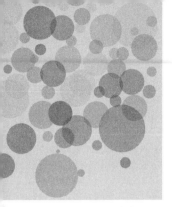

About the Author

Photo by Norbert Schiller

BRUCE SCHNEIER is an internationally renowned security technologist who studies the human side of security. A prolific author, he has written hundreds of articles, essays, and academic papers, as well as eleven books that together have sold more than 400,000 copies. He has testified before Congress, is a frequent guest on television and radio, and is regularly quoted in the press. His blog and monthly newsletter at www.schneier.com reach over 250,000 devoted readers worldwide.

"The closest thing the security industry has to a rock star." —*The Register*

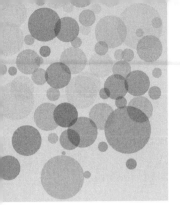

Index